WORKSHOP MANUAL

FOR 500cc AND 650cc TWINS

MODELS

- A50 STAR
- A50 CYCLONE ROAD
- A50 CYCLONE COMP.
- A65 STAR
- A65 ROCKET
- A65 THUNDERBOLT ROCKET
- A65 LIGHTNING ROCKET
- A65 SPITFIRE HORNET
  AND CLUBMAN MODELS

Service Department
B.S.A. MOTOR CYCLES LTD.
BIRMINGHAM 11

Telephone **VIC**toria **2381**
ARMOURY ROAD

INTRODUCTION

Welcome to the world of digital publishing ~ the book you now hold in your hand was printed using the latest state of the art digital technology. The advent of print-on-demand has forever changed the publishing process, never has information been so accessible and it is our hope that this book serves your informational needs for years to come. If this is your first exposure to digital publishing, we hope that you are pleased with the results. Many more titles of interest to the classic automobile and motorcycle enthusiast, collector and restorer are available via our website at www.VelocePress.com. We hope that you find this title as interesting as we do.

NOTE FROM THE PUBLISHER

The information presented is true and complete to the best of our knowledge. All recommendations are made without any guarantees on the part of the author or the publisher, who also disclaim all liability incurred with the use of this information.

TRADEMARKS

We recognize that some words, model names and designations, for example, mentioned herein are the property of the trademark holder. We use them for identification purposes only. This is not an official publication.

INFORMATION ON THE USE OF THIS PUBLICATION

This manual is an invaluable resource for those interested in performing their own maintenance. However, in today's information age we are constantly subject to changes in common practice, new technology, availability of improved materials and increased awareness of chemical toxicity. As such, it is advised that the user consult with an experienced professional prior to undertaking any procedure described herein. While every care has been taken to ensure correctness of information, it is obviously not possible to guarantee complete freedom from errors or omissions or to accept liability arising from such errors or omissions. Therefore, any individual that uses the information contained within, or elects to perform or participate in do-it-yourself repairs or modifications acknowledges that there is a risk factor involved and that the publisher or its associates cannot be held responsible for personal injury or property damage resulting from the use of the information or the outcome of such procedures.

WARNING!

One final word of advice, this publication is intended to be used as a reference guide, and when in doubt the reader should consult with a qualified technician.

1962 to 1965 WORKSHOP MANUAL FOR BSA A50 & A65 UNIT CONSTRUCTION TWINS

This publication is a faithful reproduction of the 1962-1965 BSA Factory Workshop Manual part number 00-4113 that covers the A50 (500cc) and A65 (650cc) unit-construction twins manufactured between August 1961 through the end of July 1965.

It should be noted that BSA model years ran from August through July. For example, the 1962 models were released in August 1961, the 1963 models in August 1962 etc. This can, at times, cause confusion and the only sure method of determining 'what year is it?' is by the serial number. The various engine and frame numbers for the 1962 to 1965 unit constructions twins are shown in the table below. Note that the pre-1966 engine and frame numbers seldom matched.

MODEL KEY: C = Cyclone, CC = Cyclone Competition, L = Lightning, LC = Lightning Clubman, LR = Lightning Rocket, R = Rocket, S = Star, SH = Spitfire Hornet, TR = Thunderbolt Rocket.

EXTENSION (-) KEY: CB = Cable (Rear) Brake, CR = Close Ratio Gearbox, PM = Police Model, RB = Rod (Rear) Brake, RC = Rev Counter, UK = United Kingdom Model, US = USA Model.

1962	Engine/Frame
A50S-CB	A50-101/A50-101
A50S-RB	A50-101/A50A-101
A65S-CB	A65-101/A50-101
A65S-RB	A65-101/A50A-101

1963	Engine/Frame
A50S-CB	A50-823/A50-2288
A50S-RB	A50-823/A50-2701
A65S-CB	A65-1947/A50-2288
A65S-RB	A65-1947/A50-2701

1964	Engine/Frame
A50S	A50A-101/A50-5501
A50-PM	A50AP-101/A50-5501
A50C-US	A50B-101/A50B-101
A50C-CR	A50B-C101/A50B-101
A65S	A65A-101/A50-5501
A65-PM	A65AP-101/A50-5501
A65R	A65B-101/A50B-101
A65R-RC	A65C-101/A50-5501
A65TR	A65B-101/A50-5501
A65LR	A65D-101/A50B-101
A65SH	A65E-101/A50B-101

1965	Engine/Frame
A50S	A50A-686/A50-8437
A50-PM	A50AP-121/A50-8437
A50C-US	A50D-101/A50B-4001
A50CC-US	A50B-507/A50B-4001
A50C-UK	A50DC-101/A50B-4001
A50CC-UK	A50DC-101/A50B-4001
A65S	A65A-1134/A50-8437
A65-PM	A65AP-267/A50-8437
A65R	A65B-334/A50-8437
A65R-RC	A65C-1082/A50-8437
A65LR	A65D-1742/A50B-4001
A65SH	A65E-701/A50B-4001
A65L	A65DC-2158/A50B-4001
A65LC	A65DC-2158/A50B-4001

NOTES:

(1) An additional 'C' included in the engine number denotes 'Close Ratio' gearbox. (See 1964 Cyclone A50C-CR as an example).

(2) Some engines also carry additional letters such as 'HC' for 'High Compression'.

WORKSHOP MANUALS AND SERVICE SHEETS

In 1945, after the war had ended, BSA resumed production of their civilian line of motorcycles. However, they continued their pre-war practice of publishing repair, overhaul and technical information in the form of (dealer only) individual 'Service Sheets'. It was not until the early 1960's that BSA discontinued the service sheet program and eventually started publishing model specific workshop manuals that were available to the general public.

Consequently, owners of BSA motorcycles are subjected to considerable confusion surrounding the appropriate selection from the multitude of 'workshop manual' reprints that have recently flooded the on-line marketplace. Many of the reprints found on internet websites are from 'bedroom sellers' at enticingly low prices by individuals that really have no idea what they are selling. Many are nothing more than poor quality comb-bound photocopies that are scanned and printed complete with greasy pages and thumbprints and, as such, are deceptively described as 'pre-owned', 'used' or even 'refurbished'! In addition, they are often advertised for the incorrect series and/or model years of motorcycles.

However, VelocePress has been producing high-quality reprints of out-of-print motorcycle and automotive manuals and books since 2000. Therefore, you can be assured that this publication has received the utmost care and attention in its preparation.

BSA PART NUMBERS

This manual includes many references to BSA part numbers and it should be noted that they are not in the final format that was introduced in the late 1960's. The original part numbers utilized a 5-4 number series such as 83961-3340 these can be converted to the later 2-4 part numbers by deleting the first 3 digits of the number. For example 83961-3340 becomes 61-3340.

SUPPLEMENT

The following pages include a supplement that was inserted into the original 'Instruction Manual' that was provided with each new model sold in the USA. However, it is often missing and, while some of the information it contains is covered within the manual, it is included for the sake of completeness.

FOR U.S.A. MACHINES ONLY

SUPPLEMENTARY INSTRUCTIONS FOR A50 CYCLONE — A65 THUNDERBOLT ROCKET — A65 LIGHTNING ROCKET AND A65 SPITFIRE HORNET

In general, the details given in the instruction manual will apply to the above models but major differences, requiring special instructions, are described below.

TECHNICAL DATA

	A50 — 2C Cyclone	A65 — 2L Lightning Rocket	A65 — S.P.H. Spitfire Hornet	A65 — lT Thunderbolt Rocket
ENGINE:				
Carburettor	2 — 1 1/16″ dia.	2 — 1 1/8″ dia.	2 — 1 1/8″ dia.	1 — 1 1/8″ dia.
Main jet	*180	220	220	310
Pilot jet	25	25	25	25
Throttle valve	376/3½	389/3½	389/3½	389/3½
Needle position	*3	3	3	3
Needle jet	.106	.106	.106	.106
Compression ratio	9 (Standard)	9 (Standard)	9 (Standard)	9 (Standard)
Ignition timing	.287″ (33°)	.376″ (38°)	.376″ (38°)	.376″ (38°)
	B.T.D.C.	B.T.D.C.	B.T.D.C.	B.T.D.C.

*Corresponding figures for carburettors used with open pipes are 170 and 2

Special Note for energy transfer ignition:— On 500cc. machines, locate the rotor hole marked "S" on peg before setting timing to 33 degrees before T.D.C. For 650cc. machines, locate the rotor hole marked "R" on peg, before setting timing to 38 degrees before T.D.C.

	Cyclone Comp.	Cyclone Road			
ELECTRICAL:					
Ignition	Energy Transfer	Twin coil	Twin coil	Energy Transfer	Twin coil
Lighting	None	Battery	Battery	None	Battery
Battery	None	Lucas MLZ9E	Lucas MLZ9E	None	Lucas MLZ9E

	Cyclone Comp. EAST U.S.A.	Cyclone Road WEST U.S.A.			
TRANSMISSION:					
Top gear	5.17	5.17	4.56	4.93	4.56
3rd	5.92	5.92	6.66	5.65	6.66
2nd	8.3	7.62	7.29	7.9	7.29
1st	13.0	10.5	11.43	12.38	11.43
Engine sprocket	28	28	28	28	28
Clutch sprocket	58	58	58	58	58
Gearbox sprocket	21	21	20	21	20
Rear wheel sprocket	50	50	42	50	42

WHEELS:					
Type—front	Q.D. spindle	Q.D. spindle	Q.D. spindle	Q.D. spindle	Det. wheel
rear	Q.D. spindle	Q.D. spindle	Q.D. spindle	Q.D. spindle	Det. wheel
front tyre	†3.25×19 G.S. K70	3.25×19 G.S. K70	3.25×19 G.S. K70	3.50×19 Tri. Uni. (WEST U.S.A.) G.S. K70	3.25×18 G.S. K70
rear tyre	†4.00×18 G.S. K70	3.50×19 G.S. K70	3.50×19 G.S. K70	4.00×18 Tri. Uni. (WEST U.S.A.)	3.50×18 G.S. K70
front brake	8″ dia offset	8″ dia offset	8″ dia. offset	8″ dia. offset	8″ dia. full width
rear brake	7″ dia. offset	7″ dia. offset	7″ dia. offset	7″ dia. offset	7″ dia. full width

†Trials Universal for Comp. model (West U.S.A. only)

Wiring diagram for energy transfer ignition system, with lighting circuit shown for use when required.

W 549 350 06

allow it to settle. Mark the uppermost part of the tyre and repeat the operation to make sure that the wheel always stops in the same position.

The point marked is obviously the lightest point on the wheel and weight must be added at this point until the wheel is properly balanced.

Wheel balance on new machines leaving the factory can only be approximate due to general stiffness of the moving parts.

IMPORTANT

RUNNING-IN The engines of these machines have been "bench tested" but this does not absolve the rider from carrying out the normal 'running-in' process as this applies not only to the engine but to all other working parts.

ENERGY TRANSFER IGNITION SYSTEM

(Models: Cyclone (Comp. model), Spitfire Hornet)

This system incorporates certain characteristics of both magneto and coil ignition.

Electrical energy for ignition (and lighting when fitted) is provided by the alternator. It has six stator windings of which four are used for ignition purposes the remaining two coils being available to serve the needs of any lighting circuits—exclusive of the stop lamp which, when fitted, is fed from a tapping off one of the ignition coils.

Energy Transfer Ignition

The four stator ignition windings are series-connected (*a*) with each other, and (*b*) with the primary windings of two separately-mounted 3ET ignition coils (these being designed specially to operate on the energy transfer principle). A twin-lever model contact breaker provides the necessary low tension circuit interrupting mechanism, each contact set being parallel-connected across an associated 3ET coil primary winding. Thus when both sets of contacts are closed, short-circuiting of the primary windings occurs, whilst a closed circuit of the four ignition stator windings is simultaneously created. Under this condition, movement of the alternator rotor causes an alternating current to flow in the stator windings. At the instant that either pair of contacts open—timed to occur at a moment of peak stator current—the energy developed in the stator windings is discharged as a pulse through the primary winding of the 3ET coil associated with the opened contacts. The effect of this energy pulse in the primary winding is to induce a high voltage in the ignition coil secondary winding, this high tension current being discharged in the usual way across the appropriate plug gap. Contact closure is completed (allowing regeneration of the stator winding current) before the second contacts are opened to provide high tension current in a similar fashion to plug number 2.

Timing

Accurate ignition timing is an important requirement in the operation of the energy transfer system. The contact breaker is arranged to open only at the moment of peak value in the alternating current cycle in order that maximum electromagnetic energy is transferred from the alternator to the ignition coil and a good spark obtained at the plug.

Front Wheel Removal. (Models: Cyclone, Lightning Rocket, Spitfire Hornet)

Slacken off the brake adjuster to remove tension from the cable, lift the operating lever on the brake plate and withdraw the inner cable from its quick-release slot in the fork end. Unscrew the cable adjuster completely at its anchorage, so that the cable is then entirely free from the brake.

Remove the torque link nut on the brake cover plate, slacken the nuts at the opposite end of the link, and release the pinch bolt at the bottom of the left fork leg.

Insert a tommy bar into the hole in the spindle head and unscrew the spindle. It is important to note that it has a left-hand thread and therefore unscrews by turning in a clockwise direction. Support the wheel as the spindle is withdrawn and when it is clear the wheel can be pulled away from the fork leg and removed from the machine.

After removal, do not allow the wheel to fall on to the bush which projects from the brake side of the hub, because although the bush is pressed into position, it may be pushed into the hub if subjected to a sharp blow.

When replacing the wheel and the spindle has been screwed up, before the pinch bolt is tightened, the forks must be depressed sharply two or three times to enable the left fork leg to align itself on the spindle. If this precaution is not observed, the fork leg may be clamped out of position, preventing proper functioning of the forks.

Rear Wheel Removal. (Models: Cyclone, Lightning Rocket, Spitfire Hornet)

Removal of the wheel does not affect the chain or brake adjustment. Insert a tommy bar into the hole in the spindle head and unscrew the spindle. It has a right-hand thread and unscrews by turning in an anti-clockwise direction. The spacer sleeve between wheel and swinging fork end falls clear as the spindle is withdrawn and the wheel can then be drawn out of engagement with the brake drum and removed from the machine.

When removing the wheel it is not necessary to release the brake drum spindle nut on the left side of the machine as this will release the drum and possibly interfere with the easy removal of the wheel.

Rear Brake Adjustment. (Models: Cyclone, Lightning Rocket, Spitfire Hornet)

The rear brake and the foot pedal are on the same side of the machine and consequently there is no cross over shaft. The brake is adjustable at the operating lever on the brake shoeplate by means of the self-locking adjuster as on the other models.

Wheel Balancing

Wheels which are out of balance can have a detrimental effect on steering, particularly at high speeds. As soon as the machine has been run-in, the wheels should be balanced and they should be re-balanced whenever new tyres or other components have been fitted.

Support the machine so that the wheel is off the ground and make sure that it spins freely, i.e. remove the rear chain, check brakes, etc. If there is any sign of stiffness investigate the cause, as unless the wheel is free it will be impossible to balance it correctly. Rotate the wheel slowly and

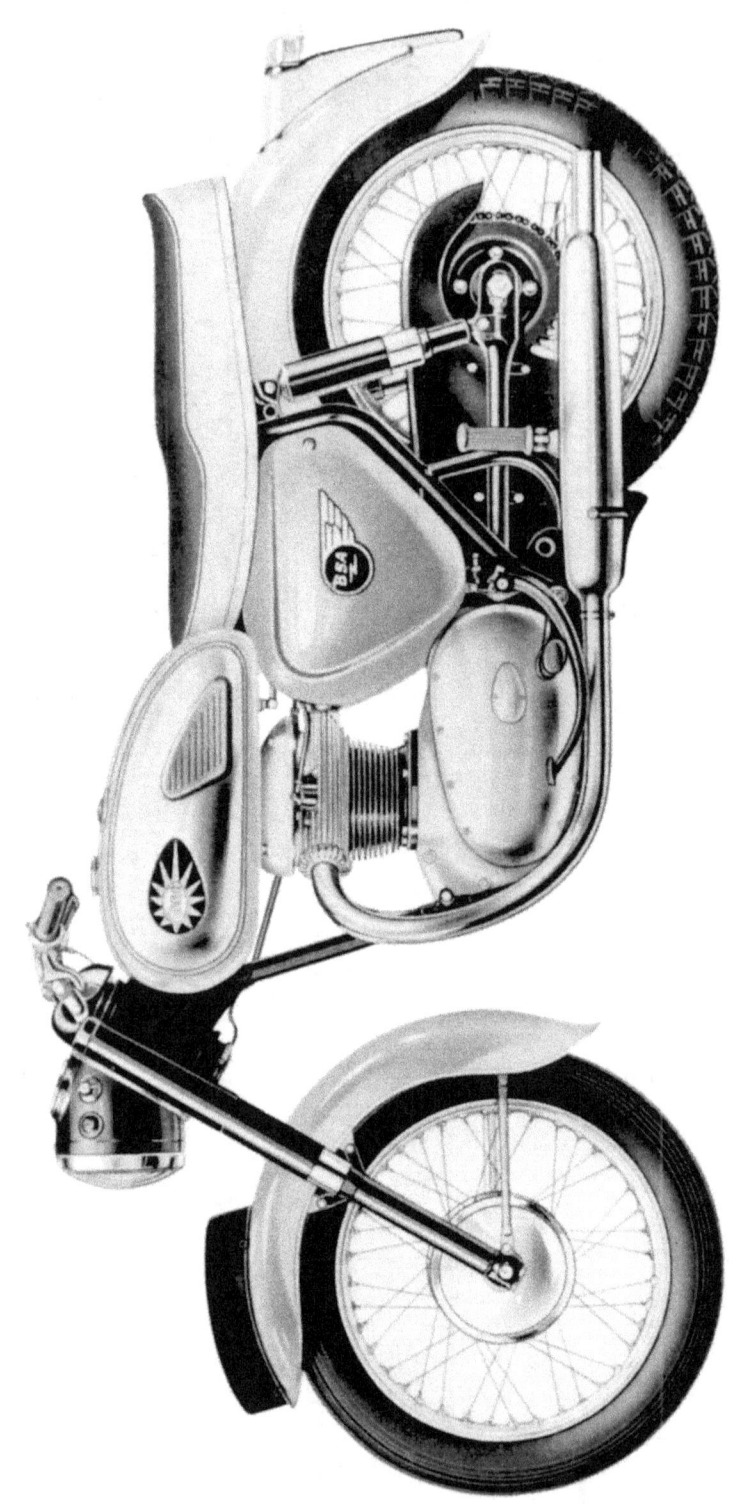

BSA 500cc OHV STAR MODEL A50

BSA 500cc CYCLONE A50C
650cc LIGHTNING A65L

BSA 500cc CYCLONE ROAD MODEL A50

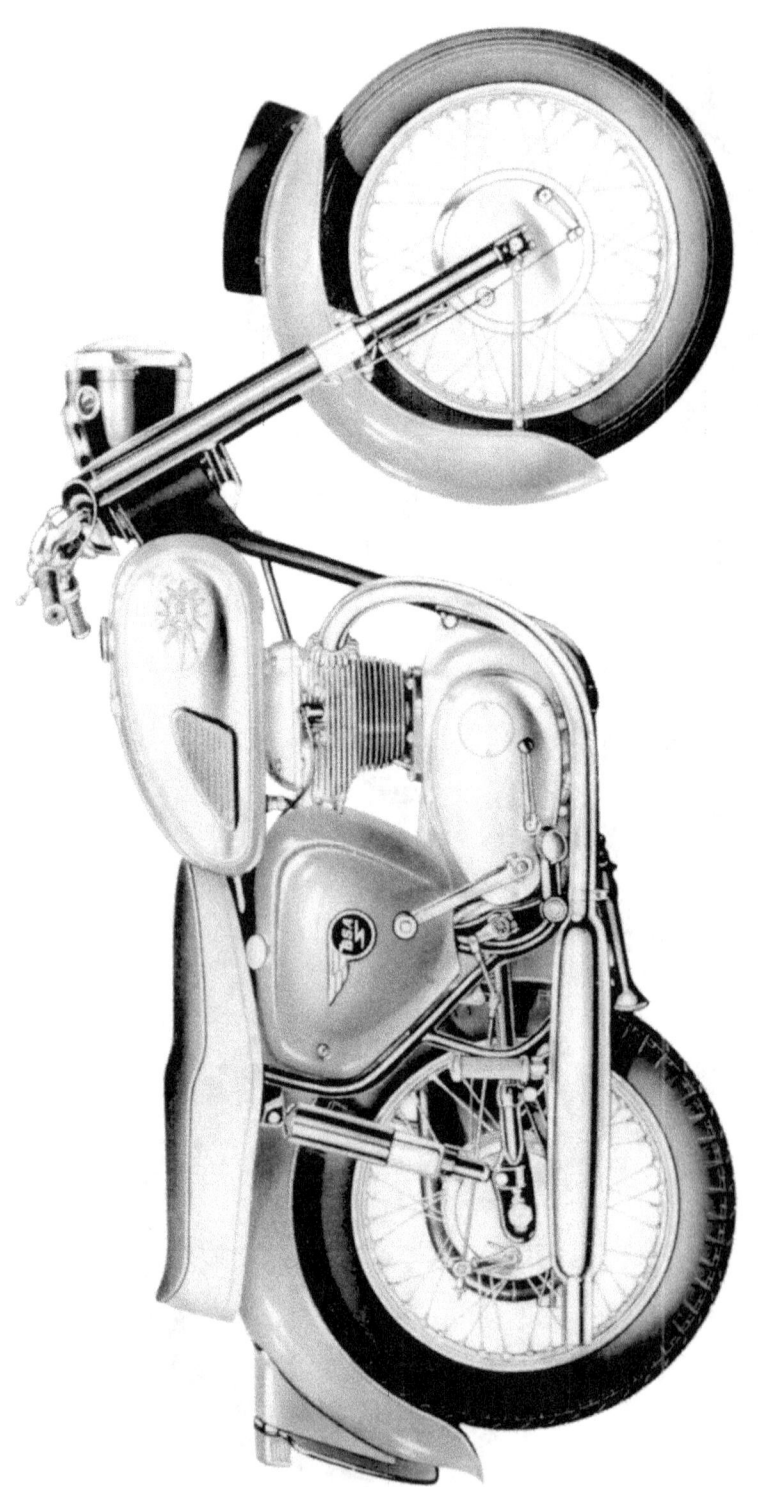

BSA 650cc OHV STAR MODEL A65

BSA 650cc OHV ROCKET MODEL A65R

BSA 650cc THUNDERBOLT ROCKET A65

BSA 650cc SPITFIRE HORNET A65 S/H

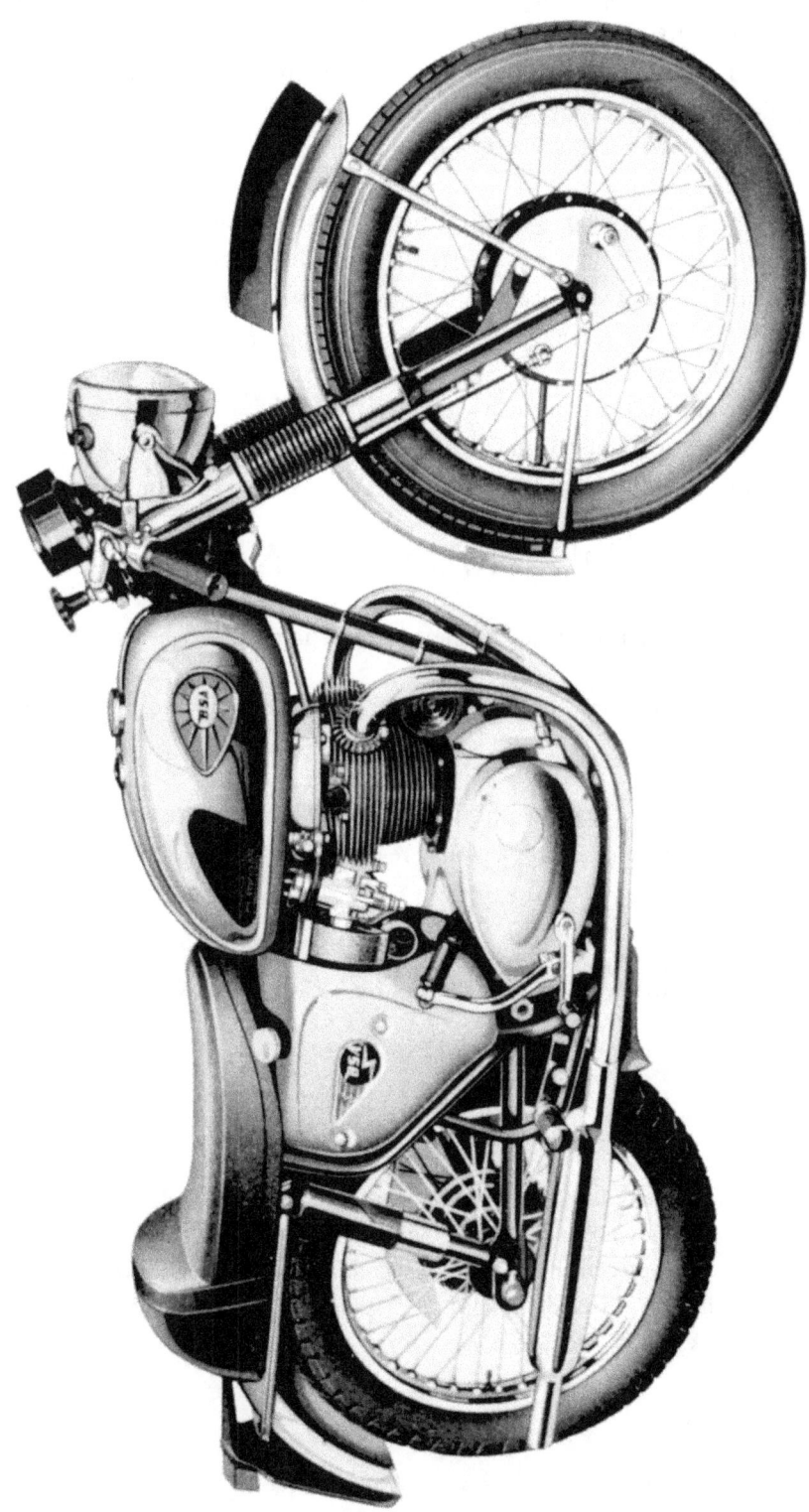

BSA 500cc CYCLONE CLUBMAN A50CC
650cc LIGHTNING CLUBMAN A65LC

INTRODUCTION

This manual has been compiled to provide comprehensive service information for the B.S.A. owner and for the workshop fitter wishing to carry out basic maintenance or major repair work. It is written in great detail, nevertheless, because of the specialized skills or equipment required to carry out some of the repair work described, the inexperienced owner is strongly advised to consult his B.S.A. dealer whenever he is in doubt as to his own ability to carry out a satisfactory job.

All the information given in this manual is correct at the time of publication but, since in the course of the constant development of B.S.A. motor cycles changes in specifications are inevitable, anyone finding the information given in this book to be at variance with the machine in his possession is advised to contact the Service Department. In such cases we will provide up-to-date information.

The manual is sub-divided into sections dealing with major assemblies and these are again broken down into the individual operations required for maintenance or repair. It is hoped that by this arrangement the manual will be useful as a quick work of reference even to the skilled mechanic.

ENGINE AND FRAME NUMBERS

The engine number is stamped on the left-hand side of the crankcase immediately below the cylinder base.

The frame number is stamped on the left-hand side of the frame steering head lug just forward and below the petrol tank.

Both the engine and frame numbers, together with prefix and suffix letters must be quoted in full in any correspondence relating to the machine or any enquiry regarding this manual, to either the dealer or the service department.

FACTORY SERVICE ARRANGEMENTS

UNITED KINGDOM.

REPLACEMENT PARTS

B.S.A. replacement parts and exchange units are distributed through a national network of B.S.A. dealers, each of whom holds a stock of fast moving parts. Approximately 200 of these dealers have been selected for appointment as specialist B.S.A. replacement part stockists and each of these stockists holds a comprehensive stock of B.S.A. replacements. Lists of appointed stockists are available on request, and their names are printed in every B.S.A. Parts Catalogue.

GUARANTEE CLAIMS

In the interests of all concerned it is best that any owner of a new motor cycle wishing to claim assistance under the guarantee should do so through the dealer from whom his machine was purchased. All B.S.A. dealers are familiar with the procedure designed by B.S.A. to give quick service to any owner of a B.S.A. motor cycle who may find himself in difficulty.

REPAIRS

Most appointed B.S.A. dealers are able to carry out even major repair work, and owners are asked to make all repair arrangements through their chosen dealer.

In the great majority of cases local repair will be possible and this will avoid the expense, inconvenience and the possibility of the machine being damaged in transit to or from the Works for repair.

Should your B.S.A. dealer decide that Service Department attention is required he will know best how to make suitable arrangements with the factory. It is important to remember that no machine can be accepted at the Works without a prior appointment. This appointment can be made either by letter or by telephone.

Labour time will be greatly reduced if proprietary articles such as legshields, safety bars, carriers or fibre glass fairings are removed before handing the machine over for repair. Accessories such as mirrors or badges should always be removed before entrusting a machine to an independant carrier.

EXCHANGE REPLACEMENT SERVICE

We have operated for many years an exchange service of Works re-conditioned units including such items as engines, front forks, frames, wheels, brakes shoes and re-bored cylinder barrels.

These parts can, if necessary, be supplied through your B.S.A. dealer before the original parts are returned, so reducing to a minimum the time that the machine is off the road. Details of the units available under this scheme are given at the end of this manual.

TECHNICAL ADVICE

B.S.A. Service Department staff have long experience in dealing with technical problems of all kinds and will be pleased to help in the event of difficulty. The correct address of the Service Department is as follows:—

> B.S.A. MOTOR CYCLES LIMITED,
> SERVICE DEPARTMENT,
> ARMOURY ROAD, BIRMINGHAM 11.
>
> *Telephone No.*: VICtoria 2381

In all communications the full engine and frame numbers with all prefix or suffix letters and figures must be quoted.

SERVICE ARRANGEMENTS OVERSEAS.

In most markets of the world B.S.A. has an appointed distributor to whom all service enquiries should be addressed.

The names of these distributors appear in all B.S.A. Replacement Part Catalogues and they are repeated in a supplement to this manual when it is supplied overseas.

PROPRIETARY PARTS

Equipment not of our manufacture which is fitted to our motor cycles is of the highest quality and is guaranteed by the manufacturers and not by us. Any complaints or repairs should be sent to the manufacturer concerned or their accredited agents who will give every possible assistance. The following are the manufacturers concerned.

CARBURETTORS	Amal Limited, Holdford Road, Witton, BIRMINGHAM 6.
CHAINS	Renold Chains Limited, Wythenshawe, MANCHESTER.
ELECTRICAL EQUIPMENT	Joseph Lucas Limited, Gt. Hampton Street, BIRMINGHAM 18.
REAR DAMPERS	Girling Limited, Kings Road, Tyseley, BIRMINGHAM 11.
SPARK PLUGS	Champion Sparking Plug Company Limited, Feltham, Middlesex.
SPEEDOMETERS	Smith's Motor Accessories Limited, Cricklewood Works, LONDON N.W.2.
TYRES	Dunlop Rubber Company Limited, Fort Dunlop, BIRMINGHAM 24.

A5065

CONTENTS

	Section	Page
GENERAL DATA	GD	20
LUBRICATION	A	57
ENGINE	B	73
CARBURETTOR AND CARBURATION	C	135
FRAME AND FITTINGS	D	147
FRONT FORKS	E	165
WHEELS, BRAKES AND TYRES	F	179
ELECTRICAL EQUIPMENT	G	203
SERVICE TOOLS	H	231
CONVERSION TABLES	J	239

GD1   GENERAL DATA   A5065

INDEX

	Page
A65 STAR (650 c.c.)	
Pistons, Piston Rings, Gudgeon Pins, Small-End Bush	GD.2
Connecting Rods, Crankshaft, Oil Pump	GD.3
Valves, Guides, Springs, Valve Timing, Tappets	GD.4
Ignition Timing, Camshaft, Camshaft Bushes, Barrel	GD.5
Tappets, Cylinder Head, Carburettor, Clutch	GD.6
Sprockets, Primary Chain, Clutch Rod, Gearbox	GD.7
Gearbox Bearings, Kickstarter Ratchet, Selector, Quadrant etc.	GD.8
Steering Head, Swinging Arm Fork, Rear Dampers, Front Forks	GD.9
Wheels, Brakes, Tyres	GD.10
Electrical Equipment	GD.11
Spark Plugs, Capacities, Dimensions, Weights	GD.12
A50 STAR (500 c.c.) General Data	GD.13–14
A65 ROCKET (650 c.c.) ,, ,,	GD.15–16
A50 CYCLONE (500 c.c.) ,, ,,	GD.17–19
A65 LIGHTNING ROCKET (650 c.c.) ,, ,,	GD.20–21
A50 STAR U.S.A. (500 c.c.) ,, ,,	GD.22
A65 THUNDERBOLT ROCKET (650 c.c.) ,, ,,	GD.23
A65 LIGHTNING ROCKET U.S.A. (650 c.c.) ,, ,,	GD.24
A65 SPITFIRE HORNET U.S.A. (650 c.c.) ,, ,,	GD.25–26
A50 CYCLONE ROAD MODEL U.S.A. (500 c.c.) ,, ,,	GD.27
A50 CYCLONE COMPETITION U.S.A. (500 c.c.) ,, ,,	GD.28–29
Gear Ratios Available (Quick Release Hubs)	GD.30–31
Gear Ratios Available (Full Width Hubs)	GD.32
Finding the Ratio	GD.33
Speedometer Gears	GD.34
Piston Displacement and Crankshaft Degrees	GD.35
Torque Wrench Settings	GD.36

A5065 GENERAL DATA GD2

MODEL A65 STAR (650 c.c.)

PISTON

Material	"Lo-Ex" aluminium alloy	
Compression ratio	8.0 to 1	
Clearance—bottom of skirt	.0012"—.0027"	(.03048—.0685 mm.)
top of skirt	.0048"—.0051"	(.1219—.1295 mm.)
(both measured on major axis)		
Gudgeon pin hole diameter	.7498"—.750"	(19.0449—19.05 mm.)

PISTON RINGS

Material	Cast-iron	
Compression ring—lower ring is tapered to same dimensions:		
width	.0615"—.0625"	(1.5621—1.5875 mm.)
thickness	.114"—.121"	(2.9972—3.0734 mm.)
clearance in groove	.001"—.003"	(.0254—.0762 mm.)
fitted gap	.008"—.013"	(.2032—.3302 mm.)
Oil control ring:		
width	.124"—.125"	(3.1496—3.175 mm.)
thickness	.114"—.121"	(2.9972—3.0734 mm.)
clearance in groove	.001"—.003"	(.0254—.0762 mm.)
fitted gap	.008"—.013"	(.2032—.3302 mm.)

GUDGEON PIN

Material	Nickel-chrome high tensile steel	
Fit in small-end (clearance)	.0001"—.0006"	(.00254—.01524 mm.)
Diameter	.750"—.7502"	(19.05—19.055 mm.)
Length	2.368"—2.373"	(60.147—60.275 mm.)

SMALL-END BUSH

Material	Phosphor bronze	
Outside diameter (before fitting)	.8775"—.8785"	(22.2885—22.3139 mm.)
Length	.940"—.950"	(23.876—24.130 mm.)
Finished bore (fitted)	.7503"—.7506"	(19.0576—19.0652 mm.)
Interference fit in rod	.002"—.004"	(.0508—.1016 mm.)

GENERAL DATA

CONNECTING RODS

Length between centres	6.0"	(152.394 mm.)
Big-end bearing type	Vandervell VP.D2	
Rod side clearance	.024"	(.6049 mm.)
Bearing diametrical clearance	.001"—.0025"	(.0254—.0635 mm.)
Small-end bore diameter	.8745"—.8755"	(22.212—22.237 mm.)

CRANKSHAFT

Type	One-piece forged two-throw crank with bolt on flywheel.	
Main bearing (drive-side)	Hoffman M.S11 (Ball)	
Journal diameter	1.125"	(28.574 mm.)
outer diameter	2.812"	(71.435 mm.)
width	.812"	(20.637 mm.)
Main bearing (gear-side)	Vandervell VP.23	
inner diameter	1.500"—1.5005"	(38.099 mm.)
outer diameter	1.6285—1.630"	(41.375 mm.)
width	.940"—.960"	(24.209 mm.)
Crankpin diameter	1.6865"—1.687"	(42.861 mm.)
Minimum regrind	—.010"	(.254 mm.)
Second regrind	—.020"	(.508 mm.)
Third regrind	—.030"	(.762 mm.)
Gear-side journal regrind (two only)	—.010"	(.254 mm.)
	—.020"	(.508 mm.)
Crankshaft end float	.0015"—.003"	(.038—.076 mm.)
Crank throw	1.4567"	(37.00 mm.)

OIL PUMP

Pump body material	Zinc base alloy	
Pump type	Double gear	
Pump drive ratio	1 : 3	
Pump non-return valve spring free length	.8125"	(20.637 mm.)
Pump non-return valve ball, size	¼"	(6.35 mm.)
Oil pressure relief valve spring, free length	.609"	(15.478 mm.)
Oil pressure relief valve ball, size	$\frac{5}{16}$"	(7.937 mm.)
Blow off pressure	50 lbs. per square inch	

GENERAL DATA

VALVES

Seat angle (inclusive)	90°	
Head diameter:		
inlet	1.470"—1.475"	(37.338—37.465 mm.)
exhaust	1.407"—1.412"	(35.737—35.864 mm.)
Stem diameter:		
inlet	.3095"—.310"	(7.874—7.861 mm.)
exhaust	.309"—.3095"	(7.848—7.8613 mm.)

VALVE GUIDES

Material	Cast-iron (high grade)	
Bore diameter inlet and exhaust	.312"—.313"	(7.9248—7.950 mm.)
Outside diameter inlet and exhaust	.5005"—.501"	(12.7127—12.7254 mm.)
Length, inlet and exhaust	1.96"—1.97"	(49.784—50.038 mm.)

VALVE SPRINGS

Free length, inner	1⅝"	(41.275 mm.)
Fitted length, inner	1.3"	(33.02 mm.)
Free length, outer	2 1/32"	(51.5937 mm.)
Fitted length, outer	1.37"	(34.798 mm.)

VALVE TIMING (Standard Camshaft)

Tappets set to .015" (.381 mm.) for checking purposes only:

inlet opens	40° B.T.D.C.
inlet closes	60° A.B.D.C.
exhaust opens	65° B.B.D.C.
exhaust closes	35° A.T.D.C.

TIMING GEAR

Crankshaft pinion:		
number of teeth	22	
fit on shaft	—.0005" +.0005"	(.0127 mm.)
Camshaft pinion:		
number of teeth	44	
interference fit	.0000"—.001"	(.0254 mm.)
Idler pinion, number of teeth	44	
Spindle working clearance	.0005"—.002"	(.0127—.0508 mm.)

TAPPET CLEARANCE (Cold)

Inlet	.008"	(.2032 mm.)
Exhaust	.010"	(.254 mm.)

GD5   GENERAL DATA   A5065

IGNITION TIMING (Standard Ignition System)

Piston position (B.T.D.C.) full advanced ...	.358″	(9.093 mm.)
Crankshaft position (B.T.D.C.) full advanced	37°	
Contact breaker, gap setting	.015″	(.381 mm.)

CAMSHAFT

Journal diameter, left	.810″—.8105″	(20.574—20.586 mm.)
Journal diameter, right	.8735″—.874″	(22.188—22.2 mm.)
End float	Nil (spring-loaded)	
Cam lift	.306″	(7.772 mm.)
Base circle diameter	.812″	(20.624 mm.)

CAMSHAFT BEARING BUSHES

Bore diameter fitted left-hand	.8115″—.8125″	(20.612—20.637 mm.)
Outside diameter left-hand	.906—.907″	(23.012—23.037 mm.)
Interference fit in case, left-hand	.002″—.004″	(.0508—.1016 mm.)
Bore diameter fitted right-hand	.875″—.876″	(22.225—22.25 mm.)
Outside diameter, right-hand	1.065″—1.066″	(27.051—27.076 mm.)
Interference fit in case, right-hand	.002″—.004″	(.0508—.1016 mm.)
Material	"Clevite 10" and bronze	

CYLINDER BARREL

Material	Cast-iron (close grained)	
Bore size (standard)	2.9521″—2.9530″	(74.983—75.0062 mm.)
Maximum oversize	2.9921″—2.9930″	(75.999—76.022 mm.)
Tappet bore size	.3745″—.375″	(9.5123—9.525 mm.)

GENERAL DATA

TAPPETS

Material	20 Carbon steel body (stellite tipped)	
Tip radius	1.250"	(31.75 mm.)
Tappet diameter	.3735"—.374"	(9.488—9.5 mm.)
Clearance in barrel	.0005"—.0015"	(.0127—.0381 mm.)

CYLINDER HEAD

Material	DTD 24 aluminium alloy (British Standard)	
Inlet port size	1⅜"	(34.925 mm.)
Exhaust port size	1 5/16"	(33.337 mm.)
Valve seatings	Cast-iron (cast-in)	

INLET MANIFOLD

Carburettor port size	1⅛"	(28.575 mm.)
Cylinder head port size	1 1/16"	(26.987 mm.)

CARBURETTOR (Standard)

Type	Amal 389/67	
Main jet	300	
Pilot jet	25	
Needle jet size	.106"	(2.6924 mm.)
Needle position	3	
Throttle valve	389/3½	
Nominal choke size	1⅛"	(28.575 mm.)
Air cleaner type	Dry felt	
Throttle slide return spring (free length)	2½"	(63.5 mm.)
Air slide return spring (free length)	3"	(76.2 mm.)

CLUTCH

Type	Multi-plate with built-in cush drive	
Number of plates:		
driving (bonded)	5	
driven (plain)	5 loose, 1 fixed	
Clutch springs	4	
Free length	1-35/64"	(39.2907 mm.)
Working coils	7	
Spring rate	90 lbs./inch	
Clutch sprocket:		
number of teeth	58	
bore diameter	1.9565"—1.9575"	(49.6951—49.7205 mm.)
Clutch hub bearing diameter	1.4538"—1.4548"	(36.9265—36.951 mm.)
Clutch roller diameter (21)	.2495"—.250"	(6.337—6.35 mm.)
Clutch roller length	.231"—.236"	(5.8674—5.994 mm.)

GENERAL DATA

SPROCKETS

	(Number of teeth)
Engine sprocket	28
Clutch sprocket	58
Final drive sprocket	19 solo; 17 sidecar

PRIMARY CHAIN

3/8" triple, roller

CLUTCH OPERATING ROD

Length	11 1/16"	(280.987 mm.)
Diameter	7/32"	(5.5562 mm.)

GEARBOX

	Top	3rd	2nd	1st
Internal ratios (standard)	1–1	1.144–1	1.6–1	2.51–1
Overall ratios (standard)	4.579–1	5.238–1	7.32–1	11.493–1

(see page GD.32 for alternative ratios)

GEAR DETAIL:

MAINSHAFT TOP GEAR

Bush diameter (fitted)	.813"—.814"	(20.6502—20.6756 mm.)
Bush length	3 1/8"	(79.375 mm.)
Bush protrusion	31/64"	(12.3031 mm.)
Working clearance	.0027"—.0042"	(.0685—.1066 mm.)

LAYSHAFT FIRST GEAR

Bush diameter (fitted)	.7495"—.7505"	(19.0273—19.0627 mm.)
Working clearance	.0005"—.001"	(.0127—.0254 mm.)

GEARBOX SHAFTS

Mainshaft left end diameter	.8098"—.8103"	(20.568—20.581 mm.)
Mainshaft right end diameter	.7495"—.7499"	(19.057—19.047 mm.)
Length	10 5/8"	(269.875 mm.)
Layshaft left end diameter	.7495"—.750"	(19.057—19.05 mm.)
Layshaft right end diameter	.7495"—.750"	(19.057—19.05 mm.)
Length	6-11/16"	(169.862 mm.)

A5065   GENERAL DATA   GD8

GEARBOX BEARINGS

Mainshaft top gear bearing	2½" × 1¼" × ⅝" ball journal
Mainshaft bearing right side	¾" × 1⅞" × 9/16" ball journal
Layshaft bearing left side	1" × ¾" × ¾" needle roller
Layshaft bearing right side	1" × ¾" × ¾" needle roller

KICKSTART RATCHET

Pinion bore diameter	.937"—.938"	(23.799—23.825 mm.)
Bush (outside diameter)	.933"—.935"	(23.698—23.749 mm.)
Bush (inside diameter)	.750"—.751"	(19.05—19.0754 mm.)
Outer working clearance	.002"—.005"	(.0508—.127 mm.)
Inner working clearance	.0001"—.0015"	(.00254—.0381 mm.)
Ratchet spring free length	½"	(12.70 mm.)

GEAR SELECTOR QUADRANT

Plunger diameter	.3352"—.3362"	(8.514—8.539 mm.)
Housing diameter	.3427"—.3437"	(8.7045—8.729 mm.)
Working clearance	.0065"—.0085"	(.1651—.2159 mm.)

CAM-PLATE PLUNGER

Plunger diameter	.4355"—.4365"	(11.0617—11.0871 mm.)
Housing diameter	.437"—.4375"	(11.0998—11.1125 mm.)
Working clearance	.0005"—.002"	(.0127—.0508 mm.)
Spring free length	2¼"	(57.15 mm.)

SPEEDOMETER GEARS

See page GD.34 for full details of driving and driven gears with sprockets and tyre sizes.

GD9   GENERAL DATA   A5065

FRAME AND FITTINGS

STEERING HEAD

Number of steel balls	40	
Size of balls	¼"	(6.35 mm.)

SWINGING ARM FORK

Bush type	Bonded rubber	
Bush diameter	1.250"—1.253"	(31.75—31.826 mm.)
Housing diameter	1.247"—1.248"	(31.673—31.699 mm.)
Interference fit	.003"—.005"	(.0762—.127 mm.)
Spindle diameter	.810"—.811"	(20.57—20.595 mm.)

REAR SHOCK ABSORBERS

Type		Coil spring/hydraulically damped	
Springs			
Fitted length	(solo)	9.4"	(238.76 mm.)
	(sidecar)	9.4"	(238.76 mm.)
Spring rate	(solo)	90 lb./per in.	
	(sidecar)	110 lb./per in.	
Colour identification	(solo)	Green/white	
	(sidecar)	Red/white	

FRONT FORKS

Type		Coil spring/hydraulically damped	
Springs			
Free length	(solo)	10"	(254 mm.)
	(sidecar)	10½"	(266.7 mm.)
Spring rate	(solo)	32½ lb./per in.	
	(sidecar)	40 lb./per in.	
Number of coils	(solo)	21 (19½ working)	
	(sidecar)	19 (17½ working)	
Colour code	(solo)	Yellow/green	
	(sidecar)	Blue/white	

BUSHES

Material		Sintered bronze	
Outer diameter	(top)	1.475—1.4755'''	(37.465—37.477 mm.)
	(bottom)	1.473"—1.474"	(37.414—37.439 mm.)
Inner diameter	(top)	1.25"—1.251"	(31.75—31.775 mm.)
	(bottom)	1.2485"—1.2495"	(31.711—31.737 mm.)
Working clearance	(top)	.0005"—.0015"	(.0127—.0381 mm.)
	(bottom)	.001"—.004"	(.0254—.1016 mm)
Length	(top)	2⅛"	(53.975 mm.)
	(bottom)	1¼"	(31.75 mm.)
Shaft diameter		1.248"—1.249"	(31.699—31.7246 mm.)
Sliding tube bore diameter		1.477"—1.475"	(37.515—37.465 mm.)

GENERAL DATA

A5065   GD10

WHEELS, BRAKES AND TYRES

WHEELS

Rim size and type front	WM2-18
Rim size and type rear	WM2-18
Spoke sizes front (40)	8/10G × 5 3/16″ (.160″—.128″ × 5.187″) (4.064—3.251 mm. × 131.762 mm.)
Spoke sizes rear (40)	8/10G × 5 5/8″ (.160″—.128″ × 5.625″) (4.064—3.251 mm. × 142.875 mm.)

WHEEL BEARINGS

Front left-hand and right-hand	20 × 47 × 14 mm. ball journal
Rear right-hand	20 × 47 × 14 mm. ball journal
Rear sprocket bearing	1″ × 2 1/4″ × 5/8″ ball journal
Spindle diameter front	.7868″—.7873″ (19.982—19.994 mm.)
Spindle diameter rear right-hand	.7867″—.7871″ (19.989—19.992 mm.)
Spindle diameter rear left-hand	.9995″—.9997″ (25.382—25.392 mm.)

REAR WHEEL SPROCKET

Number of teeth	42
Chain size (solo)	5/8″ × 3/8″ × 99 pitch
Chain size (sidecar)	5/8″ × 3/8″ × 98 pitch

BRAKES (Floating Shoes)

Diameter	(front)	8″	(203.2 mm.)
	(rear)	7″	(177.8 mm.)
Width	(front)	1 1/8″	(28.575 mm.)
	(rear)	1 1/8″	(28.575 mm.)
Lining thickness	(front)	3/16″	(4.702 mm.)
	(rear)	3/16″	(4.702 mm.)
Lining area sq./in. (sq./cm.)	(front)	8.94 (57.66)	
	(rear)	7.74 (49.92)	

TYRES

Size	(front)	3.25″ × 18″	(82.55 × 457.2 mm.)
	(rear)	3.50″ × 18″	(88.8 × 457.2 mm.)
Pressure	(front)	18 lbs./per square inch	(1.221 atm.)
	(rear)	20 lbs./per square inch	(1.36 atm.)

GENERAL DATA

ELECTRICAL EQUIPMENT

6-VOLT MODELS

Alternator type	Lucas RM19	
Rectifier	Lucas 2DS506	
Coils	Lucas MA6 (2)	
Contact breaker	Lucas 4CA	
Battery	Lucas MLZ9E	
Battery capacity at 20 hour rate	13 A.H.	
Horn	6H 6V	
Bulbs (6-volt)	*Number*	*Type*
Headlight	Lucas 312	30/24W
Parking light	Lucas 988	3W
Stop/tail	Lucas 384	6/18
Speedometer light	Smiths	3A

12-VOLT MODELS

Alternator type	Lucas RM19	
Rectifier	Lucas 2DS506	
Coils	Lucas MA12 (2)	
Contact breaker	Lucas 4CA	
Batteries	MKZ9E (two in series)	
Battery capacity	9 A.H.	
Horn	6H 12V	
Headlamp glass diameter	7"	
Bulbs (12-volt)	*Number*	*Type*
Headlight	Lucas 446	50/40W
Parking light	Lucas 989	6W
Stop/tail	Lucas 380	6/21W
Speedometer light	Smiths	2.2W
Zener Diode	Lucas	ZD.715

GENERAL DATA

SPARK PLUGS

Type	Champion N4
Gap setting	.020" (.50 mm.)
Thread size	14 mm. diameter × 19 mm. reach

CAPACITIES

Fuel tank	4 galls. (4.8 U.S. galls., 18 litres)
Oil tank	5½ pints (3.1 litres)
Gearbox	⅞ pint (500 c.c.)
Primary drive	¼ pint (140 c.c.)
Front forks (each leg)	⅓ pint (190 c.c.)

BASIC DIMENSIONS

Wheel base	54⅛" (137 cm.)
Overall length	81" (206 cm.)
Overall width	28" (71.1 cm.)
Overall height	39¾" (101 cm.)
Ground clearance	7" (17.8 cm.)

WEIGHTS

Machine unladen	390 lbs. (176 kg.)
Engine/gearbox unit	130 lbs. (59 kg.)

GD13　　GENERAL DATA　　A5065

MODEL A50 STAR (500 c.c.)

All General Data is the same as model A65 Star (650 c.c.) except for the following:—

VALVES

Head diameter (inlet)	1.409″—1.413″	(35.788—35.890 mm.)
Head diameter (exhaust)	1.312″—1.317″	(35.337—35.464 mm.)

IGNITION TIMING (Standard Ignition System)

Piston position (B.T.D.C.): full advanced	.304″	(7.721 mm.)
Crankshaft position (B.T.D.C.): full advanced	34°	

CYLINDER BARREL

Bore size (standard)	2.578″—2.579″	(65.481—65.506 mm.)
Maximum oversize	2.618″—2.619″	(66.497—66.522 mm.)

CYLINDER HEAD

Inlet port size	1-5/16″	(33.337 mm.)
Exhaust port size	1-7/32″	(30.956 mm.)

PISTONS

Compression ratio	8.5 to 1

GENERAL DATA

CARBURETTOR (Standard)

Type	Amal 376/282	
Main jet	250	
Pilot jet	25	
Needle jet	.106"	(2.6924 mm.)
Needle position	3	
Throttle valve	376/3½	
Nominal choke size	1"	(25.4 mm.)

SPROCKETS

Final drive sprocket number of teeth ... 17 solo; 16 sidecar

GEARBOX

	Top	3rd	2nd	1st
Overall ratios (standard)	5.117	5.853	8.187	12.843

(see page GD.34 for alternative ratios)

SPEEDOMETER GEARS

See page GD.32 for full details of driving and driven gears with sprockets and tyre sizes.

FRAME AND FITTINGS

REAR WHEEL SPROCKET

Number of teeth for sidecar 43

BRAKES

Diameter (front)	7"	(177.8 mm.) or
	8"	(203.2 mm.)

WEIGHTS

Engine/gearbox unit	134 lbs.	(60 kg.)
Machine unladen	385 lbs.	(174 kg.)

GENERAL DATA

MODEL A65 ROCKET (650 c.c.)

All General Data is the same as the model A65 Star (650 c.c.) except for the following:—

PISTONS

Compression ratio ... ... 9.0 to 1

CAMSHAFT

Sports

VALVE TIMING (Sports Camshaft)

Tappets set to .015″ (.381 mm.) ... ... Inlet opens 51° B.T.D.C.
Inlet closes 68° A.B.D.C.
Exhaust opens 78° B.B.D.C.
Exhaust closes 37° A.T.D.C.

CARBURETTOR

Type	389/201	
Main jet	300	
Pilot jet	25	
Needle jet	.106″	(2.692 mm.)
Needle position	3	
Throttle valve	389/3½	
Nominal choke size	1⅛″	
Air cleaner type	Dry felt	

CLUTCH

Driving plate	Bonded segments	
Springs	Heavy duty	
Free length	1-11/16″	(42.4625 mm.)
Working coils	6¾	
Spring rate	94¼ lbs./inch	

GENERAL DATA

OIL PUMP

Type ... ... With rev-counter drive

SPEEDOMETER GEARS

See page GD.34 for full details of driving and driven gears with sprockets and tyre sizes.

WHEELS (Front and Rear)

As standard except for security bolts in each rim.

GD17   GENERAL DATA   A5065

MODEL A50 CYCLONE (500 c.c.)

All General Data is the same as the model A50 Star or A65 Star except for the following:—

CYLINDER HEAD

    Type   Twin carburettor

INLET VALVE

    Head diameter   1.450″—1.455″ (36.83—36.957mm.)

CARBURETTORS (Two)

Type	Amal 376/310
Main jet	180
Pilot jet	25
Needle jet	.106″ (2.6924 mm.)
Needle position	3
Throttle valve	376/3½
Nominal choke size	$1\frac{1}{16}$″ (26.987 mm.)

PISTONS

    Compression ratio   9.0 to 1

CAMSHAFT

Type	Sports
Valve timing	Inlet opens 51° B.T.D.C.
Tappets set to .015″	Inlet closes 68° A.B.D.C.
	Exhaust opens 78° B.B.D.C.
	Exhaust closes 37° A.T.D.C.

IGNITION TIMING

    As A50 Star

GENERAL DATA

GEARBOX

	Top	3rd	2nd	1st
Internal ratios (close)	1–1	1.107–1	1.47–1	2.03–1
Overall ratios	5.177	5.664	7.521	10.39

(see pages GD.30–31 for alternative ratios)

CLUTCH

Driving plate inserts	Special
Springs	Heavy duty
Free length	1-11/16″ (42.4625 mm.)
Working coils	6¾
Spring rate	94¼ lbs./inch

SPEEDOMETER GEARS

See page GD.34 for full details of driving and driven gears with sprockets and tyre sizes.

OIL PUMP

Type ... With rev-counter drive

INNER TIMING COVER

Incorporating rev-counter drive take-off

SPROCKETS

	Number of teeth
Engine	28
Clutch	58
Gearbox	17
Rear wheel	42

GD19   GENERAL DATA   A5065

WHEELS, BRAKES AND TYRES

WHEELS

Rim size and type (front)	WM2-19
Rim size and type (rear)	WM2-19
Spoke sizes, front left-hand (20)	8⅞″ × 10G
Spoke sizes, front right-hand (20)	5-15/16″ × 10G
Spoke sizes, rear right-hand (20)	7-29/32″ × 10G
Spoke sizes, rear left-hand (20)	7-27/32″ × 10G

WHEEL BEARINGS

Front hub left-hand and right-hand	⅞″ × 2″ × 9/16″ ball journal
Rear hub left-hand and right-hand	⅞″ × 2″ × 9/16″ ball journal
Rear sprocket	⅞″ × 2″ × 9/16″ ball journal
Spindle diameter (front)	.874″—.8745″ (22.1996—22.2123 mm.)
Spindle diameter (rear)	685″—.686″ (17.399—17.424 mm.)

BRAKES (Non-Floating Shoes)

Dimensions as A65 Star

TYRES

Size (front)	3.25″ × 19″	(82.55 × 482.6 mm.)
(rear)	3.50″ × 19″	(88.9 × 482.6 mm.)
Pressure (front)	18 lbs./per square inch (1.221 atm.)	
(rear)	20 lbs./per square inch (1.36 atm.)	

REAR CHAIN

Chain size (solo)	⅝″ × ⅜″ × 103 pitches

ELECTRICAL EQUIPMENT

As A65 Star 6-volt system

MODEL A65 LIGHTNING ROCKET (650 c.c.)

General Data is the same as A65 Star except for the following:—

CYLINDER HEAD

Type ... ...   Twin carburettor

CARBURETTORS (Two)

Type ... ...   Amal 389/206
Main jet   220
Pilot jet   25
Needle jet ... ...   .106″   (2.6924 mm.)
Needle position   3
Throttle valve 389/3½
Nominal choke size ... ...   1⅛″   (28.575 mm.)

PISTONS

Compression ratio ... ...   9 or 11 to 1

CAMSHAFT

As A65 Rocket

IGNITION TIMING

As A65 Star

OIL PUMP

Type ... ...   With rev-counter drive

INNER TIMING COVER

Incorporating rev-counter drive take-off

GD21 GENERAL DATA A5065

GEARBOX

	Top	3rd	2nd	1st
Internal gear ratios (close)	1–1	1.107–1	1.47–1	2.03–1
Overall ratios	4.579	5.068	6.731	9.295

(see pages GD.30–31 for alternative ratios)

CLUTCH

Driving plate inserts	Special	
Springs	Heavy duty	
Free length	1-11/16"	(42.4625 mm.)
Working coils	6¾	
Spring rate	94¼ lbs./inch	

SPEEDOMETER GEARS

See page GD.34 for full details of driving and driven gears with sprockets and tyre sizes.

All frame, fittings, wheel, brake, tyre and electrical details as A50 Cyclone.

SPROCKETS

Number of teeth

Engine	28
Clutch	58
Gearbox	19
Rear wheel	42

A50 STAR (U.S.A.)

General Data is the same as model A50 Star, pages GD 13-14 except for the following:—

CARBURETTOR

Type	Amal 376/284	
Main jet	260	
Pilot jet	25	
Needle jet	106"	(2.6924 mm.)
Needle position	3	
Throttle valve	376/3½	
Nominal choke size	1"	(25.4 mm.)

PISTONS

Compression ratio ... ... 9.0 to 1

PETROL TANK

Capacity ... ... 2 or 4 gallons

GENERAL DATA

MODEL A65 THUNDERBOLT ROCKET (U.S.A.)

General Data is the same as model A65 Star, pages GD.1–12 except for the following:—

PISTONS

Compression ratio	9.0 to 1

CARBURETTOR

Type	Amal 389/202	
Main jet	310	
Pilot jet	25	
Needle jet	.106"	(2.6924 mm.)
Needle position	3	
Throttle valve	389/3½	
Nominal choke size	1⅛"	(28.575 mm.)

OIL PUMP

As Lightning Rocket (pages GD.20–21)

INNER TIMING COVER

As Lightning Rocket (pages GD.20–21)

CLUTCH

As Lightning Rocket (pages GD.20–21)

WHEELS

As A65 Rocket (pages GD.15–16)

PETROL TANK

2 or 4 gallons

GENERAL DATA

MODEL A65 LIGHTNING ROCKET (U.S.A.)

General Data is the same as model A65 Lightning Rocket, pages GD.20–21 except for the following:—

GEARBOX

Internal ratios (standard)	As A65 Star
Overall ratios (standard)	As A65 Star

WHEELS, BRAKES and TYRES

As A50 Cyclone, page GD.18. Balance weights and two security bolts to each wheel.

PETROL TANK

2 or 4 gallons

GENERAL DATA

MODEL A65 SPITFIRE HORNET (U.S.A.)

General Data is the same as model A65 Lightning Rocket, pages GD.20–21 except for the following:—

IGNITION TIMING (Energy Transfer System)

Piston position (B.T.D.C.):
    full advanced ... ... .357″ (9.067 mm.)
Crankshaft position (B.T.D.C.):
    full advanced ... ... 37°

GEARBOX

	Top	3rd	2nd	1st
Internal ratios (standard)	1–1	1.144–1	1.60–1	2.51–1
Overall ratios	4.93	5.65	7.88	12.40
Internal ratios (close)	1–1	1.107–1	1.47–1	2.03–1
Overall ratios	4.93	5.457	7.247	10.00

(see pages GD.30–31 for alternative ratios)

SPROCKETS

	Number of teeth
Gearbox final drive	21
Rear wheel	50

A5065   GENERAL DATA   GD26

FRONT FORK SPRINGS

Free length	$10\frac{3}{4}''$ — $10\frac{7}{8}''$ (273.05—276.225 mm.)
Spring rate	34 lbs./per inch
Number of coils	19
Colour code	Red/green

WHEELS

Rim size and type (front)	WM2-19
Rim size and type (rear)	WM3-18
Spoke size, rear right-hand (20)	$7\frac{3}{8}'' \times 10G$
Spoke size, rear left-hand (20)	$7\frac{7}{16}'' \times 10G$

TYRES

Size (front)	$3.50'' \times 19''$
(rear)	$4.0'' \times 18''$

(two security bolts to each wheel)

REAR CHAIN

$\frac{5}{8}'' \times \frac{3}{8}'' \times 109$ pitches

PETROL TANK

Material	Fibre Glass
Capacity	2 gallon

ELECTRICAL EQUIPMENT (Energy Transfer System)

Alternator type	RM19ET Lucas
Coil type	3ET Lucas
Condensors (capacitors)	54441582 Lucas
Contact breaker	4CA.ET Lucas

GD27 GENERAL DATA A5065

A50 CYCLONE ROAD MODEL (U.S.A.)

General Data is the same as model A50 Cyclone, pages GD.17–18–19 except for the following:—

CAMSHAFT

Type ... ...   As standard A50 Star

GEARBOX

	Top	3rd	2nd	1st
Internal ratios (standard)	1–1	1.144–1	1 60–1	2.51–1
Overall ratios	5.17	5.92	8.272	13.00

FINAL DRIVE SPROCKET

Number of teeth   20
(see pages GD.30–31 for alternative ratios)

WHEELS, BRAKES AND TYRES

REAR WHEEL

Rim size and type WM3–18
Spoke size left-hand (20) ... ... $7\frac{3}{8}'' \times 10G$
Spoke size right-hand (20) ... ... $7\frac{7}{16}'' \times 10G$

REAR WHEEL SPROCKET

Number of teeth   50
Chain size ... ... $\frac{5}{8}'' \times \frac{3}{8}'' \times 108$ pitches

TYRES

Size ... ... (front)   3.25″ × 19″   (82.55 × 482.6 mm.)
            (rear)   4.00″ × 18″   (101.6 × 457.2 mm.)

A5065 GENERAL DATA GD28

A50 CYCLONE COMPETITION MODEL (U.S.A.)

General Data is the same as model A50 Cyclone, pages 17–18–19 except for the following:—

CARBURETTORS (Two)

Type	Amal 376/316
Main jet	170
Pilot jet	25
Needle jet	.106"
Needle position	2
Throttle valve	376/3½
Nominal choke size	1 1/16" (26.987 mm.)

PISTONS

Compression ratio	10.5 to 1

IGNITION TIMING (Energy Transfer System)

Piston position (B.T.D.C.): full advanced	.304" (7.7216 mm.)
Crankshaft position (B.T.D.C.): full advanced	34°

GD29 GENERAL DATA A5065

GEARBOX (U.S.A., East Coast)

As A50 Cyclone Road Model (U.S.A.), page GD.27.

GEARBOX (U.S.A., West Coast)

	Top	3rd	2nd	1st
Internal ratios (close)	1–1	1.107–1	1.47–1	2.03–1
Overall ratios	5.17	5.723	7.599	10.495

FINAL DRIVE SPROCKET

Number of teeth 20
(see pages GD.30–31 for alternative ratios)

WHEELS, BRAKES AND TYRES

REAR WHEEL

As A50 Cyclone Road Model (U.S.A.), page GD.27.

REAR WHEEL SPROCKET

As A50 Cyclone Road Model (U.S.A.), page GD.27.

ELECTRICAL EQUIPMENT (Energy Transfer System)

As A65 Spitfire Hornet (U.S.A.), page GD.26

GENERAL DATA

CLOSE RATIO GEARS AVAILABLE FOR MODELS WITH "QUICK RELEASE" HUBS
ALL WITH 28 TOOTH ENGINE AND 58 TOOTH CLUTCH SPROCKETS

REAR WHEEL SPROCKET				42	42	42	42	42	42
GEARBOX SPROCKET				16	17	18	19	20	21
INTERNAL RATIO	1.0	CLOSE RATIO GEARS	Top	5.437	5.117	4.833	4.579	4.35	4.143
	1.107		Third	6.018	5.664	5.35	5.068	4.815	4.586
	1.47		Second	7.992	7.521	7.104	6.731	6.394	6.09
	2.03		First	11.04	10.39	9.81	9.295	8.83	8.41
REAR WHEEL SPROCKET				50	50	50	50	50	50
GEARBOX SPROCKET				16	17	18	19	20	21
INTERNAL RATIO	1.0	CLOSE RATIO GEARS	Top	6.473	6.09	5.73	5.45	5.17	4.93
	1.107		Third	7.165	6.741	6.343	6.033	5.723	5.457
	1.47		Second	9.515	8.952	8.423	8.01	7.599	7.247
	2.03		First	13.14	12.36	11.631	11.063	10.495	10.00
REAR WHEEL SPROCKET				51	51	51	51	51	51
GEARBOX SPROCKET				16	17	18	19	20	21
INTERNAL RATIO	1.0	CLOSE RATIO GEARS	Top	6.6	6.214	5.871	5.53	5.282	5.03
	1.107		Third	7.306	6.88	6.499	6.12	5.847	5.57
	1.47		Second	9.702	9.134	8.63	8.129	7.764	7.394
	2.03		First	13.398	12.614	11.918	11.225	10.722	10.21
REAR WHEEL SPROCKET				52	52	52	52	52	52
GEARBOX SPROCKET				16	17	18	19	20	21
INTERNAL RATIO	1.0	CLOSE RATIO GEARS	Top	6.732	6.336	5.984	5.669	5.385	5.13
	1.107		Third	7.452	7.013	6.624	6.275	5.961	5.678
	1.47		Second	9.896	9.013	8.796	8.333	7.915	7.541
	2.03		First	13.665	12.862	12.147	11.508	10.931	10.413

GENERAL DATA

**STANDARD RATIO GEARS AVAILABLE FOR MODELS WITH "QUICK RELEASE" HUBS
ALL WITH 28 TOOTH ENGINE AND 58 TOOTH CLUTCH SPROCKETS**

REAR WHEEL SPROCKET				42	42	42	42	42	42
GEARBOX SPROCKET				16	17	18	19	20	21
INTERNAL RATIO	1.0	STANDARD GEARS	Top	5.437	5.117	4.833	4.579	4.35	4.143
	1.144		Third	6.219	5.853	5.506	5.238	4.976	4.739
	1.60		Second	8.70	8.187	7.732	7.326	6.960	6.628
	2.51		First	13.646	12.843	12.130	11.493	10.918	10.398
REAR WHEEL SPROCKET				50	50	50	50	50	50
GEARBOX SPROCKET				16	17	18	19	20	21
INTERNAL RATIO	1.0	STANDARD GEARS	Top	6.473	6.09	5.73	5.45	5.17	4.93
	1.144		Third	7.405	6.967	6.555	6.234	5.92	5.65
	1.60		Second	10.356	9.744	9.168	8.720	8.272	7.89
	2.51		First	16.247	15.28	14.382	13.679	13.00	12.40
REAR WHEEL SPROCKET				51	51	51	51	51	51
GEARBOX SPROCKET				16	17	18	19	20	21
INTERNAL RATIO	1.0	STANDARD GEARS	Top	6.60	6.214	5.871	5.53	5.282	5.03
	1.144		Third	7.55	7.108	6.714	6.326	6.042	5.754
	1.60		Second	10.56	9.942	9.393	8.848	8.451	8.048
	2.51		First	16.566	15.597	14.736	13.88	13.247	12.625
REAR WHEEL SPROCKET				52	52	52	52	52	52
GEARBOX SPROCKET				16	17	18	19	20	21
INTERNAL RATIO	1.0	STANDARD GEARS	Top	6.732	6.336	5.984	5.669	5.385	5.13
	1.144		Third	7.701	7.248	6.845	6.485	6.129	5.868
	1.60		Second	10.771	10.137	9.574	9.07	8.616	8.208
	2.51		First	16.897	15.903	15.02	14.229	13.448	12.87

GENERAL DATA

A5065   GD32

STANDARD AND CLOSE RATIO GEARS AVAILABLE FOR MODELS WITH "FULL WIDTH" HUBS, ALL WITH 28 TOOTH ENGINE AND 58 TOOTH CLUTCH SPROCKETS

REAR WHEEL SPROCKET				42	42	42	42	42	42
GEARBOX SPROCKET				16	17	18	19	20	21
INTERNAL RATIO	1.0	STANDARD GEARS	Top	5.437	5.117	4.833	4.579	4.35	4.143
	1.144		Third	6.219	5.853	5.506	5.238	4.976	4.739
	1.60		Second	8.70	8.187	7.732	7.326	6.960	6.628
	2.51		First	13.646	12.843	12.130	11.493	10.918	10.398
REAR WHEEL SPROCKET				43	43	43	43	43	43
GEARBOX SPROCKET				16	17	18	19	20	21
INTERNAL RATIO	1.0	STANDARD GEARS	Top	5.56	5.239	4.750	4.687	4.453	4.241
	1.144		Third	6.36	5.993	5.434	5.361	5.094	4.851
	1.60		Second	8.896	8.382	7.60	7.499	7.124	6.785
	2.51		First	13.93	13.149	11.922	11.764	11.177	10.644
REAR WHEEL SPROCKET				42	42	42	42	42	42
GEARBOX SPROCKET				16	17	18	19	20	21
INTERNAL RATIO	1.0	CLOSE RATIO GEARS	Top	5.437	5.117	4.833	4.579	4.35	4.143
	1.107		Third	6.018	5.664	5.350	5.068	4.815	4.586
	1.47		Second	7.982	7.521	7.104	6.443	6.394	6.09
	2.03		First	11.037	10.387	9.81	9.295	8.830	8.41
REAR WHEEL SPROCKET				43	43	43	43	43	43
GEARBOX SPROCKET				16	17	18	19	20	21
INTERNAL RATIO	1.0	CLOSE RATIO GEARS	Top	5.56	5.239	4.750	4.687	4.453	4.241
	1.107		Third	6.154	5.8	5.26	5.188	4.93	4.694
	1.47		Second	8.17	7.701	6.982	6.889	6.545	6.234
	2.03		First	11.286	10.635	9.642	9.514	9.039	8.609

FINDING THE RATIO

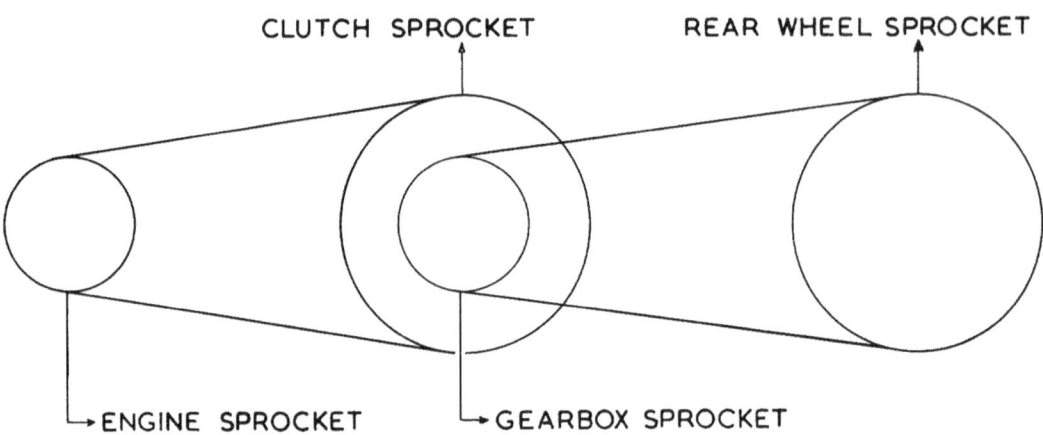

To find the gear ratios of a machine, calculate the top gear as follows:—

Divide the number of teeth on the clutch sprocket by the number of teeth on the engine sprocket and multiply the result by the number of teeth on the rear wheel sprocket, divided by the number of teeth on the gearbox sprocket, as example:—

$$\frac{\textit{clutch sprocket } (43)}{\textit{engine sprocket } (17)} \times \frac{\textit{rear wheel sprocket } (42)}{\textit{gearbox sprocket } (19)} = \frac{1806}{323} = 5.591$$

To find the intermediate gear ratio, multiply the overall top gear by the internal gear ratio concerned, as example:—

top gear 5.591 *or* 5.6 × *bottom gear internal ratio* 2.58 = 14.4 *bottom gear overall ratio*

$$\text{Gearbox internal ratio} = \frac{\textit{layshaft gear}}{\textit{mainshaft gear}} \times \frac{\textit{mainshaft top gear}}{\textit{layshaft top gear}}$$

as example:—

$$\frac{(\textit{layshaft } 3\text{rd}) \; 22\text{T}}{(\textit{mainshaft } 3\text{rd}) \; 26\text{T}} \times \frac{(\textit{mainshaft top}) \; 23\text{T}}{(\textit{layshaft top}) \; 17\text{T}} = 1.144$$

(see FIG. B52 to identify gears)

GENERAL DATA

SPEEDOMETER GEARS

Rear Tyre Size	Gearbox Sprocket	Rear Wheel Sprocket	Driving Gear Spares Number	Driving Gear Number of Teeth	Letter Marking	Driven Gear Spares Number	Driven Gear Number of Teeth
3.50×18	16T	43T	68-3148	6	G	68-0314	11
3.50×18	17T	42T	68-3131	7	C	68-3132	12
3.50×19	17T	42T	68-3143	7	B	68-3144	11
3.50×18	18T	42T	68-3143	7	B	68-3144	11
3.50×18	19T	42T	68-3146	8	D	68-3147	12
3.50×19	19T	42T	68-3134	7	A	68-3135	10
3.50×18	20T	42T	68-3134	7	A	68-3135	10
3.50×19	20T	42T	68-3140	8	E	68-3141	11
4.00×18	21T	50T	68-3143	7	B	68-3144	11

All with 1,600 r.p.m. magnetic head speedometer.

GENERAL DATA

MODEL A50 AND A65
PISTON DISPLACEMENT AND CRANKSHAFT DEGREES

Degrees	Piston Displacement		Degrees	Piston Displacement		Degrees	Piston Displacement	
	Inches	mm.		Inches	mm.		Inches	mm.
1	.0001	.00254	16	.0697	1.7703	31	.2559	6.499
2	.0010	.0254	17	.0793	2.01422	32	.2711	6.885
3	.0024	.06096	18	.0880	2.2352	33	.2876	7.305
4	.0043	.1092	19	.0980	2.4892	34	.3045	7.7343
5	.0067	.17018	20	.1084	2.7533	35	.3218	8.1737
6	.0098	.2489	21	.1194	3.0427	36	.3395	8.6233
7	.0134	.34036	22	.1307	3.3197	37	.3577	9.0855
8	.0175	.4445	23	.1427	3.6245	38	.3760	9.5504
9	.0224	.56896	24	.1551	3.9395	39	.3950	10.033
10	.0274	.69596	25	.1679	4.2646	40	.4143	10.5232
11	.0331	.84074	26	.1813	4.605	41	.4339	11.021
12	.0394	1.0007	27	.1952	4.918	42	.4538	11.5265
13	.0460	1.1684	28	.2094	5.3187	43	.4741	12.0421
14	.0535	1.3589	29	.2243	5.6972	44	.4947	12.5653
15	.0614	1.5595	30	.2393	6.0782	45	.5158	13.101

GENERAL DATA

TORQUE WRENCH SETTINGS (DRY)

FLYWHEEL BOLTS	30 lb./ft.
CONNECTING ROD BOLTS	22 lb./ft.
CYLINDER HEAD BOLTS ($\frac{3}{8}''$)	25 lb./ft.
CYLINDER HEAD BOLTS ($\frac{5}{16}''$)	25 lb./ft.
CYLINDER HEAD NUTS ($\frac{3}{8}''$)	26 lb./ft.
CYLINDER BARREL NUTS ($\frac{5}{16}''$)	18 lb./ft.
OIL PUMP STUD NUTS	7 lb./ft.
CLUTCH CENTRE NUT	70–75 lb./ft.
KICKSTARTER RATCHET NUT	60 lb./ft.
ROTOR FIXING NUT	60 lb./ft.
STATOR FIXING NUTS	10–15 lb./ft.
CRANKSHAFT PINION NUT	60 lb./ft.
MANIFOLD STUD NUTS ($\frac{5}{16}''$)	12½ lb./ft.
MANIFOLD STUD NUTS ($\frac{1}{4}''$)	6 lb./ft.
CARBURETTOR FLANGE NUTS	10 lb./ft.

NOTES

A5065   LUBRICATION   A1

INDEX

	Page
Routine Maintenance	A.2
Recommended Lubricants	A.3–4
Engine Lubrication System	A.5–6
Changing Oil and Cleaning the Filters	A.7–8
Oil Pressure and Non-Return Valves	A.9–10
Dismantling and Reassembling the Oil Pump	A.10–11
Removing and Replacing the Oil Pipe Junction	B.17
Rocker Box Oil Feed Pipe	A.6
Contact Breaker Lubrication	A.11–12
Gearbox Lubrication	A.12
Primary Drive Lubrication	A.13
Rear Chain Lubrication	A.13
Steering Head Race Lubrication	A.14
Wheel Bearings	A.15
Front Fork Lubrication	A.14
Lubrication Nipples	A.15
Control Cables	A.16
Speedometer and Tachometer Cables	A.16
Rear Brake Pedal Spindle	A.15

A2   LUBRICATION   A5065

ROUTINE MAINTENANCE

Page

DAILY

    Check Oil Level in Tank.

EVERY 2,000 MILES (3,200 Kms.)

Check Oil Level in Gearbox	A.12
Check Oil Level in Primary Chaincase	A.13
Drain and Refill Oil Tank	A.7–8
Lubricate Rear Chain	A.13
Remove and Grease Brake Cross-Shaft	A.15
Grease Brake Cam Spindles	A.15
Grease Centre Stand Pivot	D.15
Lubricate Exposed Cables	A.16
Grease Brake Rod Pivot Pin	A.15

EVERY 6,000 MILES (9,600 Kms.)

Lubricate Contact Breaker Cam	A.11
Lubricate Contact Breaker Auto-Advance	A.12
Drain and Refill Gearbox	A.12
Drain and Refill Primary Chaincase	A.13

EVERY 12,000 MILES (19,200 Kms.)

Drain and Refill Front Forks	A.14
Grease Wheel Bearings	F.2–13
Grease Steering Head Bearings	A.14

LUBRICATION

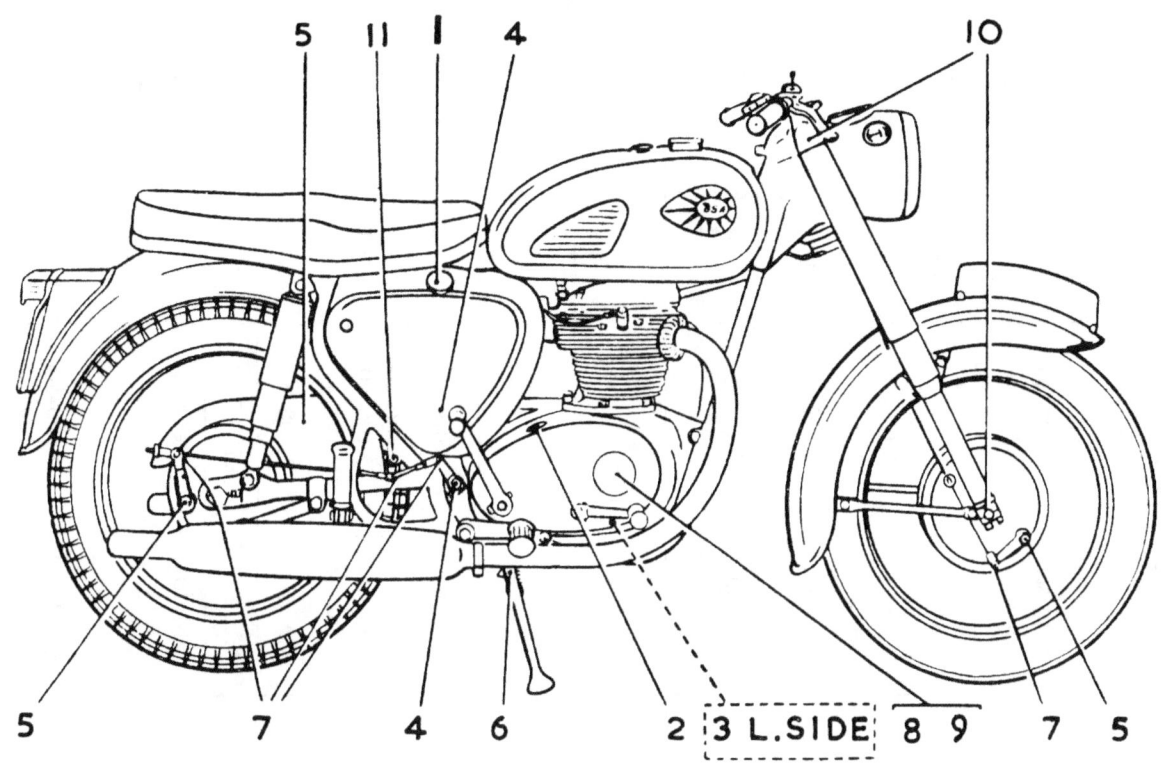

Fig. A.1.

LUBRICATION POINTS

Ref. No.		S.A.E. GRADE	
		Summer	Winter
1.	Oil Tank	40–50	20–40
2.	Gearbox	50	
3.	Primary Chaincase	20	
4.	Brake Cross-Shaft	Grease	
5.	Cam Spindles	Grease	
6.	Centre Stand Pivot	Grease	
7.	Exposed Cables and Joints	Oil or Grease	
8.	Contact Breaker	20	
9.	Contact Breaker Auto-Advance	20	
10.	Front Forks	20	
11.	Brake Rod Pivot	20	

LUBRICATION

RECOMMENDED LUBRICANTS

UNITED KINGDOM

ASSEMBLY	MOBIL	B.P.	CASTROL	ESSO	SHELL	REGENT
ENGINE: Summer / Winter	BB / A	S.A.E. 40 / S.A.E. 30	XXL / XL	Extra 40/50 / 20/30	X100-40 / X100-30	Havoline S.A.E. 40 / S.A.E. 30
GEARBOX	D	S.A.E. 50	Grand Prix	Extra 40/50	X100-50	Havoline S.A.E. 50
PRIMARY CHAINCASE	Arctic	S.A.E. 20	Castrolite	Extra 20/30	X100-20	Havoline S.A.E. 20W
FRONT FORK	Arctic	S.A.E. 20	Castrolite	Extra 20/30	X100-20	Havoline S.A.E. 20W
WHEEL BEARINGS / SWINGING ARM / STEERING HEAD	Mobilgrease MP	Energrease L2	Castrolease LM	Multi-purpose H	Retinax A	Marfak 2

OTHER COUNTRIES

ASSEMBLY	MOBIL	B.P.	CASTROL	ESSO	SHELL	CALTEX
ENGINE: Above 32°C. / 0° to 32°C. / Below 0°C.	Mobiloil AF / Mobiloil A / Mobiloil Arctic	Energol 40 / Energol 30 / Energol 20W	XXL / XL / Castrolite	S.A.E. 40/50 / S.A.E. 20W/40 / S.A.E. 10W/30	X100-40 / X100-30 / X100-20W	S.A.E. 40 / S.A.E. 30 / S.A.E. 20W
GEARBOX	Mobiloil A	Energol 50	Grand Prix	S.A.E. 50	X100-50	S.A.E. 50
PRIMARY CHAINCASE	Mobiloil Arctic	Energol 20	Castrolite	S.A.E. 20W/40	X100-20W	S.A.E. 20W
WHEEL BEARINGS / SWINGING ARM / STERING HEAD	Mobilgrease MP	Energrease L2	Castrolease LM	Multi-purpose H	Retinax A	Marfak 2
FRONT FORK: Above 32°C. / 15°C. to 32°C. / Below 15°C.	Mobiloil D / Mobiloil A / Mobiloil Arctic	Energol 50 / Energol 30 / Energol 20W	Grand Prix / XL / Castrolite	S.A.E 40 / S.A.E. 20W/40 / S.A.E. 10W/30	X100-50 / X100-30 / X100-20W	S.A.E. 50 / S.A.E. 30 / S.A.E. 20W

LUBRICATION

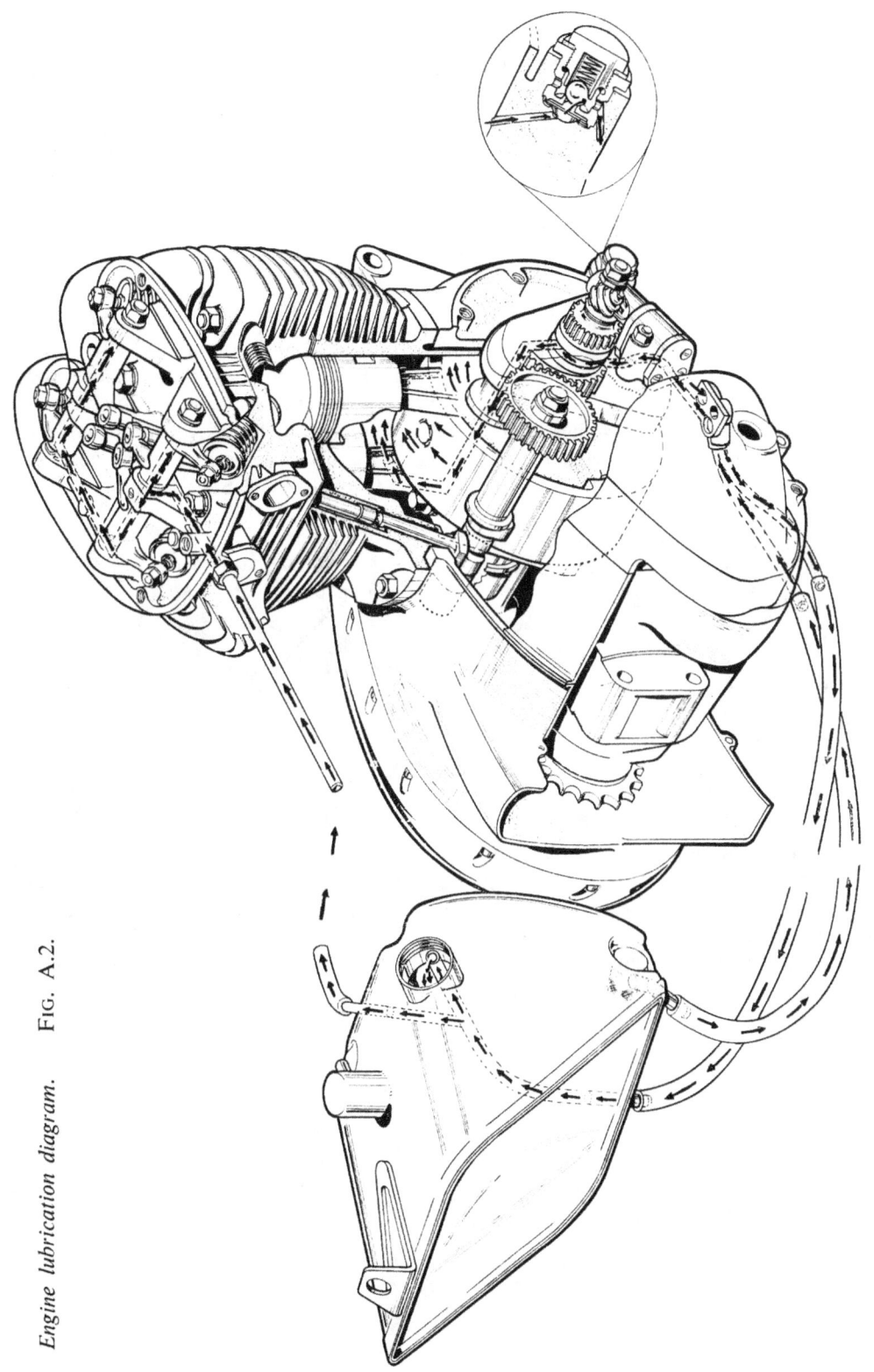

Engine lubrication diagram. Fig. A.2.

LUBRICATION

ENGINE LUBRICATION

The lubrication system is of the dry sump type, i.e. the oil is fed by gravity from a tank to the double gear type pump contained inside the crankcase on the gear-side. One set of gears in the pump draws oil from the tank through a gauze filter and delivers it under pressure past a non-return valve to the timing-side main bearing.

The oil then flows through drillings in the crankshaft past a sludge trap to the big-end bearings Excess oil is thrown off by centrifugal force on to the cylinder walls, the underside of the piston (to lubricate the gudgeon pins), and is collected in various wells to lubricate the camshaft and gears.

If the pump pressure is above the intended maximum a release valve in the base of the timing cover opens to pass the excess oil direct to the bottom of the crankcase.

After lubricating the various internal parts of the engine the oil drains down into the sump, fastened to the underside of the crankcase. From here the second, and larger set of gears in the pump, draws oil through another non-return valve and pumps it back to the tank at a greater rate than the feed side thus ensuring that the sump is not flooded; hence the term "dry sump".

Just before the oil is emptied into the tank the return pipe is tapped to provide a supply of oil at low pressure to the valve rocker gear.

This pipe is connected by means of a union to the cylinder head immediately above the carburettor intake (single carburettor models).

The oil is then fed through drillings to the inlet rocker shaft thence via the shaft and a special oilway on the left-hand side of the rocker box to the exhaust rocker spindle. From the spindles the oil also lubricates the rocker ball pins and adjuster screws, it then drains down into the crankcase, via the push rod tower, lubricating the tappets on its way down.

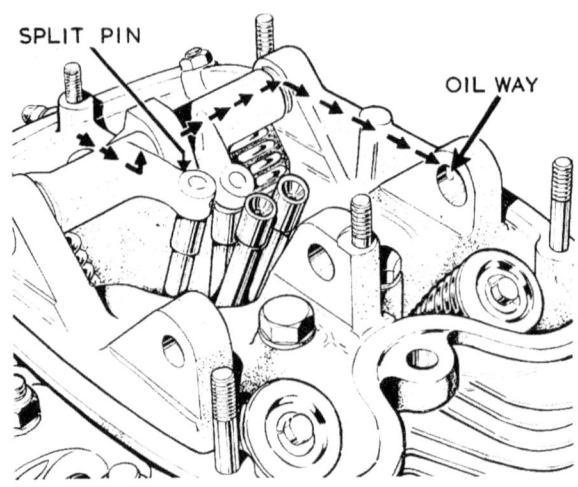

Fig. A.3. *Rocker lubrication.*

The feed to the rockers is metered by a split pin at the base of the centre pillar. Should this pin be replaced at any time one of exactly the same diameter must be used.

LUBRICATION

CHANGING THE OIL AND CLEANING THE FILTERS

The oil in new or reconditioned engines should be changed at 250, 500 and 1,000 mile (400, 800 and 1,500 kms.) intervals during the running-in period and thereafter as stated on page A.2.

It is always advisable to drain when the oil is warm as it flows more readily.

To obtain access to the oil tank take off the right-hand sidecover by turning the fasteners and pulling the cover off the carburettor stud.

Sidecovers on the twin carburettor models are of a different shape and do not use the carburettor stud as an anchorage.

The oil tank filter is screwed into the lower right-hand corner of the tank. Obtain a suitable receptacle with a piece of cardboard to use as a chute, unscrew the filter which has the normal right-hand thread, and allow the oil to drain.

Wash the filter thoroughly in petrol and allow to dry.

Lean the machine towards the right-hand side to drain off the remaining oil.

Again using a suitable receptacle to catch the oil, unscrew the four ¼ in. B.S.C. nuts holding the sump filter to the crankcase, take off the four shakeproof washers and remove the filter.

Allow the oil to drain, wash the filter thoroughly in petrol, and clean off all the old jointing material from the filter and crankcase. If there is any sign of damage to the old gasket, replace it on assembly.

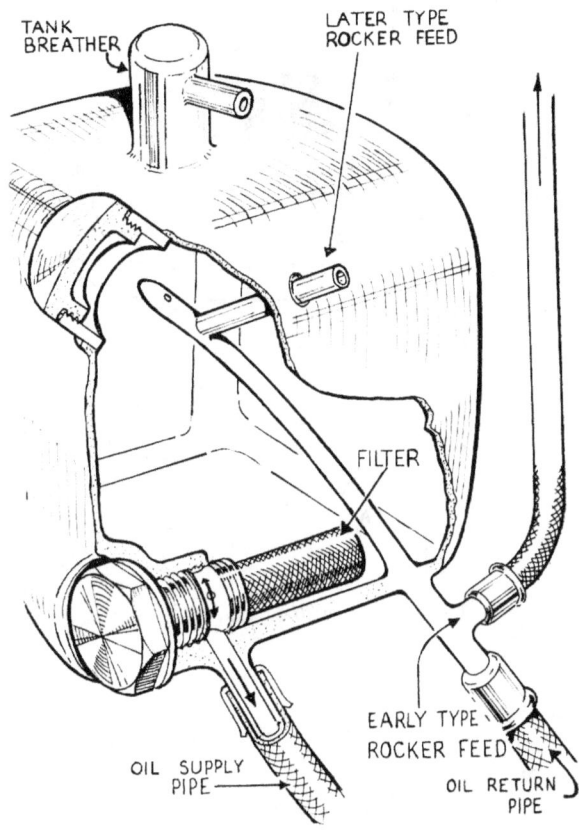

FIG. A.4. *Oil tank and filter.*

Non-Return Valves.
With the sump filter off, check the scavenge pipe non-return valve, using a piece of wire push the ball up off its seating and allow it to drop of its own weight, if it does not drop it indicates a build-up of sludge which can usually be removed by immersing the pipe in petrol for a short period.

If there has been a tendency for the crankcase to fill with oil after standing overnight so emitting clouds of smoke when the engine is started, it is quite possible that the feed line non-return valve is not seating properly thus allowing oil to run back from the tank, this is the valve behind the pump described on pages A.9 and A.10.

LUBRICATION

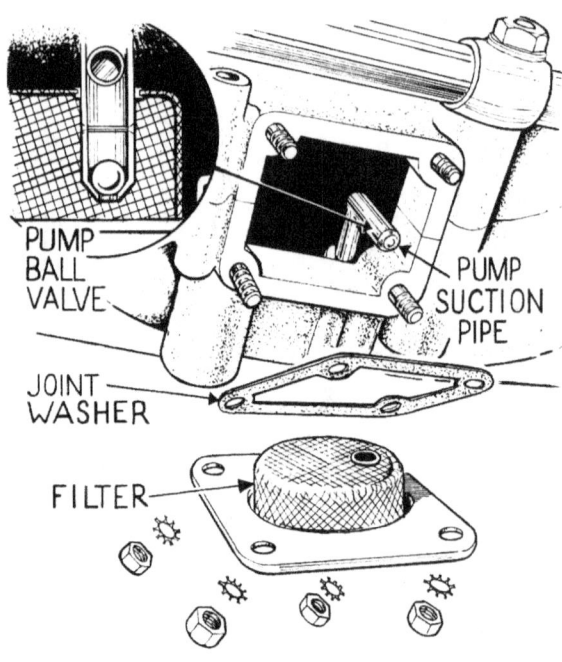

Fig. A.5. *Crankcase filter and ball valve.*

Oil Pipes.
Unscrew the single 5/16 in. B.S.F. bolt holding the oil feed and return pipes to the crankcase slightly to the right-hand of the sump filter.

On early models a plain paper gasket was used at this joint but later models use two rubber rings to provide an oil seal.

The later type can be fitted if desired but the metal pipes complete with rubber rings must be used, the rings alone cannot be used with the old pipes unless they are modified to suit.

Pull the pipes away and allow to drain.

Oil Tank.
Usually it is sufficient to drain and refill the tank. If however the machine has been used for a long period and there is an accumulation of sludge in the tank, then it is good policy to flush it out with paraffin but, **all traces of paraffin must be removed before refilling.**

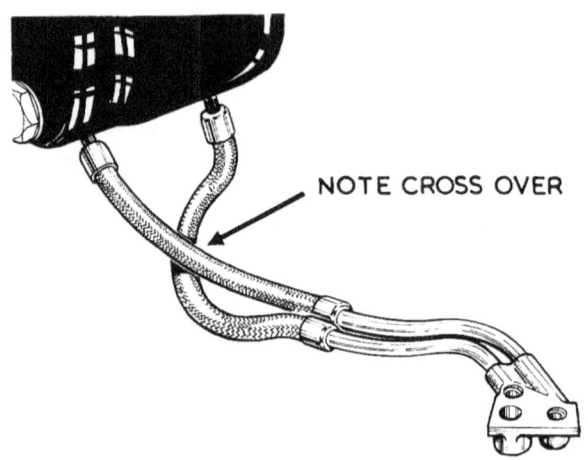

Fig. A.6. *Oil pipe connections.*

Reassembly.
After thoroughly draining and cleaning the system, replace the oil tank filter using a new fibre washer, reconnect the oil pipes to the crankcase using a new paper gasket and jointing cement sparingly, (cement is not used with the two rubber rings on later models). Replace the sump filter using a new paper gasket and cement. The four nuts must be tightened equally criss-crossing to avoid distortion.

NOTE:—The oil pipes are correctly fitted when crossed over, i.e. the outer pipe from the tank is attached to the inner connection on the crankcase.

Refill with correct grade oil.

LUBRICATION

OIL PRESSURE AND NON-RETURN VALVES

The oil pressure is controlled by the release valve situated on the right-hand side of the crankcase below the timing covers.

When the engine revolutions reach 3,000 revs per minute the oil pressure is around 50 lbs. per square inch therefore to prevent the pressure becoming excessive the valve opens and releases the excess oil direct into the crankcase whence it is returned to the tank.

The valve is pre-set at the Works and there is no point in altering the setting. However after prolonged use the spring does tend to weaken and sometimes corrode and should be replaced. The length of the spring can be checked (see page GD.3) and if there is corrosion it is wise to replace the ball also, after cleaning the valve body.

To remove the valve simply unscrew the large hexagon and to dismantle, unscrew the small hexagon. Do not attempt to remove the gauze filter and ensure that the fibre washers are fit for further use. Later models use "O" rings in place of the fibre washers but, whilst the complete valve is interchangeable, the "O" rings cannot be used with the old type valve.

There is a sludge trap built into the crankshaft and this may become blocked if oil changes are not carried out at the prescribed intervals.

Low Oil Pressure.
Low oil pressure is dangerous since insufficient oil is likely to be delivered to the engine. The possible causes of low pressure being:—

1. Insufficient oil in the tank. Check the level and the return after replenishing. If the return is correct it will show as a mixture of oil and air issuing from the return stand pipe.

2. Tank and sump filters partly blocked preventing the free passage of oil.

3. Badly worn oil pump or badly worn big-end bearing shells.

4. Oil pipes incorrectly connected at the tank when the pump would be drawing air through the return pipe.

Syphoning.
This, one of the commonest troubles, happens when one of the non-return ball valves is sticking **off** its seating. It can also be caused by a badly worn pump or one which is loose on its mounting.

Indications of syphoning are clouds of smoke from the exhaust when the engine is first started after standing overnight.

The non-return valves are located behind the oil pump body and in the scavenge pipe and consist of a ball and spring (see pages A.7 and B.3!).

DISMANTLING AND REASSEMBLING THE PUMP

Having removed the pump from the engine take out the non-return valve ball and spring and store in a safe place.

Lever up the circlip at the spindle end and pull out with a pair of pliers. The thrust washer and spindle can now be removed.

Remove the four screws at the base of the pump, take off the base plate and spindle housing to uncover the four gears.

Wash all parts thoroughly in petrol and allow to dry before examining. Look for foreign matter jammed in the gear teeth and deep score marks in the pump body. These will be evident if the oil changing has been neglected. Figure A.7 shows slight score marks which could be ignored but the metal embedded in the gear tooth must be removed.

The most likely point of wear will be on the spindle teeth, if these are worn to the extent that the sharp edge has gone then the spindle should be replaced.

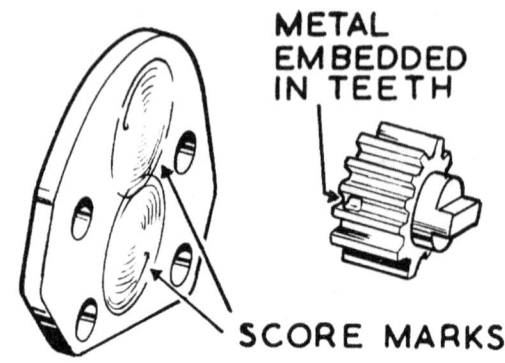

Fig. A.7.

On current model oil pumps there is an "O" ring fitted to the feed driving gear to provide an oil seal between the gear and the spindle housing. This "O" ring must be in good condition if it is to be used again otherwise it should be replaced.

The "O" ring can be used on earlier models but a new spindle housing would be required also.

LUBRICATION

REBUILDING THE PUMP

Absolute cleanliness is essential when rebuilding the pump.

Insert the feed driving gear into its housing, this is the one on the rounded side of the body, place in position the driven feed gear then insert the return gears on the lower side of the pump. Slide the spindle through the two driven gears, **apply clean oil,** and refit the spindle housing and base plate.

Place the driving spindle in position and test the pump for freedom of movement; insert the spindle thrust washer and circlip.

Finally check the joint faces for parallelity; if the housing face is not in line it will be distorted when bolted to the crankcase and may prevent the pump from working (see Fig. A.8).

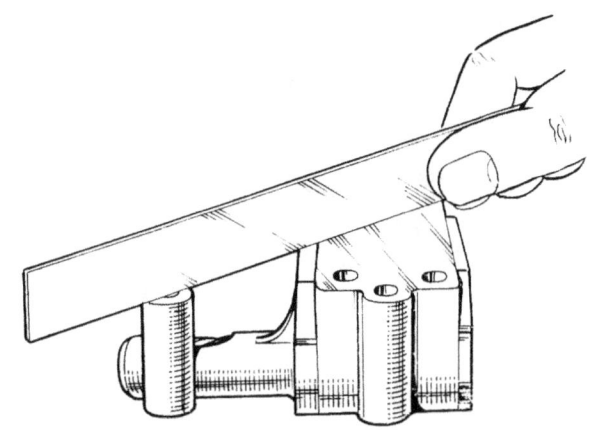

Fig. A.8. *Checking joint faces.*

CONTACT BREAKER LUBRICATION

The contact breaker is situated in the inner timing cover and it is essential that no engine oil gets into the contact breaker housing. For this purpose there is an oil seal pressed into the inner timing cover at the back of the contact breaker unit.

Lubrication of the contact breaker cam and the auto-advance unit pivot points is however necessary.

The cam is lubricated from an oil soaked felt wick which should have a few drops of engine oil (S.A.E. 20 or 30) applied every 5,000 miles (8,000 kms.)—see Fig. A.9, page A.12.

To lubricate the auto-advance unit it is necessary to remove the contact breaker plate. First place a mark across the plate and the housing so that it can be replaced in exactly the same position then take out the two contact breaker plate mounting screws and lift off the plate.

The pivot points of the auto-advance unit should be lightly oiled where indicated in Fig. A.10 again at 5,000 mile (8,000 kms.) intervals. After lubricating, replace the plate to the marks but, if the timing has been upset, follow the instructions on pages B.49–53.

A12 LUBRICATION A5065

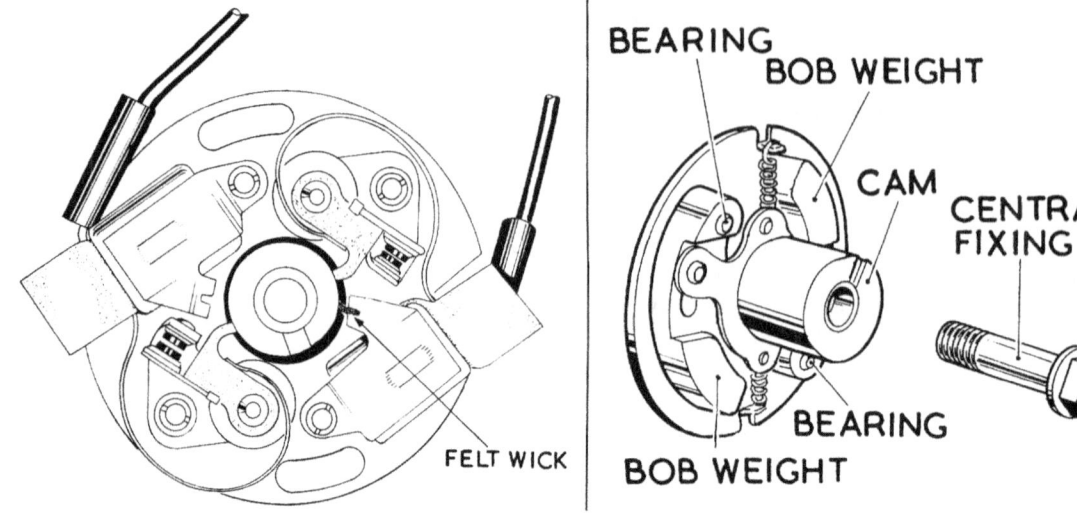

Fig. A.9. *Contact breaker.* Fig. A.10. *Auto-advance unit.*

GEARBOX LUBRICATION

The gearbox having its own oil bath is independant of the engine for lubrication but, for the same reason, the level of oil must be checked and any loss due to leakage made good.

The lower set of gears runs in the oil bath and oil being squeezed from or thrown off these gears by centrifugal force lubricates the rest of the gears, bearings, and bushes.

To drain the gearbox take out the filler plug on top of the gearbox then unscrew and take out the larger of the two plugs underneath, draining the oil into a suitable receptacle (see Fig. A.11).

After draining, replace the drain plug making sure that the fibre washer (or "O" ring) whichever is fitted, is in good condition but leave out the smaller plug.

Now replace the oil until it commences to overflow down the drain plug tube.

Replace the small plug.

Recommended grades are quoted on page A.3, capacities on page GD.12 and checking frequency on page A.2.

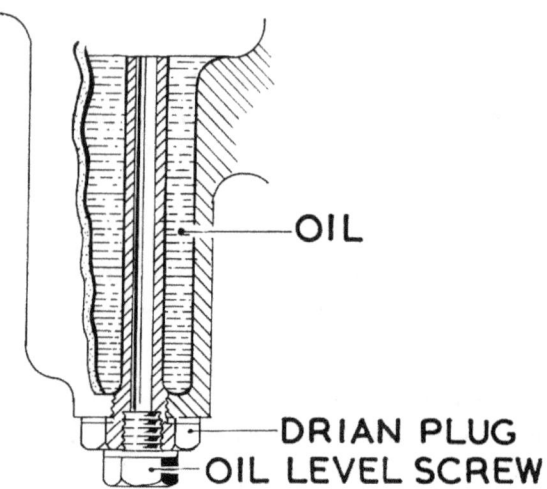

Fig. A.11. *The gearbox oil level and drain plugs.*

LUBRICATION

PRIMARY CHAINCASE LUBRICATION

Like the gearbox, the primary chaincase, having its own oil bath, is independant of the engine but the level of oil must be checked periodically and the oil drained and replaced as indicated in the routine maintenance sheet, page A.2.

The oil bath in the primary chaincase does not lubricate the chain only, the clutch being contained in the same case is dependant on this oil supply for its efficient functioning and a drip feed is also provided for the rear chain through an oil well and nozzle at the back of the chaincase.

There are two of the chaincase cover screws which have their heads painted red; they are situated midway along the lower rim of the case, the front one being the oil level screw and the rear is the drain screw.

To drain the oil, take out one of the inspection caps at the side of the case and the drain screw.

After draining, replace the drain screw, take out level screw and add oil through the inspection cap hole until it commences to run out of the level screw hole.

Oil containing molybdenum disulphide or graphite must NOT be used in the primary chaincase.

Drain the oil and use the grades as recommended on page A.4.

REAR CHAIN

Oil thrown off the primary chain is collected in a small well at the back of the primary case from which a drip feed is supplied to the rear chain.

This may not, however, be adequate in some circumstances and it may be advisable to supplement the drip feed by using an oil can occasionally on the rear chain, depending on the state of the chain. The chain should be moist with oil but not dripping.

The best method of lubrication is to remove the chain every 2,000 miles, wash thoroughly in paraffin and allow to drain, then immerse it in melted tallow to which powdered graphite has been added.

Hang the chain over the grease tin to allow the surplus grease to drain off. If the tin is covered after use it can be used many times, but always use care when melting.

LUBRICATION

STEERING HEAD

The steering head bearings are packed with grease on assembly and only require repacking at the intervals quoted on page A.2.

Removal and replacement of the steering is dealt with on pages E.4–5 in the fork section.

When the balls are removed they should be cleaned by placing in clean rag then rolling the rag between the palms of the hands, changing the position on the rag as necessary.

After cleaning examine carefully for pitting and corrosion and examine the cups and cones for pocketing and cracks.

If there is evidence of damage, it is wise to replace all the bearings, cones and cups.

The fresh grease will hold the balls in position during assembly but make sure that there is the correct number as quoted on page GD.9 and that the grease is as quoted on page A.4.

FRONT FORKS

The oil contained in the forks not only lubricates the bearing bushes, but also acts as the damping medium. It is for this latter reason essential that the amount of oil in each fork leg is exactly the same.

Oil leakage midway up the forks usually indicates that the oil seal has failed and requires replacement; this is dealt with on page E.9 covering the dismantling and reassembly of the forks.

Correct period for changing the oil as quoted on page A.2 is every 12,000 miles (19,200 kms.) but some owners may not cover this mileage in a year, in which case it is suggested that the oil be changed every 12 months.

To drain the oil, take off steering head lock bezel, remove the damper rod and take off the top fork cover. This is only applicable where the headlamp is mounted in the fork cowl. Other models have no fork top cover.

Unscrew and remove the two fork top nuts and take out the drain screws at the base of each fork leg (see Fig. A.12.)

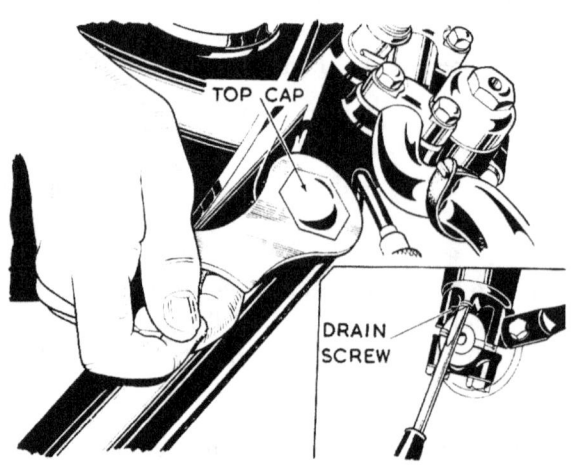

Fig. A.12.

After allowing several minutes to drain, pump the forks up and down to expel any oil remaining, then replace the drain screws taking care not to omit the fibre washers.

Refill with one-third pint (190 c.c.) of the correct grade of oil (see page A.3).

LUBRICATION

WHEEL BEARINGS

The wheel bearings are packed with grease on assembly and only require repacking at the interval quoted on page A.2.

The bearings should be removed as quoted on pages F.2–13 dealing with wheels. After removal wash thoroughly in paraffin and, if possible, use an air line to blow any grit or paraffin remaining, out of the bearings.

Pack with the correct grade of grease as quoted on page A.4 after assembling the first bearing. Do not over-lubricate and do not handle brake shoes with greasy hands.

LUBRICATION NIPPLES

There are a number of points to be lubricated by means of a grease gun and nipples as indicated on page A.3. They comprise both front and rear brake cam spindles (5), rear brake rod pivot (full width hubs)—(11), and centre stand (6). Give one stroke of the grease gun to each of these points at the period indicated on page A.2. No more than one stroke of the gun should be used at point (5) as excess grease is liable to get on the brake linings.

LEFT HAND REAR BRAKE

Models equipped with left-hand rear brake have no cross-shaft. On these models the brake pedal is provided with an oil hole to which a few drops of oil from a can should be applied every 2,000 miles or more frequently if the pivot point tends to dry up.

BRAKE PEDAL CROSS SHAFT

There is no provision for greasing the cross-shaft; like the steering and hubs, grease is applied on assembly but the shaft must be withdrawn and greased periodically as quoted on page A.2.

To do this first slacken off the brake adjustment, scribe a line across the shaft and the right-hand lever — to assist reassembly — remove the right-hand lever pinch bolt and pull the shaft complete with pedal from the left-hand side.

Clean off any accumulation of dirt and grease with a paraffin rag from both spindle and hole, apply grease and reassemble being careful to match the scribed lines.

Adjust the rear brake as necessary.

CABLES

Exposed sections of inner cables should be lubricated periodically (see page A.2). This can be done either by greasing or applying the oil can.

The most satisfactory way, however, is to induce a flow between the inner and outer casing by forming some sort of reservoir to hold the oil and leaving the cable for several hours (see Fig. A.13).

From January 1965, machines are fitted with cables, the inner wires of which, have been greased with a molybdenum based grease which forms a semi-permanent lubricant. They will give long service before needing attention.

SPEEDOMETER CABLES

It is necessary to lubricate speedometer cables particularly to prevent premature failure of the inner wire. Care is however necessary to avoid over-zealous greasing which may result in the lubricant getting into the instrument head. On models with exposed speedometer heads it is only necessary to unscrew the cable nipple below the head and to pull out the inner wire for cleaning and greasing.

On models with a headlamp cowl, the headlamp must first be removed to obtain access to the speedometer. Apply grease sparingly to the inner wire, and none at all within 6 in. of the instrument head.

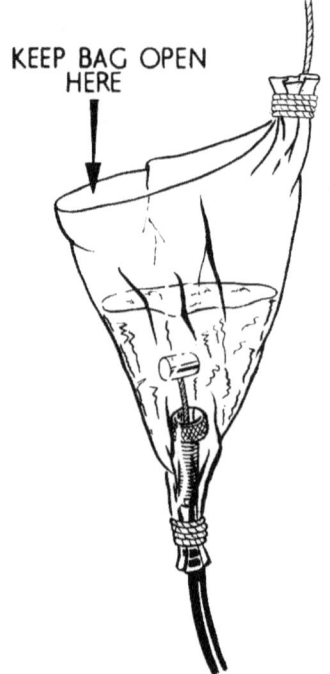

FIG. A.13. *Oiling a cable.*

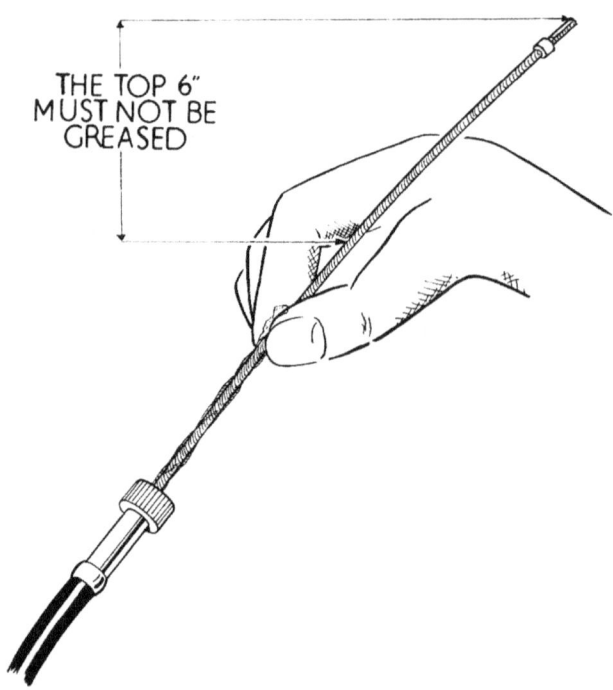

FIG. A.14. *Greasing speedometer cable.*

| A5065 | ENGINE | B1 |

INDEX

	Page
Engine Exploded	B.2
Engine Description	B.3
Decarbonising	B.4–15
Preparation	B.4
Removing the Petrol Tank	B.5
Removing the Carburettor	B.5
Rocker Box and Exhaust Pipes	B.6
Exhaust Rocker Assembly	B.6–7
Cylinder Head Bolts and Studs	B.7
Cylinder Head Removal	B.8
Valve Springs	B.8
Push Rods	B.9
Valves and Guides	B.9
Valve Grinding	B.10
Cylinder Barrel	B.10–11
Tappets	B.11
Cylinder Bores	B.12
Removing the Pistons	B.12
Piston Rings	B.13
Small-End Bushes	B.13
Reassembly after Decarbonising	B.14
Replacing the Barrel	B.14
Replacing the Head	B.14
Tappet Adjustment	B.15
Replacing the Carburettor(s)	B.15
Removing the Engine Unit	B.16–18
Footrests	B.16
Chainguard	B.16
Chaincase	B.17
Rear Chain	B.17
Clutch Cable	B.17
Speedometer and Rev-Counter Cables	B.17

B1a ENGINE A5065

INDEX

	Page
Oil Draining	B.18
Mounting Bolts	B.18
Replacing the Engine Unit	B.19–21
Dismantling the Engine Unit	B.22–44
Transmission	B.22
Primary Drive Cover	B.22
Clutch Dismantling	B.23
Generator	B.23–24
Inspecting the Clutch	B.24
Shock Absorber	B.25
Clutch Chainwheel	B.25
Final Drive Sprocket	B.25
Clutch Operation	B.26
Reassembling the Primary Drive	B.26–28
The Contact Breaker	B.29
Removing the Contact Breaker	B.30
Timing Side Cover	B.30–31
Inner Timing Cover	B.31–32
Timing Gear and Oil Pump	B.32
Replacing the Pump	B.33
Timing Gears	B.33–34
Gearbox Dismantling	B.34–36
Gearbox Reassembly	B.36–38
Splitting the Crankcase	B.39
Camshaft	B.40
Crankshaft Assembly	B.40
Crankshaft Grinding	B.42
Crankshaft Sludge Trap	B.43
Flywheel Balancing (Static)	B.44
Bearings, Bushes and Oil Seals	B.45
Reassembling the Connecting Rods	B.46
Reassembling the Crankcase	B.47
Replacing the Inner Cover	B.48
Ignition Timing	B.49–53

ENGINE

A5065 — B2

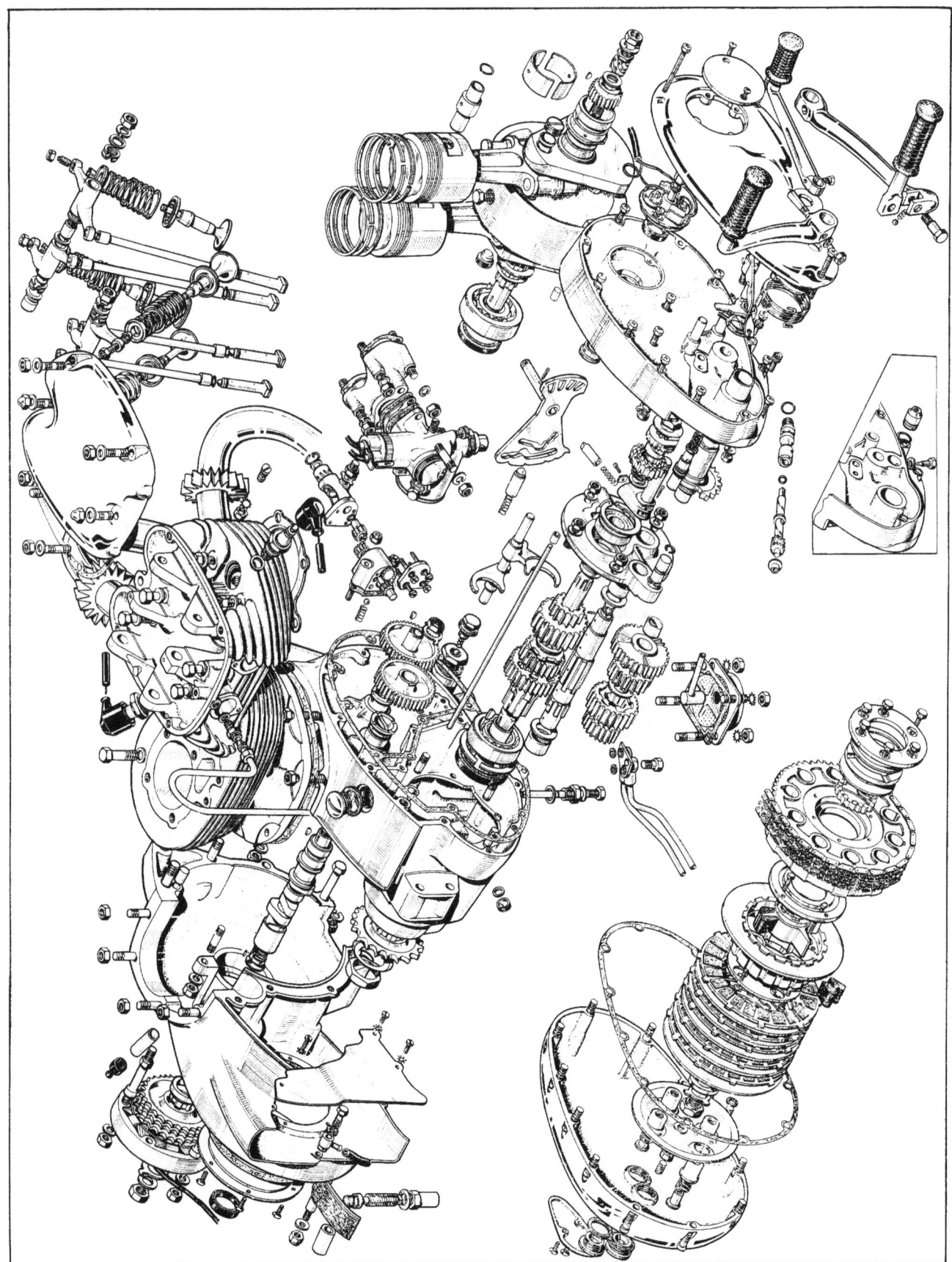

FIG B.1. 500 *and* 650 *c.c. engine exploded.*

ENGINE

DESCRIPTION (500 and 650 c.c.)

Of unit construction the engine has a twin cylinder barrel of close grained cast-iron mounted on an aluminium crankcase made from two halves bolted and machined together. The gearbox is an integral part of the gearside or right-hand half-case which also houses the oil pump and timing gears.

The primary drive case is an integral part of the left-hand or drive side half-crankcase which, in addition to housing half the crankshaft, houses the alternator, clutch and primary chain.

The aluminium alloy cylinder head has high duty cast-iron valve seat inserts cast-in, and the rocker trunnions form an integral part of the head.

"Lo-Ex" aluminium pistons having two compression rings, one of which is tapered, and one scraper ring are used on H-section connecting rods made from RR.56 hiduminium alloy. The one-piece camshaft operates in three bushes, one in "Clevite 10" and the other two made from sintered bronze.

The alternator consists of a rotor mounted on the left-hand of the crankshaft and a six-coil stator mounted on three pillar bolts.

The one-piece, forged, two-throw crankshaft, has a detachable flywheel held in position by three high-tensile steel bolts secured by "Loctite" sealant. Incorporated in the crankshaft is a tubular centrifugal sludge trap.

The double gear oil pump is driven off a crankshaft mounted worm wheel and supplies oil to the crankshaft cylinders, pistons and timing gears. When required the oil pump also drives a revolution counter.

Both the gearbox and primary chaincase have their own independent oil baths.

Power is transmitted from the engine through the engine sprocket and triple primary chain to the clutch, which has a built-in shock absorber, then to the four-speed gearbox and final drive sprocket.

An Amal monobloc carburettor is attached to an inlet manifold which in turn is bolted to the cylinder head on single carburettor models. When twin carburettors are used they are attached direct to the cylinder head.

ENGINE

DECARBONISING — DESCRIPTION

Decarbonising or "top overhaul" as it is sometimes called means the removal of carbon deposited on the top of the piston, on valve heads, around the combustion chamber and inlet and exhaust ports. It also means that while the upper portion of the engine is dismantled for this purpose the opportunity is taken to examine the various parts of the engine for general "wear and tear," hence the term "top overhaul."

Carbon, which is the result of the combustion taking place in the engine when running, is not harmful providing it is removed at the right time, that is before the deposit is too heavy and therefore likely to cause pre-ignition and other symptoms which may impair performance.

The usual symptoms, indicating the need for decarbonising are, a tendency to "pink" (metallic knocking sound when under load), a general falling off of power noticeable mainly on hills, a tendency for the engine to run hotter than usual and an increase in petrol consumption.

Decarbonising should not be carried out unnecessarily, it should only be done when the engine really needs it.

PREPARING TO DECARBONISE

Before commencing the work it is advisable to have the following equipment available:—

Spanners from $\frac{3}{16}$W—$\frac{1}{4}$ in. B.S.F. to $\frac{5}{16}$W—$\frac{3}{8}$ in. B.S.F.
Set of scrapers.
Set of feeler gauges.
Supply of fine emery cloth.
Jointing compound or cement.
Grinding paste.
Clean engine oil.
Two pieces of hardwood, 9 in. long × $\frac{5}{8}$ in. square.
Top overhaul gasket set No. 11900–3158 (A65) or No. 11900–3157 (A50).
Gudgeon pin circlips No. 40266–0954 (4).
Valve springs (set) 11040–0169, 11568–0475
Paraffin and rag for cleaning

Perfect cleanliness is essential to ensure success in any service task, so, before starting the job, make sure that you have a clean bench or working area in which to operate and room to place parts as they are removed.

ENGINE

REMOVING THE PETROL TANK

The following instructions apply equally to machines fitted with twin or single carburettors, except that with twin carburettors there will also be two fuel feeds and two air cleaners to be removed.

Turn off the petrol supply at the taps and disconnect the fuel pipes at the carburettor by unscrewing the banjo union bolt(s). Be careful not to lose the nylon filter or the fibre washers.

Take out the rubber plug in the centre of the tank and remove the nut and washer which will be exposed. On all steel tanks, both two or four gallon, there is an anti-roll bar fitted underneath the forward end, remove the two $\frac{5}{16}$ in. bolts and washers, take the bar away and lift the tank clear of the frame.

Two gallon fibre glass tanks only use the single centre fixing bolt to secure them to the frame.

REMOVING THE CARBURETTOR(S)

On single carburettor models, it is first necessary to remove both side panels. This is done by turning the catches then pulling the side covers back off the inlet manifold studs. Unscrew the air filter from the carburettor and remove the two nuts and washers holding the carburettor to the manifold.

For the purpose of decarbonising it will be sufficient to pull the carburettor off its studs and tie back out of the way.

To remove the carburettor completely, disconnect the throttle cable at the handlebar by removing the two screws securing the halves of the twist-grip, part the body and pull out the cable nipple. Withdraw the cable from the grip.

Open the air control to its fullest extent, then close it, at the same time pull the outer casing and inner wire from the stop, remove the nipple from the lever and pull both throttle and air cables from the frame clips.

The same procedure can be used with twin carburettors except that as there is no manifold the side covers are secured solely by fasteners.

ENGINE

ROCKER BOX AND EXHAUST PIPES

Remove the engine steady stay at the front of the cylinder head by taking out the bolt securing it to the cylinder head, slacken off the bolt holding the steering head end and swing the stay to one side.

Remove the bolts securing the exhaust pipes and silencers to the frame brackets, tap the pipes out of the head using a raw-hide mallet and take away complete.

With siamese pipes the clip securing the left-hand pipe must be slackened off also.

Straight through pipes have a tie rod in front of the engine which must be released before the pipes can be removed.

If this is not done the cylinder head may be seriously damaged.

To remove the rocker box cover take off the six ¼ in. nuts and plain washers, break the joint by a light tap with a mallet, and remove the cover.

There are two projections at the rear of the cover to assist in its removal. The paper gasket is cemented on one side only and should always be replaced.

Disconnect the oil feed pipe to the rocker box by unscrewing the union nut at the rear of the box. The other end pushes into a rubber sleeve adjacent to the oil tank.

EXHAUST ROCKER ASSEMBLY

The exhaust valve rocker assembly must be removed to obtain access to the two front cylinder head bolts. First slacken off the two front (exhaust) valve rocker adjusting screws until the two push rods can be removed, then unscrew the nut holding the exhaust rocker shaft—at the front right-hand side—and tap the shaft through towards the left hand, leaving the rockers in position.

To avoid damaging the end of the shaft use a blunt centre punch. Take careful note of the position of the spring and thrust washers, and remove the rockers from between the shaft pillars.

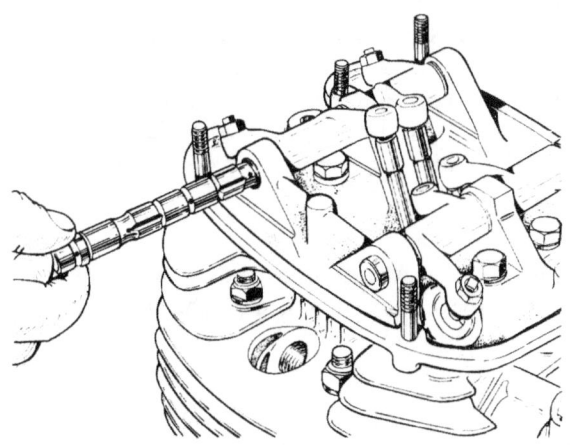

FIG. B.2. *Exhaust rocker spindle.*

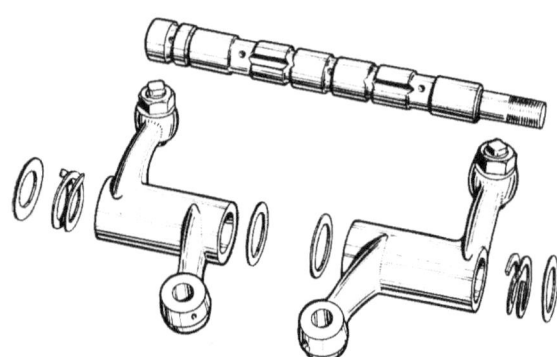

FIG. B.3. *Exhaust rocker assembly*

From left to right, the assembly should be:—

thrust washer
spring washer
left-hand rocker
thrust washer
                centre post
                        thrust washer
                        right-hand rocker
                           spring washer
                             thrust washer

Spring washers are always fitted next to the rockers, they must never be fitted next to the shaft pillars.

There is no need to disturb the inlet rocker assembly, except for replacement purposes or, if there is doubt about the oil supply to the rockers. See page A.6 for details of the rocker lubrication.

CYLINDER HEAD BOLTS AND STUDS

The cylinder head is secured by four $\frac{3}{8}$ in. B.S.C. nuts and washers on studs screwed into the barrel adjacent to the spark plug holes, two $\frac{3}{8}$ in. B.S.F. bolts at the front, two $\frac{5}{16}$ in. B.S.F. bolts at the rear, and one $\frac{3}{8}$ in. B.S.F. bolt in the centre at the bottom of the push rod tower. This latter bolt is short and the push rods must be removed to obtain access to it.

Lift out the exhaust push rods, slacken off the inlet rocker adjusting screws, and take out the inlet push rods.

Pull off the spark plug high-tension leads and remove the spark plugs.

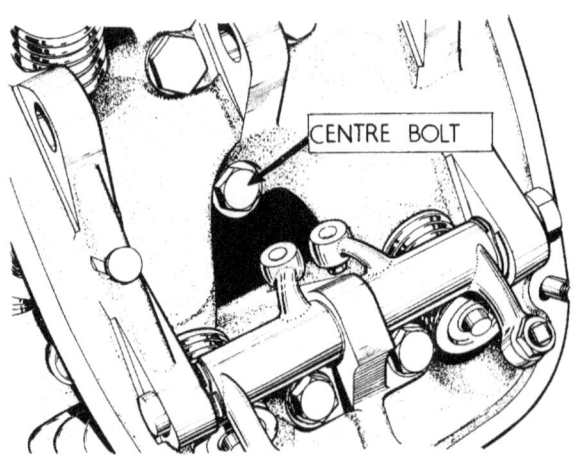

FIG. B.4. *Centre head bolt.*

CYLINDER HEAD REMOVAL

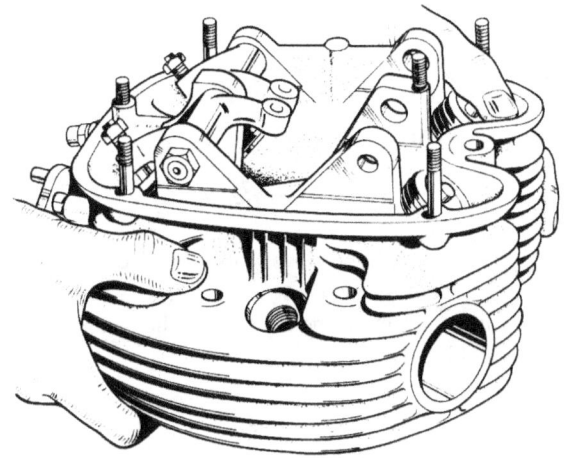

FIG. B.5. *Removing the head.*

Slacken off the nuts and bolts starting with the four long centre bolts then the short one in the push rod tunnel and finally the four nuts, unscrewing each a little at a time to avoid distorting the head. When all the nuts and bolts are removed, break the joint by tapping the exhaust ports gently with a hide mallet, and lift the head clear. Do not disturb the inlet manifold, unless it is to be changed, or the gaskets are to be renewed. Twin carburettors are fitted direct to the head and do not require a manifold.

VALVE SPRINGS

Using service tool number 83961–3340, or any other good valve spring compressor, compress the springs until the split collets can be removed. If the tool is given a sharp blow with a hammer on the spring side after the spring has been compressed a little, it will release the collets from the tapered hole in the valve cap.

When the collets are out, the valve springs and top collars can be lifted from the valve stems, swilled in paraffin, then placed on a numbered board indicating their position in the head.

The springs may have settled through long use and they should therefore be checked in accordance with the dimensions quoted on page GD.4.

If the springs have settled more than $\frac{1}{16}$ in. (1.587 mm.), or there are signs of cracking, they should be replaced.

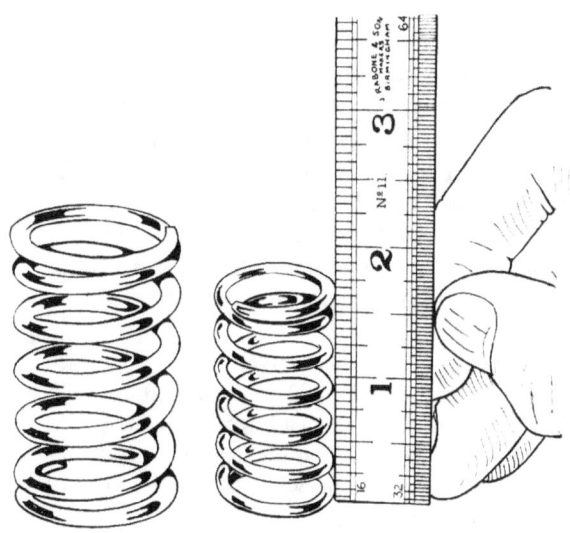

FIG. B.6. *Checking the springs.*

PUSH RODS

Examine the push rod end cups to see if they are chipped, worn or loose, and check the rods by rolling on a flat surface, such as a piece of plate glass, to see if they are bent. If any of these faults are evident the rod should be replaced.

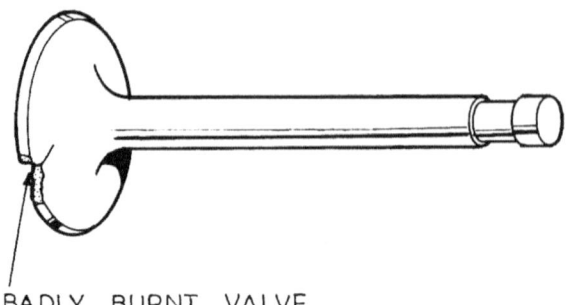

BADLY BURNT VALVE

Fig. B.8. *Burnt valve.*

When a new valve guide has been fitted, or if a new valve is necessary, the valve seat in the head must be re-cut at the correct angle of 45 degrees.

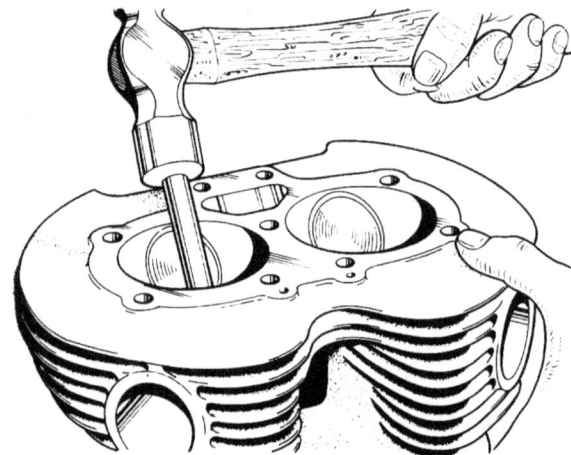

Fig. B.7. *Driving out the guide.*

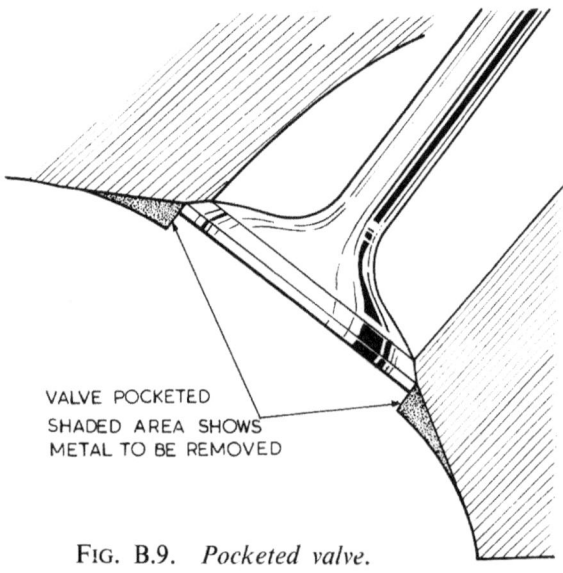

VALVE POCKETED
SHADED AREA SHOWS
METAL TO BE REMOVED

Fig. B.9. *Pocketed valve.*

VALVES AND GUIDES

Check the valves in the guides, there should be no excessive side play or evidence of carbon build-up on that portion of the stem which operates in the guide. Carbon deposits can be removed by careful scraping and very light use of fine emery cloth. If there are signs of scoring on the stems indicating seizure, both valve and guide should be replaced.

An old guide can be driven out with service tool number 81661–3382 but, the aluminium head should first be heated by immersing in hot water. The new guide can be driven in with the same punch while the head is still warm (see Fig. B.7).

Valve heads can be refaced on a valve refacer but if pitting is deep or the valve head is burnt, then a new valve must be fitted and ground-in.

Sometimes, when the engine has been decarbonised many times, valves become "pocketed", that is the head and seat is below the surface of the combustion chamber so impairing the efficiency of the valve and affecting the gas flow. When this happens it is necessary to remove the pocket using a special 30° angle cutter before re-cutting the seat or grinding-in the valve.

The valve seats can be re-cut with pilot number 83661–3293 and cutter number 85561–3299 which has a 45° angle one side and 30° angle on the other.

ENGINE

VALVE GRINDING

During decarbonisation, all valves must be ground-in, each to its own seat, whether new or old. This operation is carried out only after all the carbon deposit has been removed from the combustion chamber.

Removal of carbon from the head, inlet and exhaust ports, can be done with scrapers or rotary files but whichever method is used great care must be taken to avoid damage to the valve seats due to the tools slipping across the seats. For final "polishing" the careful use of fine emery cloth wetted by paraffin is recommended.

Having removed the carbon smear a small quantity of fine grinding paste over the face of the valve and return it to its seat.

Hold the head of the valve with tool number 11465-9240 and rotate the valve backwards and forwards maintaining steady pressure.

Every few strokes raise the valve and turn to a new position.

Take the valve out, clean off the paste and examine both face and seat, continuing the grinding until both show a uniform matt finish all round. After grinding remove all traces of grinding paste and smear the valve stem with clean engine oil before reassembling the valve to the head.

Prolonged grinding does **not** produce the same results as re-cutting and must be avoided at all costs.

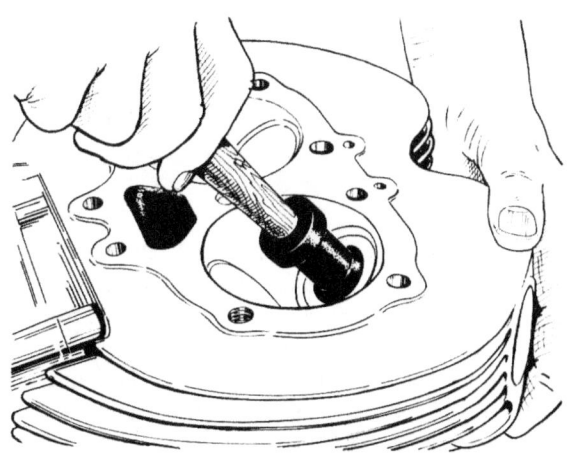

Fig. B.10. *Grinding-in valve.*

CYLINDER BARREL

In the ordinary course of events it should rarely be necessary to remove the cylinder barrel, since top overhaul, already described, usually suffices to keep the engine in first-class working condition for thousands of miles. Unless the condition of the engine indicates that the pistons, rings or cylinder bores require attention, the cylinder barrel should not be disturbed.

If the bores are worn this can sometimes be detected by placing the fingers on top of the piston and pushing backwards and forwards in the direction of rotation. Symptoms indicating faulty piston rings might include heavy oil consumption, and poor compression (but only if the valves are in good order, otherwise they are much more likely to be the cause). Excessive piston slap when warm may indicate a worn bore or severe damage through seizure.

ENGINE

Worn bores can be measured with cylinder bore dial gauges, by moving the pistons to the bottom of the bores thus exposing them for examination (see page B.12).

If the barrel is not being removed bring the pistons to the top of the bores, plug the push rod tower with clean rag, and proceed to remove the carbon from the piston crowns using a suitable scraper such as a stick of tinsmiths solder flattened on the end to form a scraper.

Always leave a ring of carbon round the edge of the piston crown and do not remove the ring of carbon at the top of the cylinder bore.

After cleaning the pistons again rotate the engine to lower the pistons and wipe all loose carbon from the cylinder walls.

The cylinder barrel and head joint faces

Fig. B.11. *Removing carbon.*

must also be cleaned and great care taken not to damage the faces by scoring with the scraper. Such score marks would result in gas leakage, loss of compression and even burning of the cylinder head face.

REMOVING THE BARREL

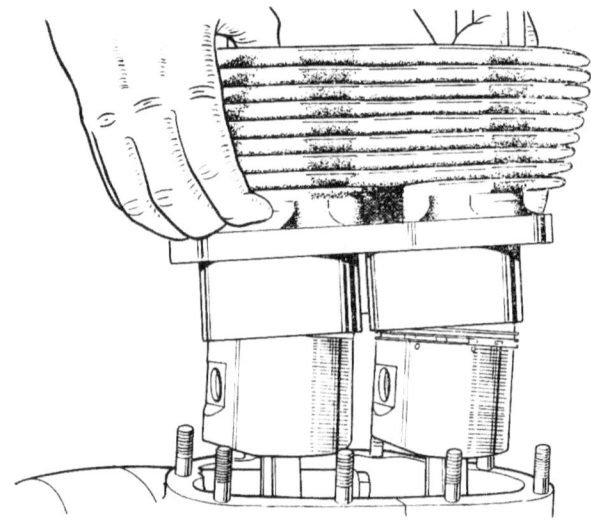

To remove the barrel, unscrew and remove the eight cylinder base nuts, revolve the engine until the pistons are at bottom dead centre, then carefully lift the barrel until the pistons are clear of the bores. While this is being done get an assistant to steady the pistons as they emerge from the barrel.

After removal cover the mouth of the crankcase with clean rag to prevent grit and dust falling in.

Fig. B.12. *Removing barrel.*

TAPPETS

The tappets are retained in the barrel by circlips around their upper ends.

Examine both ends for signs of wear or chipping and make sure that they are quite free to move in the block. If there are signs of "scuffing" on the feet they should be replaced but, the camshaft should be examined too, as this also may be damaged.

To remove a tappet drive it out of the barrel using a soft metal punch on the upper end, as soon as the circlip is free the tappet can be removed from the lower end.

To replace, insert the tappet into the barrel, preferably in the same place if it is being refitted, then fit the circlip from above using service tool number 81961-5702. Slip the circlip over the tool "pilot" shaft and press in the handle to transfer it to the tappet ring.

CYLINDER BORES

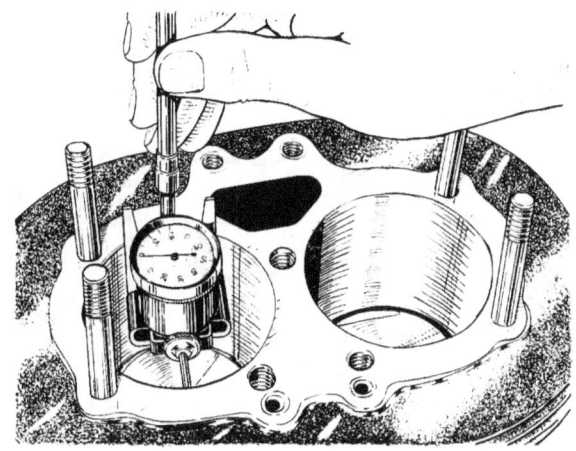

Fig. B.13. *Checking bore size.*

Examine the bores for signs of seizure or scoring and check for bore wear, the maximum usually being the top 1 in. in the direction of rotation. Bore wear anti-rotation and at the base of the cylinder is usually negligible. If the original bore size is unknown the amount of wear can therefore be considered as the difference between the base measurement and the point of maximum dimension shown by the dial.

If wear exceeds .005 in. (.127 mm.) at the top (rotation) then a rebore with new piston is indicated.

REMOVING THE PISTONS

To remove a piston from its connecting rod it is first necessary to remove one of the gudgeon pin circlips. This is best accomplished with a pointed instrument such as the tang end of a file suitably ground to enter the slot in the piston. If the gudgeon pin bush or piston are worn the pin will come out easily otherwise it may be necessary to heat the piston with rags dipped in hot water and wrung out.

Then, supporting the piston, tap out the gudgeon pin using a light hammer and punch.

When the piston is free, mark the inside of the piston skirt, so that it can be replaced the correct way round and on the same connecting rod.

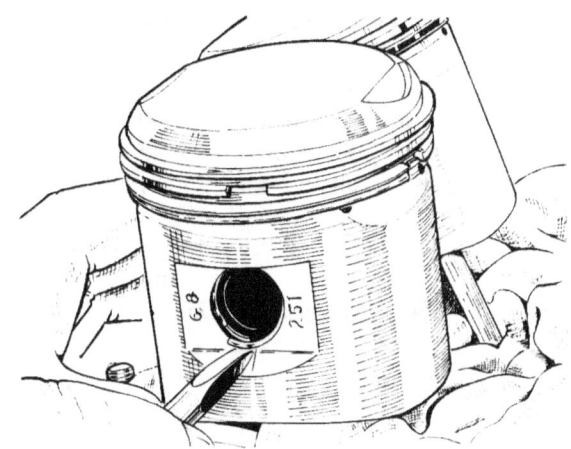

Fig. B.14. *Removing circlip.*

PISTON RINGS

If the rings are stuck in their grooves they will need to be carefully prised free and removed from the piston. All carbon should be carefully scraped from the grooves and the back of the rings. An old broken ring is useful for cleaning the grooves in the piston. If any rings show brown patches on the faces, replace them with new rings. Check the ring gaps by inserting each piston in its bore then slide the ring up to the piston to square it up and measure the gap with feeler gauges. Fit new rings if gaps greatly exceed figures quoted on page GD.2.

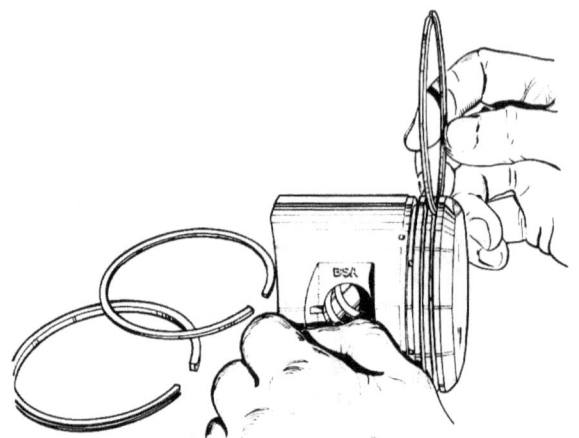

Fig. B.15. *Checking ring grooves.*

REPLACING THE RINGS

It is always advisable to check the gap of new rings before fitting, and if the gap is less than the minimum stated on page GD.2, the ends of the rings should be carefully filed to the correct limit.

When the ring gaps are measured the rings should be in the position of minimum bore wear which is usually at the bottom of the stroke.

Piston rings are very brittle and unless handled carefully are easily broken.

Reassembly is in the reverse order to that for dismantling, that is the scraper ring is replaced first. The middle ring on each piston is tapered this being indicated by the letter "T" marked on one face which must always be uppermost on the piston.

The ring gaps must always be equally spaced round the piston, that is, at 120° apart to restrict gas leakage through the gaps to the absolute minimum.

SMALL-END BUSHES

Small-end bush wear is normally very slight but when excessive it can cause an unpleasant high pitched tapping sound. The gudgon pin should be a good sliding fit in the bush with no appreciable up and down movement, if there is considerable up and down movement then the bush should be changed.

To change a bush, push the old one out and at the same time press the new one in with service tool number 83261-3652. The new bush must be correctly lined up with the oil hole and reamed to .7503—.7506" (19.0576—19.0652 mm.) after pressing into the connecting rod.

ENGINE

REASSEMBLY AFTER DECARBONISING

Having ground-in and replaced the valves and springs in the cylinder head taking great care to correctly fit the tapered cotters, replace the pistons on the connecting rods so that they are the same way round as previously. Always use new gudgeon pin circlips and see that they are pressed well down into their grooves.

If the circlips come adrift or if one is omitted the cylinder barrel will soon be damaged and will require replacement.

Use a new cylinder base washer and support the pistons with two pieces of hardwood placed across the crankcase under the piston skirts. See Fig. B.4 for measurements.

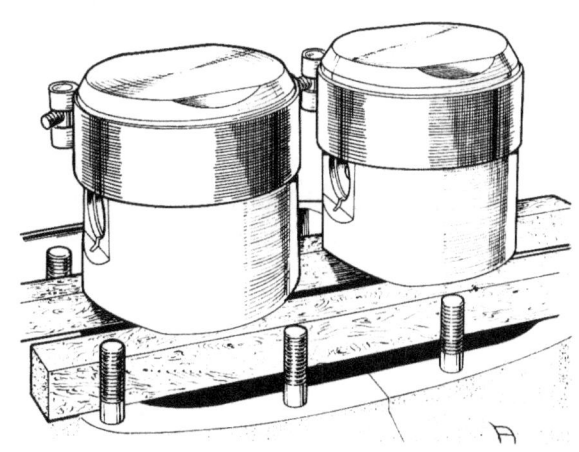

FIG. B.16. *Piston ring slippers.*

REPLACING THE BARREL

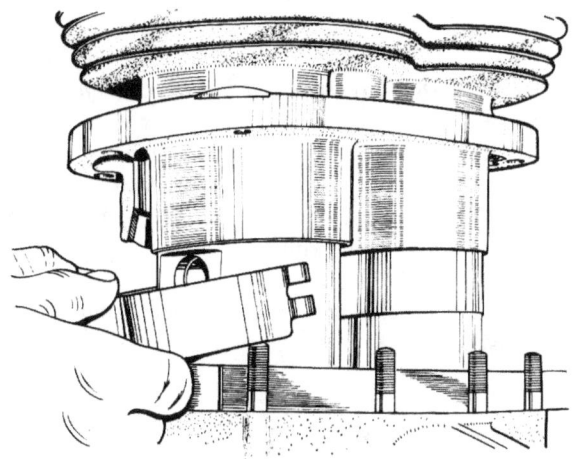

FIG. B.17. *Removing slippers.*

Apply a coating of clean engine oil to the pistons and position the ring gaps at 120°. Using two piston ring slippers, service tool number 81361–3682 (A50) or 81361–3707 (A65) compress the rings so that they are just free to move, then replace the barrel which will displace the slippers as the rings enter the bores. Remove the slippers after the rings have entered the barrel.

Take out the two pieces of wood to drop the barrel over the studs, replace the stud nuts and tighten down evenly to avoid distortion.

REPLACING THE HEAD

Place the cylinder head gasket in position. Slacken off the inlet valve rockers completely and place the head in position over the four studs. Screw in the five cylinder head bolts and replace the four nuts and washers on the studs, tighten down each a little at a time criss-crossing the head from the centre outwards.

Do not forget the short bolt inside the push rod tower, this bolt cannot be fitted with the push rods in position.

Using a torque wrench tighten the bolts and nuts to the figures quoted on page GD.36.

When the head is finally pulled down replace the two short push rods on the two outer tappets and under the inlet (rear) rocker arms.

Assemble the exhaust (front) rockers in the order detailed on page B.7 with the adjuster screws over the valves and fit the two long push rods on to the two inner tappets and under the exhaust rocker ball pins. Reconnect the rocker oil feed pipe.

ENGINE

TAPPET ADJUSTMENT

To set the tappets (or valve clearance) the valve must be in the correct position, that is with the cam follower (tappet) on the base circle of the cam as follows:—

Left-hand inlet valve spring fully compressed (valve fully open).
Set the right-hand inlet valve.
Right-hand inlet valve spring fully compressed (valve fully open).
Set the left-hand inlet valve.
Left-hand exhaust valve spring fully compressed (valve full open).
Set the right-hand exhaust valve.
Right-hand exhaust valve spring fully compressed (valve full open).
Set the left-hand exhaust valve.

With the valve in the correct position check the gap with the appropriate feeler gauge .008 in. (.2032 mm.), .010 in. (.254 mm.) exhaust.

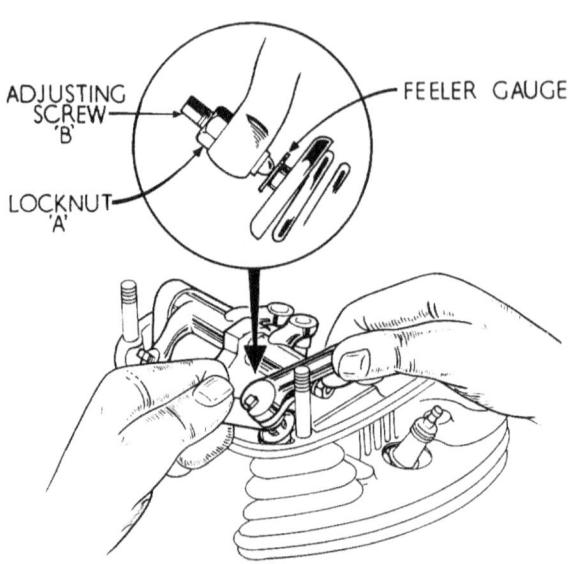

FIG. B.18. *Measuring the valve clearance.*

If adjustment is required slacken off the locknut (A) and screw the adjuster (B) in or out as necessary. Re-check the setting after tightening the locknut.

Replace the rocker box cover using a new gasket.

REPLACING THE CARBURETTOR(S)

The fitting of the carburettor(s) is the same whether there are single or twin carburettors.

Place the paper gasket next to the head (twin) or the inlet manifold (single) then position the tufnol block(s) ensure that the rubber O-ring(s) in the carburettor flange is sound and in position, place the carburettor in position and secure with two spring washers and two $\frac{5}{16}$ in. B.S.C. nuts. Be very careful to tighten the nuts equally and avoid over-tightening, this only distorts the carburettor flange and results in an air leak and unsatisfactory control operation.

Thread the cables through the frame clips and reconnect to the twist-grip and air controls.

To complete the work of decarbonising, replace the air cleaner(s) reconnect the petrol pipes and engine steady stay, and replace the petrol tank and sidecovers.

Note, when replacing the air cleaners see that the water deflectors are so positioned that water cannot drip off the tank into the filter.

ENGINE

COMPRESSION PRESSURES

The Table below gives compression pressures for engines in good condition taken at starter cranking speed with both plugs removed, throttle fully open and engine hot.

Taken with Crypton BX.35 gauge.

Model	Comp. Ratio	First Kick	Average
A65 Star	7.5 : 1	65—70	120/125
A65 Rocket	9.0 : 1	65—70	140/145
A65 Lightning Rocket	9.0 : 1	65—70	140/145
A50 Star	8.5 : 1	65—70	135/140
A50 Cyclone	9.0 : 1	65—70	150/155

Figures quoted are in pounds per square inch. To obtain grammes per square centimetre, multiply by 70.3.

If readings obtained are substantially below those quoted the engine concerned is in need of attention to valves, rings or possibly a rebore.

ENGINE

REMOVING THE ENGINE UNIT

During the process of removing the engine unit keep careful watch for any nuts or bolts which have been loose and chafing, such parts are no longer safe and should be replaced. Examine the wiring for places where the insulation may have rubbed through and protect with a few turns of insulating tape.

Remember a bare wire can cause an electrical short-circuit which can set the machine on fire.

Proceed as for decarbonising described on pages B.5 to B.6, but do not remove the rocker box cover at this stage.

FOOTRESTS

The left-hand footrest is secured by a washer and nut which has a left-hand thread. Unscrew the nut, turning clockwise, remove the washer and give the footrest a sharp blow with a mallet to release it from its taper.

The right-hand footrest is secured to the frame in a similar manner but in this case the nut has the conventional right-hand thread.

FIG. B.19. *Removing footrest nut.*

CHAINGUARD

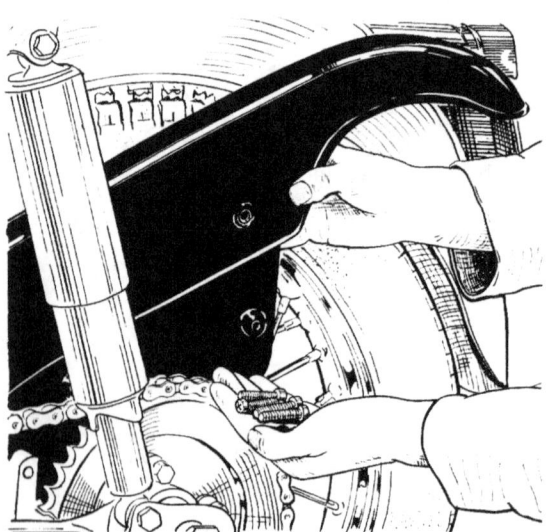

FIG. B.20. *Removing chainguard.*

On models fitted with full-width hubs the rear chainguard is secured by four bolts which screw into captive nuts, remove the four bolts to take the chainguard away.

Models fitted with quick-release hubs use a different chainguard and the lower rear bolt is extended to secure the rear brake anchor strap. On these models take out the split-pin in the anchor strap bolt, remove the nut, washer and distance piece then the two Philips head screws to remove the chainguard. Replacement is the reversal of the above.

ENGINE

CHAINCASE

The full chaincase is only fitted to models with full-width hubs. To remove take out the four Philips head screws when the two halves can be taken away upwards and downwards respectively. Replacement is the reversal of this procedure.

REAR CHAIN

After removing the chainguard or chaincase whichever is fitted, disconnect the rear chain by removing the spring link and run the chain off the gearbox sprocket. Disconnect the generator leads at the couplings and remove the low-tension wires from the terminals on the coils. Battery ignition, single and twin carburettor models will require the left-hand coil to be removed.

Models with "energy transfer" ignition system, where both coils are immediately above the gearbox will require both coils removed, as they are attached to the top engine mounting plate bolt, they can be removed at the same time as this bolt.

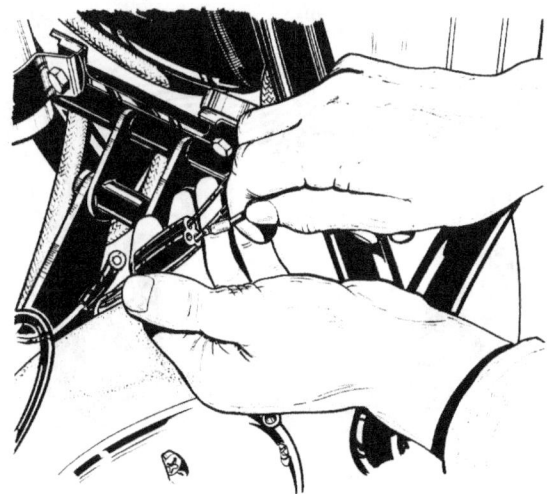

Fig. B.21. *Generator couplings.*

CLUTCH CABLE
(Early Type)

On early models the clutch cable is removed with the unit by disconnecting at the handlebar end.

To do this, screw the adjuster right home. take off the lever fulcrum pin and nut. slip the lever off the bracket and prise out cable nipple. The cable and adjuster can now be removed from the bracket.

To remove the early type cable from the lower end, take off both footchange and kickstart pedals, remove the three screws holding the timing side outer cover and remove the cover when the cable can be disconnected from the lever.

CLUTCH CABLE
(Current Type)

To remove the clutch cable on later models the procedure is the same at the handlebar end.

At the lower end, pull back the rubber cover to expose the cable connections. Pull back the cable and take out the short slotted abutment, this will allow the long abutment to be pulled back exposing the cable nipple which can then be removed from the connector.

SPEEDOMETER AND REV-COUNTER CABLES

Disconnect the speedometer and rev-counter cables (if fitted), the former from underneath the gearbox adjacent to the footchange and the latter from the front of the timing case. Simply unscrew the outer casing nipple and pull out the inner cable.

ENGINE

OIL DRAINING

Unscrew the oil filter from the oil tank and drain into a suitable receptacle. Replace the filter when the tank is empty.

Remove the single $\tfrac{5}{16}$ in. bolt which holds the oil feed and return pipes to the underside of the crankcase. A new gasket will be required for this joint on the older models, later models use two rubber seals which must be sound and unbroken. Seals which have softened and swollen should be replaced. Use jointing cement both sides of a gasket but not at all with the oil seals.

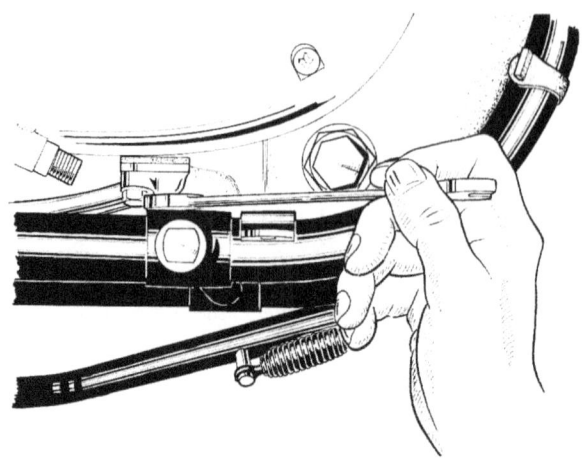

FIG. B.22. *Oil pipe connection.*

MOUNTING BOLTS

The engine/gearbox unit is now held solely by its mounting bolts.

Unscrew and remove the two nuts and washers securing the rear engine plates to the frame. Drive the bolts out towards the right-hand side leaving the plates attached to the engine but, slacken off the engine plate crankcase bolts (early models have only one bolt).

Remove the front mounting bolt and the long bolt underneath the crankcase. This latter bolt usually has a packing washer inserted between the crankcase and the frame, take note of its position.

The unit will now be free and ready to be lifted out. To do this tilt the engine forward so lifting the rear upwards and the front downwards, then twist the unit and lift out on the left-hand side complete with the rear engine plates.

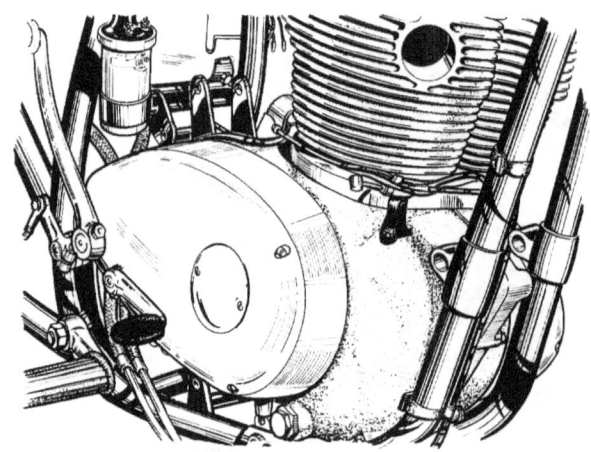

FIG. B.23. *Engine loose.*

ENGINE

REPLACING THE ENGINE UNIT

Having completed the overhaul of the engine/gearbox unit, it should be complete with kickstart and footchange levers and rear engine plates loosely fitted. Older machines having the clutch cable fitted direct to the clutch lever inside the timing cover, should have the cable coiled round the cylinder barrel for the time being. Models with quickly detachable clutch cable need not have it fitted at this stage.

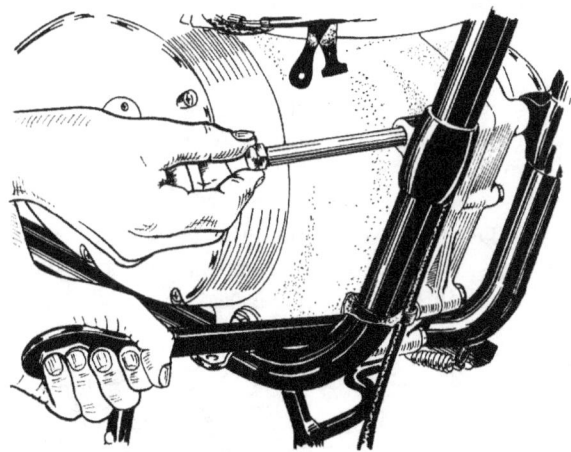

FIG. B.24. *Positioning the engine.*

Lift the unit into the frame from the left-hand side and position the front mounting lug below the frame lug and the rear mounting above the frame lug, then lever the mountings into position. Insert the mounting bolts through the front lug then the rear lug (refit energy transfer coils if applicable) and finally the bottom lug. Do not omit the packing piece which is usually on the lower engine bolt between the frame and the crankcase. Replace the nuts and washers and make absolutely tight. Replace the engine steady-stay to the front of the cylinder head.

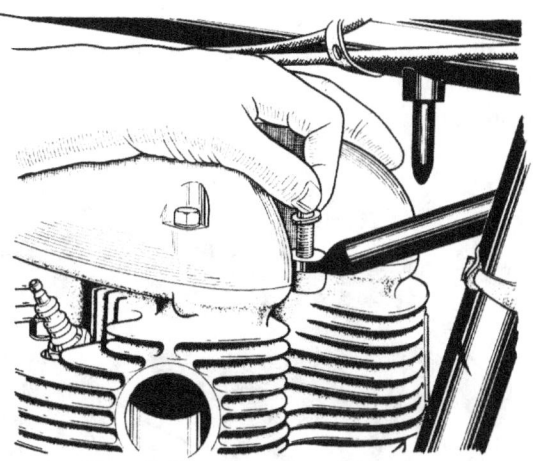

FIG. B.25. *Engine steady-bolt.*

Connect the rocker box oil feed pipe to its union at the rear of the cylinder head and then the oil feed and return pipes to the crankcase and oil tank. To ensure that the crankcase connection is oil-tight use a new gasket and jointing cement sparingly (if it is the older type). Later models which have two rubber seals do not require jointing cement. "Loctite" cement should however be used on the threads of the centre bolt on **both** types to ensure that the bolt does not work loose.

Feed the clutch cable through the frame clips (or replace it) pass the nipple and adjuster through the handlebar bracket, then insert the nipple into the lever and secure the lever with the fulcrum pin and nut. Adjust the cable as necessary.

On battery ignition models the coils can now be replaced.

Reconnect the generator leads ensuring that the colours are correctly matched and replace the low-tension wires on to the coils. The black/yellow wire to the (+) positive terminal on the right-hand coil and the black/white wire to the (+) positive terminal on the left-hand coil.

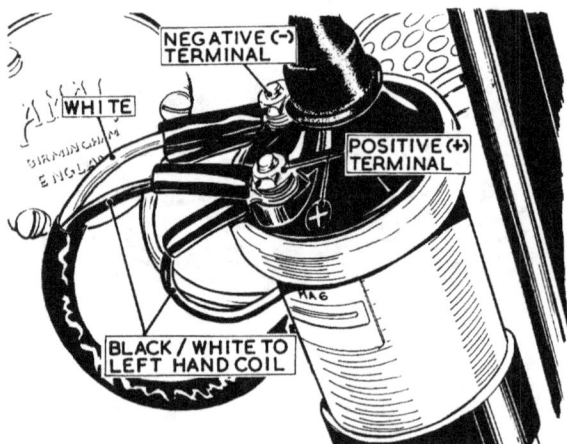

Fig. B.26. *Coil connections.*

Replace the rear chain with the closed end of the connector link spring facing the direction of chain travel and refit the chainguard or chaincase.

On those models fitted with quick release rear hub, do not omit the split pin from the brake anchor strap bolt, which also secures the chainguard.

See that the O-ring(s) is(are) in position in the carburettor(s) and that the insulating block or blocks are undamaged.

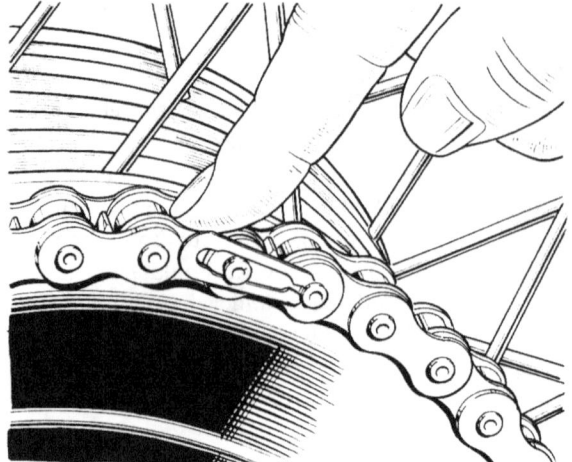

Fig. B.27. *Chain link.*

Replace the carburettor(s) using a new gasket between the block and the manifold or cylinder head.

Do not over-tighten the carburettor flange nuts, such action can result in a buckled flange and subsequently an air leak.

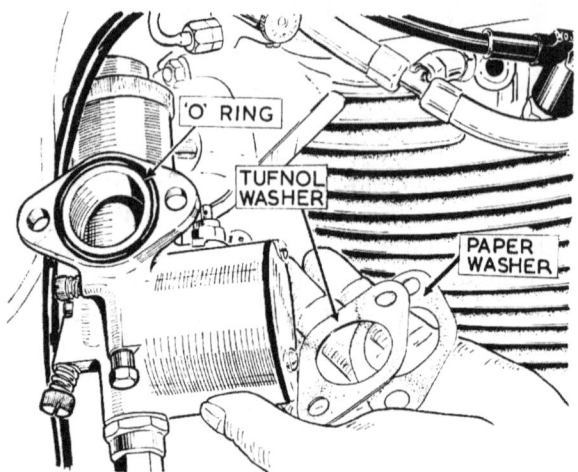

Fig. B.28. *Carburettor joint.*

Press the exhaust pipes well down into the exhaust ports, replace the silencers and secure to the brackets at the front and rear of the frame.

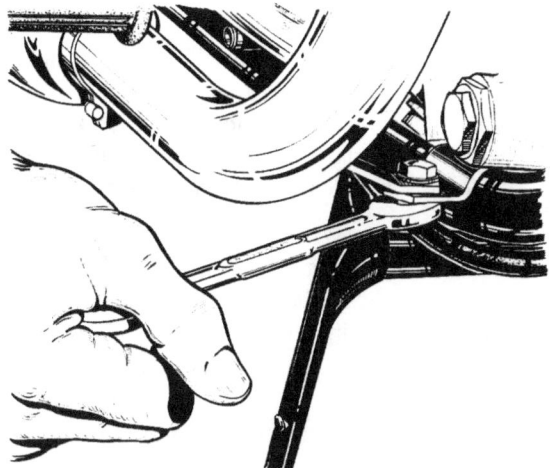

Fig. B.29. *Exhaust pipe bolt.*

On models fitted with straight through pipes on each side of the machine the front tie rod is fitted last. At the rear fastening the longest distance piece is on the left-hand side.

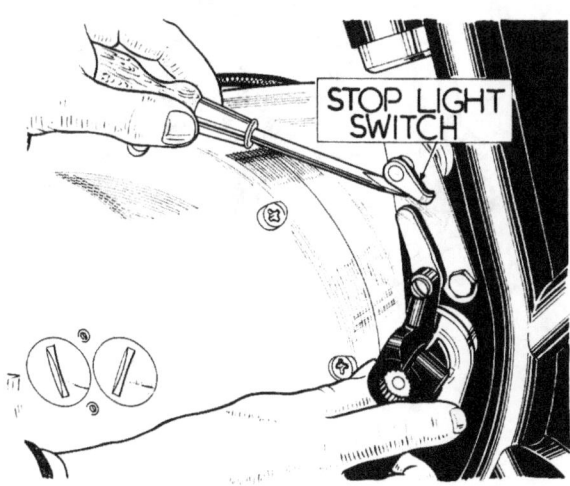

Fig. B.30. *Stop light switch.*

Replace the left-hand footrest which is secured by a washer and nut having a left-hand thread.

Sometimes the rear brake pedal is removed to facilitate removal of the engine in which case the pedal can now be refitted but, it must be adjusted on the splines to suit both the footrest and the stop light switch. Do not omit to tighten the pinch bolt.

These latter remarks do not apply where quick release hubs are fitted.

If the right-hand footrest has been lowered this can be replaced, but this time the nut has the normal right-hand thread.

Replace the petrol tank, position the holding down bolt in the centre tube, then press the tank down on to the mounting rubbers and secure with the large diameter washer and nut. If a steel tank is fitted, replace the anti-roll bar underneath the tank, ensuring that it is correctly fitted and not being strained.

Replace the carburettor air filter or filters, reconnect the fuel pipes, and after completing the assembly of the side covers etc., refill the oil tank, primary drive case and gearbox.

Before starting the motor or turning on the fuel supply, turn the engine over several times by means of the kickstart, to prime the oil pump and start the oil circulating.

TRANSMISSION

Power from the engine is transmitted through the engine sprocket and primary drive chain to the clutch chainwheel, thence via the clutch driving and driven plates to the shock absorber unit and the gearbox mainshaft, through the gearbox to the final drive sprocket, the rear chain and rear wheel.

The shock absorber unit, as its name implies, is necessary to smooth out the drive as the power impulses fluctuate.

The clutch not only provides a means of stopping and starting the machine without stopping the engine, but also provides a means of changing from one gear ratio to another smoothly.

Thus it will be evident that the satisfactory functioning of one part of the system is very often dependent on another part. In other words if one part is worn or faulty it can very often prevent other parts from working properly.

The dismantling and reassembly of the primary drive can be carried out if necessary without removing the engine unit, but will be treated in this case as though the unit were on the bench.

PRIMARY DRIVE COVER

Take out the twelve screws securing the primary chaincase outer cover, two of these, which have fibre or aluminium washers under the heads are the oil level and drain screws. If the joint has not already been broken to release the oil, break it by tapping the cover gently with a hide-mallet and remove the outer cover, but have a receptacle underneath to catch the oil.

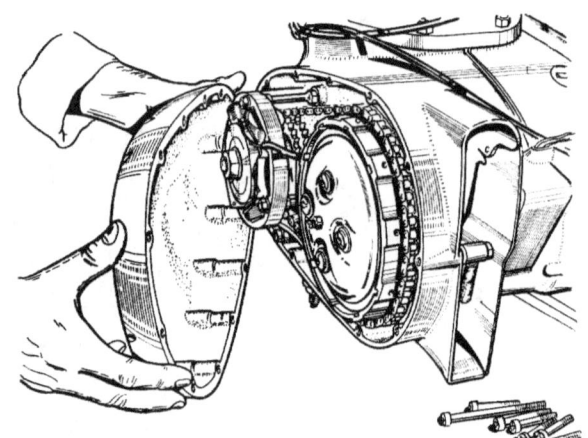

FIG. B.31. *Primary cover.*

ENGINE

CLUTCH DISMANTLING

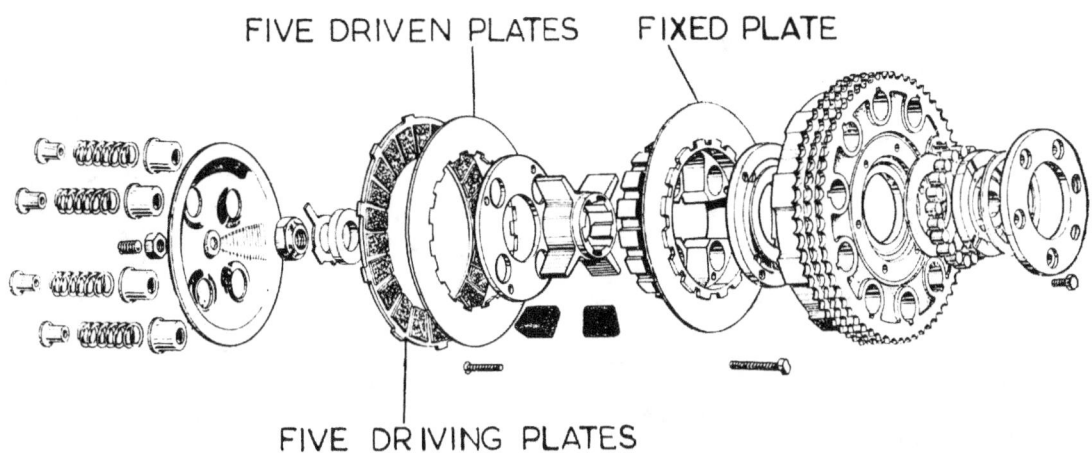

FIG. B.32. *Clutch exploded.*

Unscrew the four spring nuts which have the normal right-hand thread. Some of these may be difficult because there is a projection on each nut to prevent it working loose and it may be necessary to destroy the spring in the process of removal.

Take out the nuts, springs, pressure plate, driving and driven plates and pull out the clutch push rod. There is one driven plate at the back of the clutch centre, this is a press-fit on the centre and should not be disturbed if it appears to be undamaged.

To unscrew the clutch centre nut it will be necessary to lock the chainwheel and centre together with service tool number 00061-3760 and to support the connecting rods with a bar through the small-end bushes, resting on hardwood pads on the crankcase to avoid damage.

Flatten the tab-washer under the clutch centre nut and unscrew the nut which has a right-hand thread. Take off the nut, tab-washer and distance piece but do not attempt to remove the chainwheel at this stage.

Slacken off the chain tensioner adjusting screw until the tensioner blade is completely free from the chain.

GENERATOR

The generator comprises the rotor which is the circular component fitted to the engine mainshaft and the stator which is mounted on three studs around the rotor, both being dealt with in the electrical section.

To remove the clutch chainwheel, chain or engine sprocket, however, the generator must first be removed.

Flatten the tab-washer under the crankshaft nut and using the bar through the connecting rods, unscrew the nut which has a right-hand thread.

Do not omit to use the hardwood pads on the crankcase face to avoid damaging the joint face.

Take off the three stator plate nuts and washers, being careful not to damage the windings of the coils, and pull the stator plate off the studs.

ENGINE

Pull off the rotor to expose the engine sprocket and take out the engine shaft key (if fitted). Machines fitted with energy transfer ignition equipment have a timing disc between the rotor and the engine sprocket, the disc can be removed with the rotor. There is no key on these models.

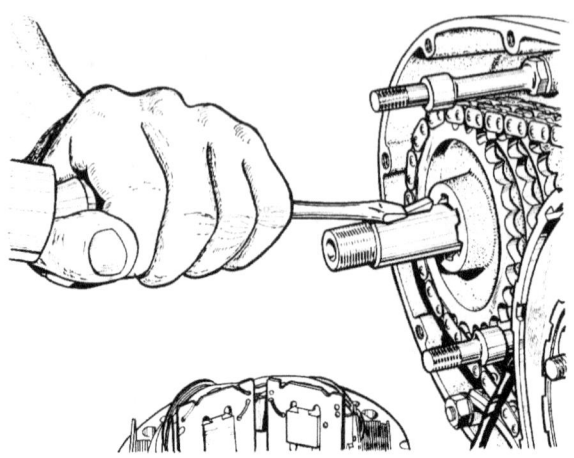

Fig. B.34. *Crankshaft key.*

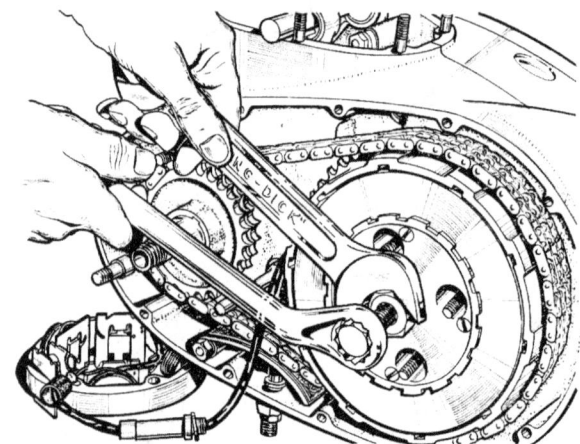

Fig. B.33. *Removing clutch.*

The engine sprocket, primary chain and clutch chainwheel must be removed together. Free the clutch sleeve with service tool number 82561-1912 then withdraw all the components together. If the engine sprocket is tight, it can be drawn off the shaft with service tool number 84861-3676, and two bolts ¼ in. by 26 t.p.i. by 3 in. long.

INSPECTING THE CLUTCH

The driving plates have segments of special friction material bonded to the metal, these segments should all be complete, unbroken and not displaced.

The tags on the outer edge should be a reasonable fit in the chainwheel slots and not hammered up. If there are burrs on the tags, or the segments are displaced, the plates should be replaced. Even if there is no apparent wear or damage the overall thickness of the plate and segments should be measured and if the extent of the wear is more than .030 in. (.75 mm.) the plate should be replaced.

Standard thickness is .140—.145 in. (3.556—3.683 mm.).

The plain driven plates should be free from score marks and perfectly flat. To check the latter lay the plate on a piece of plate glass. If it can be rocked from side to side it is buckled and should be replaced.

SHOCK ABSORBER

To inspect the shock absorber rubbers which are inside the clutch centre, take out the four countersunk head screws adjacent to the clutch spring housings and prise off the retaining plate.

The rubbers should be quite firm and sound, if there is any tendency for the rubbers to disintegrate they should be replaced. To remove prise out the smaller rebound rubbers first. When refitting do not use oil or grease, if lubricant is required it is better to use a liquid soap.

CLUTCH CHAINWHEEL

Examine the slots for wear, if they are corrugated or the teeth are hooked and thin, the chainwheel should be replaced. Check the chainwheel bearing for up and down play, slight play is permissible otherwise the bearings should be renewed.

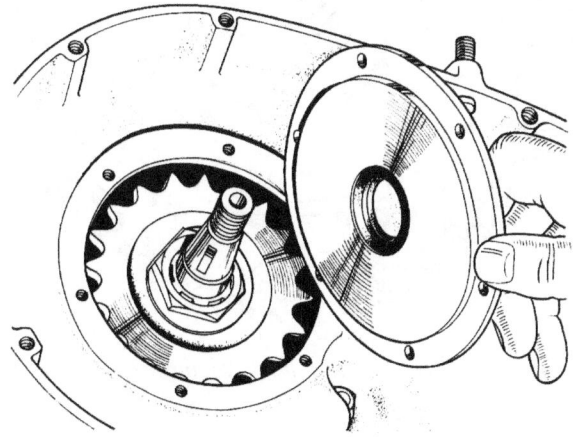

FIG. B.35. *Primary case back-plate.*

GEARBOX OR FINAL DRIVE SPROCKET

Access to the gearbox sprocket can only be obtained when the clutch is removed. Take out the six screws holding the circular plate at the back of the primary case, break the joint and remove the plate which also carries an oil seal. Look for signs of leakage down the back of the cover, if leakage is evident change the oil seal taking care to see that it is fitted the correct way round with the lip of the seal to the inside of the chaincase.

To change or renew the sprocket, flatten the tab-washer, place a length of chain round the sprocket and lock in a vice or with a suitable bolt and unscrew the sprocket nut which has a right-hand thread.

When the nut and tab-washer are removed the sprocket can be pulled off its splines. If there has been oil leakage from the back of the sprocket it indicates that the gearbox oil seal requires renewal. This can be done but great care is necessary when fitting the replacement, also if the sprocket boss is worn this also will require replacement.

Fitting a new seal on its own would be useless as the old sprocket would ruin the new seal.

If the sprocket boss is smooth and not scored it can of course, be replaced but it must be lightly oiled to avoid damaging the seal as the sprocket is pressed home. Reassembly is in the reverse order but do not omit to turn the tab-washer over the nut after tightening.

CLUTCH OPERATION

As already indicated, the clutch being part of the transmission system transmits power to the rear wheel, and by separating the driving and driven plates this connection is broken. This is done by pulling the left-hand handlebar lever towards the rider, the force imposed is transmitted via the clutch cable to the clutch lever in the timing side case, thence by means of the push rod in the hollow gearbox mainshaft to the clutch pressure plate, so compressing the clutch springs and freeing the plates.

To ensure the smooth operation of the clutch it is essential that the spring pressure is equal and the pressure plate runs true. Adjustment for the cable is provided at the handlebar lever and at the clutch pressure plate.

REASSEMBLING THE PRIMARY DRIVE

Replace the circular cover at the back of the primary case using jointing cement on one side only of the paper gasket.

If the clutch chainwheel has been removed from the sleeve, grease the roller track, assemble the 21 rollers and slide the chainwheel over the rollers.

Of the eight cush drive rubbers the four thick driving rubbers are fitted on the right-hand side of the centre vanes and the four

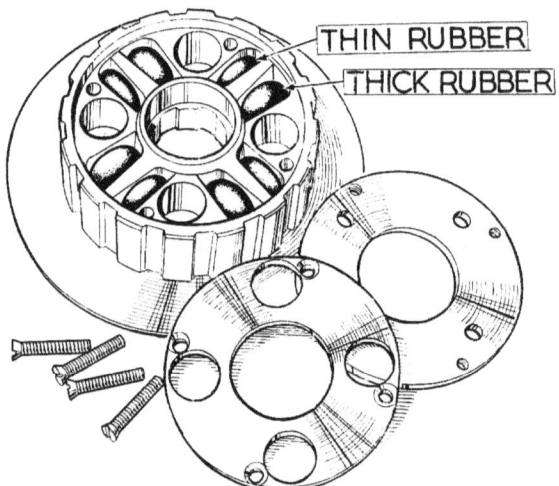

FIG. B.36. *Cush drive.*

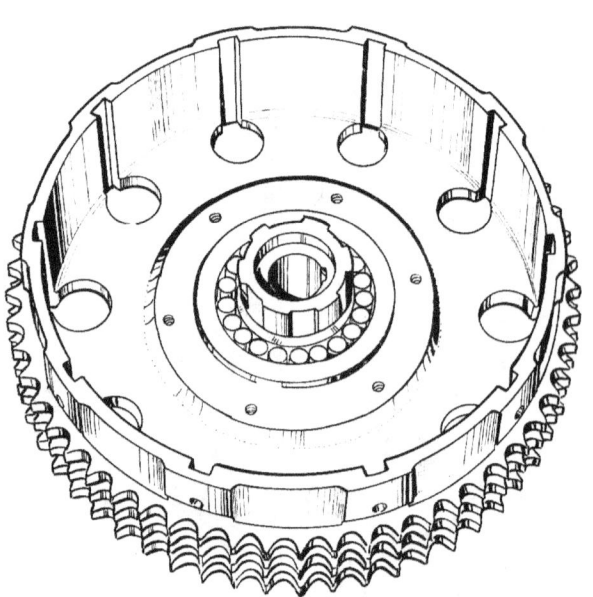

FIG. B.37. *Clutch chainwheel.*

thin rebound rubbers are on the left-hand side, the outer plate being secured by four countersunk head screws. The driven plate at the back of the clutch centre is a press-fit and should not normally be disturbed, if it has been removed and replaced it should be pressed flat against the rear wall of the clutch centre.

ENGINE

Insert the spring bolts from the rear and slide the assembly into the chainwheel.

Pass the stator leads through the back of the primary chaincase and screw in the cable guide. On later models this guide is a plain press-in tube.

NOTE:—It is easier to do this operation at this stage rather than after the chain and sprockets are fitted.

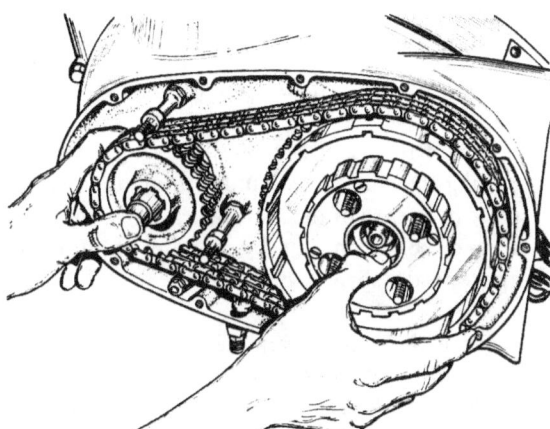

FIG. B.38. *Fitting primary drive.*

Make sure that the crankshaft distance piece is in position behind the engine sprocket.

With both the clutch chainwheel and the engine sprocket lying on the bench, place the chain round both, pick up engine sprocket, chainwheel and chain, pass the stator plate through the chain and slide both sprockets and chain over the shafts at the same time.

Secure the clutch by replacing the distance piece, recessed side outwards, tab-washer and nut turning the tab-washer over the nut after tightening.

On models fitted with "energy transfer" ignition equipment the timing disc is fitted next to the engine sprocket with the peg facing outwards at approximately 9 o'clock and the piston at top dead centre.

The rotor for these models has two holes at the rear, the one marked "S" is for A50 models and the one marked "R" is for A65 models. Locate the peg in the appropriate hole for the model and secure the rotor with its nut and washer turning the washer on to the nut after tightening.

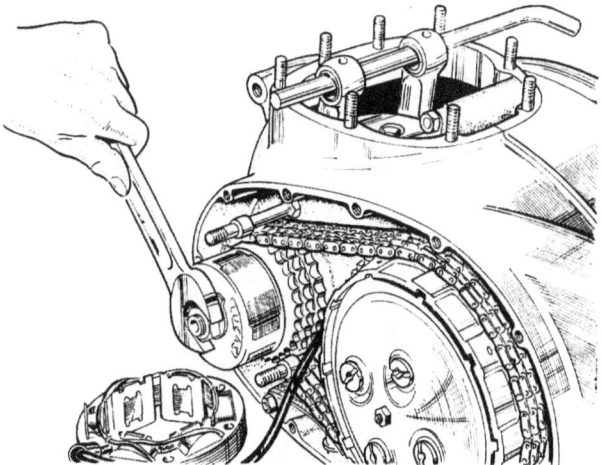

FIG. B.39. *Fitting the rotor.*

On models with battery ignition equipment, replace the Woodruff key in the crankshaft, replace the rotor and secure with nut and washer.

Slide one segmented driving plate into the clutch chainwheel then one plain plate and so on, until all the plates are assembled, there being five of each excluding the fixed back-plate.

Insert the clutch push rod into the hollow gearbox mainshaft (if it has been removed) and replace the pressure plate, spring cups, springs and nuts. It is essential that the spring nuts are tightened evenly to keep the plates parallel. Normal setting is for the outer face of the nut to be flush with the end of the stud.

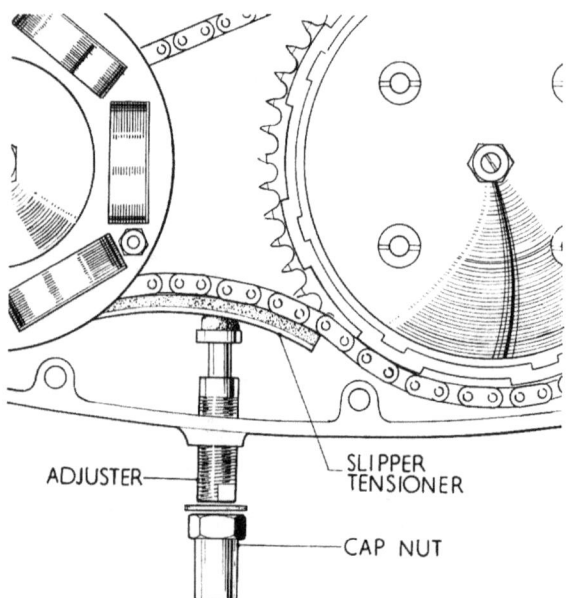

Fig. B.40. *Adjustment of the primary chain.*

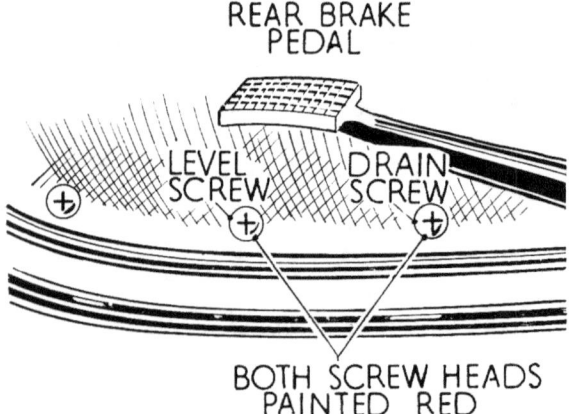

Fig. B.41. *The primary chaincase oil level.*

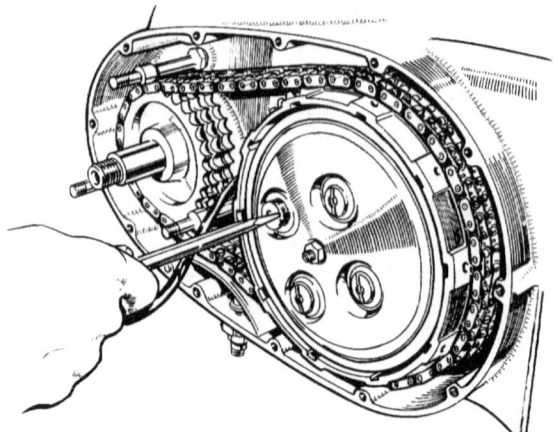

Fig. B.42. *Adjusting clutch springs.*

Check the accuracy of the spring setting by pulling the clutch lever and rotating the pressure plate by means of the kickstarter. Any unevenness should be taken out by re-adjustment of the appropriate springs.

Place the stator over the three studs so that the leads are on the outside at approximately 2 o'clock and replace the three plain washers and nuts.

It is important that the air gap between the rotor and stator is equal so, if there is any variation due to the studs having been displaced, the studs should be very carefully set over. The gap can be checked with feeler gauges between the stator pole pieces and the rotor.

Replace the chain tensioner and adjust the chain so that there is slight up and down movement on the top run of the chain, no more than $\frac{1}{8}$ in.

Apply jointing cement to both faces of the chaincase and, using a new gasket, replace the cover tightening the screws evenly to avoid distortion.

See that the oil level and drain screws are correctly positioned on the lower run with fibre or aluminium washers under the heads of the screws.

THE CONTACT BREAKER

The contact breaker assembly is contained in a circular compartment in the inner timing cover on the right-hand side of the machine, its circular cover forming part of the outer timing cover.

The assembly comprises the contact breaker plate on which are mounted the two sets of contacts and two condensers (capacitors).

Underneath the contact plate is the automatic-advance and retard assembly comprising two bob-weights and springs and the contact breaker cam. This assembly is locked into the tapered hole in the idler pinion by its central bolt.

Oil is prevented from reaching the assembly by an oil seal set in the back of the housing.

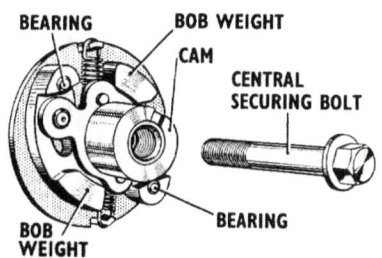

FIG. B.44. *Auto-advance mechanism.*

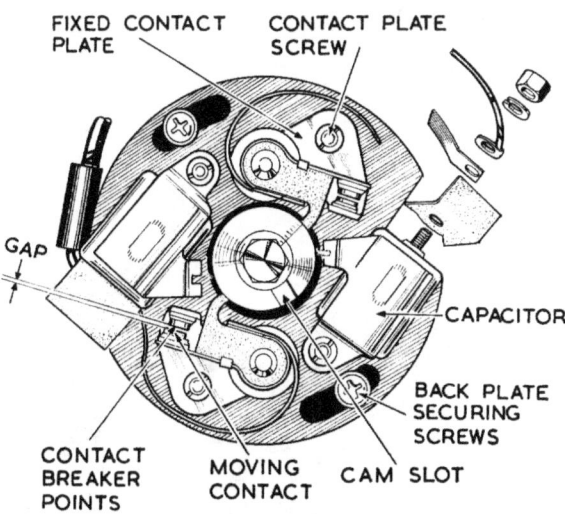

FIG. B.43. *Contact breaker unit.*

When the engine is first started the ignition is in the retarded position because of the two springs which are holding the two bob-weights and the cam. This makes starting easier and prevents "kick-back" on the kickstart lever.

As the engine revolutions increase, centrifugal force carries the bob-weights outwards and this in turn progressively turns the cam and advances the ignition.

The elongated holes in the contact plate enable the plate to be moved to right or left, so providing a means of fine adjustment for ignition timing.

To obtain access to the contact breaker take out the two screws holding the circular cover to the outer timing cover. Early models had four screws.

REMOVING THE CONTACT BREAKER

Before removing the two screws holding the contact plate, scribe a mark on the plate and housing to assist in reassembly, otherwise it will be necessary to retime the ignition. The plate can be removed, complete with contacts and condensers after the two bolts are removed.

To remove the auto-advance unit and cam it is necessary to take out the centre bolt, the unit can then be freed from its taper with service tool number 81461–5005.

This tool is screwed in until resistance is felt, further screwing will then release the assembly.

Do not however, remove the auto-advance unit unnecessarily as the timing will have to be reset, this is detailed on pages B.48–50.

To change a set of points unscrew and remove the barrel nut inside the C-shaped spring and remove the nut holding the spring and lead to the condenser, lift off the movable contact, fibre washer, then the fixed contact (see Fig. B.43).

Replacement is in the reverse order but do not omit the fibre washer between the contacts on the pillar or the insulating strip from the condenser, this is fitted over the terminal and before the spring or the lead (see inset Fig. B.43).

After changing a set of points revolve the engine until the fibre heel is on the peak of the cam, slacken off the contact plate screw and move the fixed contact point in or out to obtain the correct gap of .015 in. (.381 mm.).

Re-check the timing.

TIMING SIDE COVER

To obtain access to the timing gears or the gearbox internals, it is necessary to remove the covers on what is known as the timing or gear-side, that is the right-hand side of the machine.

Take off the kickstart and footchange pedals, take out the three screws retaining the outer cover and remove the cover complete with the contact breaker cover.

This now reveals the contact breaker unit, kickstart return spring, clutch lever and footchange return spring.

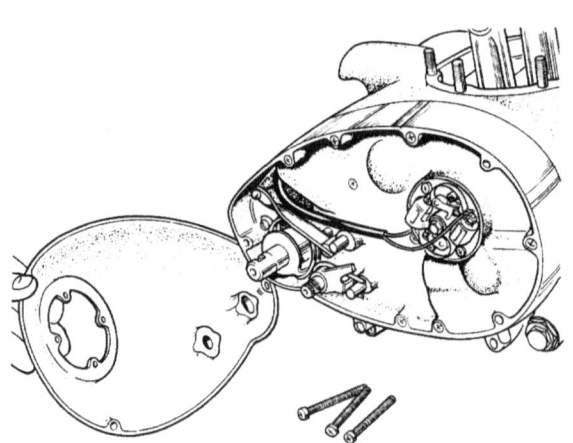

FIG. B.45. *Gear-side cover.*

ENGINE

Disconnect the clutch cable from the lever (if the machine is of the older type), if of the later type with the cable connector, then the connector can remain on the lever.

Take out the clutch lever ball and pull off the kickstart return spring, anchor plate, and the footchange return spring and stop plate.

On later models there is a grub or set-screw securing the footchange return spring stop plate, this screw must be slackened off before the plate can be removed.

Remove the long key from the footchange spindle.

INNER TIMING COVER

Revolution Counter.
If the machine is equipped with a revolution counter (or tachometer) remove the two bolts holding the cable connection to the front of the timing cover, remove the connector and pull out the revolution counter drive spindle.

The inner timing cover can now be removed. Take out the eight screws round the outer edge, two in the centre and one under the clutch lever, but do not remove the slotted screw at the rear, this is the kickstart spring anchorage.

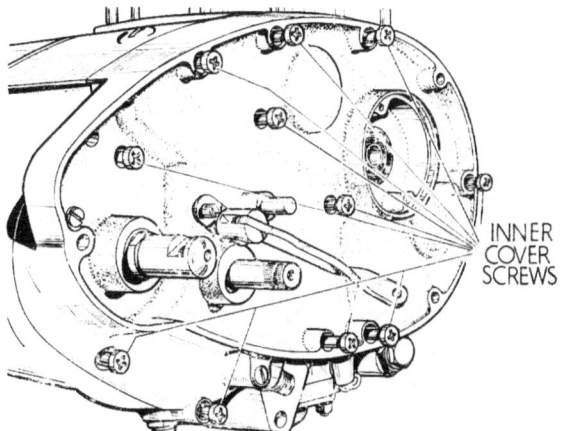

Fig. B.47. *Inner cover screws.*

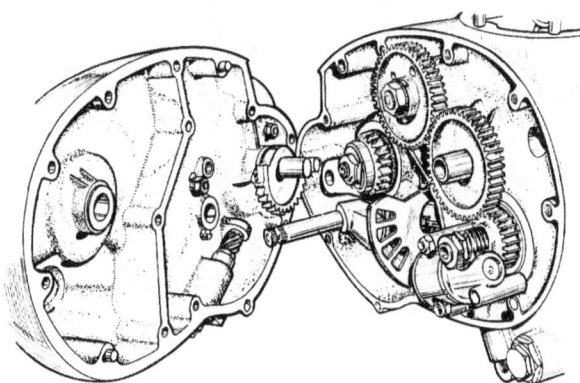

Fig. B.46. *Removing inner cover.*

Tap the cover gently with a hide-mallet round the edges to break the joint and pull off the cover complete with the speedometer drive spindle and clutch lever.

There is no need to disturb the speedometer drive unless the spindle bush or O-rings are to be replaced in which case remove the screwed peg from the underside and pull out the speedometer drive bush.

There is an O-ring fitted to both the spindle and the bush and if there has been any sign of oil leakage either from the bush or into the cable, both rings should be replaced.

Do not omit the thrust pad for the small end of the spindle or the thrust washer fitted over the long end.

Early models used only one pair of driving and driven gears but later models—fitted with magnetic speedometer heads—have a choice of five pairs of gears according to the gear ratio and tyre size (see page GD.34).

The clutch lever pivot post is retained by a single nut and washer on the inside and need not be disturbed.

The gearchange selector quadrant and kickstart quadrant are simply push-fits into the cover and can be withdrawn from the inside.

TIMING GEAR AND OIL PUMP

Oil Pump Removal.
Removal of the inner timing cover exposes the oil pump, timing gears, kickstart ratchet assembly and gearbox outer cover.

Flatten the tab-washer under the crankshaft nut, unscrew the nut which has a left-hand thread, then unscrew the oil pump worm-drive which also has a left-hand thread and is therefore turned in a clockwise direction to unscrew.

To remove the oil pump, unscrew the two nuts and remove the washers from the main body of the pump. On later models flatten the tab-washer under the other nut and unscrew the nut. Early models use a Philips head screw in this position.

As the pump is removed it will release the oil feed non-return valve ball and spring which are fitted into the crankcase behind the pump.

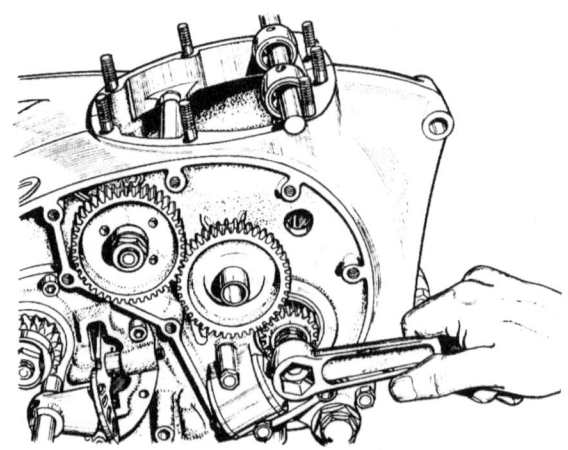

Fig. B.48. *Crankshaft nut.*

It is not advisable to dismantle the oil pump unless it is suspected that there is some fault or possible damage. Internal damage can occur if the periodical oil changes have been neglected.

Dismantling and reassembly is described on pages A.10-11.

REPLACING THE PUMP

Take out the oil pump studs, and ensure the faces are clean, apply a smear of grease to a new gasket and place the gasket in position on the crankcase face. Insert the non-return valve spring, apply a dab of grease to the countersunk hole in the joint face of the pump and press the ball into the grease, position the pump carefully and screw in the studs securing the nuts equally to avoid tilting the pump.

If the engine is being completely dismantled the pump will of course be left off until the engine is rebuilt.

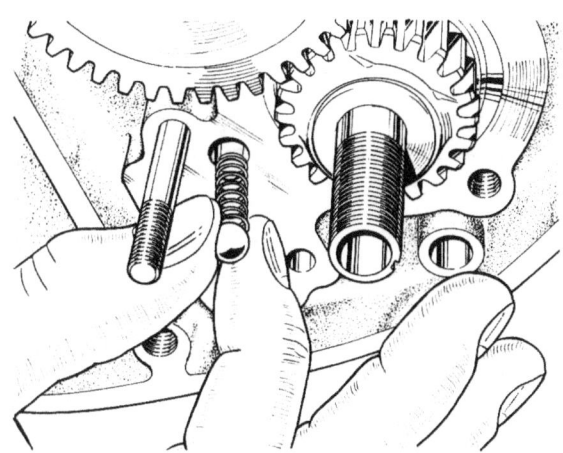

FIG. B.49. *Oil pump non-return valve.*

TIMING GEARS

Careful examination of the timing gears will show that there are marks on the faces of the gears adjacent to the gear teeth.

These marks are to assist in the correct reassembly and it is good practice to familiarise oneself with them before removing the gears (see Fig. B.50).

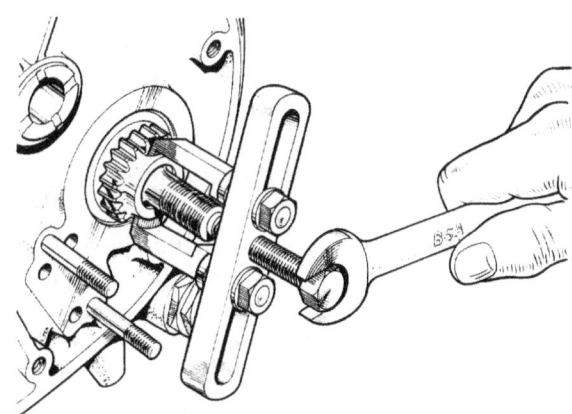

FIG. B.51. *Removing pinion.*

FIG. B.50. *Timing marks.*

Take off the crankshaft distance piece then pull off the pinion using extractor number 84961–3676.

The idler pinion is simply a push-fit in the case and can be withdrawn without a tool.

To unscrew the camshaft nut it is necessary to leave the gears in position and lock the assembly with a bar through the connecting rods. Great care must be taken to avoid damaging the crankcase.

Having locked the assembly, flatten the tab washer, unscrew the nut, and withdraw the camshaft pinion with extractor 84961–3676.

Take out the Woodruff key.

Replacement of the timing gear is simply the reversal of the above procedure except that care must be taken to match the timing marks as the idler pinion is inserted last into the case.

GEARBOX DISMANTLING

If the purpose of dismantling is to obtain access to the connecting rods or flywheel assembly there is no need to remove the gear cluster unless the assembly is suspect.

The gearbox internal cluster can be removed without interfering with the timing gears but the clutch must be removed first (see pages B.22–28).

Take off the five $\frac{5}{16}$ in. B.S.C. nuts holding the gearbox end cover (some very early models used socket screws) break the joint with a hide mallet, and remove the cover complete with the gear cluster, cam-plate and selector forks.

To remove the cam-plate from the circular cover straighten and remove the split pin in the fulcrum, take out the fulcrum then remove the cam-plate, selector forks and shaft.

Pull out the layshaft and remove the sliding pinion (layshaft third gear), first gear and kickstart quadrant.

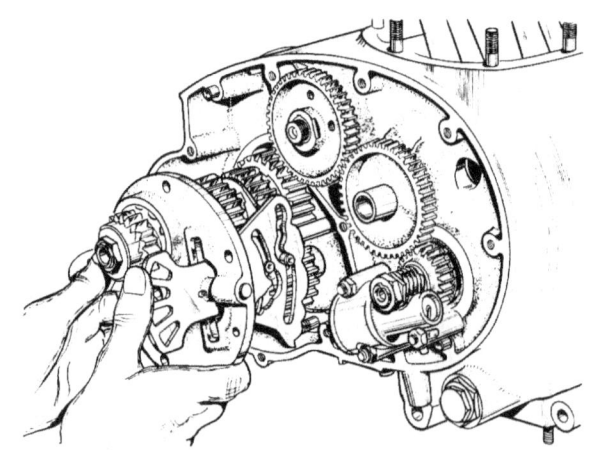

FIG. B.52. *Removing cluster*.

To remove the mainshaft grip the shaft in a vice using soft metal clamps, flatten the tab washer under the kickstart ratchet nut, unscrew and remove the nut and take off the ratchet, ratchet pinion, spring and bush.

The mainshaft complete with its gears can now be driven out of the cover bearing.

ENGINE

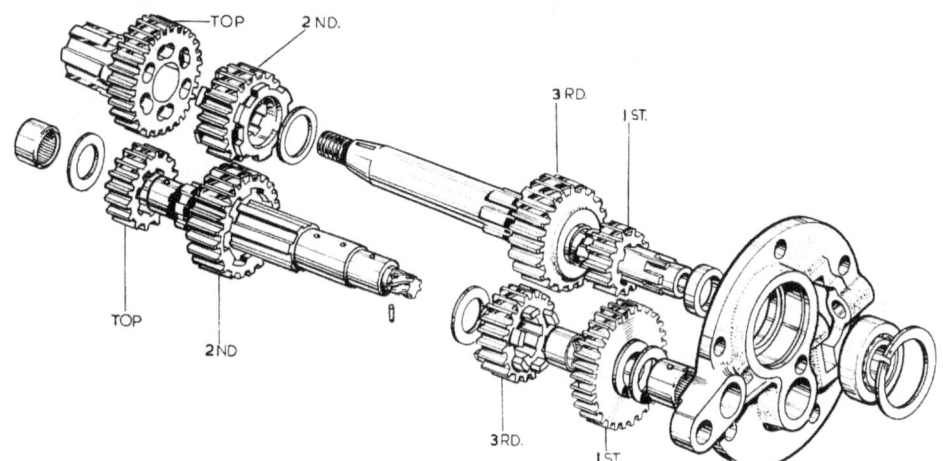

FIG. B.53. *Gear cluster exploded.*

After taking off the sliding pinions both shafts are left with two gears, the mainshaft first and third gears and the shorter layshaft with its top and second gears.

In both cases the smaller gear is a press-fit on to the shaft so retaining the larger gear which has a thrust washer between it and the end of the splines.

If it is necessary to change either of these gears the shaft must be pressed out of both gears at the same time, an operation which requires a good press properly mounted on bench or floor.

When examining the various bearings and bushes for wear do not overlook the phosphor bronze bushes in the layshaft first gear and the mainshaft top gear, this gear is at this point still in the gearbox.

The layshaft has needle roller bearings at each end, one in the back of the box and one in the end cover. Both can be driven out with a suitable size drift.

The mainshaft has ball journal bearings at each end. To remove the left-hand bearing the gearbox sprocket must be removed (see page B.25) then the top gear pinion is driven through, into the gearbox, the oil seal prised out from the outside and the circlip removed. The bearing can then be pressed out from inside the gearbox, but before any bearing or bush is removed from an aluminium case, the case should be heated, the bearing pressed out and the replacement pressed in while the case is still hot.

The right-hand mainshaft bearing can be removed from the cover, pressing from the inside, after the circlip is removed.

When examining the gears look for cracked, chipped or scuffed teeth, the latter will show (if present) on the thrust faces of the teeth and in severe cases might even have broken through the case hardening.

IMPORTANT NOTE:—Both first and top gears have been modified at various times and as the modified gears are not interchangeable individually, should it be necessary to replace either of the mainshaft or layshaft first or top gears of the early type, the mating gear must also be changed.

Check the cam-plate for wear in the cam-track by offering up the selector forks and check the gear notches at both ends. At the large end look for burrs and at the small end for wear on the edges of the slots.

The plunger at the back of the box must be quite free in its housing and the gearchange quadrant plungers must not be chipped or worn on the toothed end and again must be

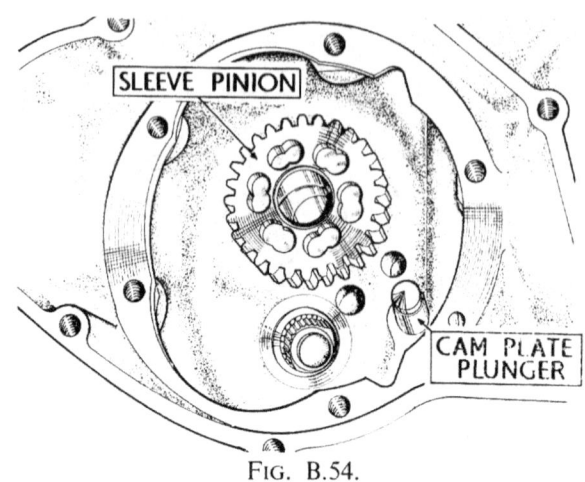

Fig. B.54.

quite free in their housings. Any damage to these parts will make good gearchanges impossible.

GEARBOX REASSEMBLY

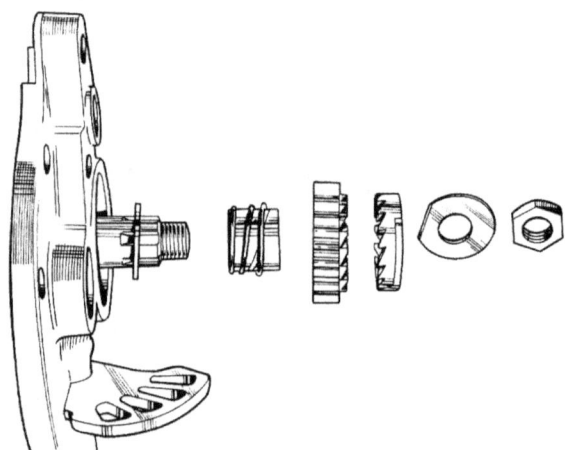

Fig. B.55. *Kickstart ratchet.*

It will be assumed that all bearings, bushes or oil seals have been replaced as necessary.

Press the mainshaft through its bearing in the outer cover ensuring that the distance piece is in position between the bearing and the small gear. Grip the shaft in a vice using soft metal clamps and replace the kickstart ratchet gear washer, bronze bush, spring, ratchet pinion, ratchet, tab washer and nut in that order. Turn the washer over the nut after tightening.

The mainshaft being locked to the cover bearing does not need checking for end float but the layshaft has thrust washers at each end, it must therefore be assembled into the case with the low gear pinion and standard thrust washer (.113—.115 in.) at each end when there should be just perceptible end float. If the end float is excessive there are two thicker washers available (.120—.122 in. and .127—.129 in.) which should be used at the sprocket end.

Having checked the layshaft end float the cluster can be assembled on to the end cover.

Clean all jointing compound off the joint faces in readiness for the assembly.

Note that whilst the mainshaft (second) and layshaft (third) sliding gears are interchangeable (with standard ratios) the selector forks are not. The latter can be identified thus: with forks on the shaft and both rollers below the shaft as in

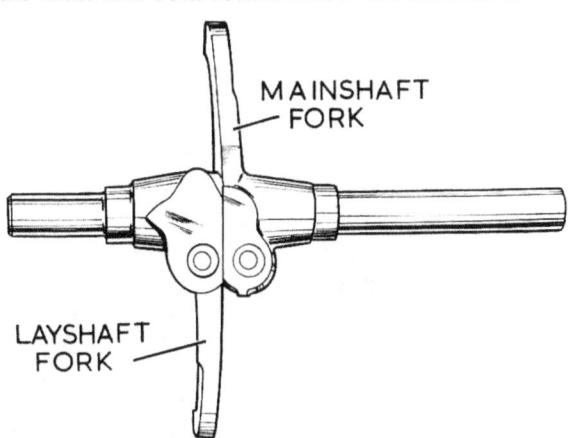

FIG. B.56. *Selector forks.*

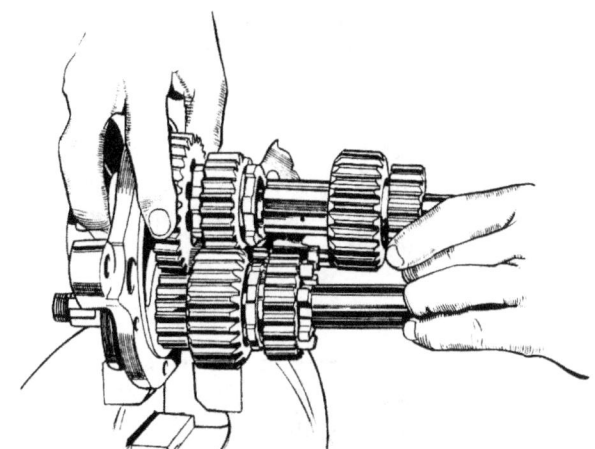

FIG. B.57. *Assembling the gears.*

Fig. B.56, the layshaft fork is on the left and the mainshaft fork on the right.

Place one of the standard thrust washers in position on the inside face of the cover, position the layshaft first gear with the dogs facing inwards and insert the layshaft complete with its sliding gear second and top gears.,

Position the layshaft selector fork, slide the mainshaft sliding gear onto the shaft and position the mainshaft selector fork.

Insert the cam-plate through the slot in the cover with the long end of the outer track at the bottom. Fit the cam-plate fulcrum pin and split pin and insert the selector fork spindle.

If the mainshaft top gear has not already been fitted, press the gear through its bearing, replace the gearbox sprocket and secure with the locknut and tab-washer.

See that the cam-plate plunger and spring are in position at the back of the gearbox.

Pick up the gearbox outer cover complete with the gear cluster, place the other thrust washer over the end of the layshaft and slide the whole assembly into the box.

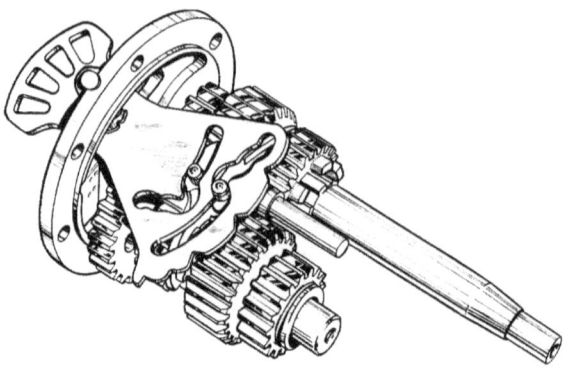

Fig. B.59. *Cluster assembled.*

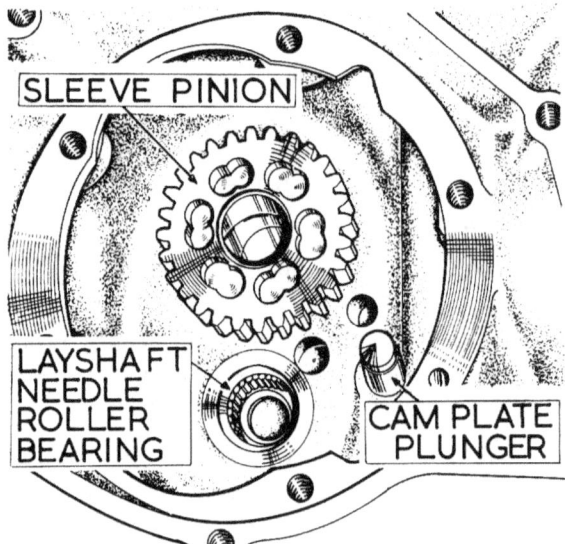

Fig. B.58. *Inside the box.*

Position the cam-plate midway in the slot and insert the small end of the gear selector quadrant into the small hole in the cover at the same time engaging the quadrant plungers in the cam-plate.

Place the small end of the kickstart quadrant into the steel bush on the left-hand side of the cover before replacing the inner timing cover.

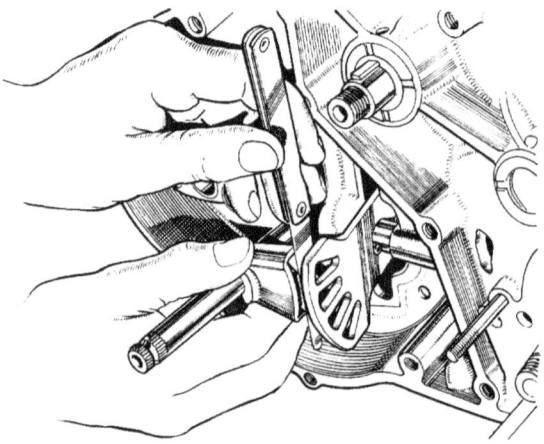

Fig. B.60. *Fitting the selector.*

To facilitate the meshing of the top gear pinions revolve the shafts gently. Secure the cover with the nuts and washers (or screws if fitted) when the cover is right home.

Do not attempt to force the cover home.

SEQUENCE OF GEAR CHANGING

To understand this description of the gear changing sequence, it is necessary to refer to the various drawings and to understand some of the terms used.

(1) CAM-PLATE — this is the large fan-shaped part with notches at one end and windows at the other end.

(2) LARGE PLUNGER — this operates at the large end of the cam-plate to locate the gear positions.

(3) SELECTOR PLUNGERS — these operate at the small end of the cam-plate in the "windows."

(4) SELECTOR FORKS — these only show as small spots in the wavy cam-tracks at the large end of the cam-plate. They are the rollers which move the selector forks up and down the tracks.

(5) SLIDING GEARS — there are two gears in the box which move along the splined shafts. These are operated by the selector forks, there being one on each shaft.

The gears must always be in the neutral position for starting the engine, this is the position shown in Fig. B.60A.

The large plunger is holding the cam-plate by the second notch. At the other end of the cam-plate the selector quadrant plungers are compressed ready to operate either way the pedal is moved.

When the pedal is moved down, to engage first gear, the plunger will enter the cam-plate and move it to first gear position, this in turn will operate the layshaft selector fork and will mesh the layshaft sliding gear with the layshaft first gear.

Reference to Fig. B.60B will now show the quadrant plunger in the second window ready to move the cam-plate from first to second gear.

This time the cam-plate moves in the opposite direction and again operates the layshaft selector fork moving the layshaft sliding gear in the opposite direction to mesh with the second gear.

Reference to Fig. B.60C will show two quadrant plungers in the cam-plate windows ready to move the gears from second to first or neutral or back again.

When the cam-plate is moved to third gear position as will be seen by reference to Fig. B.60D, the action moves **both** selector forks, drawing the layshaft sliding gear to a neutral position and moving the mainshaft sliding gear into mesh with the mainshaft third gear. Again the quadrant plungers are ready to move the gears either way.

Finally, the move into fourth or top gear (Fig. B.60E) operates the mainshaft selector fork only, again sliding the gear the opposite way to mesh with the sleeve pinion. After each movement of the gearchange pedal the quadrant returns to a static position so that the plungers are ready to operate the cam-plate. The large plunger at the large end of the cam-plate is the positive gear location and it also serves to steady the cam-plate whilst the quadrant plungers are returning to their static position.

SEQUENCE OF GEAR POSITIONS

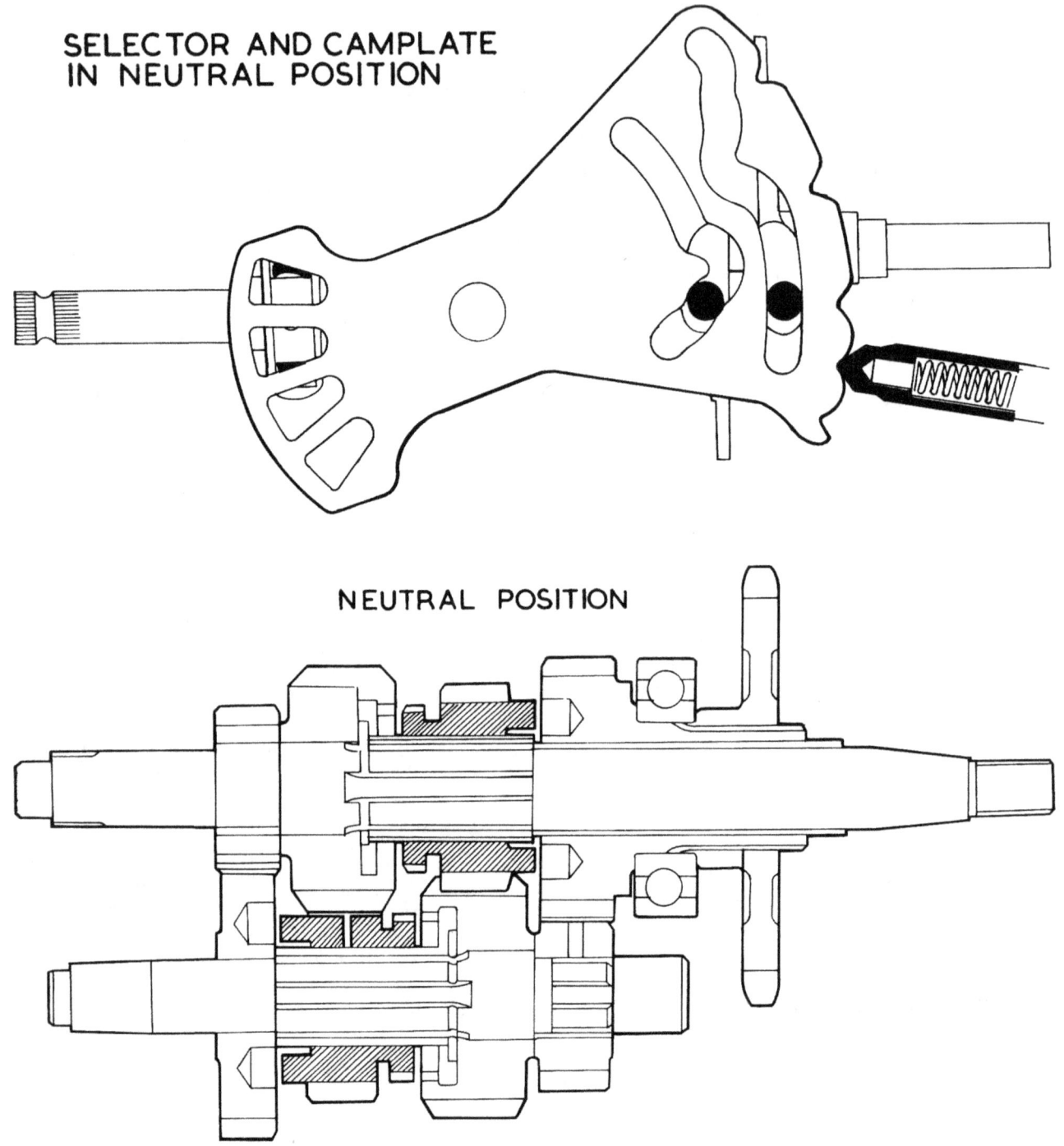

Fig. B.60A.

ENGINE

SEQUENCE OF GEAR POSITIONS

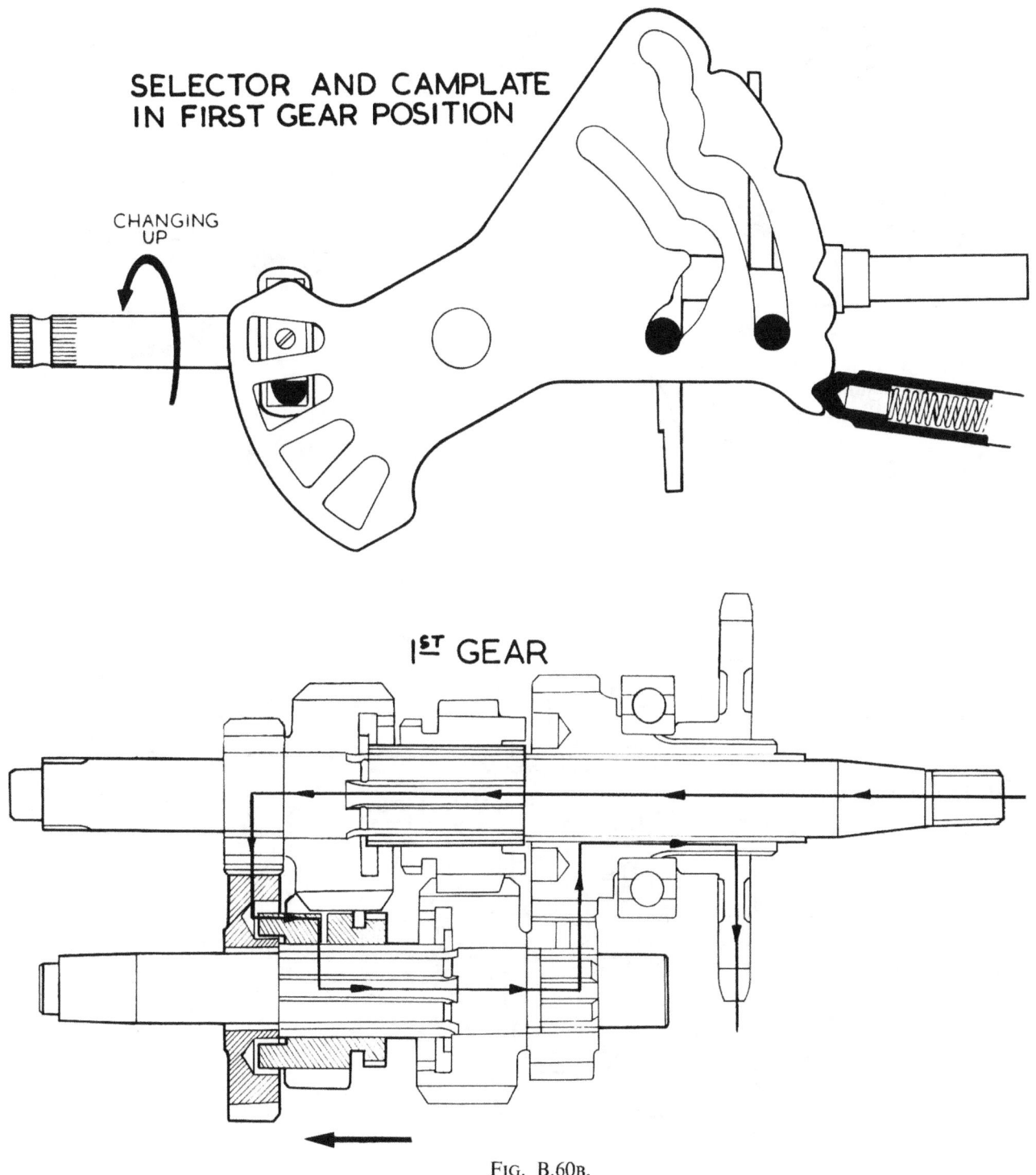

Fig. B.60B.

SEQUENCE OF GEAR POSITIONS

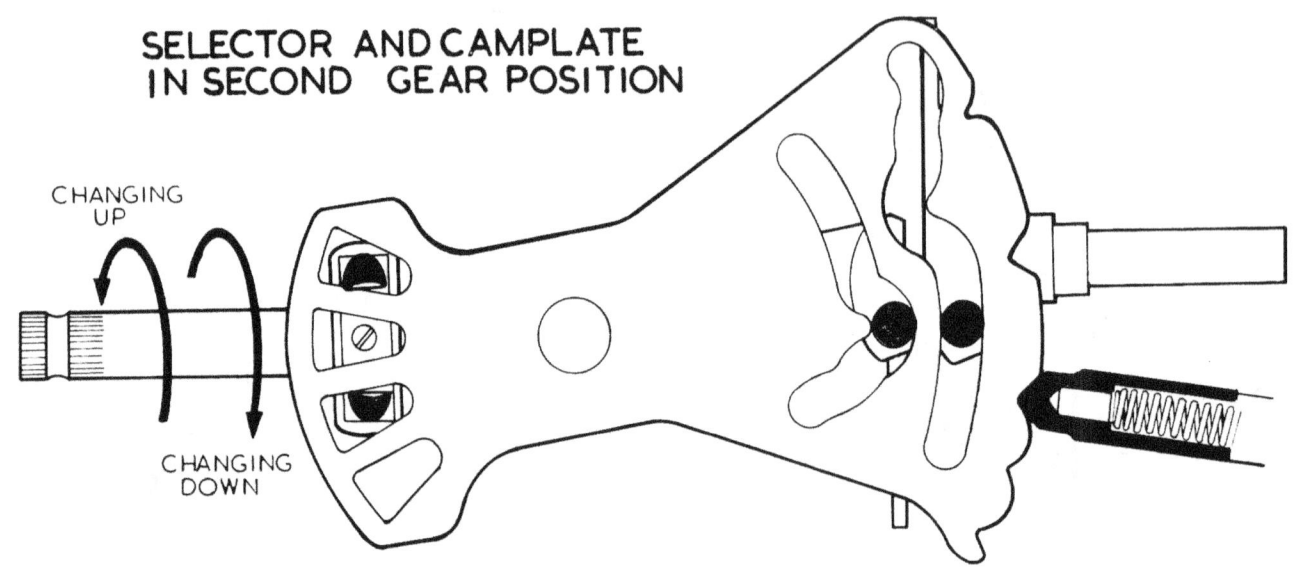

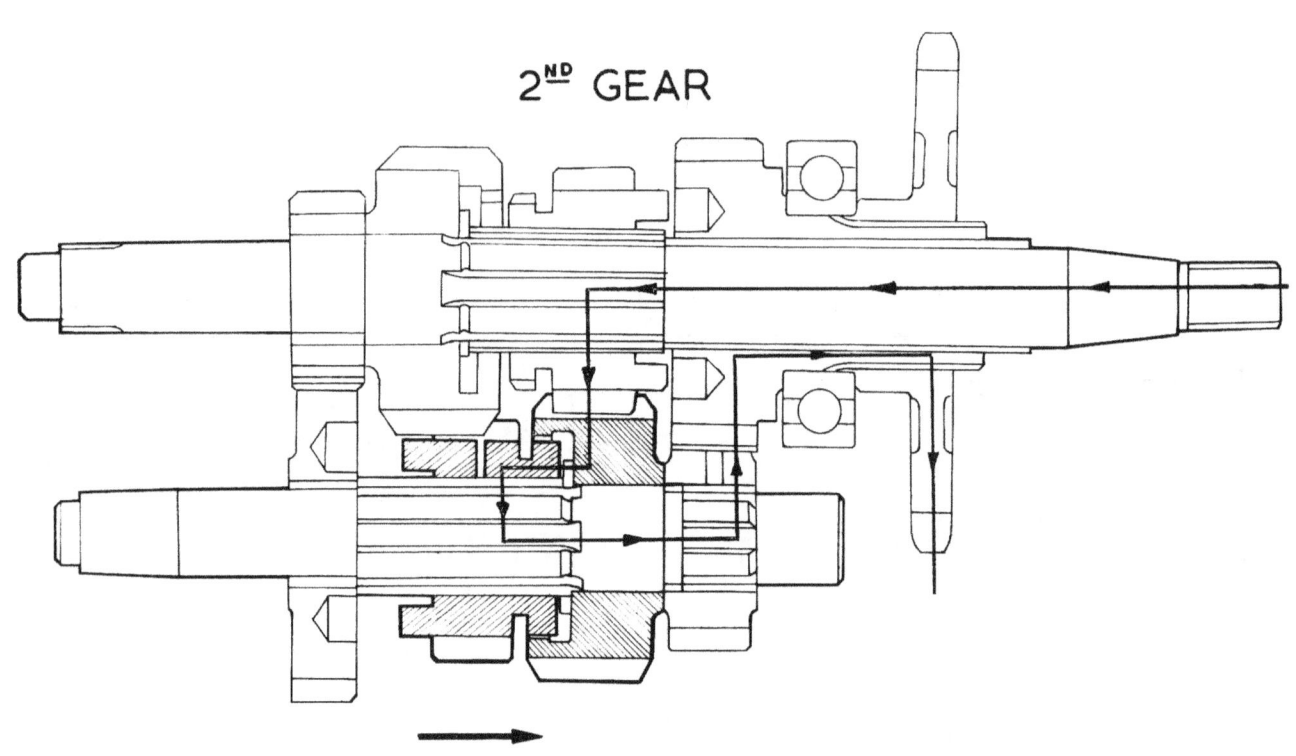

Fig. B.60c.

ENGINE

SEQUENCE OF GEAR POSITIONS

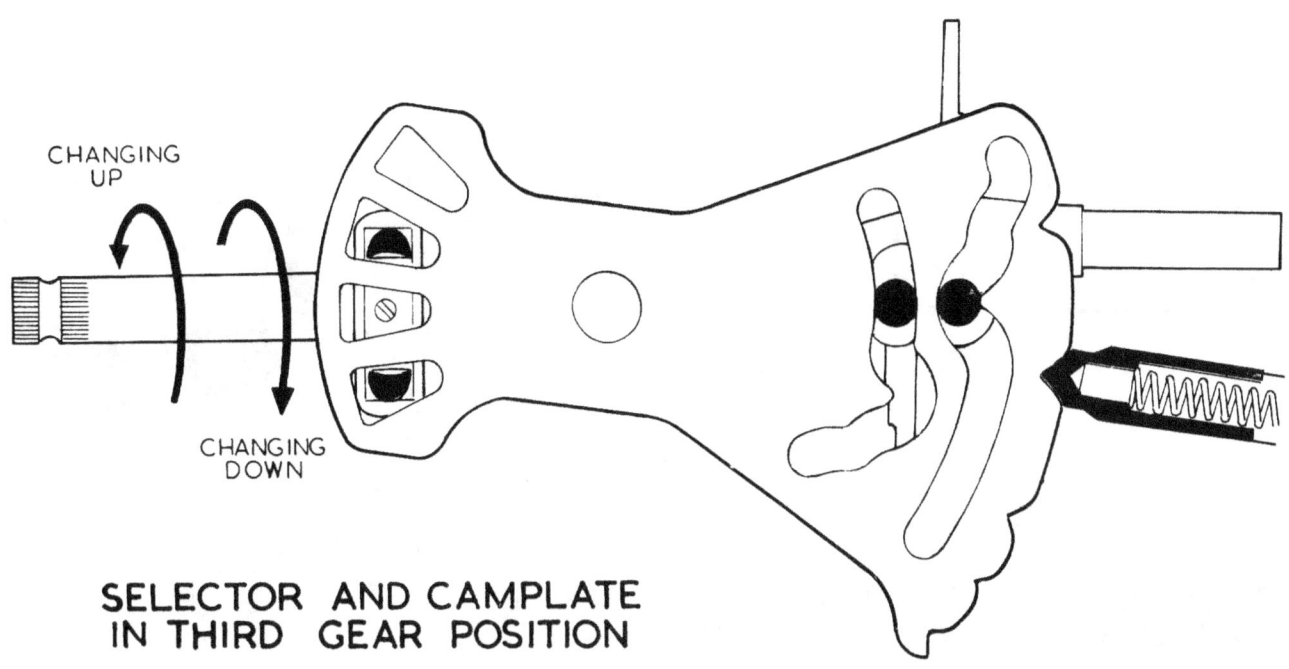

SELECTOR AND CAMPLATE IN THIRD GEAR POSITION

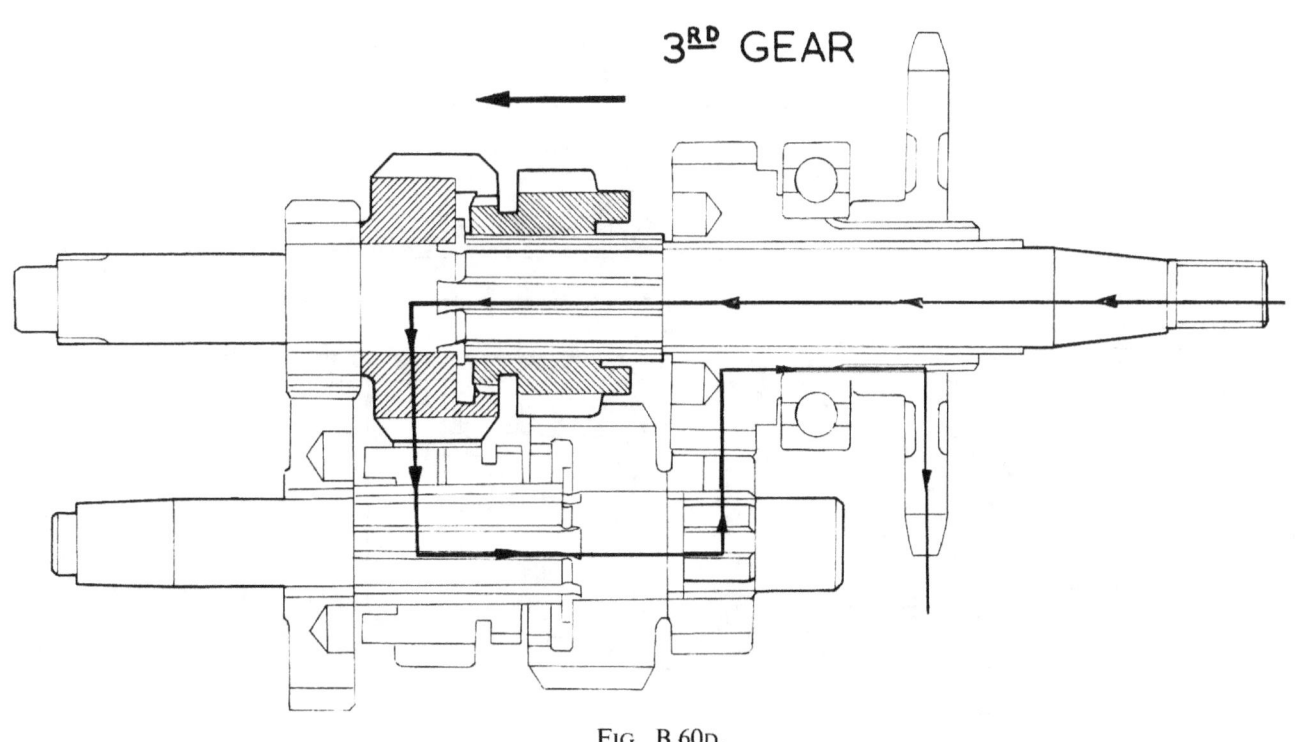

Fig. B.60D.

ENGINE

SEQUENCE OF GEAR POSITIONS

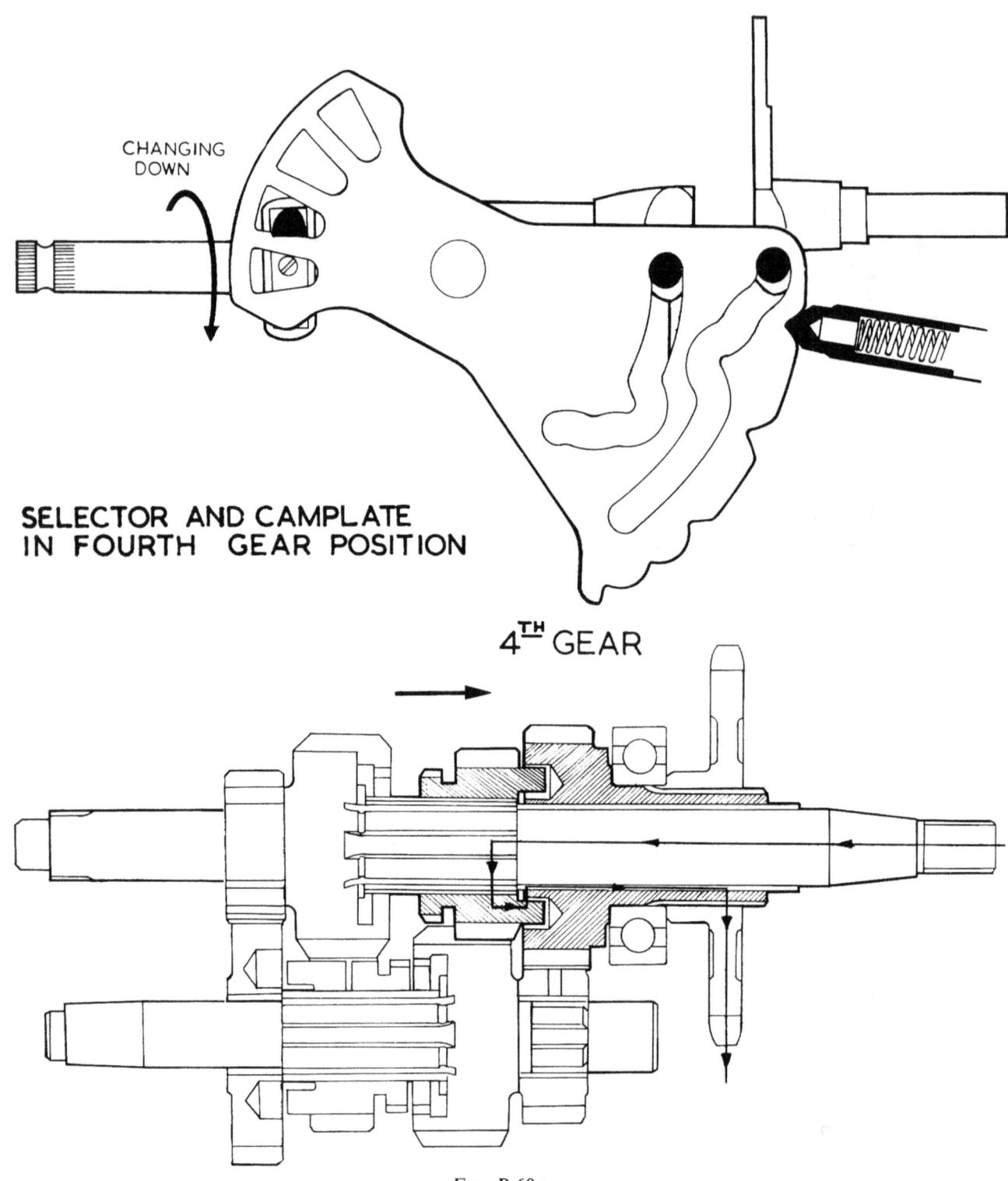

FIG. B.60E.

SPLITTING THE CRANKCASE

Before attempting to part the two halves of the crankcase all the timing gear must have been removed as detailed on pages B.32–34 and the primary drive gear as detailed on pages B.22–25.

It is not absolutely necessary to remove the gear cluster but, since the work already involved constitutes a major operation it is sometimes good policy to examine the gears at the same time. Removal and replacement of the gear cluster is detailed on pages B.34–38.

Remove the nuts and washers from the two bolts (A) at the lower front of the case, the two bolts (B) at the upper front and the three studs (C), Fig. B.61.

There is also one nut and washer on the bridge piece across the mouth of the crankcase.

Take off the four nuts holding the sump filter and remove the filter.

There is no need to disturb the oil pump scavenge valve which is now exposed, unless it is known to be defective but, care must be taken during subsequent handling to avoid damage.

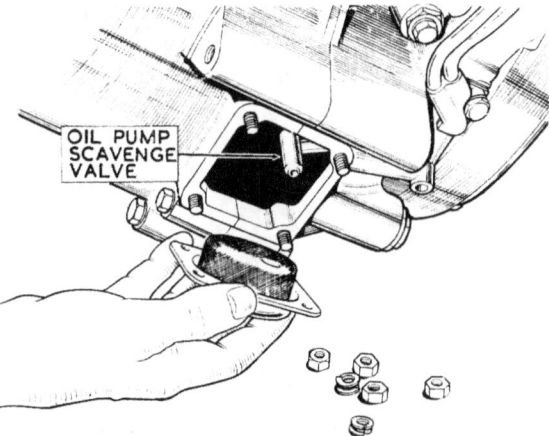

FIG. B.62. *Scavenge valve.*

Remove any Woodruff keys which may still be in the shafts noting their particular locations, break the joint by tapping gently with a hide mallet and take away the gear-side half-case. Do not attempt to prise the two halves of the case apart using a screwdriver or other tool between the joint, this will only damage the joint faces and result in oil leakage.

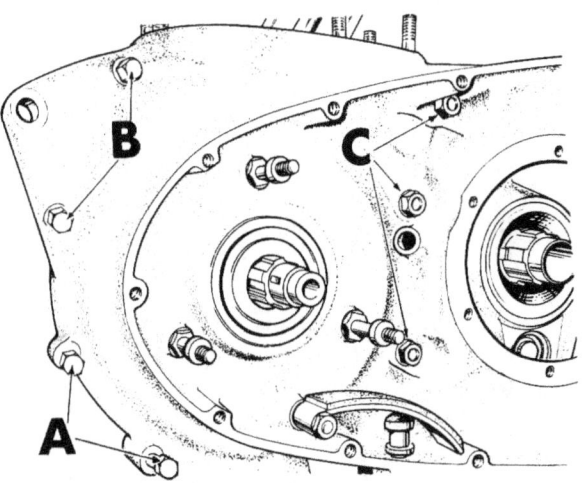

FIG. B.61. *Crankcase bolts.*

CAMSHAFT

The camshaft can now be removed, it may come away with the breather valve and spring or these parts may remain behind the camshaft bearing in the drive-side half-case.

The breather is of the rotary disc valve type, the rotating half being driven off the end of the camshaft and the static half being secured by a peg at the base of the drive-side camshaft bearing. The bearing must be removed to gain access to the static half.

Examine the peaks of the cams for wear or scuffing. If the peaks are worn the valves will not open completely and the camshaft should be replaced.

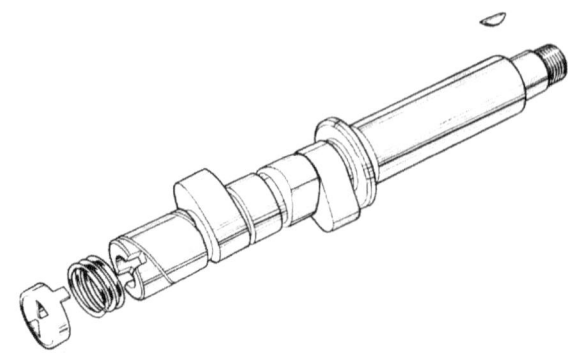

FIG. B.63. *Camshaft and breather.*

The crankshaft assembly can now be removed and placed to one side.

CRANKSHAFT ASSEMBLY

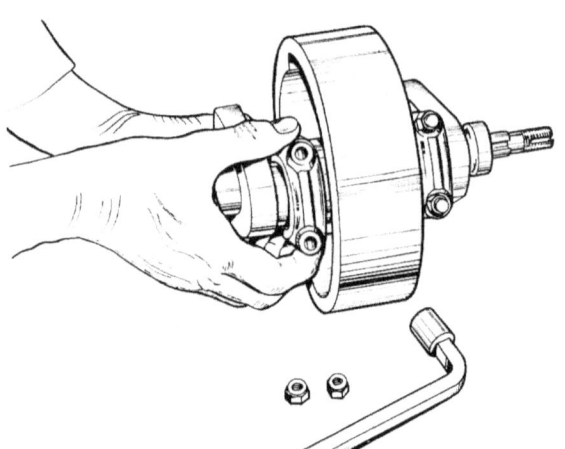

FIG. B.64. *Removing connecting rod.*

Removal of the connecting rods from the crankshaft is quite straight forward but, the rods, bolts and caps must be marked so that they can be replaced in the same positions if they are being used again.

If the crankshaft is to be reground it is essential that the correct regrind sizes are used to suit the undersize big-end bearing shells and gear-side bush.

There are three undersize bearing shells available but only two gear-side bushes.

ENGINE

CRANKSHAFT GRINDING

It will be necessary to regrind the bearing surfaces if the overall wear of the crankpins or gear-side journal exceeds .002 in. or if the surfaces have been damaged by seizure. Worn bearings will develop a distinct "knock" and the engine will become generally very rough.

GEAR-SIDE JOURNAL

Shafts No. 68-0175 or 68-0179.
Grind journal to: 1.4885—1.489 in. with .050—.060 in. radius and use .010 in. undersize bush number 68-0334 or grind to 1.4785—1.479 in. with .050—.060 radius and use .020 in. undersize bush number 68-0332.

FIRST REGRIND

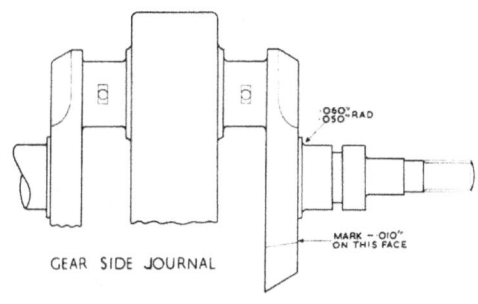

MARK CRANKSHAFT WEB FACE AS SHOWN.

FIG. B.65.

Reground crankshafts complete with big-end bearing shells and gear-side bush are available from the Service Department.

SECOND REGRIND

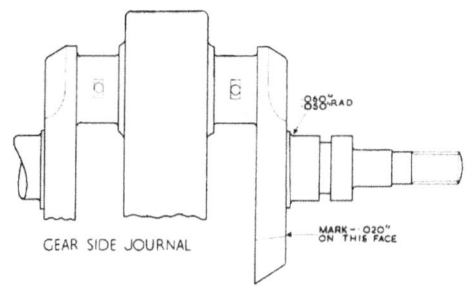

MARK CRANKSHAFT WEB FACE AS SHOWN.

FIG. B.66.

This service, only available to owners in the British Isles, is operated through the dealer network.

BIG END JOURNALS

FIRST REGRIND

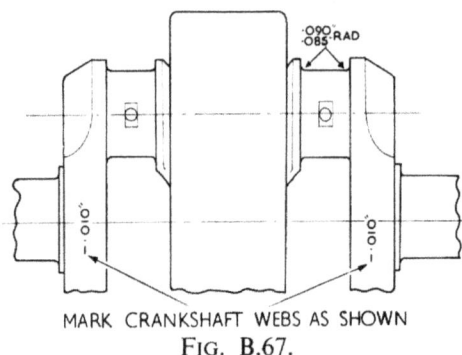

FIG. B.67.

Grind the crankpins to 1.677—1.6765 in. diameter with .085—.090 in. face radius. Fit bearing shell 67-1431 (4 off) marked .010 in. undersize.

SECOND REGRIND

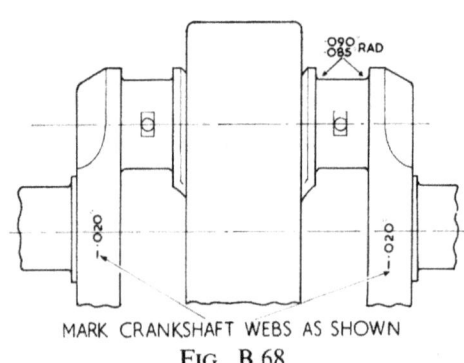

FIG. B.68.

Grind the crankpins to 1.667—1.6665 in. diameter with .085—.090 in. face radius. Fit bearing shell 67-1432 (4 off) marked .020 in. undersize.

THIRD REGRIND

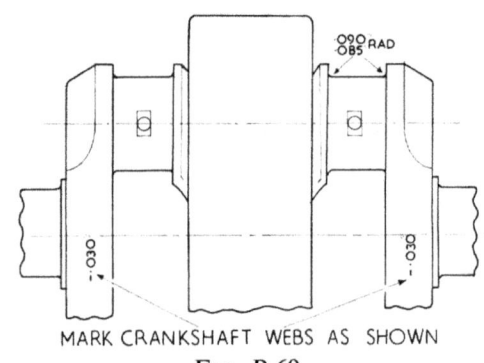

FIG. B.69.

Grind the crankpins to 1.657—1.6565 in. diameter with .085—.090 in. face radius. Fit bearing shell 67-1433 (4 off) marked .030 in. undersize.

CRANKSHAFT SLUDGE TRAP

The opportunity should be taken while the crankshaft is out of the case (assuming it is being refitted) to clean the sludge trap.

To remove the trap, take out both end plugs (early type shaft) and the flywheel bolt on the crankpin side and tap the sludge trap out. The oilways should be thoroughly cleaned with paraffin and if possible blown out with a high pressure air line.

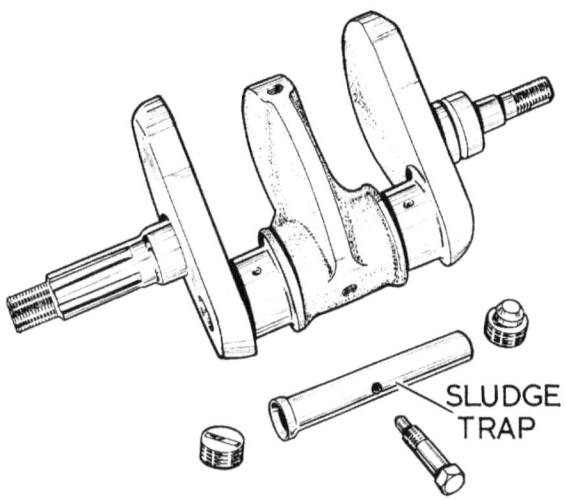

FIG. B.71. *Sludge trap.*

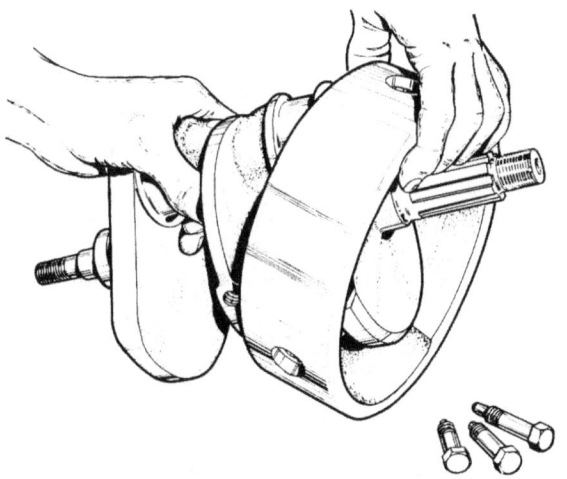

FIG. B.70. *Removing the flywheel.*

NOTE:—The later type crankshaft has only one sludge trap plug and neither plugs or traps are interchangeable with each other. If replacements are required the correct parts must be used.

When replacing the sludge trap locate with the flywheel bolt first then screw in the end plug or plugs, all should be secured with "Loctite" seal or if this is not available the plugs should be centre punched into the thread to secure.

Should it be necessary the crankshaft balance can be checked using service tool 85161-3710 for the 650 c.c. or tool number 85161-3711 for the 500 c.c. machines. Crankshaft balancing does however, call for the services of a skilled mechanic and should not be undertaken without access to precision workshop equipment.

FLYWHEEL BALANCING (STATIC)

For all general purposes the crankshafts and flywheel assemblies are sufficiently balanced when they leave the works.

There should be no need to rebalance when fitting new connecting rods or oversize pistons.

Flywheel balancing should not be undertaken except by an expert mechanic who has access to the equipment necessary.

The equipment required is a drilling machine with depth stop and knife-edge rollers as illustrated, the latter must be set up perfectly horizontal.

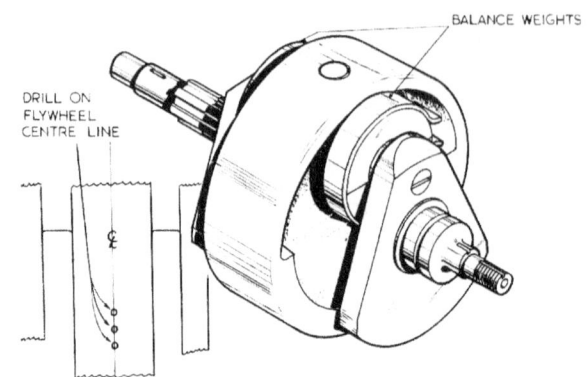

Fig. B.73.

Fig. B.72. *Knife-edge rollers.*

For balancing purposes a weight equivalent to 70% of the reciprocating weight is attached to each crankpin journal (see Fig. B.73), the crankshaft is then placed on the rollers and allowed to revolve until it stops, when a chalk mark is made at the lowest point.

This procedure is repeated several times to ensure accuracy.

The next step is to find the amount of out-of-balance so, plasticine is applied to the rim of the flywheel diametrically opposite the heaviest point until the shaft remains stationary when placed in any position on the rollers.

The wheels must now be drilled at the heaviest spot to remove metal equal to the weight of plasticine.

Drilling must be carried out on the periphery of the flywheel and must be central and not deeper than $\frac{3}{16}$ in.

It is better to start with a small diameter hole, which can be opened out if necessary, rather than a large hole to then find that too much metal has been removed.

BALANCE WEIGHTS

MODEL	TOOL NO.	NO. REQD.	WEIGHT
A50	61–3711	2	22 ozs. 14 drms.
A65	61–3710	2	21 ozs.

BEARINGS, BUSHES AND OIL SEALS

With the crankcase split the opportunity should be taken to examine and replace all bushes and bearings which may be worn or damaged.

Ball journal bearings should be checked for roughness indicating damaged balls or ball tracks.

Most bearings and bushes can be pressed out, and in, quite normally but the crankcase must always be heated first and well supported.

The blind camshaft bush in the drive-side half-case can be removed with service tool number 84961–3159 but the replacement bushes must be reamed in line to the sizes quoted on page GD.4. To do this the two half-cases must be bolted together after the bushes have been changed, they are then carefully reamed to the required size, unbolted and the swarf very carefully removed by high pressure air line.

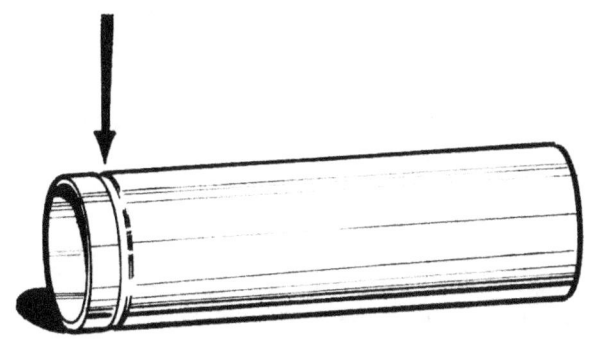

FIG. B.75. *Sleeve pinion bush.*

When replacing oil seals they must be handled very carefully to avoid damaging the knife-edge of the seal and they must be pressed into the housing squarely, with the open side always towards that part which is to be sealed.

Never reassemble a component which is deeply scored by the seal, to a new seal, it will be useless, the component should be replaced as well as the seal.

Figure B.75 shows sleeve pinion bush with groove worn by the primary drive case oil seal. This is a case where both components must be replaced.

Check all oilways to see that they are clear and see that the oil scavenging non-return valve in the base of the crankcase is quite free. If there is any possibility of sludge in the return pipe obstructing the ball, immerse the pipe in a container of petrol and allow to soak for a time.

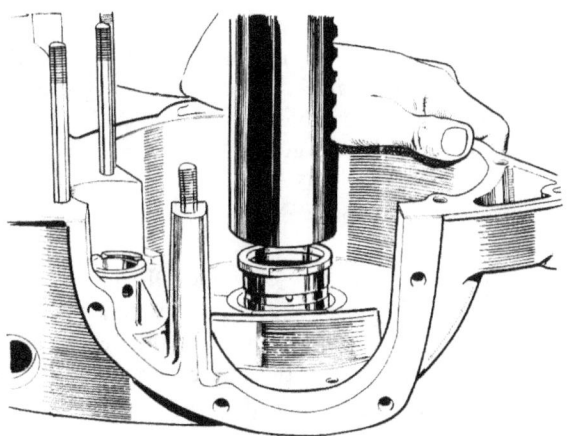

FIG. B.74. *Gear-side bush.*

REASSEMBLING THE CONNECTING RODS

The need for cleanliness cannot be over emphasized, all parts should be clean and free from grit or rust. As the various parts are assembled all bearing surfaces should be coated with clean engine oil.

Place the bearing shells in both the caps and connecting rods. If the old shells are being refitted see that they go into their original positions. No scraping is necessary with these bearing shells and must not be attempted or damage will result.

Connect each rod in turn to its crank journal making sure that the marks on rod and cap correspond and that the rods are the right way round, insert the bolts and secure the new self-locking nuts with a torque wrench set to 22 lbs./ft.

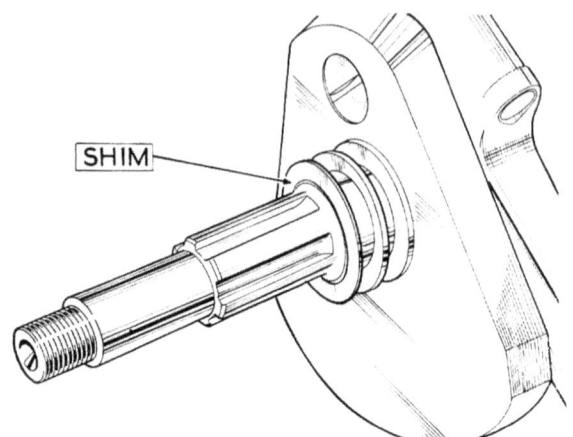

FIG. B.77. *Crankshaft shim.*

Maximum crankshaft end float must not exceed .003 in. (.0762 mm.). This is controlled by shims fitted between the inner race of the drive-side bearing and the crankshaft web. If the original shaft is being replaced it it only necessary to see that the shims are fitted.

When a new or reground crankshaft is being used, it must first be assembled into the case and the two halves bolted tightly together to enable the end float to be checked. If the float amounts to say .010 in. then two shims of .003 in. and .005 in. should be used leaving .002 in. end float.

At this point it is of great help to obtain a block or box measure approximately 8 in. by 8 in. by 6 in. with a hole in the centre large enough to accept the drive-side end of the crankshaft.

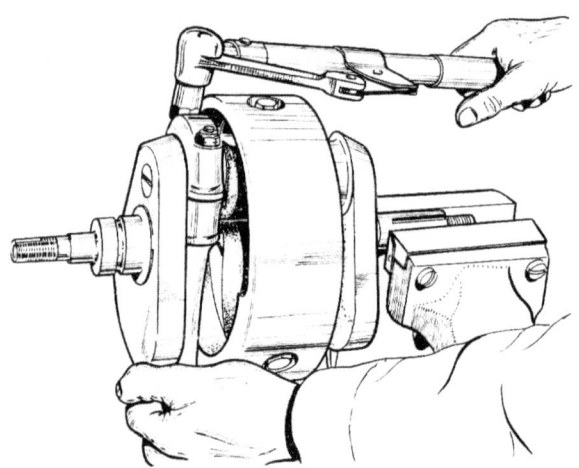

FIG. B.76. *Using torque wrench.*

REASSEMBLING THE CRANKCASE

Place the crankshaft assembly on the block or box with gear-side end in the block, see that the shims are in position on the drive-side end and place the drive-side half-case in position being careful to enter the bearing squarely and to ensure that it goes right home.

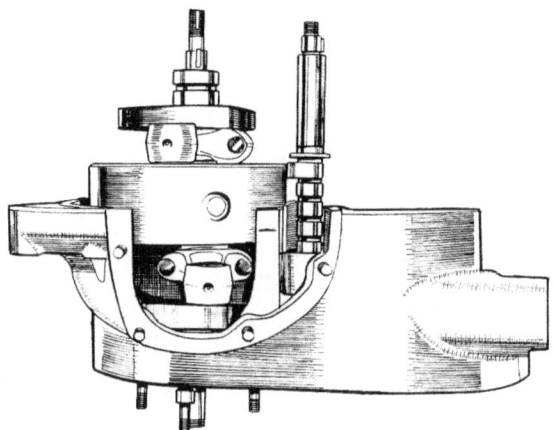

Fig. B.78. *Assembling drive-side.*

Reverse the assembly on the block and enter the rotary breather disc with the driving pegs uppermost, enter the spring and finally the camshaft carefully engaging the driving dogs in the end of the camshaft.

Having previously cleaned off the joint faces, smear both faces with a thin coating of jointing cement, place the gear-side half-case in position and bolt the two halves together. There are four bolts at the front (two with nuts and washers) and four nuts with plain washers on studs, three inside the primary case and one on the bridge piece across the mouth of the case.

Check that both the crankshaft and camshaft rotate quite freely, if they do not, then the alignment is incorrect and the cause of the trouble must be found and rectified.

Camshaft end float does not matter at this stage, it will be eliminated when the pinion is fitted.

Replace the sump plate and filter using a new gasket cemented both sides.

Replace the Woodruff key in the crankshaft and refit the crankshaft pinion with the timing mark on the outside.

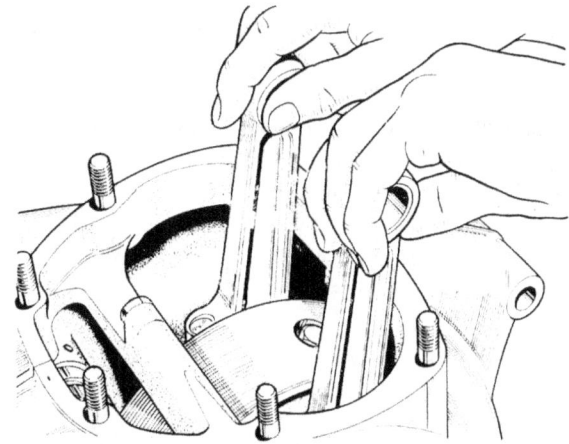

Fig. B.79. *Testing for freeness.*

Replace the crankshaft distance piece then screw on the oil pump worm gear, this has a left-hand thread and is therefore replaced screwing anti-clockwise. Place the tab-washer in position and secure with the nut which also has a left-hand thread.

ENGINE

Fig. B.80. *Camshaft pinion.*

Replace the oil pump as detailed on page B.33.

Replace the Woodruff key in the camshaft and refit the camshaft pinion with the timing mark outside (flat face inside). Do not omit to turn the tab-washer over the nut after tightening.

The idler pinion is now replaced so that the timing marks match with both the camshaft and the crankshaft pinions (see Fig. B.50, page B.33).

If the gear cluster has not yet been replaced it can now be assembled as detailed on pages B.36–38.

REPLACING THE INNER COVER

On older machines the inner timing cover can now be fitted. On later models (1964 onwards) the speedometer driving gear has an outrigger bearing in the inner cover, (see page GD.34 for range of gears). Assembly procedure for this type is as follows:—

Replace the timing cover using a new paper gasket cemented both sides, insert the speedometer driving gear into the layshaft, place the thrust washer over the speedometer gear, then insert the outrigger bush complete with its O-ring into the inner cover, and secure with the grub- or set-screw and washer after the eleven inner cover screws have been tightened.

Check that the ball is in position in the clutch lever cup and connect the cable to the lever (older models).

On later models see that the cable connector is in position on the lever.

Replace the long key in the gear selector spindle and fit the return spring and stop plate together so that one end of the spring is lying each side the lower pin, secure with the grub- or set-screw (when fitted).

There is no grub-screw used on the older models.

Replace the kickstart return spring and stop plate winding the plate round to engage the flats on the spindle and so place the spring under tension.

If a rev-counter is fitted, replace the driving pin so that it engages with the oil pump spindle and replace the cable nipple on the front edge of the case.

Replace the automatic-advance unit loosely, together with the contact breaker plate, and leave the retiming of the engine until later.

Replace the primary drive as detailed on pages B.26–28.

Replace the upper part of the engine as detailed for decarbonising on pages B.14–15.

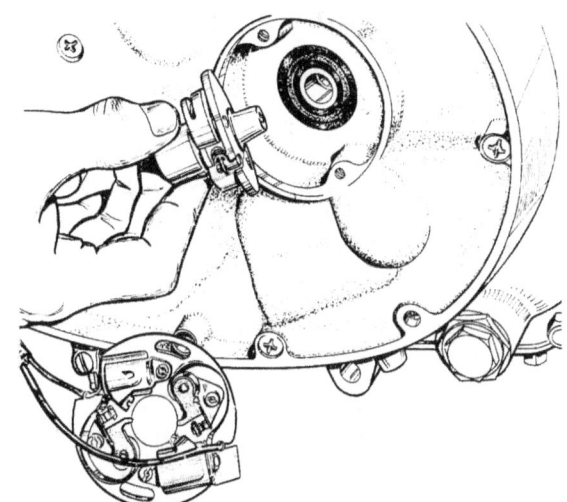

FIG. B.81. *Auto-advance unit.*

IGNITION TIMING

The simplest way to set the ignition timing, that is the point at which the compressed charge in the combustion chamber is ignited, is to set it statically.

Unfortunately, due to manufacturing tolerances this is not the ideal because, whilst it will set the timing of the engine for tick-over speeds, the firing at wide throttle openings can be varied due to differences in the amount of automatic-advance.

The automatic-advance functions by centrifugal force acting in spring-loaded bob weights and advances the ignition timing as the engine revolutions rise. Since exact timing accuracy is required at operating speeds it is better to time the engine in the fully advanced position so transferring any variations in the firing to the tick-over or low engine speeds when it can least affect the performance.

PISTON POSITION BEFORE TOP DEAD CENTRE (FULL RETARD)

A50, $\frac{1}{16}$ in. (1.5875 mm.) 15° crankshaft angle.

A65, .039 in. (1 mm.) 12° crankshaft angle.

IGNITION TIMING—MODELS WITHOUT FLYWHEEL LOCATING PEG

INITIAL PREPARATION

Continue from the point reached during re-building of the engine unit (see page B.49) where the auto-advance and the contact breaker were left loosely assembled.

(1) Remove both spark plugs if not already out.

(2) Mount a dial indicator on the cylinder head with a long thin pointer projecting into the cylinder through the right-hand spark plug hole.

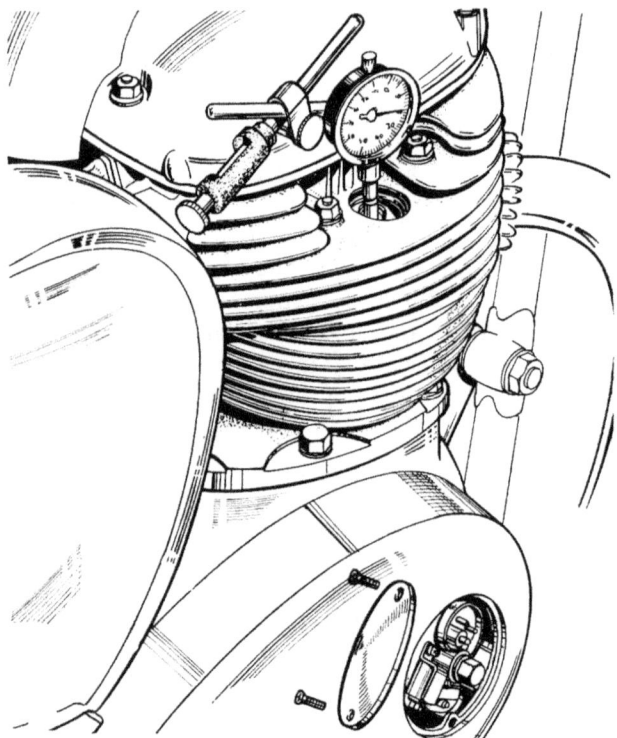

FIG. B.82.

(3) Revolve the engine so that the right-hand piston is on top dead centre with both valves closed. If either valve is open revolve the engine one complete turn. Set the dial indicator to zero. If an indicator is not available use a thin rod and make a mark in line with a clear point on the head.

(4) Revolve the engine backwards and then forwards until the piston is the required distance before top dead centre on the compression stroke. To do this using a thin rod, it will be necessary to make a second mark, to the required distance above the first mark (see Table on page B.51).

An alternative is to mount a timing disc on the crankshaft with a pointer mounted adjacent to the disc. Set the pointer to zero with the piston at top dead centre, revolve the engine backwards until the required number of degrees of advance are indicated by the pointer. Crankshaft angles are as indicated in the Table overleaf.

(5) Secure the contact breaker back-plate with the two screws midway in the slots.

(6) Without moving the pistons and lightly pressing the auto-advance cam inwards, turn the cam until the upper set of contact breaker points are just about to open, and secure the auto-advance unit by securely tightening the centre bolt.

After tightening revolve the cam to the limits of the auto-advance and check the fully open gap which should be .015 in. (.381 mm.). If the gap has to be adjusted repeat the timing procedure to obtain the static timing. To adjust the gap slacken off the circular slotted nut inside the "C"-shaped spring adjacent to the points being adjusted.

Do not, at this stage, alter the back-plate screws.

Check the fully open gap of the lower set of points (left-hand cylinder).

ENGINE

IGNITION TIMING—FULLY ADVANCED

Timing should always be set in the advanced position.

To check the opening of the contacts more accurately connect a battery and bulb in circuit with the points.

Attach one lead from the "C"-spring to the battery terminal, take another lead from the other battery terminal to a bulb then from the other side of the bulb to a good earth on the machine.

When the points open the light will go out. The leads must of course be changed to whichever set of points is being used.

(1) Position the right-hand piston before top dead centre on the compression stroke (both valves closed) as Table below.

(2) Slacken off the contact breaker back-plate screws. By holding the cam and turning anti-clockwise open the bob weight to the fully advanced position, then still holding the cam turn the contact breaker plate so that the upper set of points are just opening. Lock the plate in this position and re-check the setting. There should be no change in the fully open gap setting.

(4) Position the left-hand piston the required distance before top dead centre on the compression stroke.

PISTON POSITION BEFORE TOP DEAD CENTRE—FULL ADVANCE

A50, .304 in. (7.216 mm.) — 34° crankshaft angle.   A65, .357 in. (9.067 mm.) — 37° crankshaft angle.

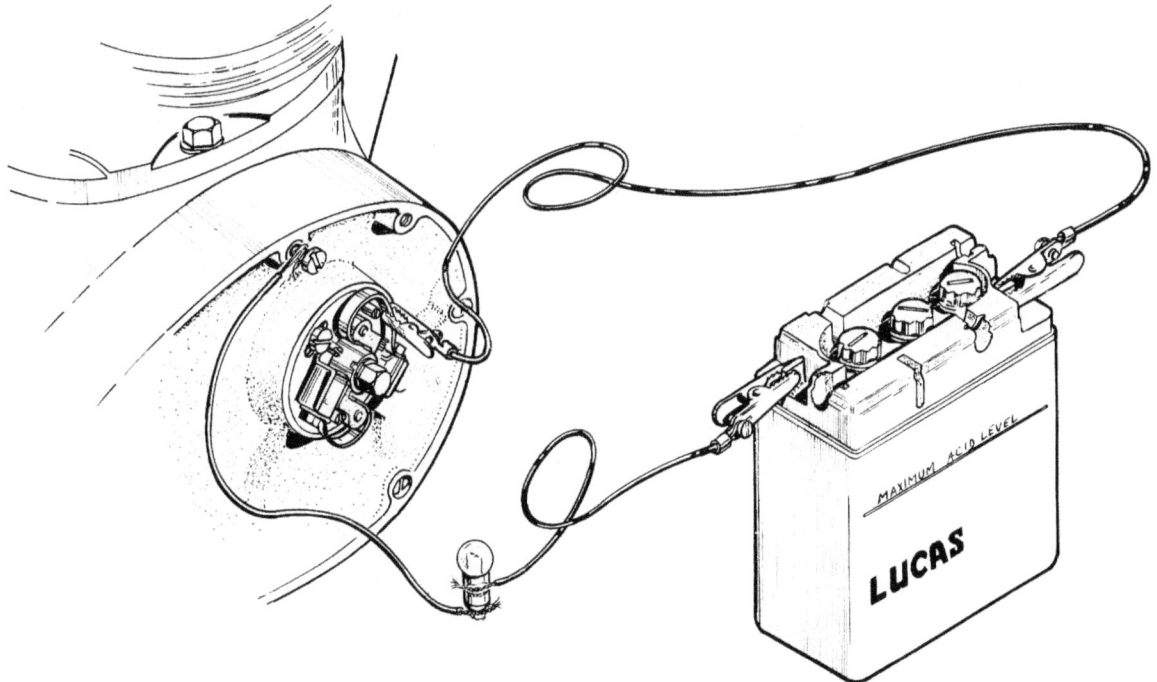

Fig. B.83. *Battery and bulb in circuit.*

(5) Now holding the cam in the fully advanced position check the opening of the points. This time do not move the back-plate but adjust the points gap to obtain the setting.

To advance the spark open the points approximately .001 in. for each engine degree required and to retard close the gap. If the setting on the left-hand cylinder (or lower set of points) is say now .013 in. this figure should be recorded and always used when retiming.

It should not be necessary to alter the gap by more than .003 in. + or — to obtain correct timing.

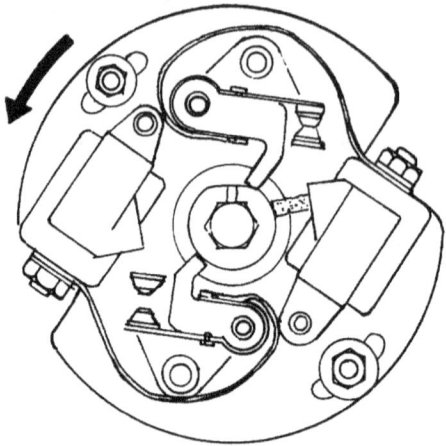

Fig. B.85. *Points just opening on right-hand cylinder (upper set).*

The right-hand gap setting must, of course, remain at .015 in. (.381 mm.).

Note:—When checking the ignition timing with the engine in position in the frame the ammeter on the machine can be used in place of the battery and bulb, if the ignition switch is turned to ON, the needle will flick to zero when the points open, unfortunately the help of an assistant will be required to observe this. Also the piston position can be obtained more easily if top gear is engaged and the rear wheel is rocked backwards or forwards.

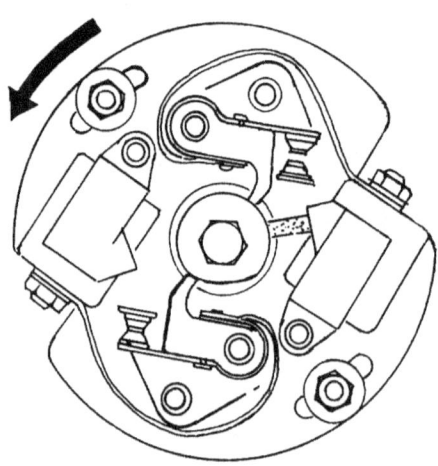

Fig. B.84. *Points just opening on left-hand cylinder (lower set).*

ENGINE

IGNITION TIMING
(with crankcase plug)

Later models have a plug included in the toolkit for setting the piston position to time the ignition in the fully advanced position.

This plug is used through the aperture on the right-hand front of the crankcase and it has two positions one for 500 c.c. models and the other for 650 c.c. models.

TIMING PROCEDURE

First see that the contact breaker points gap is correct at .015 in.

Take off the contact breaker plate, remove the centre screw holding the auto-advance mechanism and free the assembly from its taper by tapping the cam with the wooden handle of the screwdriver.

Remove the crankcase cover and insert the peg with the appropriate model number uppermost and using light finger pressure on the plug, turn the crankshaft slowly until the plug drops into the groove in the flywheel.

Do not revolve the crankshaft whilst the timing plug is in position.

The engine can be turned by means of the kickstart lever but it can be done easier with both spark plugs out and in top gear by turning the rear wheel.

Having located the flywheel by means of the plug check which cylinder is on compression stroke and proceed to time the engine as described on page B.50 from paragraph 6.

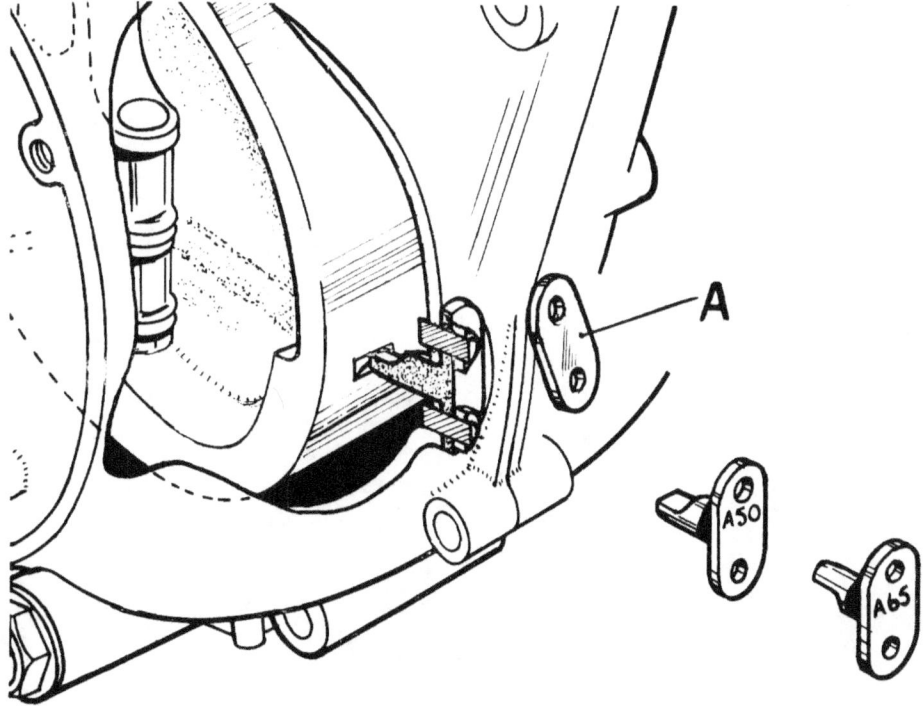

Fig. B.86.

NOTES

A5065 CARBURETTOR C1

INDEX

	Page
Carburettor (Exploded Drawing)	C.2
Description	C.3
Dismantling and Reassembling	C.4
Inspecting the Components	C.5
Hints and Tips	C.5–6
Reassembling	C.7
Tracing Faults	C.7–8
Variable Settings and Parts	C.8–9
How to Tune (Single Carburettor)	C.10–11
Tuning Twin Carburettors	C.12

CARBURETTOR

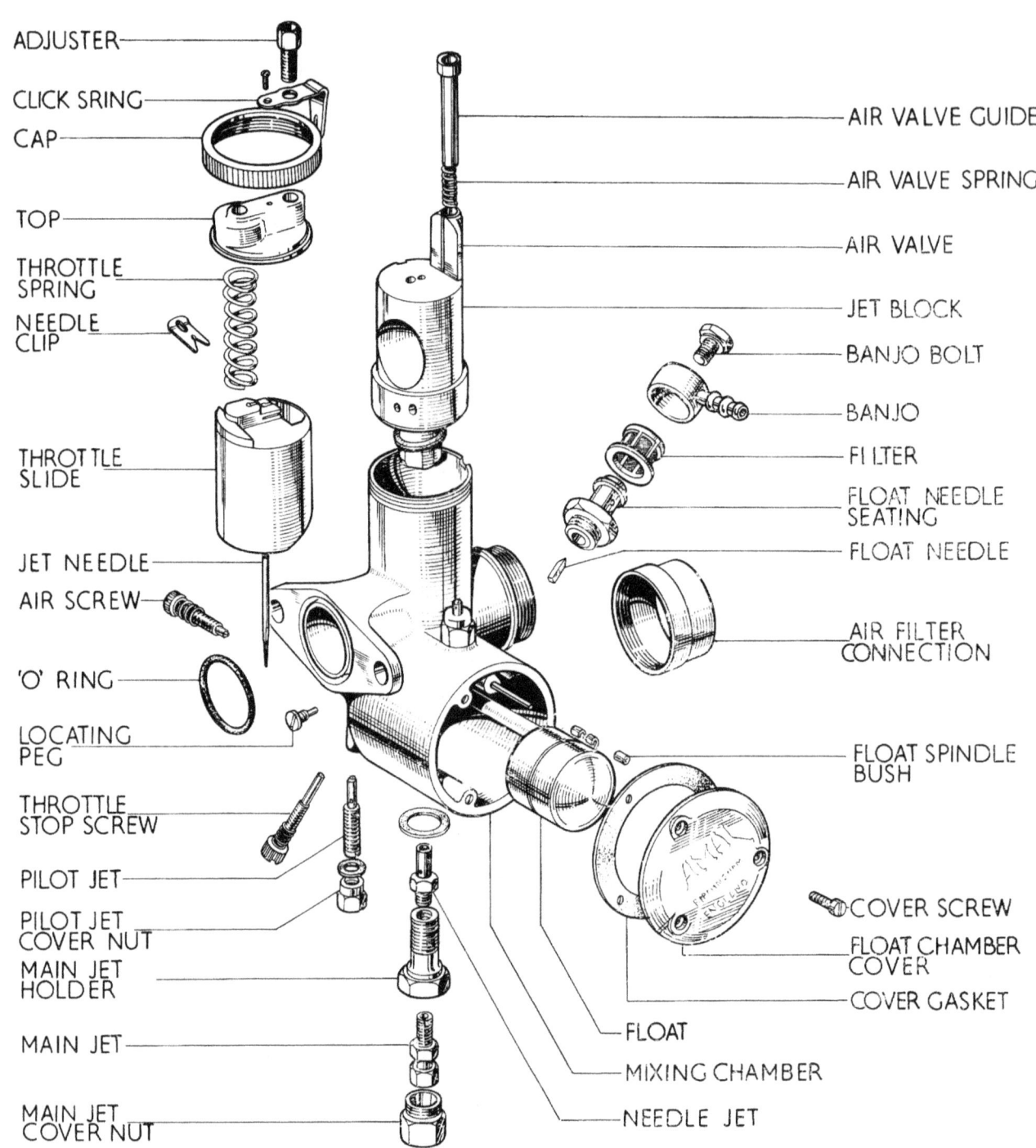

Fig. C.1. *Carburettor exploded.*

CARBURETTOR

DESCRIPTION

All the 500 c.c. (A50) and 650 c.c. (A65) models are fitted with the Amal Monobloc, the only variation being on the A50 Cyclone, A65 Lightning and A65 Spitfire models which have twin monobloc carburettors.

The carburettor, because of its jets and choke bore, proportions and atomises just the right amount of petrol with the air that is drawn into the engine and provides a highly inflamable mixture which is ultimately burnt inside the cylinder head, hence the term "combustion chamber."

The float chamber maintains a constant level of fuel at the jets and incorporates a valve which cuts off the supply when the engine stops.

The throttle, being operated from the handlebar twist-grip, controls the volume of mixture and therefore the power.

At tick-over the mixture supply is from the pilot jet system, then as the throttle is opened via the pilot by-pass, the mixture is augmented from the main jet, the earlier stages of which action is controlled by the needle in the needle jet.

The pilot system is supplied by a jet which is detachable for cleaning purposes and which, when assembled in the carburettor body, is sealed by a cover nut.

The carburettor also has a separately operated mixture control known as an air valve, for use when starting from cold, and until the engine is thoroughly warm. This control partially blocks the passage of air through the main choke and is operated from the handlebar.

The design of the carburettor is such that it provides quite simple and effective tuning facilities.

The main jet does not spray directly into the mixing chamber, but discharges through the needle jet into the primary air chamber, and goes from there as a rich petrol/air mixture, through the primary air choke, into the main air choke. This primary air choke has a compensating action in conjunction with bleed holes in the needle jet, which serve the double purpose of compensating the mixture from the needle jet and allowing the fuel to provide a well outside and around the needle jet, which is available for snap acceleration.

DISMANTLING AND REASSEMBLING THE CARBURETTOR

After removing the carburettor from the cylinder as described on page B.4 the procedure for dismantling is the same whether for single or twin except that twin carburettor cables are connected at junction boxes. Removal of the cable nipples from the junction boxes is quite simple and straight forward after the single cables have been disconnected from the lever and twist-grip.

First remove the throttle and air slides from the body by unscrewing the mixing chamber top cap, then withdraw the slides and throttle needle.

Remove the needle retaining spring clip, compress the slide return spring, then push the cable nipple down and out of the slide.

To release the air slide, compress the spring and slip the nipple out of the bottom of the slide.

Unscrew three slotted screws and withdraw the float chamber cover and remove the float spindle bush, the float, then withdraw the triangular section float needle.

Unscrew the banjo bolt which secures the fuel pipe banjo connector to the float needle seating block and withdraw the banjo, filter and junction washers. Unscrew the needle seating block. Unscrew the tickler body then withdraw the tickler and spring.

Remove the air screw and throttle stop screw, then the main jet cover nut from the bottom of the body. Unscrew the main jet, main jet holder and needle jet. To release the jet block re-insert the main jet holder, until a few threads are engaged then tap it with a hide mallet. This will release the jet block through the carburettor body.

Unscrew the pilot jet cover, and unscrew the pilot jet. All that remains to be removed then is the hexagonal locating peg, the end of which can be seen protruding within the mixing chamber.

Thoroughly clean all parts in petrol (gasoline). Deposits on the carburettor body are best removed by a light grade wire brush. It is advisable to wash the parts several times each in a clean quantity of petrol, to avoid particles of dirt remaining. Allow the parts to drain, preferably using a jet of compressed air from such as a hand pump to ensure that all holes and drillings are free from blockage.

Inspect the component parts for wear and check that the jets are in accordance with the recommended sizes given in GENERAL DATA.

Apart from one or two points that are mentioned below, reassembly is a reversal of the above instructions, referring to Fig. C.1 for guidance.

Do not replace any fibre washer that looks unserviceable. It is advisable to purchase replacement washers before removing the carburettor.

When replacing the jet block, ensure that the fibre washer is in position; align the location slot in the jet block with the locating peg in the carburettor housing and drive the block home.

Finally, note that the float spindle bush fits on the outside end of the spindle, and that the float pressure pad is uppermost so that the float needle rests on it.

CARBURETTOR

INSPECTING THE CARBURETTOR COMPONENTS

The parts liable to show wear after considerable mileage are the throttle valve slide, mixing chamber and the air slide.

(1) Inspect the throttle valve slide for excessive scoring to the front area and check the extent of wear on the rear slide face. If wear is apparent the slide should be renewed. In this case, be sure to replace the slide with the correct degree of cut-away (see GENERAL DATA).

(2) Examine the air valve for excessive wear and check that it is not actually worn through at any part. Check the fit of the air valve in the jet block. Ensure that the air valve spring is serviceable by inspecting the coils for wear (see page GD.6).

(3) Inspect the throttle return spring for efficiency and check that it has not lost compressive strength by measuring its length and comparing it to the figure given in page GD.6.

(4) Check the needle jet for wear or possible scoring and carefully examine the tapered end of the needle for similar signs.

(5) Examine the float needle for efficiency by inserting it into the inverted float needle seating block, pouring a small amount of petrol (gasolene) into the aperture surrounding the needle and checking it for leakage.

(6) Ensure that the float does not leak by shaking it to see if it contains any fuel. Do not attempt to repair a damaged float. A new one can be purchased for a small cost.

(7) Check the petrol filter, which fits over the the needle seating block, for any possible damage to the mesh. Ensure that the filter has not parted from its supporting structure, thus enabling the petrol (gasolene) to by-pass it unfiltered.

HINTS AND TIPS

Cable Controls.
See that there is a minimum of backlash when the controls are set back and that any movement of the handlebar does not cause the throttle to open: this is done by the adjusters on the top of the carburettor. See that the throttle shuts down freely.

Petrol Feed.
Later models are fitted with a filter gauze at the inlet to the float chamber. To remove the filter gauze unscrew the banjo bolt, the banjo can then be removed and the filter gauze withdrawn from the needle seating.

Ensure that the filter gauze is undamaged and free from all foreign matter. To check fuel flow, before replacing the banjo, turn on petrol tap momentarily and see that fuel gushes out.

Flooding.
May be due to a worn needle or a leaky float, but is more likely due to impurities (grit, fluff, etc.) in the tank, so clean out the float chamber periodically till the trouble ceases. If the trouble persists, the tank must be drained and swilled out.

CARBURETTOR

Fixing Carburettor and Air Leaks.
Erratic slow running is often caused by air leaks, so verify there are none at the point of attachment to the cylinder or inlet pipe, check by means of an oilcan and eliminate by new washers and the equal tightening up of flange nuts. On later models a sealing ring is fitted into the attachment flange of the carburettor. In old machines look out for air leaks caused by a worn throttle or worn inlet valve guides.

Banging in Exhaust.
May be caused by too weak a pilot mixture when the throttle is closed or nearly closed, also it may be caused by too rich a pilot mixture and an air leak in the exhaust system: the reason in either case is that the mixture has not fired in the cylinder and has fired in the hot silencer. If the banging happens when the throttle is fairly wide open the trouble will be ignition, not carburation.

Bad Petrol Consumption.
Which cannot be corrected by normal adjustment, may be due to flooding, caused by impurities from the petrol tank lodging on the float needle seat so preventing its valve from closing.

It may also be caused by a worn float needle valve. High consumption will be apparent if the needle jet has worn; it may be remedied or improved by lowering the needle in the throttle, but if it cannot be—then the only remedy is to get a new needle jet.

There are many other causes of high fuel consumption not connected with the carburettor.

Air Filters.
These may affect the jet setting. If a carburettor is set with an air filter and the engine is run without, take care not to overheat the engine due to too weak a mixture; testing with the air valve will indicate if a larger main jet and higher needle position are required.

Effect of Altitude on Carburettor.
Increased altitude tends to produce a rich mixture. The greater the altitude, the smaller the main jet required. Carburettors ex-works are set suitable for altitudes up to 3,000 feet approximately. Carburettors used constantly at altitudes 3,000 to 6,000 feet should have a reduction in main jet size of 5%, and thereafter for every 3,000 feet in excess of 6,000 feet altitude further reductions of 4% should be made.

No adjustment can compensate for lost power due to rarified air.

CARBURETTOR

REASSEMBLING THE CARBURETTOR (see page C.4)

TRACING FAULTS

There are two possible faults in carburation, either richness or weakness of mixture.

Indications of Richness
Black smoke in exhaust.
Petrol spraying out of carburettor.
Four-strokes, eight-stroking.
Two-strokes, four-stroking.
Heavy, lumpy running.
Sparking plug sooty.

Indications of Weakness
Spitting back in carburettor.
Erratic slow-running.
Overheating.

Engine goes better if: throttle is not wide open or air valve is partially closed.

If richness or weakness is present check if caused by:—

(1) Petrol feed—check that jets and passages are clear, that filter gauze in float chamber banjo connection is not choked with foreign matter, and that there is ample flow of fuel. Check there is no flooding.

(2) Air leaks—at the connection to the engine or due to leaky inlet valve stems.

(3) Defective or worn parts—as a loose fitting throttle valve, worn needle jet, loose jets.

(4) Air cleaner choked up.

(5) An air cleaner having been removed.

CARBURETTOR

(6) Removal of the silencer or running with a straight-through pipe, this requires a richer setting.

Having verified the correctness of fuel feed and that there are no air leaks, check over ignition, valve operation and timing. Now test to see if mixtures are rich or weak. This is done by partially closing the air valve, and if engine runs better weakness is indicated, but if engine runs worse richness is indicated.

To remedy, proceed as follows:—

To Cure Richness
Position 1. Fit smaller main jet.
Position 2. Screw out pilot air adjusting screw.
Position 3. Fit a throttle with larger cut-away (paragraph E, page C.9.)
Position 4. Lower needle one or two grooves (paragraph D, page C.9).

To Cure Weakness
Position 1. Fit larger main jet.
Position 2. Screw pilot air adjusting screw in.
Position 3. Fit a throttle with smaller cut-away (paragraph E, page C.9).
Position 4. Raise needle one or two grooves (paragraph D, page C.9).

NOTE.—It is not correct to cure a rich mixture at half-throttle by fitting a smaller jet because the main jet may be correct for power at full throttle: the proper thing to do is to lower the needle.

VARIABLE SETTINGS AND PARTS

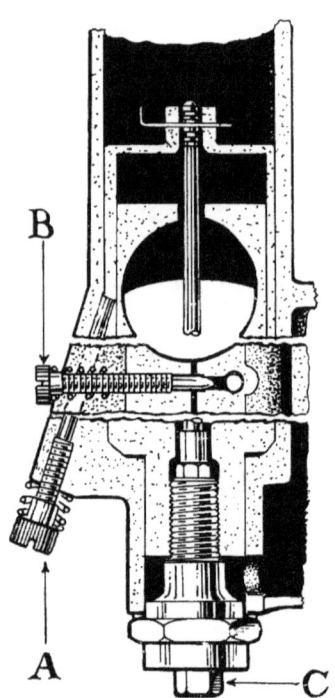

FIG. C.2.

Figure C.2 is three diagramatic sections of the carburettor to show the throttle adjusting screw (A), and the pilot air adjusting screw (B).

(A) THROTTLE ADJUSTING SCREW.
Set this screw to hold the throttle open sufficiently to keep the engine running when the twist-grip is shut off.

(B) PILOT AIR ADJUSTING SCREW.
This screw regulates the strength of the mixture for "idling" and for the initial opening of the throttle. The screw controls the depression on the pilot jet by metering the amount of air that mixes with the petrol.

CARBURETTOR

(C) MAIN JET.

The main jet controls the petrol supply when the throttle is more than three-quarters open, but at smaller throttle openings although the supply of fuel goes through the main jet, the amount is diminished by the metering effect of the needle in the needle jet.

Each jet is calibrated and numbered so that its exact discharge is known and two jets of the same number are alike. **Never ream out a jet, get another of the right size.** The bigger the number the bigger the jet.

To remove the main jet unscrew the main jet cover, the exposed main jet can then be unscrewed from the jet holder.

(D) NEEDLE AND NEEDLE JET (Fig. C.1.)

The needle is attached to the throttle valve and being taper—either allows more or less petrol to pass through the needle jet as the throttle is opened or closed throughout the range, except when idling or nearly full throttle. The taper needle position in relation to the throttle opening can be set according to the mixture required by fixing it to the throttle valve with the jet needle clip in a certain groove, thus either raising or lowering it. Raising the needle richens the mixture and lowering it weakens the mixture at throttle openings from quarter- to three-quarters open.

(E) THROTTLE VALVE CUT-AWAY.

The atmospheric side of the throttle is cut away to influence the depression on the main fuel supply and thus gives a means of tuning between the pilot and needle jet range of throttle opening. The amount of cut-away is recorded by a number marked on the throttle valve, viz. 376/3 means throttle valve type 376 with number 3 cut-away; larger cut-aways, say 4 and 5, give weaker mixtures and 2 a richer mixture.

(F) AIR VALVE.

Is used only for starting and running when cold, and for experimenting with, otherwise run with it wide open.

(G) TICKLER.

A small plunger spring-loaded, in the float chamber wall. When pressed down on the float, the needle valve is allowed to open and so "flooding" is achieved. Flooding temporarily enriches the mixture until the level of the petrol subsides to normal. This valve is operated on some models through a metal strip immediately in front of the left side cover.

CARBURETTOR

HOW TO TUNE THE CARBURETTOR

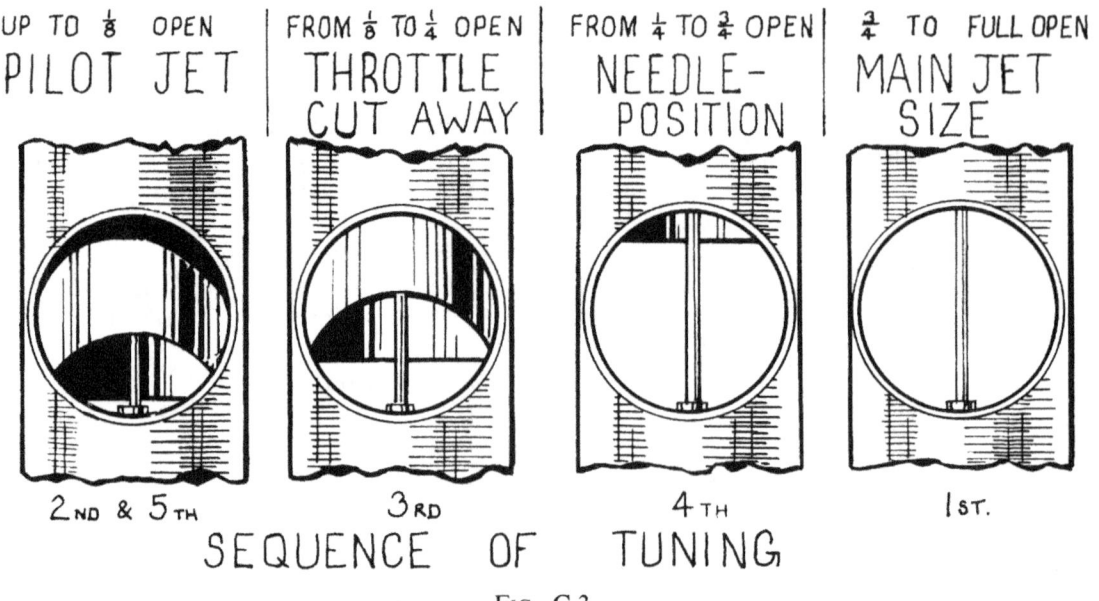

Fig. C.3.

TUNE UP IN THE FOLLOWING ORDER

NOTE:—The carburettor is automatic throughout the throttle range—the air valve should always be wide open except when used for starting or until the engine has warmed up. We assume normal petrols are used.

READ REMARKS ON PAGES C.8-9 for each tuning device and get the motor going perfectly on a quiet road with a slight up gradient so that on test the engine is pulling.

1st MAIN JET with throttle in position 1, Fig. C.3. If at full throttle the engine runs "heavily" the main jet is too large. If at full throttle by slightly closing the throttle or air valve the engine seems to have better power, the main jet is too small.

With a correct sized main jet the engine at full throttle should run evenly and regularly with maximum power.

If testing for speed work ensure that the main jet size is sufficient for the mixture to be rich enough to keep the engine cool, and to verify this examine the sparking plug after taking a fast run, declutching and stopping the engine quickly. If the plug body at its end has a cool appearance the mixture is correct: if sooty, the mixture is rich; if, however there are signs of intense heat, the plug being very white in appearance, the mixture is too weak and a larger main jet is necessary.

CARBURETTOR

2nd PILOT JET (Fig. C.3) with throttle in positions 2 and 5. With engine idling too fast with the twist-grip shut off and the throttle shut down on to the throttle adjusting screw, and ignition set for best slow-runnng: (1) Screw out throttle adjusting screw until the engine runs slower and begins to falter, then screw pilot air adjusting screw in or out, to make engine run regularly and faster. (2) Now gently lower the throttle adjusting screw until the engine runs slower and just begins to falter, adjust the pilot air adjusting screw to get best slow-running, if this 2nd adjustment leaves the engine running too fast, go over the job again a third time.

3rd THROTTLE CUT-AWAY with throttle in position 3 (Fig. C.3). If, as you take off from the idling position, there is objectionable spitting from the carburettor, slightly richen the pilot mixture by screwing in the air screw. If this is not effective, screw it back again, and fit a throttle with a smaller cut-away. If the engine jerks under load at this throttle position and there is no spitting, either the jet needle is much too high or a larger throttle cut-away is required to cure richness.

4th NEEDLE with throttle in position 4 (Fig. C.3). The needle controls a wide range of throttle opening and also the acceleration. Try the needle in as low a position as possible, viz. with the clip in a groove as near the top as possible; if acceleration is poor and with air valve partially closed the results are better, raise the needle by two grooves; if very much better try lowering the needle by one groove and leave it where it is best. If mixture is still too rich with clip in groove number 1 nearest the top, the needle jet probably wants replacement because of wear. If the needle itself has had several years' use replace it also.

5th FINALLY go over the idling again for final touches.

CARBURETTOR

TUNING TWIN CARBURETTORS

First of all, slacken the throttle stop screws and put the twist-grip into the shut off position to allow the throttles to shut off. There should be a slight back-lash in the cables which can be obtained, if necessary, by screwing in the cable adjusting screws on the top of the carburettor. Then with the handlebars in the normal position and with the throttles closed, adjust the cable adjusting screws so that on the slightest opening of the twist-grip, both throttles begin to open simultaneously.

To set the carburettors, follow the procedure as given on previous pages and bear in mind these "hints", which may be useful:—main jet sizes are of course selected by checking the effect of the mixture on the sparking plugs after taking a run at full throttle over a straight piece of road; the smallest pair of jets that give the best maximum speed are usually correct provided that the plugs do not show any signs of excessive heat. It might be that for really critical tuning, one carburettor might require a slightly different jet size from the other. For slow running, set the twist-grip to make the engine run slowly but just faster than a "tick-over"; then gently screw in the throttle stops to just hold the throttles in that position, and return the twist-grip into the shut position, leaving the engine running on the throttle stops. Set each carburettor according to operation 2, on previous page.

Regarding the setting of the pilot a fairly satisfactory method is to detach one sparking plug lead, and set the pilot air adjusting screw on the other cylinder, as a single unit, and then reverse the process to the other cylinder. It may be found that when both leads are connected to the sparking plugs, the engine runs slightly quicker than desirable, in which case, a slight re-adjustment of the throttle stop screws will put this right. It is essential that the speed of idling on both cylinders is approximately the same, as this will either make or mar the smoothness of the get-away on the initial opening of the throttle.

It is essential with twin carburettors that the throttle slides are a good fit in the bodies and also that there is no suspicion of air leaks at either of the flange attachments to the cylinder.

The lower end of the throttle range, is always more difficult to set and one can only take extra care to make quite sure that the control cables are perfectly adjusted, without any excessive back-lash or difference in the amount of back-lash between one carburettor and another; otherwise one throttle slide will be out of phase with the other, and so resulting in lumpy running.

To check the opening of the throttles simultaneously, shut the twist-grip back so that the throttles are resting on the throttle stop screws in their final position of adjustment; then insert the fingers into the air intakes and press then on the throttles and ask a friend to gently open by the twist-grip and feel that the throttles lift off their stops at the same time.

A5065 FRAME and FITTINGS D1

INDEX

	Page
A50, A65 Star Model Frame	D.2
A50 Cyclone, A65 Spitfire Hornet, A65 Lightning Rocket Frame	D.3
Frame Alignment	D.4–6
Chaincase and Chainguard	D.6
Swinging Arm	D.7–10
Rear Shock Absorbers	D.11
Swinging Arm Bushes	D.12
Dual Seat	D.12
Sidecovers	D.12
Rear Mudguard	D.13
Battery Carrier	D.13
Toolbox	D.13
Oil Tank	D.14
Centre Stand	D.15
Petrol Tank Removal	B.4
Throttle Control Cable Replacement	D.16–17
Air Control Cable Replacement	D.17–18
Clutch Control Cable Replacement	B.16
Twin Carburettor Cables	D.18
Front Brake Cable Replacement	D.18

D2 FRAME and FITTINGS A5065

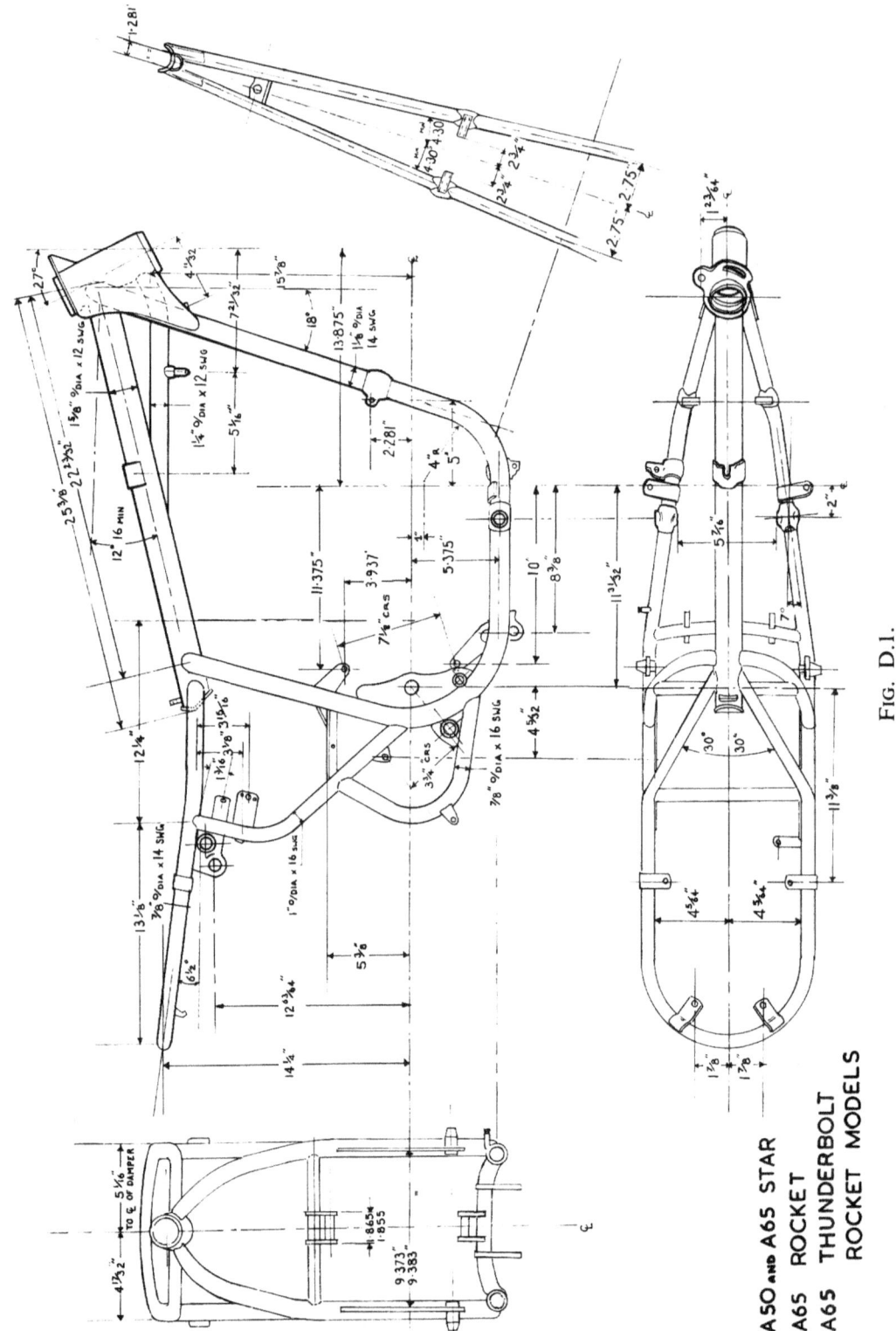

Fig. D.1.

A50 and A65 STAR
A65 ROCKET
A65 THUNDERBOLT ROCKET MODELS

A5065 FRAME and FITTINGS D3

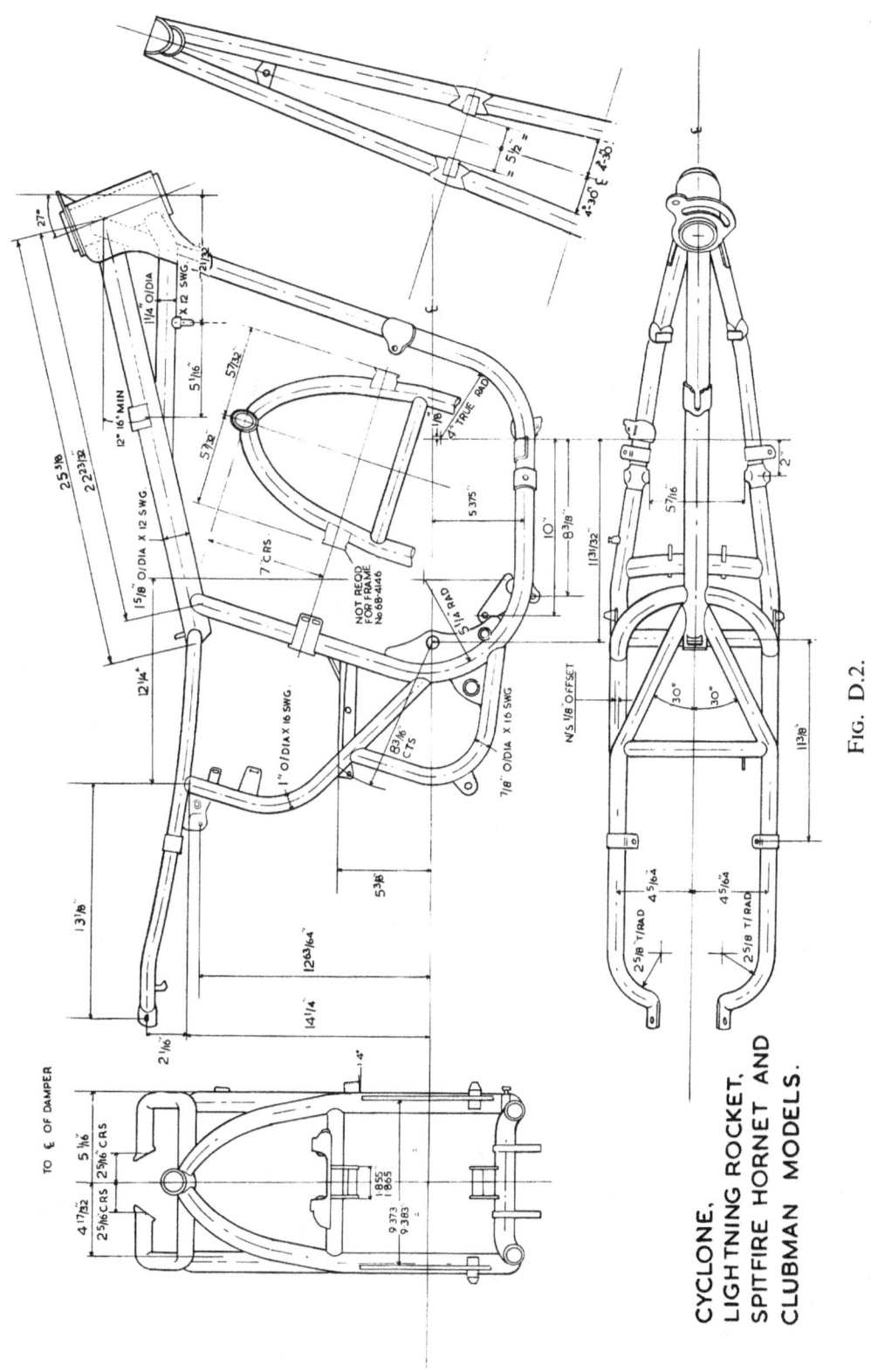

Fig. D.2.

CYCLONE, LIGHTNING ROCKET, SPITFIRE HORNET AND CLUBMAN MODELS.

D4   FRAME and FITTINGS   A5065

FRAME ALIGNMENT

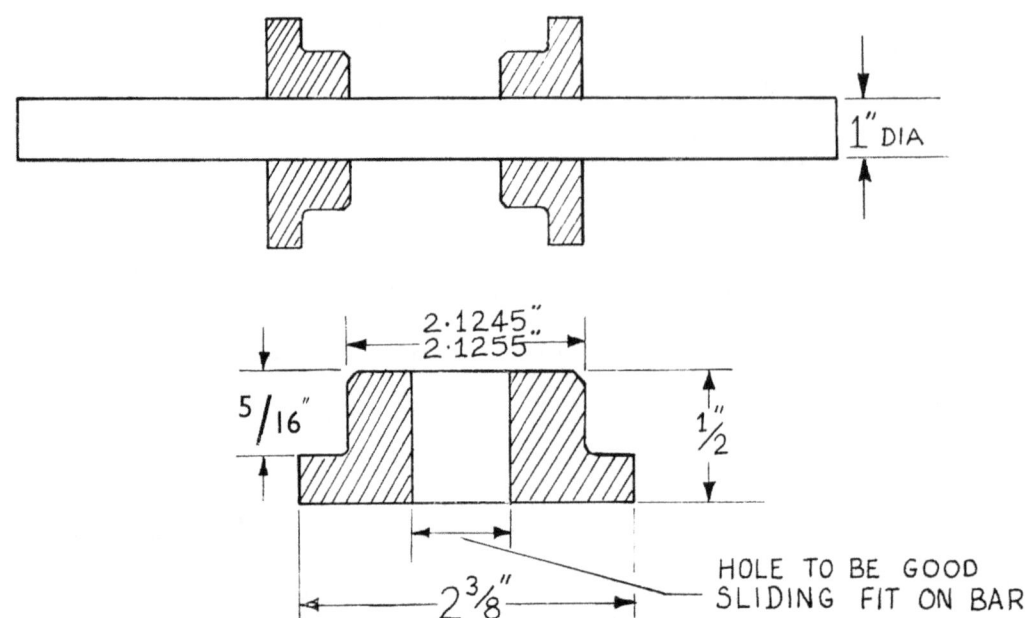

FIG. D.3. *Steering head mandrel.*

ONE OFF MILD STEEL BAR.

24 IN. × 1 IN. TO SUIT BLOCKS.

TWO OFF MILD STEEL BLOCKS.

The only satisfactory way of checking the A50/65 frame for alignment is on an engineers setting-out table. The drawings on pages D.2 and D.3 will help in checking the basic dimensions.

In addition to the table which should be approximately 5ft. × 3ft. the following equipment will also be necessary.

One mandrel and two blocks as in Fig. D.3.

One mandrel or bar for swinging arm pivot 13/16 in. dia. × 12 in.

One large set-square.

One 18 in. vernier height gauge or large scribing block.

One pair of large "V" blocks and several adjustable height jacks.

A5065   FRAME and FITTINGS   D5

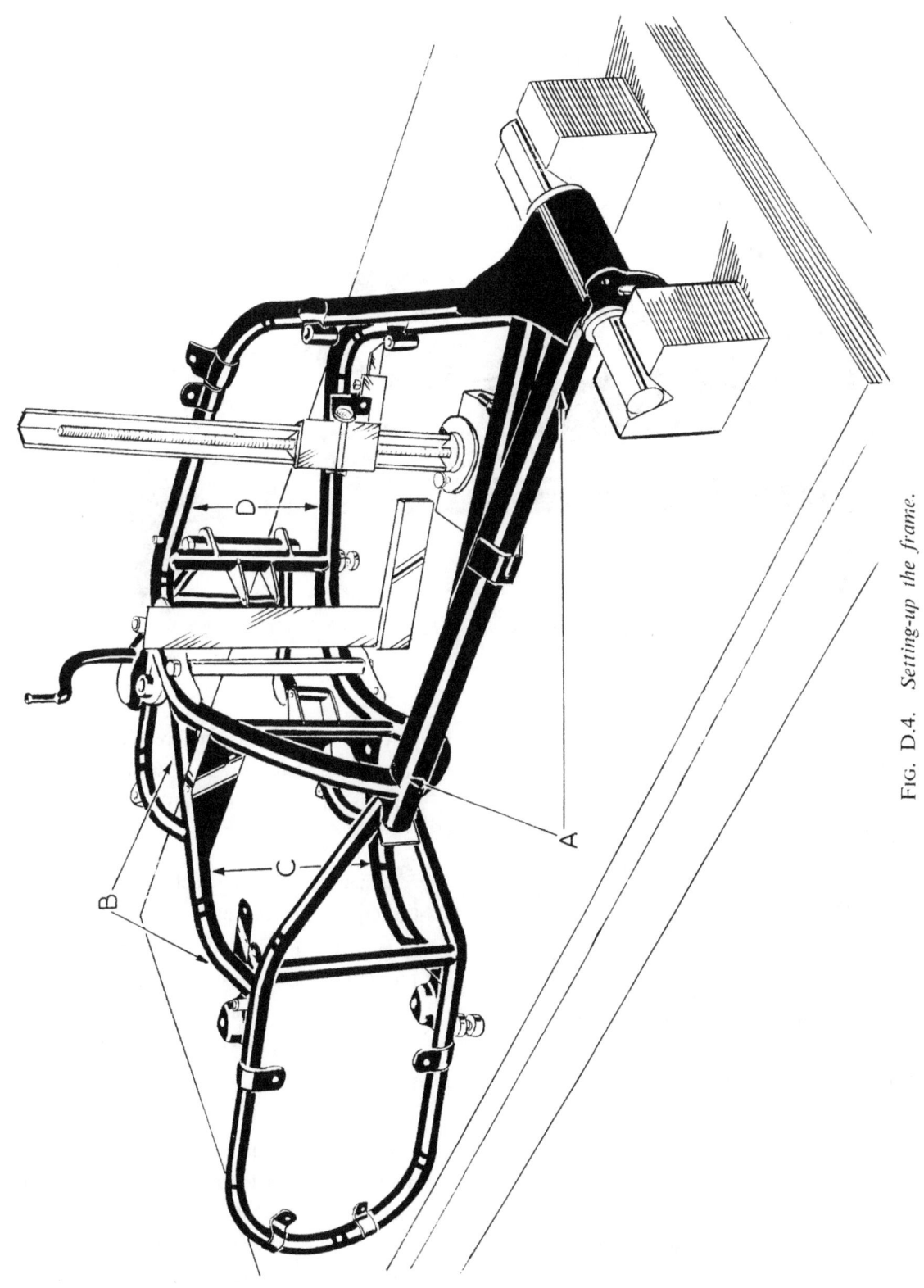

Fig. D.4. *Setting-up the frame.*

FRAME ALIGNMENT

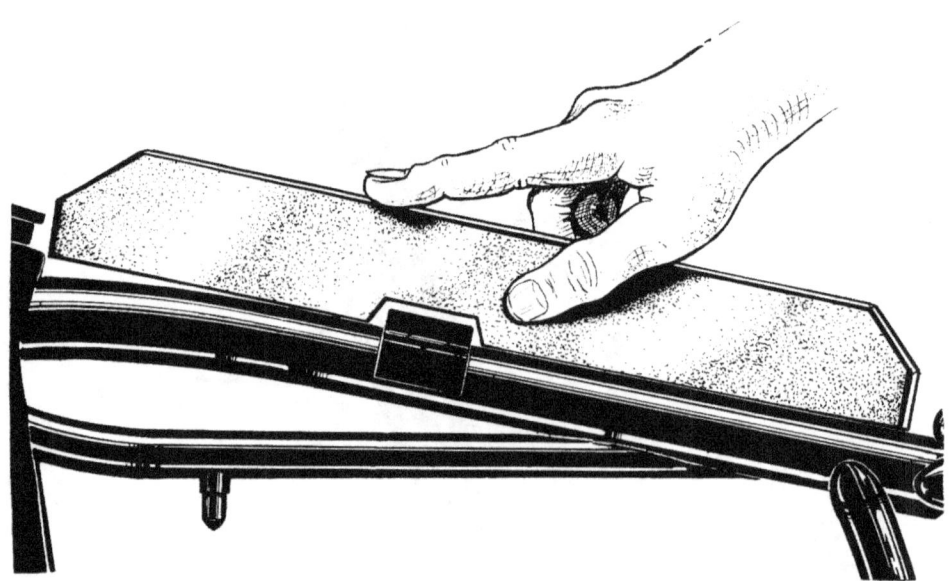

Fig. D.5. *Showing bent top tube.*

If a scribing block is used then an 18 in. steel rule will also be required. The mandrels must be straight and round, otherwise measurements will be affected. The basic set-up for checking is shown in Fig. D.4, variations can of course be used according to the facilities available.

Place the mandrel and blocks in the steering head and "V" blocks and position the blocks at one end of the setting-out table.

Check the mandrel at each end to ensure that it is parallel with the surface of the table.

Insert the 13/16 in. diameter mandrel through swinging arm pivot holes.

Using jacks or packing pieces set the frame horizontal to the table so that checks taken at points (A) are the same.

If the frame has suffered damage in an accident, it may not be possible to set points (A) parallel in which case points (B) can be used.

Sometimes if the machine has suffered a frontal impact, the main tube will be parallel at points (A) but will be bent as shown in Fig. D.5. The straight edge can be made quite easily from say a piece of good quality hardboard but, the checking edge must be quite straight.

When set parallel to the surface table the mandrel through the swinging arm pivot holes should be vertical in all directions, this can be checked using the set-square and internal calipers or a slip gauge between the mandrel and the square.

FRAME and FITTINGS

The set-square should touch the upper and lower tubes together at points (C) and (D) if the frame is true and correctly set-up on the table.

To find the frame centre line take the height of the main tube and subtract half the diameter of the tube, checks can then be taken of the engine mounting lugs and other points of the frame.

Errors at any point should not exceed 1/32 in. (.75 mm.).

CHAINCASE AND CHAINGUARD

The full chaincase or chainguard used with the full-width hubs is retained in position by four Phillips head screws in captive nuts.

To remove either component it is only necessary to take out the four screws. The chaincase is in two halves and can be removed upwards and downwards.

The chainguard used with quick release type hubs with the brake rod on the left-hand side, has only the two upper screws in captive nuts and one bolt in the rear lower position.

This bolt also retains the rear brake anchor strap, with a distance piece between the strap and the rear portion of the guard, and a loose nut—retained by a split pin—at the back of the guard.

To remove, take out the split pin, remove the nut, bolt and distance piece, and take out the two upper screws.

Replacement is simply the reversal of the removal procedure.

SWINGING ARM REMOVAL

The swinging arm fork fits between two plates welded to the frame and is retained in position by the pivot spindle. When full-width hubs are used the rear brake pedal is fitted to the left-hand end of a cross-shaft which passes through the swinging arm pivot.

The brake cable (early models) or brake rod (later models) is attached to a lever on the right-hand end of the cross-shaft.

When quick release hubs are fitted the brake rod is on the left-hand side of the frame and the pedal is fitted to a separate lug.

FRAME and FITTINGS

Remove the chaincase or chainguard as described on page D.7.

Remove the rear chain from the chainwheel after disconnecting the spring link.

Remove the rear wheel and chainwheel according to whichever type of hub is fitted, full-width hub pages F.4–6, quick release type pages F.10–13.

Remove the rear shock absorbers (page D.11).

Scribe a line across the right-hand end of the cross-shaft and the lever and remove the pinch bolt from the lever. The line will assist reassembly of the lever. Pull off the lever by drawing out the cross-shaft, complete with brake pedal, from the left-hand side.

NOTE:—The above does not apply when the brake rod is on the left-hand side of the machine.

Unscrew and remove the large 13/16 in. B.S.C. nut fitted to the right-hand end of the hollow pivot spindle.

Remove the single $\frac{5}{16}$ in. bolt and washer holding the pivot spindle anchor plate on the left-hand side of the machine and pull out the spindle.

When the brake rod is on the left-hand side it may be necessary to move the small stop light lever on the brake pedal to allow free passage for the anchor plate.

If the spindle has corroded use a drift not more than .805 in. diameter to drive the spindle out.

The swinging arm fork is now ready to be removed, using a raw-hide mallet, tap the left-hand side downwards and the right-hand side upwards to release it from the plates.

Replacement is simply the reversal of removal procedure but, do not lock the large 13/16 in. B.S.C. nut until the shock absorbers have been refitted.

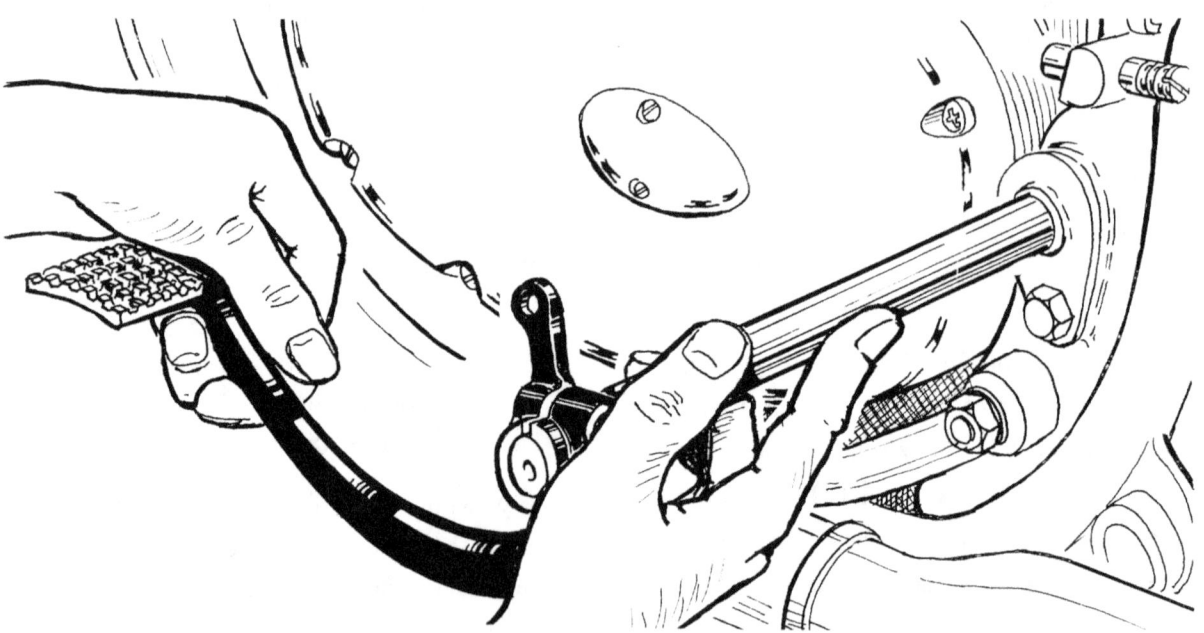

FIG. D.6. *Drawing out the cross-shaft.*

FRAME and FITTINGS

To check the fork, the silent bloc bushes must be in good condition or, be renewed.

Using the same mandrel that was used for the swinging arm pivot on the frame, and the rear wheel spindle, set the swinging arm in "V" blocks as shown in Fig. D.7. In this position both the spindle and mandrel should be parallel to the surface table.

Should there be less than ¼ in. malalignment of the swinging arm fork it is permissible to correct it by means of a suitable lever but, great care is necessary if further damage is to be avoided.

To check that the forks are square to the pivot they must be set-up at 90° to the position illustrated, that is the pivot must be vertical.

Next find the centre of the pivot and check the fork ends etc., in accordance with the drawing dimensions (see page D.10 for dimensions of the swinging arm forks).

There may also be variation in the rear dampers and a careful examination should be made of the overall length between the mounting eyes. It is possible that one damper may be weaker than the other, this may be due to "settling" of one spring in which case it is advisable to renew both springs.

When there is considerable malalignment in either frame or swinging arm owners in the British Isles can obtain works reconditioned units through the dealer network.

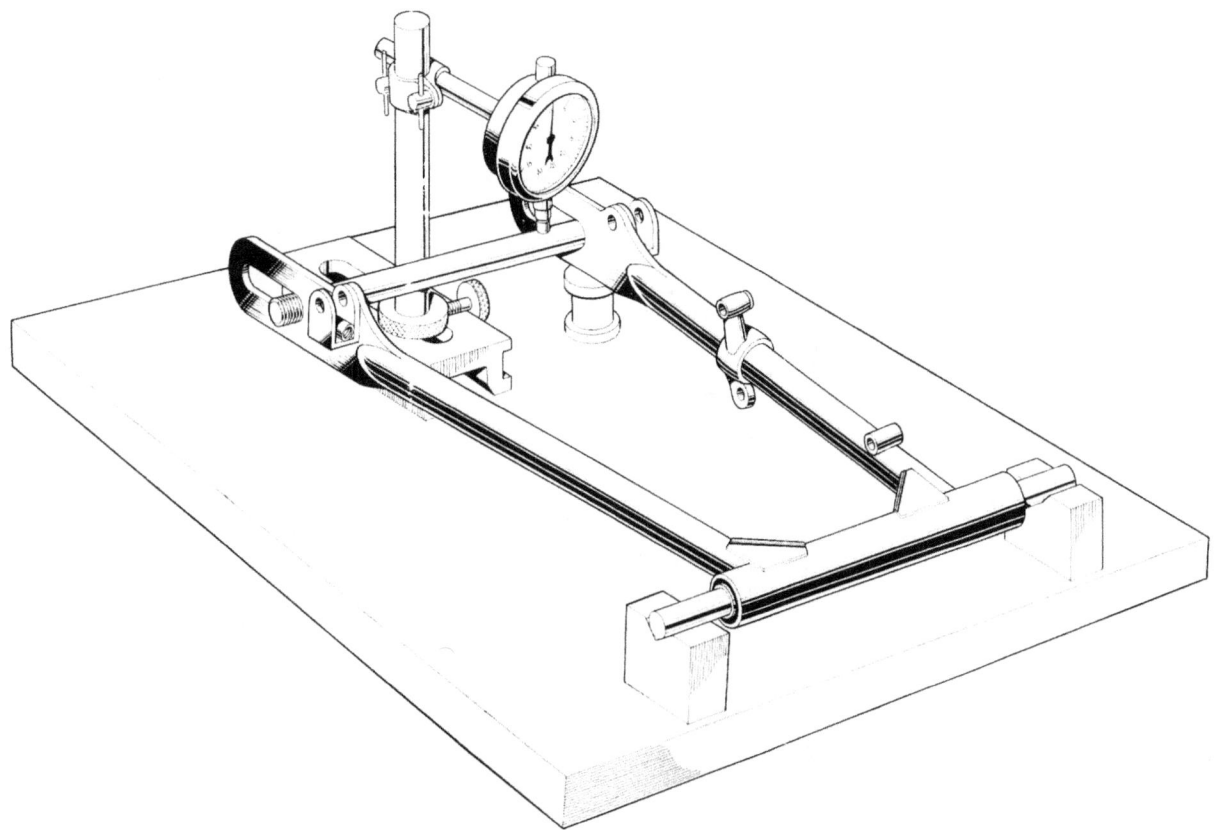

FIG. D.7. *Checking the swinging arm fork.*

FRAME and FITTINGS

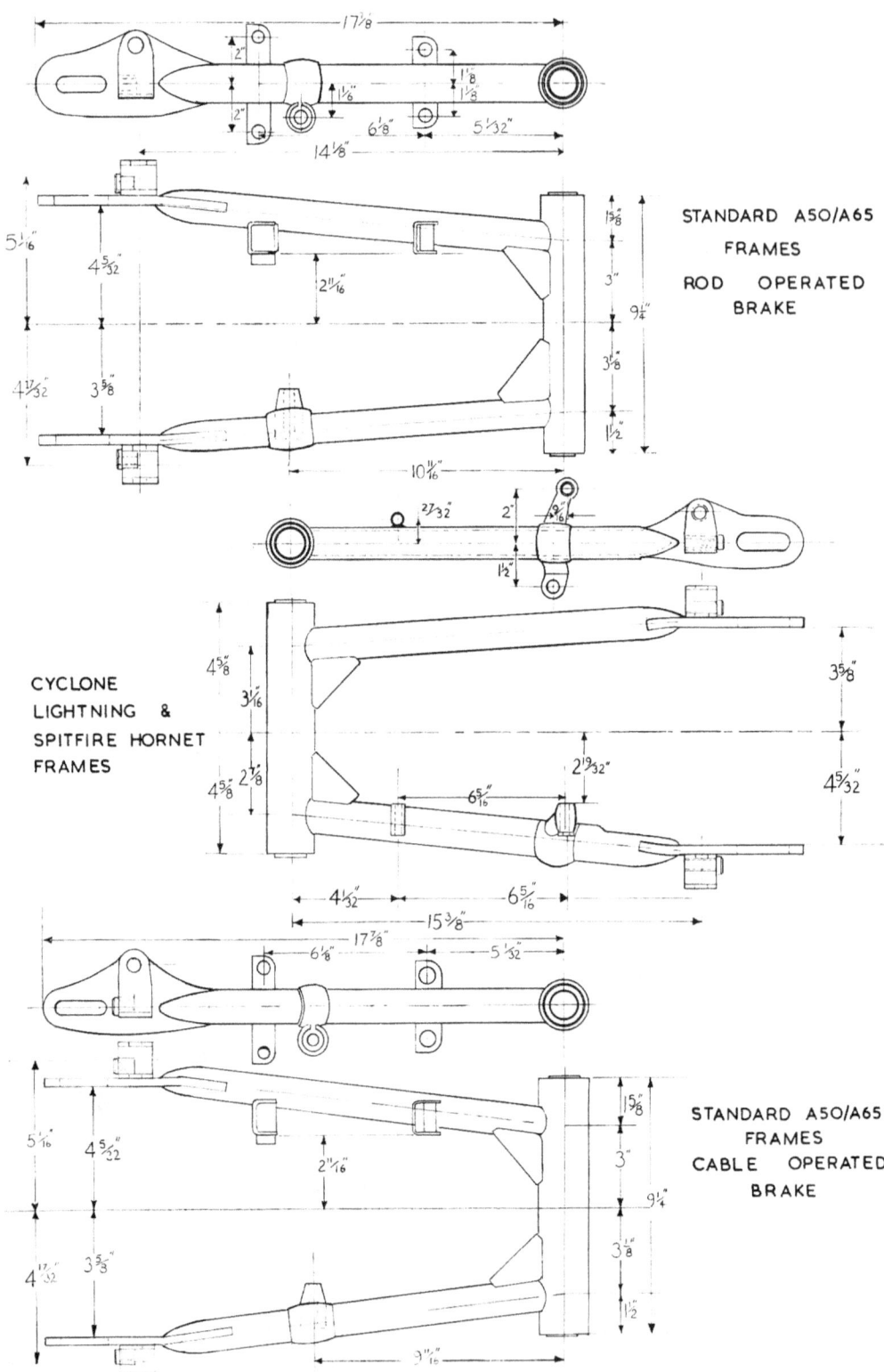

Fig. D.8. *Swinging arm dimensions.*

FRAME and FITTINGS

REAR SHOCK ABSORBERS

The rear shock absorbers are the coil spring type, hydraulically damped, with bonded rubber mounting bushes at each end. The only dismantling possible is for the removal and replacement of the springs.

To remove the dampers take out the upper and lower mounting bolts after placing a suitable block of wood between the rear tyre and the mudguard.

Take careful note of the various distance pieces and washers used with the top mounting.

If the springs are to be changed the spring must first be compressed with service tool number 61–3503 and the split collets removed, the tool is then removed, the spring changed and the new spring compressed to replace the split collets.

FIG. D.10. *Cam ring positions.*

Solo springs are graded at 90 lbs./in. rate and have green/white marking. Sidecar springs are graded at 110 lbs./in. and are marked with red/white paint for identification.

The dampers have three load positions, light, medium and heavy and they must be in the "light-load" position before dismantling.

The mounting bushes at each end can be driven out quite easily, and new ones fitted, if a little liquid soap is used to assist.

Squeaking is usually due to the spring rubbing on the lower dust shield and can be eliminated by smearing high-melting point grease on the spring and inside the shield.

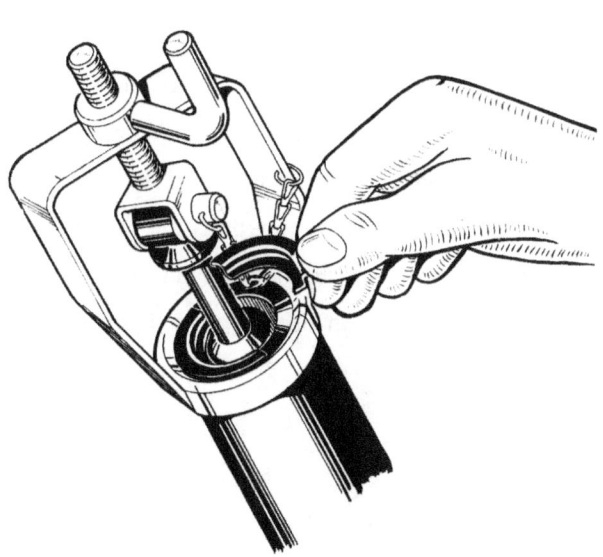

FIG. D.9. *Using tool 61–3503.*

Do not lubricate the plunger rod.

FRAME and FITTINGS

SWINGING ARM BUSHES

The bushes fitted to the swinging arm fork take the form of two steel bushes bonded together with rubber, the inner bush being slightly more in length than half the width of the fork pivot.

When the swinging arm is assembled in the frame the two inner bushes are locked together on the end faces and the rubber is then under tension as soon as the fork moves.

Under normal circumstances the bushes will last the life of the machine but, if they do require renewal, then the rubber should first be removed by burning it out. This can be done by heating thin rods or strips of metal and then progressively burning out the rubber. When sufficient rubber has been removed, drive out the inner bushes after which the outer bushes can be removed with a suitable drift which should not be more than 1.245 in. (31.623 mm.) in diameter.

DUALSEAT

The dualseat is retained in position by two nuts and washers on studs underneath the seat at each side of the guard. To remove take off the nuts and washers and unhook the seat at the front end.

Replacement is the reversal of this procedure.

SIDECOVERS

Sidecovers are made of steel or glass fibre according to the model. Steel covers which are used on single carburettor models have one special fastener and they also use the manifold stud extensions as anchorage points.

Glass fibre covers which are used with twin carburettor models have two special fasteners only. Removal and replacement of the covers is quite straight forward. It is only necessary to give the fastener a half-turn to release it or to lock it.

SIDECOVER FASTENERS

The fastener bolt in the cover is known as an "Oddie" stud and is retained in the cover by the rubber bush. If at any time it is necessary to replace a stud, simply press the old one out, place a new bush in the hole and press the new stud into position using a little liquid soap as a lubricant.

The fasteners on the frame brackets are known as "Oddie" clips and are retained in position by $\frac{1}{8}$ in. Whitworth bolts and nuts.

FRAME and FITTINGS

REAR MUDGUARD

Two types of rear mudguard are used, the valanced, and the blade type, which has no valance.

The mountings are basically the same except at the shock absorber. All valanced guards have the top shock absorber bolt passing through the valance with the nuts inside the guard, whereas the blade type uses a bridge piece, the guard then being bolted to the bridge piece separately.

Removal.

Remove the dualseat as described on page D.12 and disconnect the rear lamp at the connectors under the seat.

Take out the rear wheel as described on pages F.4 (full-width hub) or F.10 (quick release hub) but, do not disturb the chainwheel.

Valanced Type.

Remove all the bolts and nuts attaching the guard to the frame taking particular note of the disposition of any distance pieces or washers.

The damper bolts need be drawn out only sufficient to release the mudguard which can be removed complete with the number plate.

Blade Type.

Proceed as for valanced guard but do not disturb the damper bolts, release the mudguard by taking out the two bolts and nuts attaching the guard to the bridge piece. In some cases it may be necessary to move the rectifier to avoid damaging it.

Replacement of both types is simply the reversal of dismantling procedure.

BATTERY CARRIER

The battery carrier is retained on its platform by two $\frac{1}{4}$ in. B.S.C. bolts and nuts with two distance pieces between the carrier base and the platform.

Removal and replacement is quite straight forward after the left-hand side cover has been removed.

Always see that the rubber mat and the rubber buffer at the back of the carrier are in position.

TOOLBOX

The toolbox is retained by two $\frac{1}{4}$ in. B.S.C. bolts and nuts which pass through both the box and the bag with the nuts inside the bag. To remove or replace the bag, it is only necessary to remove the two nuts and washers, after taking off the right-hand sidecover.

If the toolbox is to be removed the rear wheel must be taken out, as described on pages F.4 or F.10 according to the type of wheel, and the mudguard removed as detailed previously. The box can only be positioned from inside the frame.

OIL TANK

The oil tank rests on three rubber buffers and is retained in position by a single rubber-mounted bolt at the top of the tank, thus insulating the tank from vibration.

To remove the tank, first drain the oil as described on pages A.7–8.

Remove the dualseat and disconnect the oil feed and return pipes from underneath the tank and the rocker box oil feed pipe. On older models this latter pipe is connected to the return pipe at the base of the tank but, on later models, the connection is at the top of the tank.

Take out the rear wheel, as described on pages F.4 or F.10 according to the type of wheel, and remove the rear mudguard as described on page D.13.

Remove the oil tank mounting bolt noting the position of the rubbers etc., and lift the tank out. NOTE:—It may be necessary in some cases to move the rectifier to avoid damage.

The rubber buffers below the tank are simply a press fit into the frame brackets and need not be disturbed unless they have become saturated with oil, in which case, they should be replaced.

Replacement of the oil tank is simply the reversal of dismantling but, it is advisable to replace all the pipes and check for leakage before replacing the mudguard and wheel.

Do not forget that the oil feed and return pipes cross over on the way to the engine.

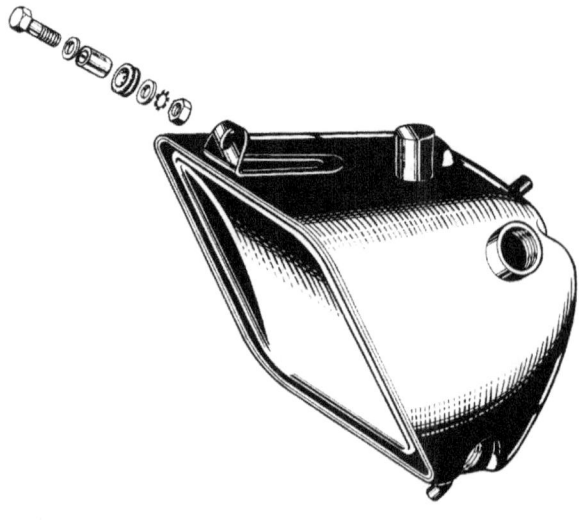

FIG. D.11. *Tank mounting.*

FRAME and FITTINGS

CENTRE STAND

Two types of central stand are used. One with an extension on the left-hand side for use with twin exhaust pipes and silencers, the other, which is minus the extension, being used with "siamesed" exhaust pipes and single silencer.

Both types are fitted in the same manner, that is, with a plain steel bar drilled at both ends for split pins, centre distance piece, two spring washers and two plain washers.

To remove the stand it is only necessary to remove the split pin from one side and draw the pivot pin out from the opposite side.

When replacing the stand, note that the spring washers are fitted outside the stand, then the plain washer and finally the split pin.

Grease nipples are provided in each stand lug to lubricate the pivot.

Stand Spring.

The simplest way to replace the stand spring is to use a Phillips type screwdriver. Place the eye of the spring over the frame anchorage, insert the screwdriver in the other eye, place the screwdriver slot under the hook on the stand and lever downwards to press the spring over the hook (see Fig. D.12).

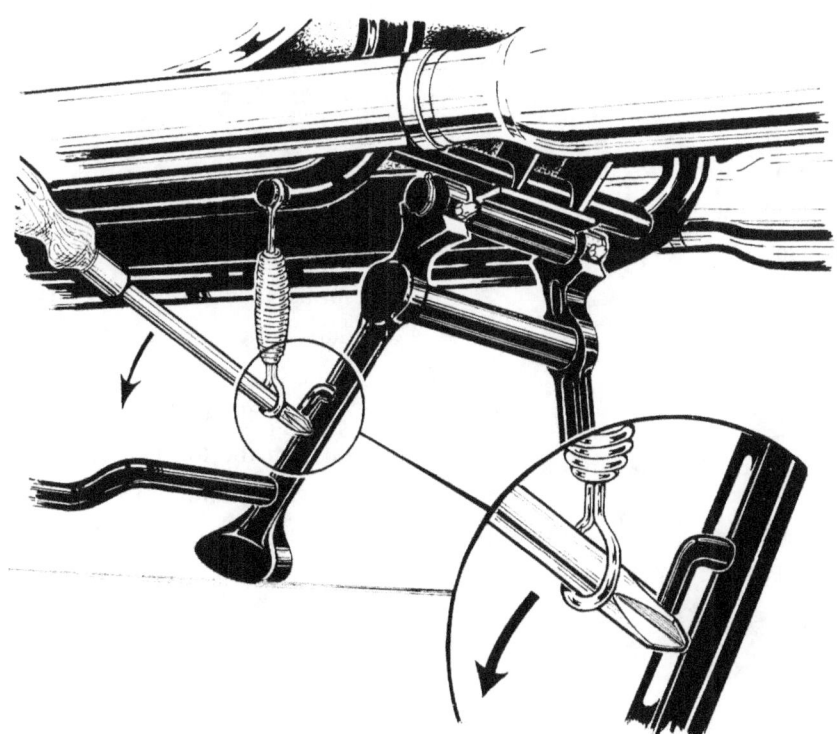

Fig. D.12. *Fitting the spring.*

THROTTLE CABLE REPLACEMENT

Throttle cable replacement is an operation which the private owner should practice once or twice so that in the event of a cable failure on the road, the replacement can be quickly carried out.

It is also good practice to carry spare throttle and air cables taped to the existing cables.

Single Carburettor Models.

First turn the twist-grip to open the throttle, then release it and at the same time pull the cable out of the grip to release the slotted cable stop.

Now remove the two slotted screws from the twist-grip control and take off the top half to expose the cable nipple.

Ease the nipple out of the grip and remove the cable.

Fit the replacement cable to the grip by passing it up through the lower half to insert the nipple in its slot.

Replace the top half of the grip tightening the screws equally and ensuring that the grip turns freely.

Do **not** replace the cable stop at this stage.

Remove the petrol tank and carburettor as described on page B.4.

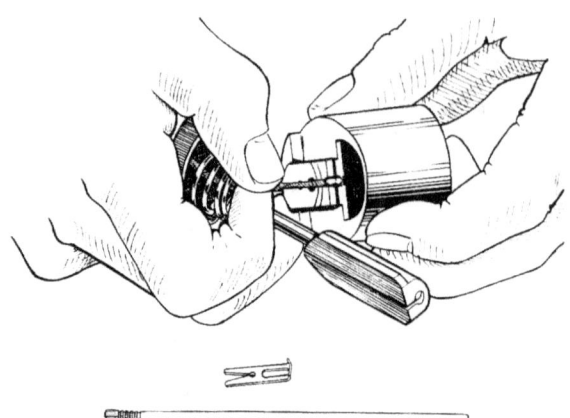

FIG. D.13. *Removing throttle cable from slide.*

Pull the cable from the frame clips and unscrew the knurled ring holding the mixing chamber top cap on the carburettor (see Fig. C.1).

Very carefully draw out the slide assembly.

Take careful note of the position of the throttle needle clip and remove the clip and needle. Compress the throttle slide return spring then push the cable nipple down and out of the slide (see Fig. D.13).

To fit the replacement cable, pass the nipple through the top cap and the spring, compress the spring and slip the cable through the slot so that the nipple is seated to one side of the centre hole.

Replace the throttle needle and secure with the spring clip in the correct groove (see page GD.6).

Carefully pass the needle down through the carburettor body so that the needle goes into the needle jet.

Locate the slides so that they slip freely down into the body and replace the top cap and ring. Make absolutely sure the ring goes completely down on its seat and that threads are in good condition.

Check the action of the controls before replacing the carburettor on the engine.

Secure the cable to the frame, replace the cable stop at the twist-grip, and adjust the cable as necessary by means of the adjuster in the top cap or on the cable.

AIR CONTROL CABLE

To replace an air control cable first open the control to its fullest extent then close it pulling the cable out of the body at the same time. Release the cable nipple.

Remove the petrol tank and carburettor as described on page B.4 and remove the slide assembly as described for changing the throttle cable.

Slip the air slide up and out of the throttle slide and compress the spring to release the cable nipple.

To fit the replacement pass the nipple through the top cap, spring guide tube, and spring, compress the spring and slip the nipple into the slide.

Replace the air slide in the throttle slide and proceed as for the replacement of the throttle cable.

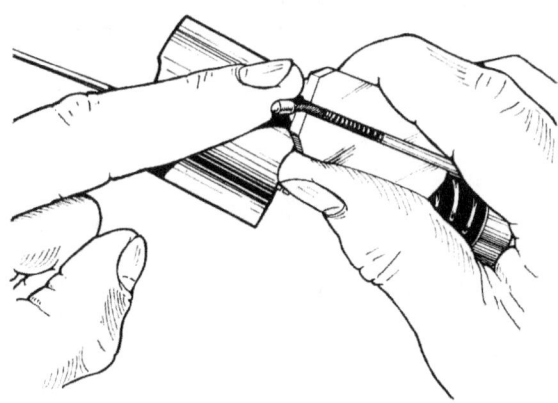

Fig. D.14. *Air slide and cable.*

TWIN CARBURETTORS

The procedure for replacement of cables is similar to the single carburettor models except that there is no need to remove the carburettors from the engine, and the twin cables from the carburettors enter a junction box to emerge as single cables.

Remember that the adjustment of the cables for twin carburettors is very critical otherwise the tune will be upset.

There are two adjusters for the throttle cables but only one on the top cap for the air cable.

If either of the long cables are to be replaced remove the petrol tank as described on page B.4.

This will expose the junction boxes underneath the tank, it is then only necessary to unscrew the one cap off the junction box to expose the cable nipple.

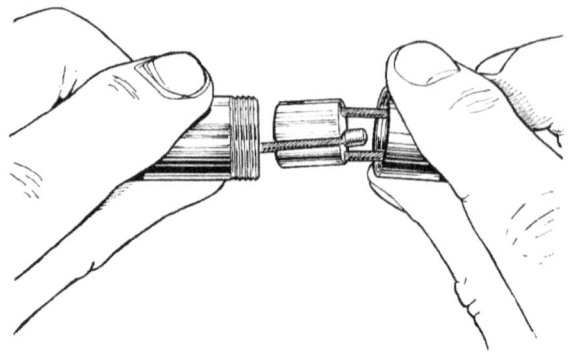

FIG. D.15. *Junction box.*

If either of the short cables require replacement, unscrew the carburettor top caps and draw out the slides, unscrew the junction box caps at that end to expose the nipples and proceed as for single carburettors.

After reassembly synchronise the carburettors as detailed on page C.12.

FRONT BRAKE CABLE

To remove a front brake cable first unscrew and remove the handlebar lever fulcrum pin and nut.

Swing the lever out from the bracket and slip the cable nipple out of the lever, the adjuster can then be removed from the bracket with the cable.

Remove the screw and nut holding the toggle to the lever on the brake cover plate and remove the outer casing from the stop on the cover plate.

Replacement is simply the reversal of the above procedure but, do not omit to re-adjust the brake cable, and test brake deliberately before using the machine as usual.

A5065   FRONT FORK   E1

INDEX

	Page
Removing and Refitting the Top Cover	E.2
Removing and Refitting the Headlamp	E.6
Renewing Steering Head Races	E.4–5
Adjusting Steering Head Races	E.2–3
Removing Fork Legs	E.6–7
Dismantling Fork Legs	E.8–9
Rebuilding Fork Legs	E.9–10
Replacing Fork Legs	E.10
Fork Alignment	E.11–12
Changing Fork Springs	E.7
Oil Seals	E.9
Hydraulic Damping	E.13

FRONT FORK

DESCRIPTION

The front forks fitted to all A50 and A65 models are basically the same in that they are telescopic, hydraulically damped and the oil used for damping also lubricates. The quantity of oil required is the same for all the forks the only variations being in the fittings, such as spring covers, headlamps and fork ends.

Some models with full-width hubs have metal spring covers and clamp type fork ends, whereas other models with quick release type hubs have rubber gaiters and the wheel spindles screw into the fork end.

The forks are of robust design and only require the minimum of maintenance amounting to oil changing at the periods quoted on page A.2.

REMOVING AND REFITTING THE TOP COVER

Unscrew and remove the steering damper rod then unscrew the headlock bezel which has a normal right-hand thread. The cover which is only fitted to the standard Star models, can now be lifted clear of the forks to expose the two top caps, steering head nut, the top yoke pinch bolt, and handlebar clip bolts.

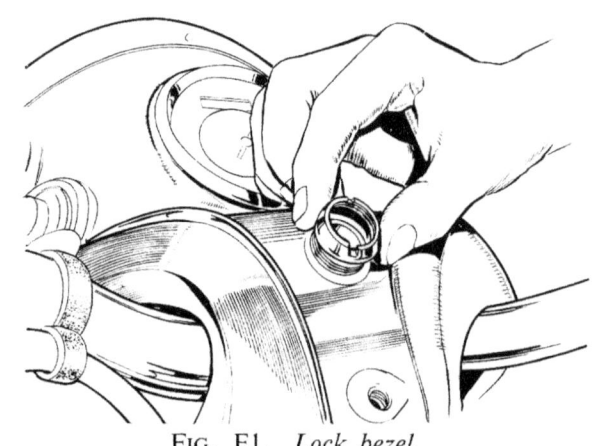

FIG. E1. *Lock bezel.*

ADJUSTING STEERING HEAD RACES

It is most important that the steering head races are correctly adjusted.

There should be no play evident between the races but great care must be taken not to overtighten, the latter can indent the balls into the races and make steering extremely difficult and dangerous.

Place a strong support underneath the engine so that the front wheel is lifted clear of the ground, then standing in front of the wheel, push and pull alternately on the lower fork legs to determine if there is play in the steering head (Fig. E.3).

FRONT FORK

Care is necessary to distinguish between play in the head races and play in the fork bushes. In some cases there may be both.

If possible get a friend to place the fingers of one hand lightly round the top head races whilst the forks are being pushed and pulled, if play is there, it will be felt quite easily by the fingers.

It should also be possible to move the forks from side to side quite smoothly and without any jerky movement. If the movement is jerky the balls are indented into the races, or broken, in either case they and the cups and cones should be renewed. The damper must of course be completely free while testing.

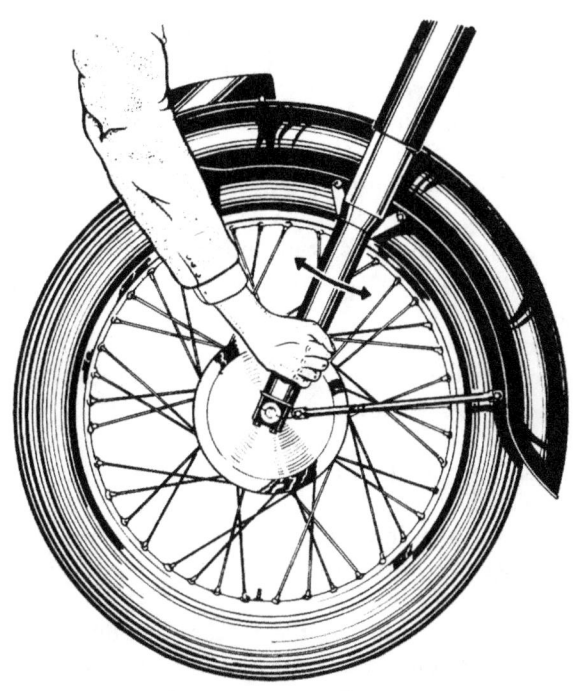

FIG. E.3. *Testing the steering head for play.*

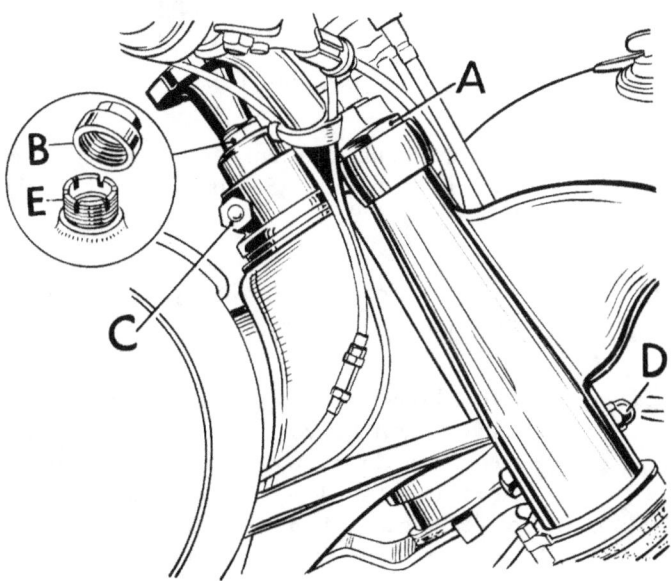

FIG. E.2. *Steering head adjustment.*

To adjust the steering, remove the damper rod and top fork cover (if fitted) then remove the top cap (B) Fig. E.2 to expose the adjuster sleeve (E).

Slacken off the pinch bolts (C) and (D) and using service tool number 00061–3008 screw the sleeve (E) in (clockwise) to reduce steering play or, out (anti-clockwise) to increase steering play.

Having adjusted the steering tighten the pinch bolts (C) and (D), replace the top cap (B), top cover (if fitted) and the damper rod.

FRONT FORK

RENEWING HEAD RACES

The steering can be dismantled to change the head races without stripping the forks but the lighting cables must be removed by pulling them from the socket at the back of the switch and the reflector in the headlamp (see page E.6). Disconnect the front brake cable at the handlebar lever.

Remove the damper rod, lock bezel and fork top cover (when fitted).

Disconnect both speedometer and rev-counter cables (when fitted) by unscrewing the cable nipples at the instrument heads and pulling out the inner wire.

Place a piece of cloth over the fuel tank, remove the four bolts securing the handlebar clips, and place the handlebars to one side on the tank.

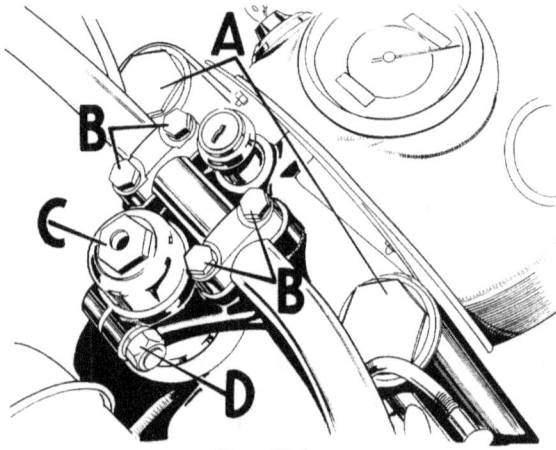

Fig. E.4.

Slacken the pinch bolt (D), remove the caps (A) and (C), and unscrew and remove the adjusting sleeve which is underneath cap (C) Fig. E.4.

Using a raw-hide mallet strike the sides of the top yoke alternately to release it from the tapered legs. Lift the top yoke to one side and draw the steering column down and out of the head, but be careful to catch the bearings which will be released as the column is withdrawn.

Fig. E.5.

There should be twenty ¼ in. diameter steel balls in each race. See page A.14 regarding lubrication.

The two cones differ slightly in size but the two cups are identical.

The lower cone can be prised off the column but care is required when fitting the replacement. For this purpose a piece of steel tubing 10 in. by 12 in. long, 1¼ in. inside diameter, of heavy gauge, is most useful for driving the cone on to its seat squarely and firmly (see Fig. E.5).

FRONT FORK

The two cups can be removed with service tool number 61-3063.

Slacken off the nut on the tool sufficient to allow the tool to be screwed into the cup then tighten the nut until the tool is expanded tightly into the cup threads.

Drive out the cup with a suitable bar from inside the head tube.

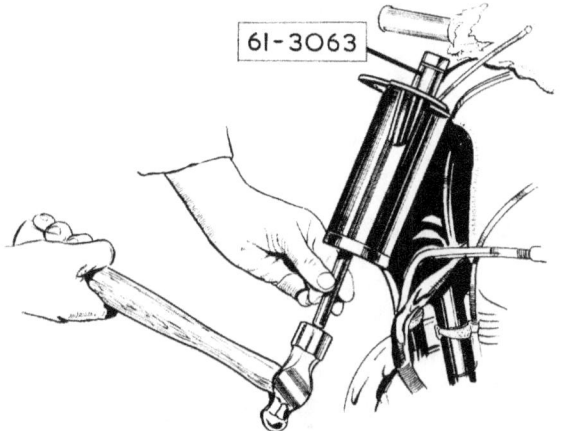

FIG. E.6. *Removing the top cup.*

Remove the tool by slackening off the nut and repeat the procedure on the other cup.

When fitting the replacement cups see that they enter the housings squarely and be very careful to avoid cracking the cup. If possible use a piece of steel bar or tube slightly less than the outside diameter of the cup. Do not drive the cup in with a drift resting on the radius of the ballrace, this will impose undue strain and is liable to fracture the cup. A suitable drift would be as Fig. E.7.

Reassembling the Steering Head.
After replacing the cups and bottom cone grease the cups, assemble 20 balls in each cup then slide the column back into the head. Replace the top cone and dust cover then the top yoke and screw in the adjusting sleeve. Adjust as quoted on pages E.2–3 and complete the reassembly in the reverse order to that used for dismantling.

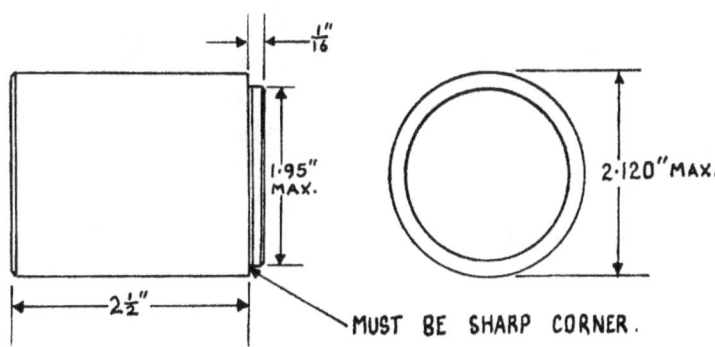

FIG. E.7. *Cup drift.*

FRONT FORK

REMOVING THE HEADLAMP

Cowl Type.
Take out the screw on top of the headlamp cowl adjacent to the rim, pull out the headlamp and disconnect the leads.

Disconnect the leads to the ammeter and speedometer and pull out the harness plugs from the lighting and ignition switches.

Unscrew the speedometer cable nipple and pull out the inner wire.

To remove the headlamp shell take out the four bolts securing the shell to the fork cover.

Non-Cowl Type.
Procedure is the same as for the cowl type except that the headlamp shell is secured to the two arms by two bolts which are plainly visible. Replacement of either type of lamp is simply a reversal of the removal procedure.

REMOVING THE FORK LEGS

Before commencing work on the forks it is advisable to have the following tools and replacements available:—

10129–5334	Shim .005 in.	
10129–5335	Shim .010 in.	as
10129–5336	Shim .020 in.	reqd.
10129–5337	Shim .030 in.	
12565–5451	Oil seal (2)	
13265–5424	Top bush (2)	
12929–5347	Lower bush (2)	
84161–3350	Service tool	
84161–3005	Service tool	
84361–3006	Service tool	
84361–3007	Service tool	

and a length of number five twine approximately 15 in. long.

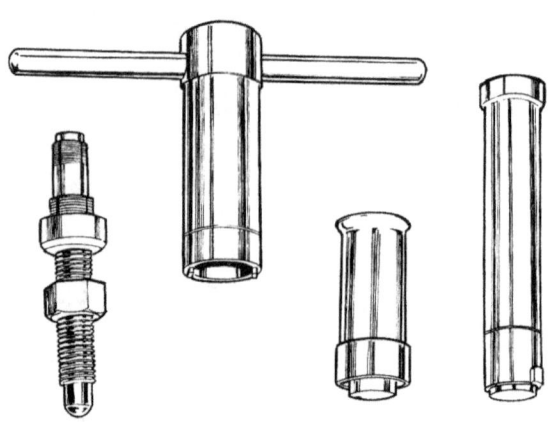

FIG. E.8. *Fork tools*.

FRONT FORK

Remove the front wheel as described on pages F.2 or F.7 according to the type of wheel fitted, then remove the front mudguard by taking out the bolts from the fork ends and midway up each leg.

Remove the damper rod, lock bezel and top cover as described on page E.2.

On those models fitted with twin speedometer and rev-counter heads on a bracket above the forks, pull out the light bulbs and disconnect the drive cables after unscrewing the cable nipples.

Remove the instrument heads and the bracket after taking out the two front handlebar clip bolts.

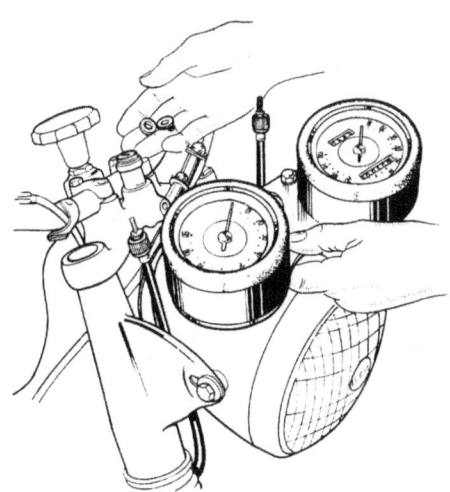

FIG. E.9.

Drain the oil from the forks as described on page A.14. Screw service tool number 84161-3350 (minus the large nut and washer) into the top of the fork leg and slacken off the pinch bolt in the bottom fork yoke (D) Fig. E.2, page E.3.

On those models fitted with rubber gaiters, remove the top clip, and push the top of the gaiter off the fork cover.

Now take a firm grasp of the lower sliding member with one hand and strike the top of the tool sharply with a hammer or mallet, this will release the leg from its taper in the top yoke and the complete leg can be drawn down and removed from the machine. Repeat the operation on the other leg.

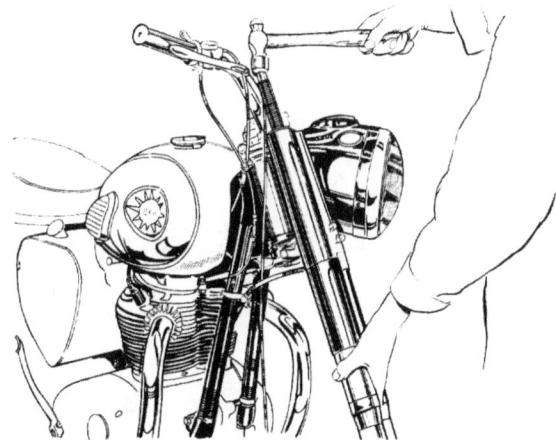

FIG. E.10. *Removing fork leg.*

Spring Changing.
At this stage—if no other work is required—the springs can be changed. All that is necessary is to pull out the old springs, apply a liberal coat of grease to the new springs and to replace.

Replacing the fork leg is described on page E.10.

FRONT FORK

DISMANTLING THE LEG

To dismantle the lower section of the fork hold the sliding tube by gripping the wheel spindle lug in a soft-jawed vice. If rubber gaiters are fitted slacken off the clip and pull off the gaiter.

To remove the oil seal holder slide service tool number 84161-3005 over the main tube and enter the dogs in the slots at the bottom of the oil seal holder.

Pressing down firmly on the tool and turning anti-clockwise at the same time, unscrew the oil seal holder complete with the extension tube.

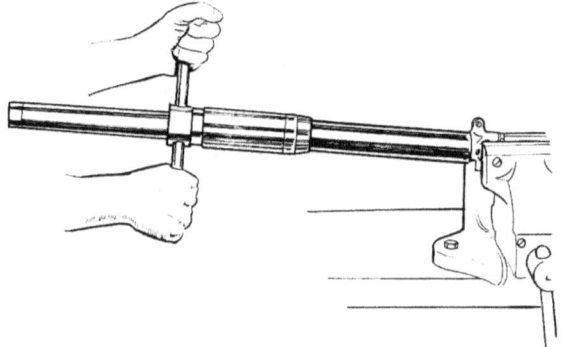

Fig. E.11. *Removing oil seal holder.*

Remove the tool and slide the holder up the shaft until it becomes tight on the tapered section of the shaft, but do not use force or the oil seal may be damaged.

The circlip which retains the top bush in the sliding member, is now exposed and can be prised out with a sharp tool such as the tang end of a file.

Underneath the circlip there may be a number of shims, these are to remove any play there may be between the bush and the circlip and should be retained for use on reassembly.

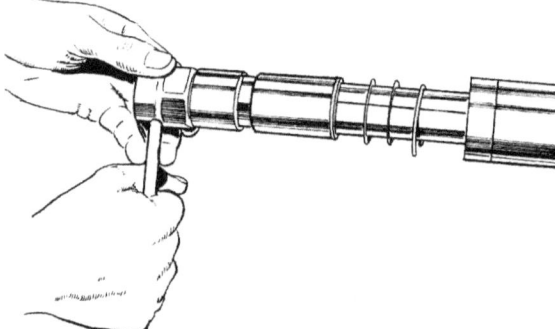

Fig. E.12. *Removing lower nut.*

After the circlip is removed the main tube complete with bushes can be withdrawn from the sliding member.

Grip the tube in a vice using soft clamps on the unground portion of the shaft and unscrew the nut at the lower end of the shaft.

This nut secures the lower bush and after its removal the oil seal holder, circlip, shims and bushes can be slid off the shaft.

FRONT FORK

OIL SEALS

If it is necessary to change the oil seal, place the lower edge of the holder on a wooden block and enter service tool number 84361-3006 into the top of the holder, give the tool a sharp blow with the hammer and the seal will be driven out.

To fit a replacement seal, coat the outside with a good jointing compound and whilst still wet enter the seal squarely into the holder with the open side upwards and drive home with service tool number 83661-3007.

Great care is required to avoid damaging the feather edge of the oil seal and this should be greased before reassembly.

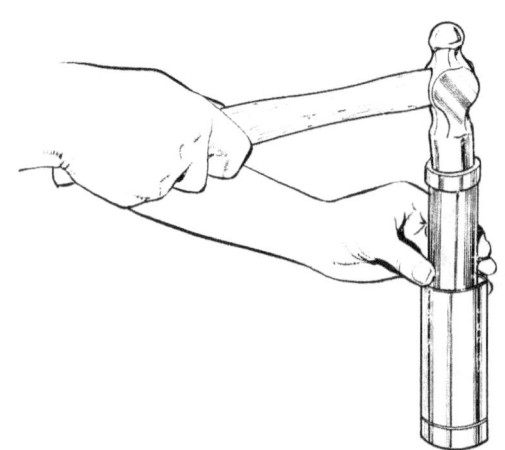

FIG. E.13. *Removing oil seal.*

REBUILDING THE FORK LEG

Reassembly is carried out in the reverse order to dismantling.

Cleanliness is essential and before attempting to reassemble, clean all parts thoroughly and the work bench on which the forks have been dismantled.

Slide the oil seal holder over the shaft until it is on the tapered section but do not use force or the seal may be damaged.

Place the circlip over the shaft followed by the packing shims, then the top bush, the bottom bush and finally the bottom nut.

Tighten the nut securely, grip the lower sliding tube in the vice and enter the main-shaft, with the assembled parts, into the sliding tube.

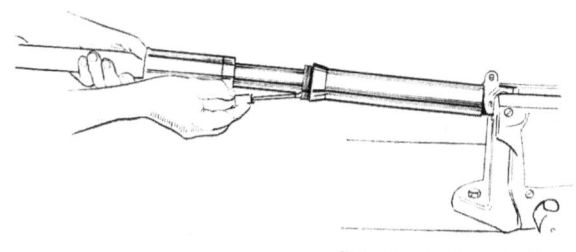

FIG. E.14. *Testing for play.*

Fit the circlip over the top bush and check for up and down movement of the bush. This can be done by holding a screwdriver against the flange of the bush then by pulling the main tube out to its fullest extent, push and pull alternately (see Fig. E.14, page E.9).

If a new bush has been fitted, it may be necessary to add to, or take from, the existing shims.

As already indicated shims are avilable in .005, .010, .020, .030 in. sizes.

If the bush is not properly shimmed a tapping noise may be heard when the machine is ridden.

Having shimmed up the bush correctly and fitted the circlip firmly in position, screw down the oil seal holder on to one turn of twine round the groove at the end of the thread. This will provide an additional seal.

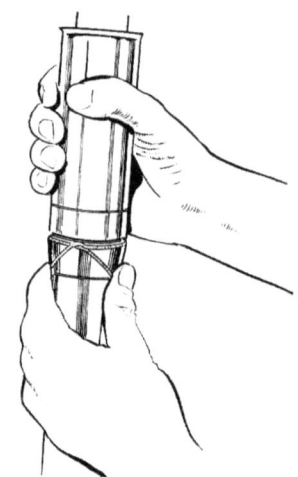

FIG. E.15. *Using the twine*.

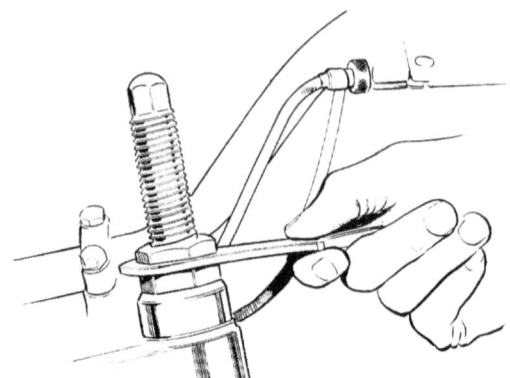

FIG. E.16. *Using tool* 00061-3350.

Repeat the operations on the other leg. Before refitting the leg to the steering head, apply a liberal coating of grease to the spring and place the spring in position in the oil seal holder.

Replacing the Fork Leg.
Now screw service tool number 84161-3350 minus the nut and collar—into the top of the tube and pass the tube up through the two yokes, fit the collar and nut and draw the tube firmly home into its taper.

Tighten the pinch bolt in the bottom yoke before removing the tool.

Repeat the operation on the other leg then refill with the correct amount of oil (⅓ pint to each leg), see page A.4 for grades, and replace the top caps.

Final assembly is simply the reversal of dismantling.

FRONT FORK

FORK ALIGNMENT

It is possible, during reassembly of the forks, for them to be incorrectly aligned.

For this reason, after the mudguard has been replaced, replace the wheel so that the two fork end clamps are just pinched—but not tight—and the rest of the bolts, in the bottom yoke, top caps, and the pinch bolt in the top yoke are slackened off.

When quick release type wheels are fitted, as in the Cyclone and Lightning models, the front spindle should be screwed up tight into the right-hand leg but the pinch bolt in the left-hand leg must be slack.

The forks should now be pumped up and down several times to line them up and then tightened up from bottom to top, that is, wheel spindle, bottom yoke pinch bolts, top caps, and finally the steering stem pinch bolt in the top yoke.

If the forks do not function satisfactorily after this treatment, either the fork tubes are bent or one of the yokes is twisted.

The tubes can only be accurately checked for straightness with special equipment such as knife-edged rollers and dial gauges and special gauges are required to check the yokes.

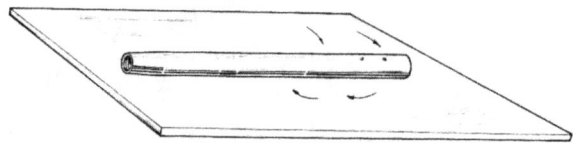

FIG. E.17. *Testing for straightness.*

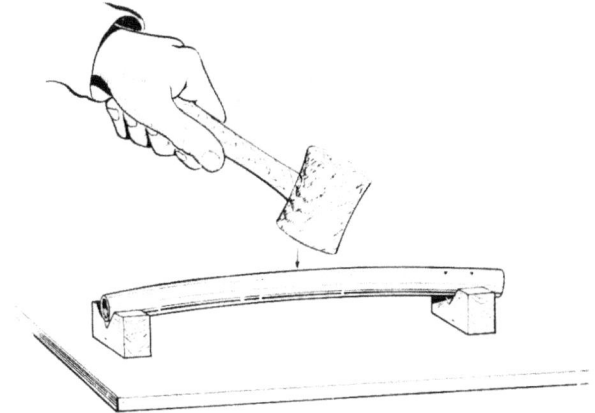

FIG. E.18. *Straightening.*

It is possible however to take a reasonable check of the tubes by rolling them on a good flat surface such as a piece of plate glass, but it is not a simple operation to straighten a bent tube, it is far better to obtain a factory serviced unit if the owner is resident in the British Isles.

If the tube is obviously bent but not kinked, then it may be possible to effect a reasonable repair with patience and care.

Find the highest point on the bend then with the two ends resting on wood blocks and with a wood block to protect the tube from the hammer give the tube a hard blow and re-check. The measure of success will of course depend on the extent of the damage and the skill of the operator.

This job is vastly improved and simplified if a press is available to the repairer.

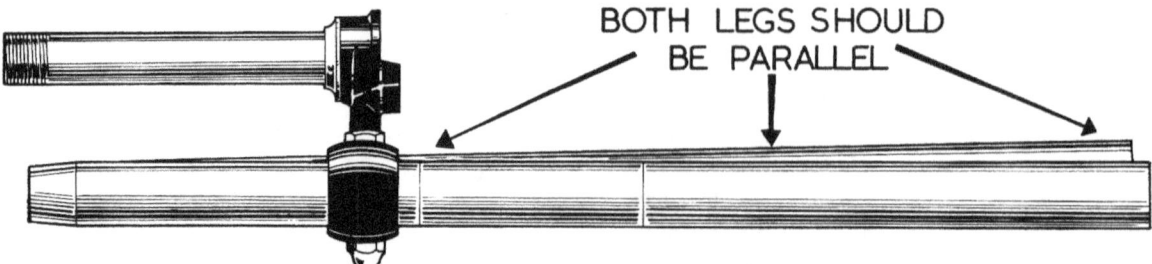

FIG. E.19. *Bottom yoke twisted.*

Having checked the tubes for straightness and reset as necessary, the top and bottom yokes can be checked.

First assemble the two tubes into the bottom yoke so that a straight edge across the lower ends is touching all four edges of the tubes, tighten the pinch bolts.

Now view them from the side, when the two tubes should be quite parallel, or, place the lower 12 in. of the tubes on a surface plate when there should be no rocking.

If the tubes are not parallel as in Fig. E.19, then the yoke can be set providing the error is not excessive.

To reset hold the one tube in a vice, on the unground portion, using soft clamps and set the other tube using a longer and larger diameter piece of tube for leverage.

Having set the tubes one way, check the gap between them on the ground portion.

The next step is to place the top yoke in position when the steering column should be quite central, Fig. E.20 shows a bent steering column.

Final step is to check with the two tubes assembled into the top yoke only, in this case use the bottom yoke loosely assembled on the tubes simply as a pilot.

It is permissible to rectify slight errors in alignment by resetting, but when there is excessive malalignment it is safer to replace the part affected.

Works reconditioned forks are available to owners in the United Kingdom through the dealer network.

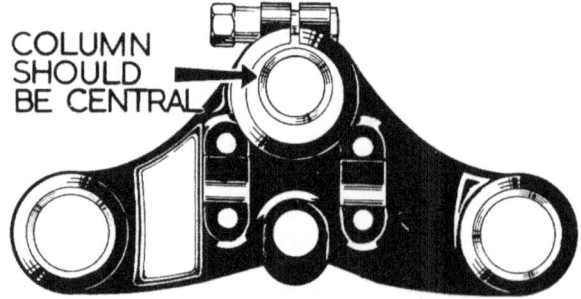

FIG. E.20. *Bent steering column.*

FRONT FORK

HYDRAULIC DAMPING

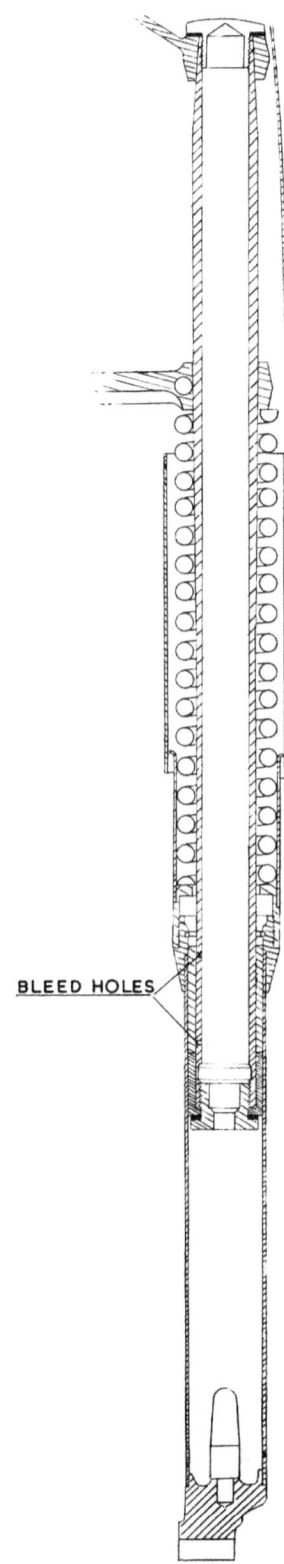

Figure E.21 shows a sectional view of the forks fully extended. In the lower portion—the main oil reservoir—will be seen a tapered pin and in the main tube two $\frac{3}{32}$ in. diameter bleed holes.

As the forks are compressed, the air in the upper portion of the main tube is compressed and the oil being contained in the lower sliding member and rising with it reaches a point when —since oil cannot be compressed—it must escape so it passes through the bleed holes, then the transfer of oil is progressively slowed as the tapered damping pin enters the hollow nut in the base of the tube.

During the period of fork compression the oil is passing into the area between the fork bushes, an area which is increasing in size as the bushes go further apart.

Eventually the point of maximum compression is reached, this being cushioned by the remaining oil in the main reservoir.

As the forks begin to extend again, the oil in the compartment between the two fork bushes begins to be compressed, and as the only outlet is the two small $\frac{3}{32}$ in. diameter bleed holes the action is slowed down to a smooth cushioned motion.

Exactly the same amount of oil should be in each leg otherwise damping will not be uniform. The correct quantity is $\frac{1}{3}$ of a pint to each leg.

If a sidecar is fitted stronger fork springs should be used, these are available through the dealer network.

FIG. E.21.

NOTES

A5065   WHEELS, BRAKES and TYRES   F1

INDEX

	Page
Front Wheel (Full-Width Hub)	F.2–3
Rear Wheel (Full-Width Hub)	F.4–6
Front Wheel (Quick Release Hub)	F.7–9
Rear Wheel (Quick Release Hub)	F.10–13
Wheel Building	F.13–14
Renewing Brake Linings	F.17
Wheel Alignment	F.16
Wheel Balancing	F.14
Removing and Refitting Tyres	F.18–22
Security Bolts	F.15
Tyre Maintenance	F.23
Sidecar Alignment	F.24

WHEELS, BRAKES and TYRES

FRONT WHEEL REMOVAL
(FULL-WIDTH HUB)

With the machine resting on its centre stand place a box or small wooden trestle underneath the crankcase so that the front wheel is clear of the ground. Disconnect the brake cable at the drum end by removing the bolt, nut and washer, securing the cable toggle to the lever and withdraw the cable from the lug on the cover plate.

Remove the fork end caps by unscrewing the four bolts (two in each cap). Support the wheel as the bolts are finally removed to avoid damage to the screw threads (Fig. F.1).

The wheel will now be free and can be dropped down and out of the forks.

FIG. F.1. *Removing fork caps.*

FRONT BRAKE SHOES

To remove the brake cover plate, apply the brake by means of the lever and unscrew the large spindle nut next to the cover plate. Take off the cover plate complete with brake shoes etc.

The brake shoes can be prised off the cover plate complete with the springs.

It is important to note that the brake shoes are fully floating and there is a leading and trailing shoe which must be fitted as shown in Fig. F.2.

Relined brake shoes are available to owners in the United Kingdom through the dealer network.

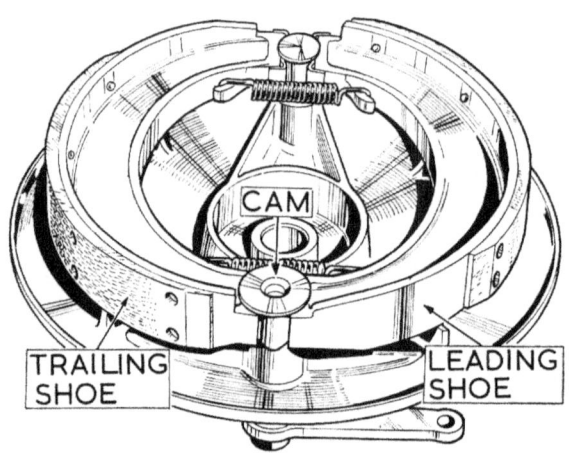

FIG. F.2. *Front brake shoes.*

A5065   WHEELS, BRAKES and TYRES   F3

FRONT HUB DISMANTLING
(FULL-WIDTH HUB)

Remove the cover as detailed on page F.2, this will expose the bearing retainer which has a left-hand thread.

Remove the retainer by unscrewing in a clockwise direction with peg spanner number 82661-3694.

Drive out the right-hand or brake side bearing by striking the left-hand end of the spindle resting a piece of hardwood against the end of the spindle to avoid damage.

To remove the left-hand side bearing prise out the circlip, reverse the spindle through the bearing and drive out the bearing and dust cover from the right-hand side, again using the wood to protect the spindle.

Both bearings are the same size and are therefore interchangeable.

Wash the bearings thoroughly in paraffin and if possible blow out with a high pressure air hose.

Examine carefully for excess play or roughness indicating damaged balls or races. If there is any sign of roughness it is safer to replace the bearing as it may suddenly disintegrate in further use. This could be very dangerous.

Fitting New Bearings.
The fitting of new bearings is an operation which is best done on a bench arbor press or similar equipment if available.

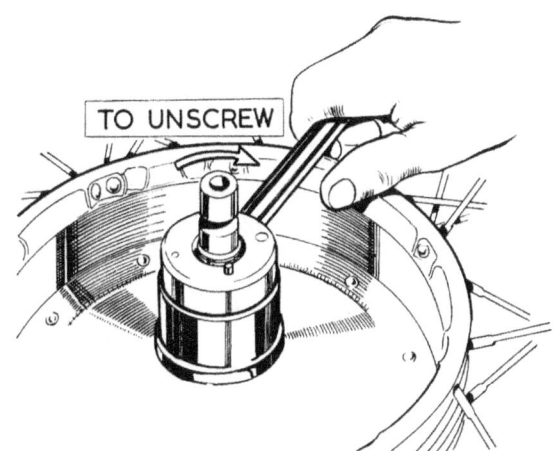

Fig. F.3. *Removing the retainer.*

It is essential that the bearings are pressed in absolutely square to the housing and the force applied must be on the outer ring not on the inner ring.

Place the right-hand bearing squarely in position and if a press is not available use a piece of tube which will go inside the housing and will press on the inner ring only. Drive the bearing home until it rests on the abutment face in the hub then screw in the lock-ring with service tool number 82661-3294 turning anti-clockwise since the ring has a left-hand thread. Insert the spindle, threaded end first from the left-hand side, and tap it gently home so that the inner ring of the bearing is resting against the shoulder on the spindle.

Pack the hub with grease, place the left-hand bearing over the spindle and drive it into the housing until the dust cap just clears the circlip groove then replace the circlip.

WHEELS, BRAKES and TYRES

REAR WHEEL
(FULL-WIDTH HUB)

Removal.
To remove the wheel only, take out the four extension nuts on the chainwheel (Fig. F.4).

When a full chaincase is fitted these can be removed through the hole in the chaincase which is closed with a rubber plug.

Unscrew the brake adjuster nut completely and remove the nut and washers securing the torque arm to the cover plate. The nut at the forward end of the arm can be slackened off as far as the split-pin to enable the arm to be removed from the plate.

Unscrew the wheel spindle from the right-hand side, take out the distance piece, and pull the wheel away from the sprocket at the same time freeing the brake lever.

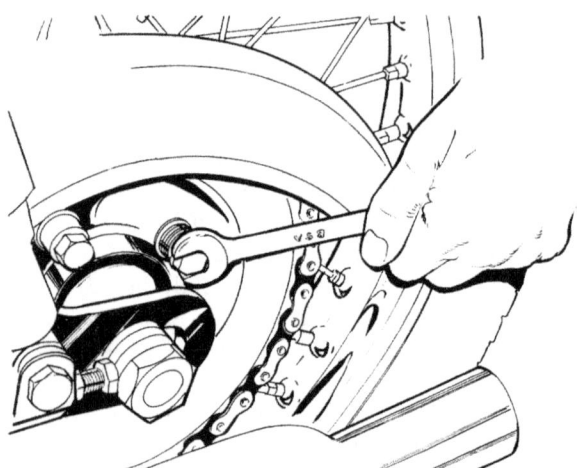

FIG. F.4. *Removing rear wheel.*

Lean the machine over slightly towards the left-hand side and remove the wheel from the right-hand side.

Rear Brake Shoes.

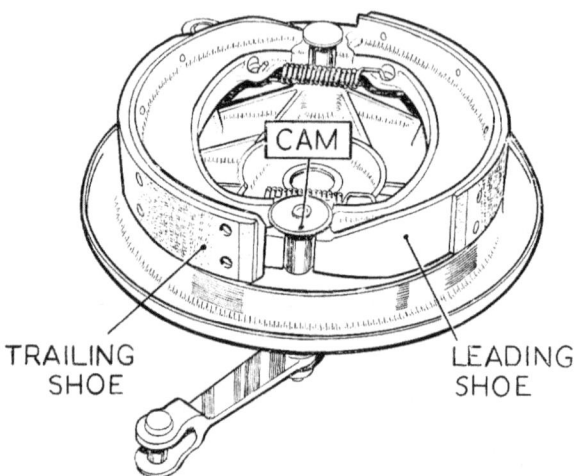

FIG. F.5. *Rear brake shoes.*

The brake cover plate can be lifted off complete with the shoes and springs. The shoes can be sprung off the plate in exactly the same way as the front and it is essential that they are replaced in the same way with the leading and trailing shoes in their correct positions (see Fig. F.5).

On the A65 models and the latest A50 models the rear brake shoes are not interchangeable with the front shoes since the rear are 7 in. diameter and the front are 8 in. diameter, but the early A50 models had 7 in. diameter brakes for both wheels.

A grease nipple is provided for lubricating the cam spindle and it is advisable to check that the hole is not blocked by dirt. Be careful not to over-lubricate, grease must not get on to the linings

Relined shoes are available to owners in the United Kingdom through the dealer network.

WHEELS, BRAKES and TYRES

REAR HUB DISMANTLING
(FULL-WIDTH HUB)

To obtain access to the bearings unscrew the bearing retainer which has a left-hand thread and is therefore removed by using the peg spanner number 82661-3694 in a clockwise direction.

Using a suitable drift, drive the hollow spindle through from the left-hand side so driving out the brake drum side bearing (Fig. F.6)

The four bolts in the hub shell are splined and a press-fit into the shell, they can if necessary be replaced by pressing into the brake drum then fitting the replacements from the drum side but, care is required to mate the splines before pressing in.

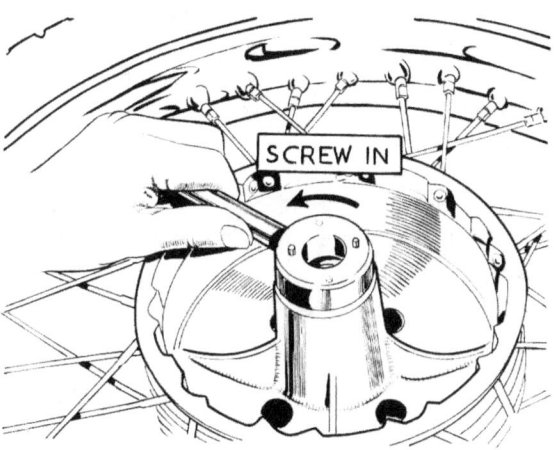

FIG. F.7. *Replacing the retainer.*

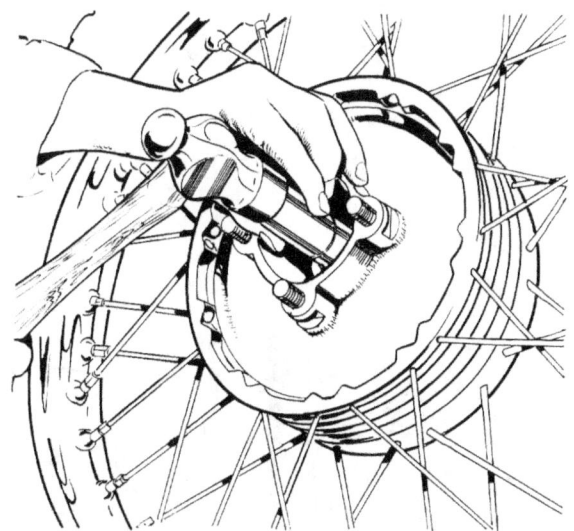

FIG. F.6. *Removing the bearing.*

There is no need to disturb the grease retainer unless it is to be replaced in which case it can be driven out from the right-hand side.

A new bearing can be fitted in the reverse order but be sure that it is square with its housing and apply pressure to the outer ring only.

After pressing the replacement in, pack with grease, enter the hollow spindle with the flanged end against the bearing then press in the grease retainer on the left-hand side.

Replace the bearing retainer which has a left-hand thread (see Fig. F.7).

CHAINWHEEL

To remove the chainwheel, disconnect the chain, unscrew the spindle nut on the left-hand side, remove the washer and then the chainwheel. To renew the bearing drive the spindle through from the left-hand side then drive out the bearing and grease retainer from the same side (see Fig. F.8).

The replacement bearing is fitted in the reverse order but care should be taken to enter the bearing squarely in the housing. Pack with grease and press the retainer and spindle in from the right-hand or wheel side.

The outer distance piece must always be fitted with the larger diameter next to the bearing.

FIG. F.8.

REAR WHEEL REPLACEMENT

Procedure for replacement is the reverse of removal but care is required not only to see that chain adjustment is correct but to see also that the wheels are in alignment with each other (see Page F.16).

Always ensure that the spring of the chain connecting link is correctly fitted and the right way round with the closed end to the front on the top run of the chain.

See that all nuts and bolts are securely tightened particularly those on the brake anchor strap (see Fig. F.9).

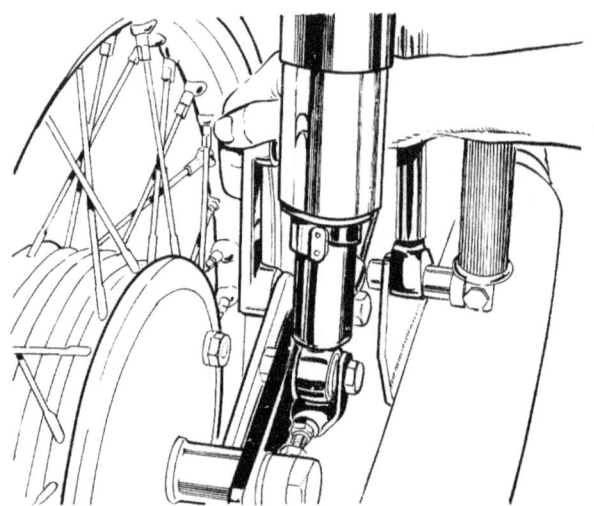

FIG. F.9. *Tightening anchor strap bolt.*

WHEELS, BRAKES and TYRES

FRONT WHEEL REMOVAL AND REPLACEMENT
(QUICK RELEASE HUB)

To remove the front wheel, first disconnect the cable from the lever on the cover plate. This can usually be done by screwing in the adjuster completely then operating the brake by means of a spanner on the lever nut so providing sufficient slack to release the nipple. Having released the nipple unscrew and remove the cable adjuster and cable (see Fig. F.10).

FIG. F.10. *Removing cable adjuster.*

Remove the brake anchor strap nut from the cover plate and slacken off the nuts at the other end to enable the removal of the strap from the plate.

Slacken off the pinch bolt in the left-hand fork end and using a bar through the head of the spindle unscrew the spindle in a clockwise direction (left-hand thread).

Support the wheel as the spindle is withdrawn and when it is clear the wheel can be pulled away from the right-hand leg and clear of the machine.

Try not to let the wheel fall on the brake side as this may displace the bush through the cover plate, if it does happen the bush can be retrieved and replaced with the wheel spindle.

Front Wheel Replacement.
Lift the wheel between the fork legs and position the bush in the right-hand fork leg. Screw the spindle in anti-clockwise (left-hand thread) until it is nearly tight, position the brake plate and replace the anchor strap. Tighten the spindle then pump the forks up and down to position the left-hand leg and tighten the pinch bolt in the left-hand fork end.

Finally replace the brake cable and adjust as necessary using the adjuster on the cover plate.

The cable adjuster on the handlebar is for cable adjustment when riding.

FIG. F.11. *Replacing the spindle.*

F8 WHEELS, BRAKES and TYRES A5065

FRONT BRAKE SHOES
(QUICK RELEASE HUB)

The brake plate (A) is a push-fit on the bush (B) (see Fig. F.12).

To remove the brake shoes lever them upwards and outwards off the cam and fulcrum pin.

The shoes are of the conventional type (not floating) and can be fitted either side. Replacement brake shoes are available through the Exchange Service in the British Isles, but for those who cannot use this service the notes on relining on page F.17 may be of some assistance.

A grease nipple is provided for lubricating the cam spindle and it is advisable to check that the hole is not blocked by dirt. Be careful not to over-lubricate, grease must not get on to the linings.

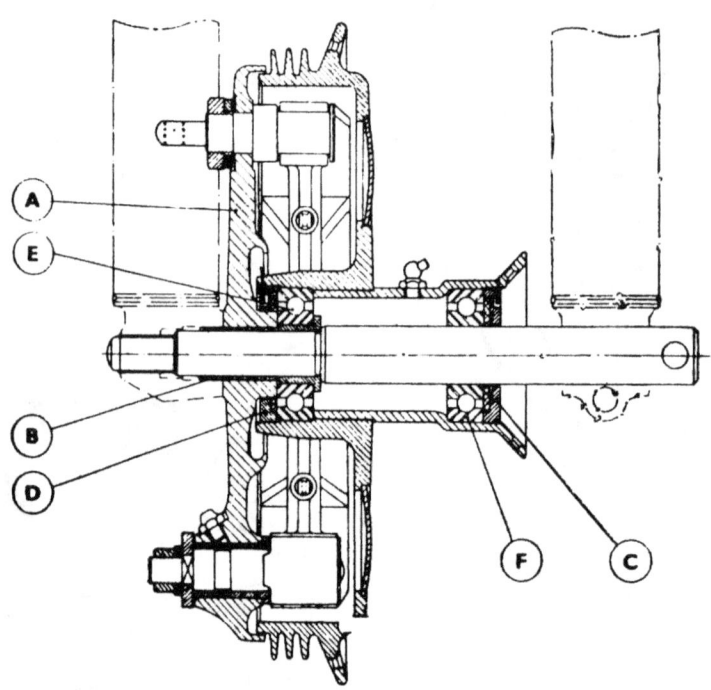

FIG. F.12. *Section of front hub.*

WHEELS, BRAKES and TYRES

FRONT HUB DISMANTLING
(QUICK RELEASE HUB)

Pull off the brake plate and remove the split-pins at each side of the hub. Unscrew the bearing retainers which have normal right-hand threads.

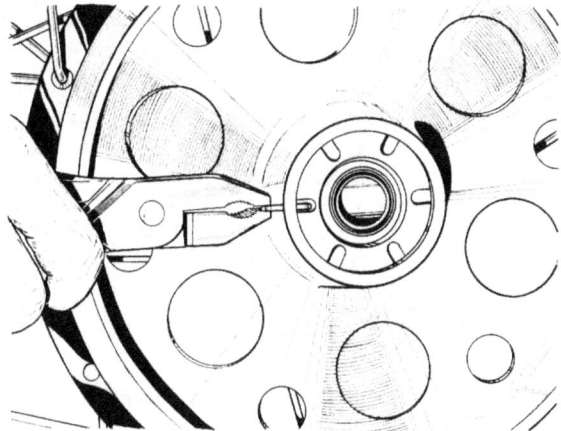

Fig. F.13. *Removing split-pin.*

Fig. F.14. *Fitting new bearing.*

Replace the spindle and drive out the brake side bearing together with the bush (B) by striking the head of the spindle with a hide-mallet. If a mallet is not available use a piece of hardwood to protect the spindle.

Only the left-hand bearing remains and this can be driven out with a suitable drift or with the spindle and bush reversed.

Both bearings are the same size and therefore interchangeable.

Replacement bearings are simply fitted in the reverse manner but, pressure must only be applied to the outer ring of the bearing.

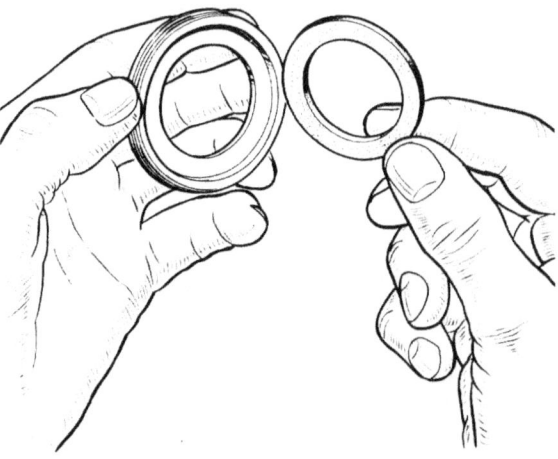

Fig. F.15.

See that the rubber grease retainers are in good condition and that the retainers are screwed down quite tight. If necessary drill new holes for the split-pin.

REAR WHEEL REMOVAL
(QUICK RELEASE HUB)

The rear wheel can be removed without any effect on the brake adjustment or chain. Remove the spindle using a bar through the head, screwing anti-clockwise (right-hand thread). If the bush on the right-hand side does not fall clear, take it away then pull the wheel away from the brake drum and clear of the machine.

Do not unscrew the spindle nut on the left-hand side.

FIG. F.16. *Removing rear wheel.*

HUB SHELL BEARINGS

The hub is fitted with two bearings which are a light press-fit on to the hollow spindle and into the hub shell. They are both the same size as the bearing used in the brake drum.

FIG. F.17. *Bearing retainer.*

To remove the bearings unscrew the retaining ring on the left-hand side, this has a left-hand thread and is therefore turned in a clockwise direction.

Using a drift slightly under .875 in. diameter drive out the right-hand bearing from the left-hand side, this will release the hollow spindle, short distance piece, pen steel washer and the dust covers from the right-hand side.

The left-hand bearing can now be driven out from the right-hand side.

The only part now left in the hub is the spacer for the left-hand bearing which need not be disturbed.

A5065   WHEELS, BRAKES and TYRES   F11

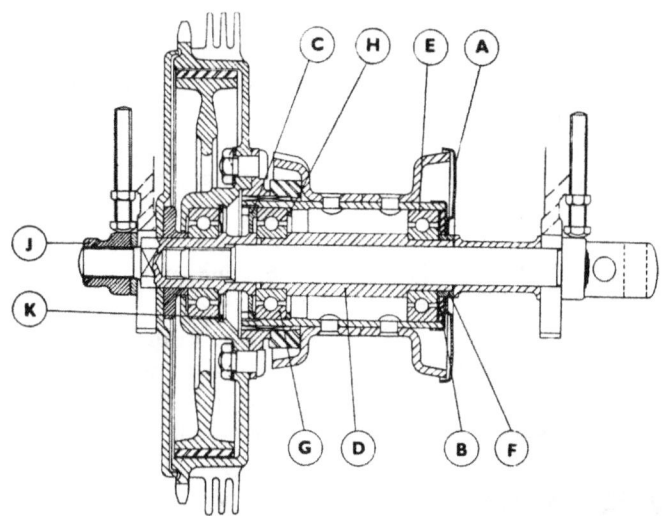

Fig. F.18. *Section through rear hub.*

To examine the bearings, wash thoroughly in paraffin and blow out with a high pressure air line if possible. Examine carefully for signs of roughness indicating broken balls or damaged tracks, or excessive play.

Reassembly is simply the reverse of dismantling but, when pressing the bearings in, apply pressure only to the outside ring of the bearing and ensure that the retainer on the left-hand side is quite tight.

Note that the short end of the hollow spindle is on the left-hand side.

REAR BRAKE DRUM (QUICK RELEASE HUB)

The brake drum is retained in the fork end by the nut (J) Fig. F.18, and the nut securing the brake anchor strap to the lower chainguard bolt. This latter nut is secured by a split-pin.

To remove the drum, disconnect the rear chain and the brake rod, remove the nut (J) Fig. F.18 and the split-pin and nut at the rear of the lower chainguard bolt. The complete assembly can now be removed from the fork end.

The brake plate and distance piece can be lifted from the spindle complete with the brake shoes. There is no need to disturb the cam spindle unless it is to be replaced in which case the position of the outrigger strap, spring, bush and lever should be noted for reassembly.

The brake shoes can be removed and replaced in the usual way and to remove the bearing take off the large distance piece, drive the spindle through and remove the bearing circlip from the rear of the drum. The bearing can now be driven out from the front of the drum using a suitable drift.

There should be no need to disturb the driving flange unless it is known to be worn and is being replaced.

Fig. F.19. *Removing bearing circlip.*

To remove the flange flatten the locking plates and remove the six nuts, drive out the six bolts and remove the flange. When fitting the new flange see that it enters the drum squarely and that the mating faces are absolutely clean before replacing the six bolts. Do not omit to turn over the locking plates after tightening the nuts.

If the brake drum teeth are hooked or inside the drum is scored it should be replaced.

The rivets of the brake linings must be well below the surface, if any rivets are flush with the linings the drum will be scored and braking efficiency impaired.

Reassembly is simply the reverse of dismantling but, do not omit to grease the bearing, or replace the pen steel washer under the circlip so that it seats on the outer ring of the bearing, not the inner ring.

Drum Replacement.
See that spindle is pressed well into the bearing, place the distance piece in position with the small diameter next to the bearing, then replace the cover plate complete with brake shoes. Fit the outer distance piece and place the assembly in the fork end.

If the chain adjustment was correct there is no need to make any alteration now but, do not tighten the spindle nut until the wheel has been replaced so that the whole assembly is in alignment.

Do not omit the split-pin from the brake anchor strap and chainguard bolt.

Fig. F.20. *Replacing the drum.*

WHEELS, BRAKES and TYRES

WHEEL REPLACEMENT

See that the dust covers are secure and that the rubber seal is in position on the left-hand side of the hub. If this seal is omitted, water can enter the driving flange and bearings and will make wheel removal difficult in addition to damaging the bearings.

Lift the wheel and engage the splines in the driver, push the wheel well home, and replace the right-hand distance piece, screw in the wheel spindle and secure.

If the brake drum has been removed, tighten the spindle nut and the anchor strap nuts.

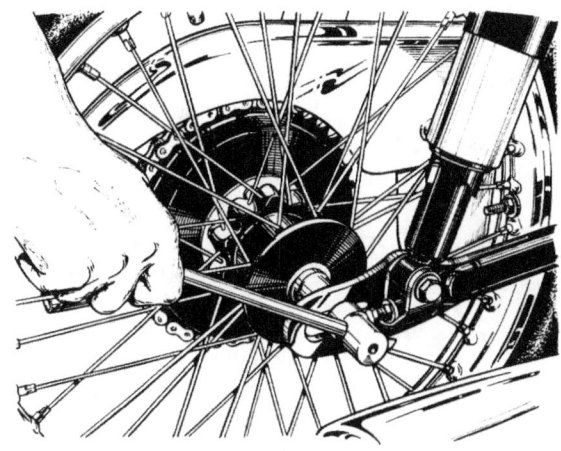

FIG. F.21. *Tightening the spindle.*

WHEEL BUILDING

This is a job which is best left to the specialist as it is essential that the wheel is laced correctly and that when truing, the spokes are correctly tensioned.

It is however possible for the less experienced to avoid trouble by periodically examining the wheels. As spokes and nipples bed down the tension will be lost and unless this is corrected the spokes will chafe and ultimately break.

Periodically test the tension either by "ringing" that is striking with a metal tool or by placing the fingers and thumb of one hand over two spokes at a time and pressing them together.

If tension has been lost there will be no ringing tone and the spokes will move freely across each other.

When a spoke needs tensioning the nipple through the rim must be screwed further on to the spoke but, at the same time, the truth of the wheel must be checked and it may be necessary to ease the tension at another part of the wheel in order to maintain its truth.

It will therefore be obvious that spoke replacement, spoke tensioning or wheel truing are not operations to be treated lightly.

F14   WHEELS, BRAKES and TYRES   A5065

Careful examination of the wheel will show that for every spoke there is another pulling in the opposite direction and that the adjacent spoke goes to the opposite side of the hub.

Increasing the tension tends to pull the rim so, to counteract this, it is sometimes necessary to increase the tension on the spoke or spokes either side to maintain the truth of the wheel.

With a little care and patience it is possible for the unskilled to at least retension the spokes but, turn each nipple only a little at a time as, when once the spoke is under tension only a fraction of a turn is sometimes sufficient to throw the rim badly out of truth.

Wheels with full-width hubs, and quick release rear wheels, are built with the rim central to the spoke flanges.

Quick release front wheels are built with the edge of the brake drum 1-15/16 in. from the centre line of the rim.

WHEEL BALANCING

When a wheel is out of balance it means that there is more weight in one part than in another. This is very often due to variation in the tyre and at moderate speeds will not be noticed but at high speeds it can be very serious, particularly if the front wheel is affected.

Weights are available for attaching to the spokes to counteract any out-of-balance but, before starting, ensure that the wheel is absolutely free and revolves quite easily. If the rear wheel is being treated remove the driving chain.

With the wheel clear of the ground spin it slowly and allow it to stop on its own. Now mark the top of the wheel or tyre and repeat two or three times to check.

If the wheel stops in the same place the extra weight must be added at the marked spot.

The next step is to ascertain how much weight is to be added, this can be done by sticking small pieces of plasticine to the nipples and recheck until the wheel will stop in any position without moving.

Having ascertained how much weight is required, a balance weight of exactly the same amount must be attached to the spokes at the spot originally marked.

If security bolts are to be used they should be fitted before balancing.

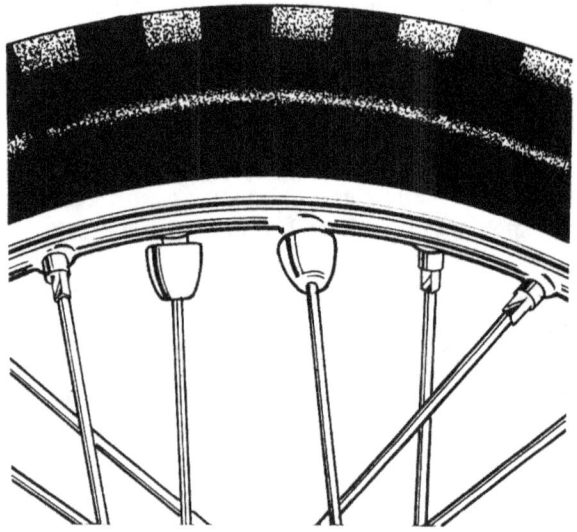

FIG. F.22. *Balance weights.*

WHEELS, BRAKES and TYRES

SECURITY BOLTS

Sometimes, particularly if a tyre is under-inflated, it will creep round the rim taking the tube with it and if not stopped will ultimately cause the valve to be pulled from the tube.

Therefore on high performance models it is usual to fit two security bolts equidistant round the rim from the valve, that is at 120° each side of the valve.

To fit the bolts remove the tyre and tube, mark the rim positions and drill the rim between

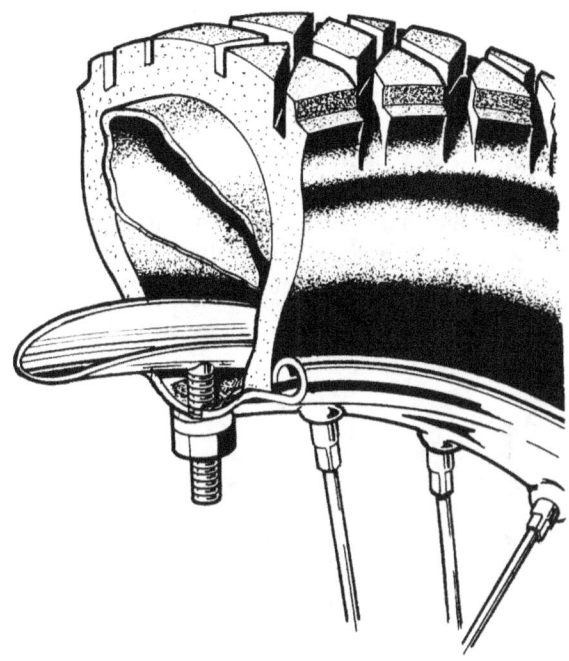

Fig. F.24. *Security bolt.*

two nipples to the required size of the bolt.

After removing any burr from the holes, fit the bolts quite loosely and replace the tyre so that the covered portion of the security bolt is inside the tyre.

Check that the tyre is correctly positioned, inflate to the required pressure and tighten the bolt nuts on to the rim.

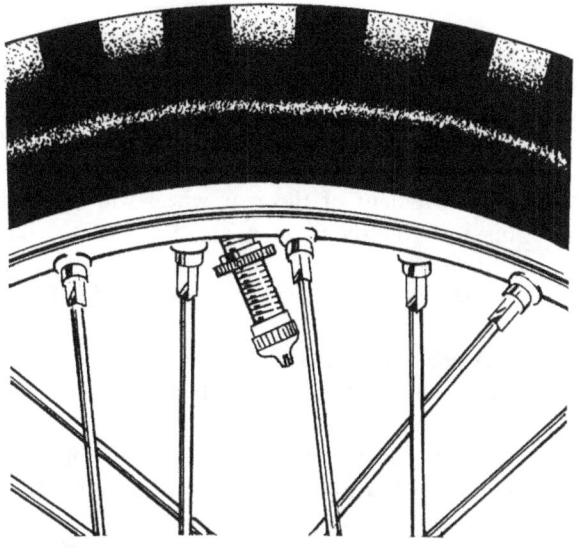

Fig. F.23. *Tyre creeping.*

WHEEL ALIGNMENT

Steering will be affected if the wheels are the slightest bit out of alignment (out of track).

Since the front wheel cannot be adjusted in this respect, it is the rear wheel which must be aligned to the front wheel. This is necessary whenever the chain is adjusted or the wheel removed. It is necessary to adjust the rear brake whenever re-alignment has been carried out.

To check the alignment of the wheels a straight edge of timber or steel is required approximately 78 in. long.

The straight edge should be laid on blocks four to six inches high (alternately) each side of the machine.

If the tyres are the same size and the wheels in alignment the straight edge will be touching the tyres at four points on each side.

If the front tyre is of smaller section then it should be as drawing (B) Fig. F.25.

If the alignment is as either (A) or (C) then the rear chain adjusters must be moved as indicated by the arrows to correct the alignment.

Assuming that the chain adjustment is correct the movement of the rear wheel will be made on the right-hand side chain adjuster which should be screwed in or out as necessary after the spindle nuts have been slackened off.

A machine suffering accidental damage may have wheels so out of alignment that they cannot be corrected in this way. Frame, fork or wheel geometry may be basically upset, in these cases a specialist repairer can probably reset any offending assembly using information in Sections D2 — D10.

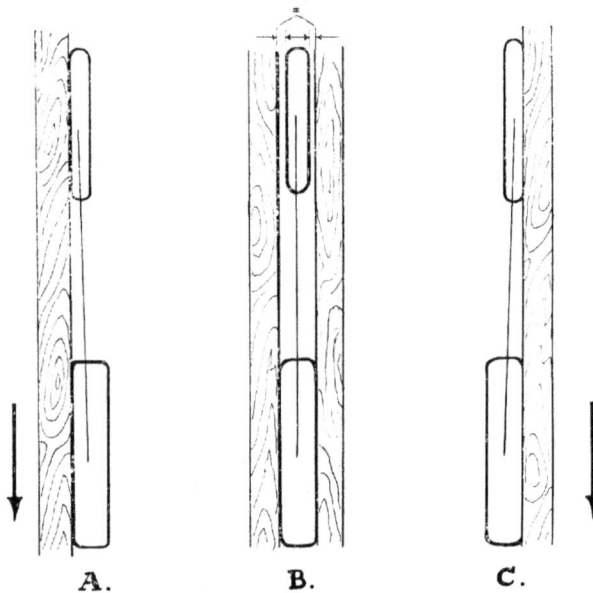

FIG. F.25. *Checking alignment.*

RENEWING BRAKE LININGS

Hold the shoe firmly in a vice and using a good sharp chisel cut off the peened over portion of the rivet.

Drive out the old rivets with a suitable pin punch. Reverse the shoe in the vice and draw file the face of the shoe to remove any burrs.

Clamp the lining in position and drill straight through with 5/32 in. diameter drill using the holes in the shoe as the jig.

Remove the clamps and holding the lining carefully in the vice counterbore or countersink, according to the type of rivet used, to no more than two-thirds the thickness of the lining, that is, if the lining is $\frac{3}{16}$ in. thick, then the counterbore must not be deeper than $\frac{1}{8}$ in.

Having prepared the linings for riveting, start at the centre and position the lining with one or more rivets.

Using either small "G" or toolmakers clamps close to the rivets and with a suitable mandril

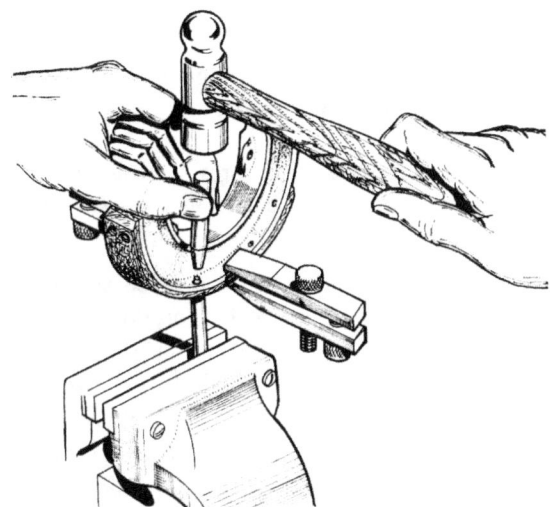

FIG. F.27. *Peening over rivets.*

in the vice, peen over the rivets working alternately outwards from the centre.

The mandril in the vice must be flat on the end and the diameter no more than that of the rivet head. It will also help to bed the rivet down if a hollow punch is used before peening.

If the clamps are used correctly, that is, next to the rivet being worked on, the linings can be fitted tight to the shoe.

Incorrectly fitted linings having a gap between the lining and the shoe will result in a spongy brake.

When the riveting is completed file a good chamfer at each end to approximately half the depth of the lining and lightly draw file the rest of the lining to remove any fraze from the drilling.

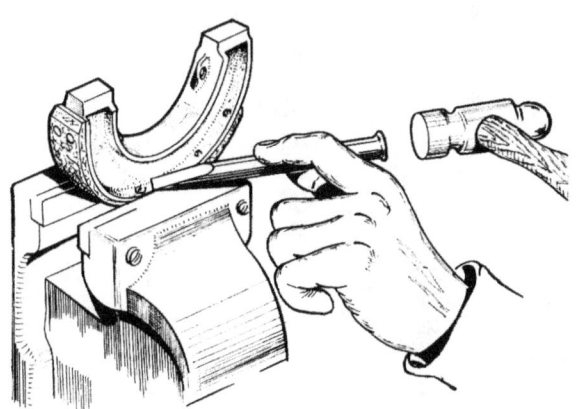

FIG. F.26. *Chopping out the rivets.*

WHEELS, BRAKES and TYRES

REMOVING AND REFITTING TYRES

TYRE REMOVAL

There are a few points about tyres which should be thoroughly understood.

(1) The beads have wire cores which cannot be stretched over the rim flanges without damage.

(2) Removal and replacement will be simpler if the beads are pressed right down into the well of the rim except at the point being "worked". The well is the centre section.

(3) The tyre beads will slip over the rim quicker and damage will be avoided if the beads and the levers are lubricated with soapy water.

Unscrew and remove the valve core to deflate the tyre.

Some valve caps are designed for this purpose but, if the cap is plain and a core removal tool is not available, depress the centre of the valve and keep "treading" the tyre to expell the air.

Press each bead off its seat into the well of the rim.

Insert the lever at the valve position, and while levering, press the bead into the well diametrically opposite the valve.

Fig. F.28.

Commencing to remove the first bead. You cannot pull the cover bead at (A) over the rim flange until the cover bead at (B) is pushed off the bead seat (C) down into the well (D). Then the cover bead at (A) comes over the rim flange easily.

WHEELS, BRAKES and TYRES

Insert a second lever close to the first and prise the bead over the flange holding the free part with the other lever.

Remove one lever and insert further along the tyre continuing every two to three inches until the bead is completely removed (see Fig. F.29).

Take care when inserting levers not to pinch the inner tube as this will result in a puncture.

Lift the valve out of the rim and remove the tube.

Fig. F.29. *Removing the first bead.*

Stand the wheel upright, insert a lever between the remaining bead and the rim and pull the cover back over the flange as in Fig. F.30. Do not forget to press the bead diametrically opposite the lever into the centre of the rim and to apply a soapy solution to the rim flange.

Fig. F.30.

WHEELS, BRAKES and TYRES

TYRE REPLACEMENT

Before a tyre—new or used—is replaced, it should be carefully checked inside and outside for loose objects or nails, flints, glass and cuts. Do not forget that although there may be nothing visible outside there could be a nail projecting inside. When repairing a tyre or tube be patient and see that the area of the repair is absolutely clean before applying solution. A rag dampened with petrol will help to clean the area but, it must be completely dry before solution is applied.

Remember that when replacing the tyre, it is very easy to cause another puncture by nipping the inner tube with the levers.

Some new tyres have balance adjustment rubbers inside the casing, they are not patches and should not be disturbed.

When there is a white spot near the bead it should be placed at the valve position or, if two security bolts are fitted, midway between the bolts.

If the spokes have been tensioned, or replaced, see that they are not projecting through the nipples. File flush any that are showing through.

Replace the rim tape with the rough side next to the rim. Place the tube in the tyre and inflate just sufficient to round it out without stretch.

Too much air makes fitting difficult, and too little will make the tube more liable to be nipped by the levers. Dust the tube and inside the cover with dusting chalk.

Lubricate the cover beads and the rim flanges with a soap and water solution or liquid soap.

Pull the tube slightly out of the cover so that it protrudes about 1 in. beyond the beads for about 4—5 in. each side the valve as in Fig. F.31.

Fig. F.31. *Cover and tube assembled ready for fitting.*

WHEELS, BRAKES and TYRES

Squeeze the beads together at the valve to prevent the tube slipping back and offer the cover to the rim as shown in Fig. F.32, at the same time passing the valve through the holes in the tape and rim.

Allow the lower bead to go into the well of the rim and the upper bead to be above the rim flange.

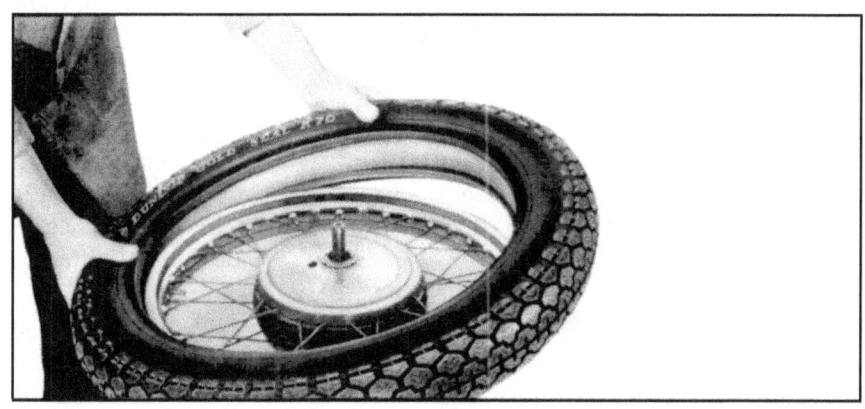

FIG. F.32. *Commencing to fit the tyre.*

FIG. F.33. *Fitting the first bead.*

Working from the valve outwards, press the lower bead over the rim flange by hand, moving along in short stretches, and ensuring that the bead lies right down in the well of the rim—this is most important—see Fig. F.33. If necessary use a tyre lever for the last few inches as in Fig. F.34.

Turn the wheel over and check that the bead is concentric with the rim before proceeding further.

FIG. F.34. *Completing the fitting of the first bead.*

WHEELS, BRAKES and TYRES

Reverse the wheel again and press the upper bead into the well of the rim diametrically opposite the valve.

Insert a lever as close as possible to the point where the bead passes over the flange, and lever the bead over at the same time pressing the fitted part into the well of the rim.

Repeat progressively round the tyre until the bead is completely over the flange, finishing at the valve (see Fig. F.35).

Push the valve inwards to ensure that the tube adjacent to the valve is not trapped under the bead, then pull the valve back firmly into position. If security bolts are fitted treat as valve.

Before inflating, check that the fitting line on the tyre wall just above the bead on each side is concentric with the rim.

If necessary bounce the wheel to help seat the tyre but, see that there is adequate pressure to prevent damaging the tyre or tube and only use moderate force. If the tyre will not seat, it is better to release the pressure, apply soap solution to lubricate and re-inflate.

Inflate to the required pressure and check fitting lines again. Inflation should not be too rapid, particularly at the commencement, to allow the beads to seat correctly on the rim.

See that the valve protrudes squarely through the valve hole before screwing down the knurled nut and replace the dust cap.

Tighten down the security bolts (if fitted).

Fig. F.35. *Completing the fitting of the second bead.*

WHEELS, BRAKES and TYRES

TYRE MAINTENANCE

Always maintain correct inflation pressures (see page GD.10). Use a tyre pressure gauge and check weekly when tyres are cold. The pressures quoted in the data pages are for a rider of 140 lbs. weight. If the rider's weight exceeds 140 lbs. pressure should be increased as follows:

FRONT TYRE:—Add 1 lb. per square inch for every 28 lbs. above 140 lbs.

REAR TYRE:—Add 1 lb. per square inch for every 14 lbs. above 140 lbs.

For sustained high speeds normal pressures should be increased by 5 lbs. per square inch. If a pillion passenger or luggage is carried, the actual load on each tyre should be taken and the pressures increased in accordance with the Table below. The load on each tyre can be found by placing each wheel in turn on a weighbridge with the rider or riders astride the machine.

Pressure should then be adjusted to the Chart.

18, 19, 20 AND 21 INCH DIAMETER RIMS

NOMINAL TYRE SECTION (INCHES)	INFLATION PRESSURE (lb. per square inch)					
	16	18	20	24	28	32
	LOAD PER TYRE (lb.)					
3.00	160	185	210	255	300	350
3.25	200	230	260	320	380	440
3.50	280	310	335	390	450	500
4.00	260	395	430	500	570	640

SIDECAR ALIGNMENT

Alignment of the front and rear wheels has been described on page F.16 and the two straight edges used can also be used for aligning the sidecar.

The combination must stand on a flat smooth surface such as concrete or paving; place one of the straight edges against the front and rear wheels and the other against the sidecar wheel as Fig. F.36.

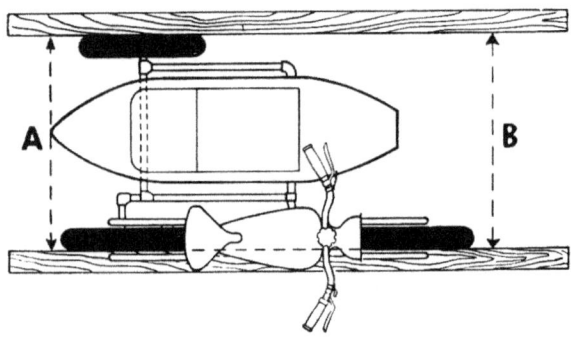

Fig. F.36. *"Toe-in"*.

Straighten the front wheel so that it touches the straight edge at each side or, if the front tyre is of smaller section, the gap is equal each side.

It is of course useless trying to align a sidecar if the front and rear wheels are not in alignment. Now measure the distance between the straight edges at (A) and (B). The distance in front at (B) should be $\tfrac{3}{8}$ in. to $\tfrac{3}{4}$ in. less than at (A). If the alignment is incorrect adjustment is usually made at the front lower coupling and it is known as "toe-in".

In addition to aligning the wheels horizontally, the machine should also be aligned vertically, if the maximum enjoyment is to be obtained from the outfit.

The machine should "lean out" approximately 1 in. from the vertical.

To check, hang a plumb-line from the handlebar, and measure the distance between top and bottom as in Fig. F.37.

Any adjustment necessary is usually carried out at the two upper sidecar connections. The measurement at (C) the top should be approximately 1 in. greater than at the bottom and should never be less.

If the machine is leaning inwards then the couplings must be adjusted to push the machine further out. To do this it may be necessary to move the connections along the sidecar chassis towards the machine, this however will depend on the type of sidecar used.

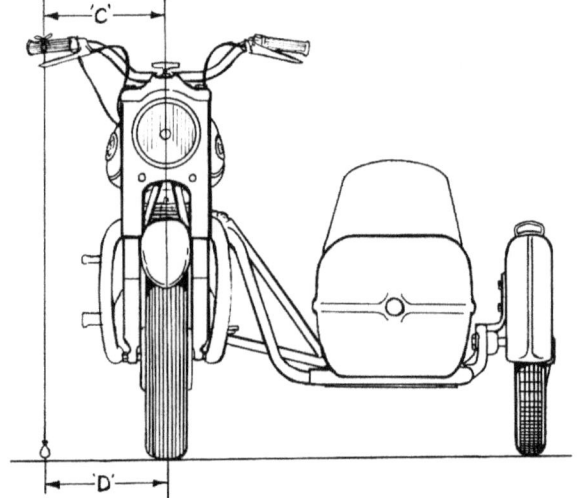

Fig. F.37. *Vertical alignment*.

ELECTRICAL SYSTEM

A5065   G1

INDEX

	Page
INTRODUCTION	G.2
BATTERY INSPECTION AND MAINTENANCE	G.2–4
Description	G.2
(A) Dry Charged Batteries	G.2–3
(B) Routine Maintenance	G.3–4
COIL IGNITION SYSTEM	G.4–8
Description	G.4
(A) Checking the Low-Tension Circuit for Continuity	G.5
(B) Fault Finding in the Low-Tension Circuit	G.5
(C) Ignition Coils	G.6
(D) Contact Breaker	G.7
(E) Checking the High-Tension Circuit	G.8
(F) Checking the Emergency Starting Circuit	G.8
SPARKING PLUGS	G.8–9
CHARGING SYSTEM	G.10–15
Description	G.10
(A) Checking the D.C. Input to Battery	G.12
(B) Checking the Alternator Output	G.12
(C) Rectifier Maintenance and Testing	G.12–14
(D) Checking the Charging Circuit for Continuity	G.15
(E) Making a 1 Ohm Load Resistor	G.15
ZENER DIODE CHARGE CONTROL	G.16–17
A.C. IGNITION (E.T.) AND A.C. LIGHTING SYSTEMS	G.18–20
Description	G.18
(A) A.C. Ignition	G.18–19
(B) Testing the A.C. Ignition System	G.19
(C) Checking the A.C. Alternator Output	G.19
(D) Direct Lighting System	G.20
ELECTRIC HORN	G.21
HEADLAMP	G.22
Description	G.22
Beam Adjustments	G.22
TAIL AND STOP LAMP UNIT	G.22
ADDITIONAL INFORMATION	G.23–24
ALTERNATOR AND STATOR DETAILS (Specifications and Output Figures)	G.25
WIRING DIAGRAMS	G.26–28
Coil Ignition Machines (6-volt)	G.25
Police 6-volt with Booster Switch	G.28
Coil Ignition Machines (12-volt)	G.26
A.C. Ignition (E.T.) Machines	G.27

ELECTRICAL SYSTEM

INTRODUCTION

The electrical system is supplied from an alternating current generator contained in the primary chaincase and driven from the crankshaft. The generator output is selected by the respective positions of the lighting and ignition switches and is then converted into direct current by a silicon diode rectifier.

On 6-volt machines the direct current is supplied to one MLZ9E battery of 12 amp./hour at 10 hour rate or 13 amp./hour at 20 hour rate; and on 12-volt machines to two MKZ9E batteries of 7 amp./hour at 10 hour rate or 8 amp./hour at 20 hour rate, the latter being connected in series with a Zener Diode in circuit to regulate the battery current.

The current is then supplied to the ignition system which is controlled by a double contact breaker driven from the timing idler gear.

The contact breaker feeds two ignition coils, one for each cylinder.

In case of a discharged battery the emergency position of the ignition switch supplies output direct from the generator through one pair of contacts and one ignition coil to enable the engine to be started.

As soon as the engine has been started the ignition switch must be returned to the normal position or burning of the contact breaker points will take place.

The routine maintenance needed by the various components is set out in the following sections. All electrical components and connections including the earthing points to the frame of the machine must be clean and tight.

BATTERY INSPECTION AND MAINTENANCE

Description.
Battery models MLZ9E and MKZ9E are six volt units and two of the latter type are connected in series on later models, to give 12 volts. The battery containers are mouled in translucent polystyrene through which the acid can be seen. The tops of the containers are so designed that when the covers are in position, the special anti-spill filler plugs are sealed in a common venting chamber. Gas from the filler plugs leaves this chamber through an elbow-shaped vent pipe union which can be inserted into one of four alternative sealed outlets. Polythene tubing may be attached to the vent pipe union to lead the corrosive fumes away from any parts of the machine where they might cause damage.

G1. Part A. Dry Charged Batteries.
Battery models MLZ9E and MKZ9E are supplied dry-charged.

Whilst these batteries leave the factory in the fully "dry-charged" condition, they may slowly lose some charge in storage. In view of this, the following filling instructions must be carefully observed:—

With the acid, battery and room temperature between 60°F., and 100°F. (15.5—37.7°C.), remove the vent plugs and fill each cell to the coloured marker line.

Measure the temperature and specific gravity of the electrolyte in each of the cells.

Allow to stand for 20 minutes and then re-check the temperature and specific gravity of the electrolyte in each cell.

The battery is then ready for service **unless** the above checks show the electrolyte temperature to have risen by more than 10°F. (5.5°C.) or the specific gravity to have fallen by more than 10 "points", i.e. by more than 0.010 specific gravity. In this event, it will be necessary to recharge the battery at the appropriatere charge rate (1.2 amperes for MLZ9E; 0.7 amperes for MKZ9E) until the specific gravity values remain constant for three successive hourly readings and all cells are gassing freely.

During charging, keep the electrolyte in each cell level with the coloured marker line by adding distilled water —**not** acid.

G1. Part B. Routine Maintenance.

Every 1,000 miles (1,500 km.) or monthly, or more regularly in hot climates the battery should be cleaned as follows. Remove the battery cover and clean the battery top. Examine the terminals: if they are corroded scrape them clean and smear them with a film of petroleum jelly, or with a silicon grease. Remove the vent plugs and check that the vent holes are clear and that the rubber washer fitted under each plug is in good condition.

Examine the level of the electrolyte in each cell. Lift the battery out of the carrier so that the coloured filling line can be seen. Add distilled water until the electrolyte level reaches this line. NOTE:— On **no** account should the batteries be topped up to the separator guard but only to the **coloured line.**

With this type of battery, the acid can only be reached by a miniature hydrometer, which would indicate the state of charge.

Great care should be taken when carrying out these operations not to spill any acid or allow a naked flame near the electrolyte. The mixture of oxygen and hydogen given off by a battery on charge, and to a lesser extent when standing idle, can be dangerously explosive.

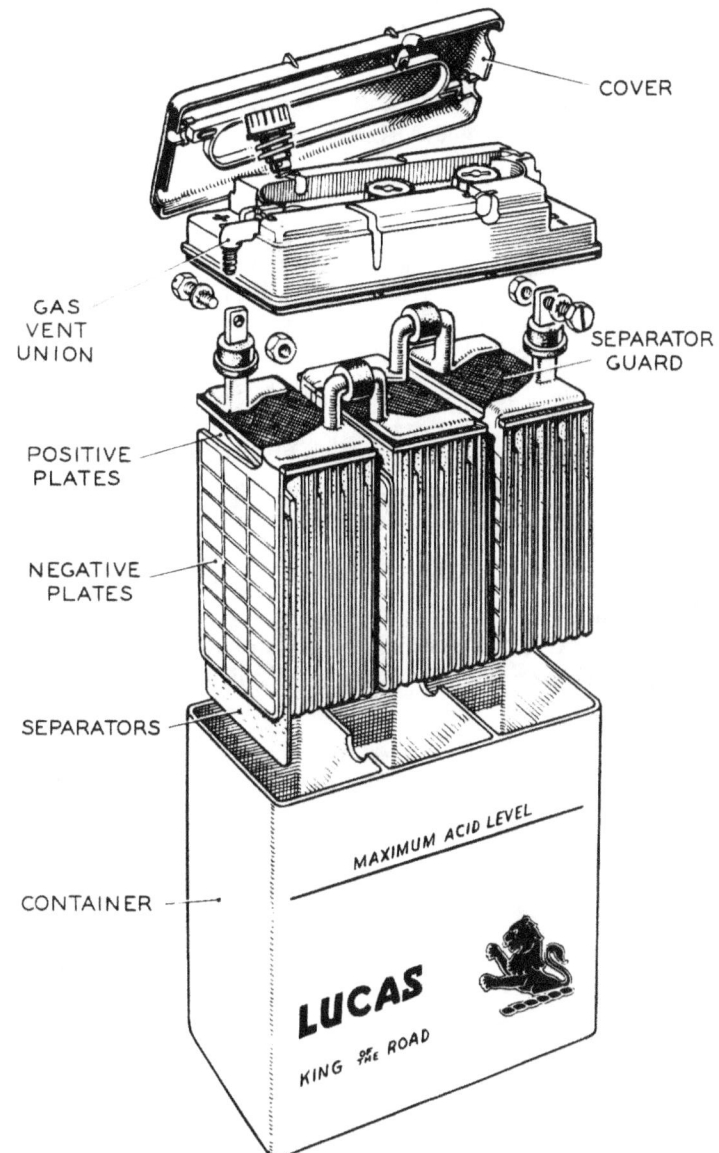

FIG. G.11. *Exploded view of battery.*

The readings obtained from the battery electrolyte should be compared with those given in Table (A). If a battery is suspected to be faulty it is advisable to have it checked by a Lucas Depot or Agent.

A leak—acid battery slowly loses its charge whilst standing—the rate of loss being greater in hot climates. If a battery is not being used, it is important to give it freshing charges at the appropriate recharge rate. These should be given monthly in temperate climates and fortnightly in the tropics.

ELECTRICAL SYSTEM

(A) **Specific Gravity of Electrolyte for filling Batteries MLZ9E and MKZ9E.**

U.K. and climates normally below 80°F. (26.6°C.)		Tropical climates over 80°F. (26.6°C.)	
Filling	Fully charged	Filling	Fully charged
1.260	1.270—1.290	1.210	1.210—1.230

To obtain a specific gravity strength of 1.260 at 60°F. (15.5°C.), add one part by volume of 1.840 specific gravity acid to 3.2 parts of distilled water.

To obtain a specific gravity strength of 1.210 at 60°F. (15.5°C.), add one part by volume of 1.840 specific gravity acid to 4.3 parts of distilled water.

(B) **Maximum Permissible Electrolyte Temperature During Charge.**

Climates normally below 80°F. (27°C.)	Climates between 80—100°F. (27—38°C.)	Climates frequently above 100°F. (38°C.)
100°F. (38°C.)	110°F. 43°C.)	120°F. (49°C.)

Notes.
The specific gravity of the electrolyte varies with the temperature. Fo convenience in comparing specific gravities, they are always corrected to 60°F., which is adopted as a reference temperature. The method of correction is as follows:—

For every 5°F. below 60°F. deduct .020 from the observed reading to obtain the true specific gravity at 60°F. For every 5°F. above 60°F., add .020 to the observed reading to obtain the true specific gravity at 60°F.

The temperature must be indicated by a thermometer having its bulb actually immersed in the electrolyte and not the ambient temperature. To take a temperature reading tilt the battery sideways and then insert the thermometer.

COIL IGNITION SYSTEM

Description.
The coil ignition system comprises two ignition coils and a contact breaker fitted in the timing cover and driven by the idler pinion. The ignition coils are mounted at the rear of the engine one either side of the frame tubes Access to the coils is achieved by removing the side covers (see page D.12). Apart from cleaning the coils in-between the terminals and checking the low-tension and high-tension connections, the coils will not require any other attention. Testing the ignition coils is amply covered in G2, Part C, page G.6, whilst testing the contact breaker is described in G2, Part D.

The best method of approach to a faulty ignition system, is that of first checking the low-tension circuit for continuity as shown in G2, Part A, and then following the procedure laid out in G2, Part B, to locate the fault(s).

Failure to locate a fault in the low-tension circuit indicates that the high-tension circuit or sparking plugs are faulty, and the procedure detailed in G2, Part E, must be followed. Before commencing any of the following tests, however, the contact breaker and sparking plugs must be cleaned and adjusted to eliminate this possible cource of fault.

G2. Part A. Checking the Low-Tension Circuit for Continuity.

To check whether there is a fault in the low-tension circuit and to locate its position, the following tests should be carried out:—

Disconnect and remove the fuel tank (Section E.1) removing the white lead which connects the SW terminals of the left and right ignition coils. Then, with the wiring harness white lead connected to the SW terminal of the left ignition coil only, turn the ignition switch to the IGN position. Slowly crank the engine and at the same time observe the ammeter needle, which should fluctuate between zero and a slight discharge, as the contacts open and close respectively.

Disconnect the wiring harness white lead from the left ignition coil and connect it to the SW terminal of the right ignition coil and then repeat the test. If the ammeter needle does not fluctuate in the described way then a fault in the low-tension circuit is indicated.

First, examine the contact breaker contacts for pitting, piling or presence of oxidation, oil or dirt etc. Clean and ensure that the gap is set correctly to .014—.016 in. (.35—.40 mm.) as described on page B.29.

G2. Part B. Fault Finding in the Low-Tension Circuit.

To trace a fault in the low-tension wiring, turn the ignition switch to IGN position and then crank the engine until both sets of contacts are opened, or alternatively, place a piece of insulating material between both sets of contacts whilst the following test is carried out:—

For this test it is assumed that the fuel tank is removed and the wiring is fully connected as shown in the appropriate wiring diagram, pages G.26–29. With the aid of a D.C. voltmeter and two test-prods (voltmeter 0—10 volts for 6-volt machines, and 0—15 volts for 12-volt electrical systems), make a point to point check along the low-tension circuit starting at the battery and working right through to the ignition coils, stage by stage, in the following manner, referring to the relevant wiring diagram.

NOTE:—On 12-volt machines it will be necessary to disconnect the Zener Diode before the test is carried out. To do this remove the white lead from the Diode centre terminal.

(1) First, establish that the battery is earthed correctly by connecting the voltmeter across the battery negative terminal and the machine frame earth. No voltage reading indicates that the red earthing lead is faulty. Also, a low reading would indicate a poor battery earth connection.

(2) Connect the voltmeter between the left ignition coil (—) terminal and earth and then the right ignition coil (—) terminal and earth the right ignition coil (—) terminal and earth. No voltage reading indicates a breakdown between the battery and the coil (—) terminal, or that the switch connections or ammeter connections are faulty.

(3) Connect the voltmeter between both of the ammeter terminals in turn and earth. No reading on the "feed" side indicates that either the ammeter is faulty or there is a bad connection along the brown and blue lead from the battery, and a reading on the "battery" side only indicates a faulty ammeter.

(4) Connect the voltmeter between ignition switch terminal 12A and earth. No reading indicates that the brown and white lead has faulty connections. Check for voltage at the brown/white lead connections at rectifier, ammeter and lighting switch terminals numbers 2 and 10.

(5) Connect the voltmeter across ignition switch number 13 terminal and earth. No reading indicates that the ignition switch is faulty and should be replaced. Battery voltage reading at this point but not at the ignition coil (—) terminals indicates that the white lead has become "open circuit" or become disconnected.

(6) Disconnect the black/white, and black/yellow leads from the (+) terminals of each ignition coil. Connect the voltmeter across the (+) terminal of the left coil and earth and then the (+) terminal of the right coil and earth. No reading on the voltmeter in either case indicates that the coil primary winding is faulty and a replacement ignition coil should be fitted.

(7) With both sets of contacts open reconnect the ignition coil leads and then connect the voltmeter across both sets of contacts in turn. No reading in either case indicates that there is a faulty connection or the internal insulation has broken down in one of the condensers (capacitors).

If a capacitor is suspected then a substitution should be made and a retest carried out.

(8) Finally, on machines with 12-volt electrical systems, reconnect the Zener Diode white lead and then connect the voltmeter between the Zener Diode centre terminal and earth with ignition "ON"). The voltmeter should read battery volts. If it does not the Zener Diode is faulty and a substitution should be made.

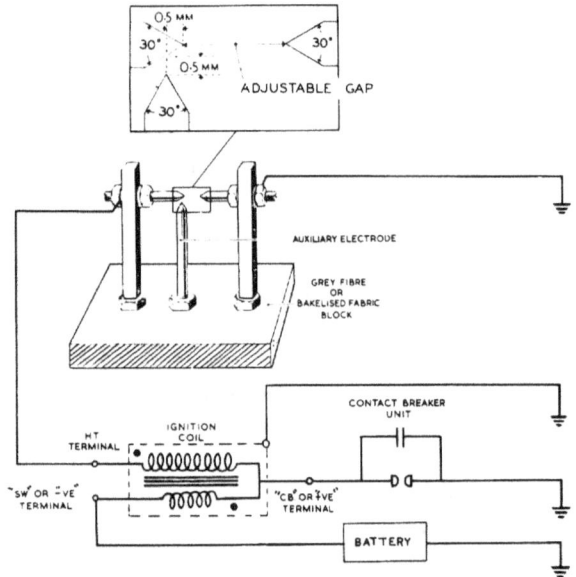

Fig. G.3. *Ignition coil test rig.*

G2. Part C. Ignition Coils.

The ignition coils const of primary and secondary windings wound concentrically about a laminated soft iron core, the secondary winding being next to the core.

The primary winding of the MA6 coil consists of 240 turns and the secondary 17,000—17,600 turns and on the MA12 coil 310 turns and 17,000—17,600 turns respectively of enamel covered wire, the seconday being much finer—also enamel covered. Each layer is paper insulated from the next on both primary and secondary windings.

To test the ignition coil on the machine, first ensure that the low-tension circuit is in order as described in G2, Part A above then disconnect the high-tension leads from the left and right sparking plugs. Turn the ignition switch to the IGN position and crank the engine until the contacts (those with the black/yellow lead from the ignition coil) for the right cylinder are closed. Flick the contact breaker lever open a number of times whilst the high-tension lead from the right ignition coil is held about $\frac{3}{16}$ in. away from the cylinder head. If the ignition coil is in good condition a strong spark should be obtained, if no spark occurs this indicates the ignition coil to be faulty.

Repeat this test for the left high-tension lead and coil by cranking the engine until the contacts with the black/white lead from the left ignition coil are closed.

Before a fault can be attributed to an ignition coil it must be ascertained that the high-tension cables are not cracked or showing signs of deterioration, as this may often be the cause of misfiring etc. It should also be checked that the ignition points are actually making good electrical contact when closed and that the moving contact is insulated from earth (ground) when open. It is advisable to remove the ignition coils and test them by the method described overleaf.

ELECTRICAL SYSTEM

Bench Testing and Ignition Coil.

Connect the ignition coil into the circuit shown in Fig. G.3 and set the adjustable gap to 8 mm. for MA6 coils and 9 mm. for MA12 types. With the contact breaker running at 100 r.p.m. and the coil in good condition, not more than 5% missing should occur at the spark gap over a period of 15 seconds. The primary winding can be checked for short-circuit coils by connecting an ohmeter across the low-tension terminals. The reading obtained should be within the figures quoted below (at 20°C.).

Coil	Primary Resistance	
	Min.	Max.
MA6	1.85 ohms.	2.1 ohms.
MA12	3.0 ohms.	3.4 ohms.

G2. Part D. Contact Breaker.

Faults occurring at the contact breaker are in the main due to, incorrect adjustment of the contacts or the efficiency being impaired by piling, pitting or oxidation of the contacts due to oil etc. Therefore, always ensure that the points are clean and that the gap is adjusted to the correct working clearance as described on page B.29.

To test for a faulty condenser, first turn the ignition switch to IGN position and then take voltage readings across each set of contacts with the contacts open. No reading indicates that the condenser internal insulation has broken down. Should the fault be due to a condenser having a reduction in capacity, indicated by excessive arcing when in use, and overheating of the contact faces, a check should be made by substitution.

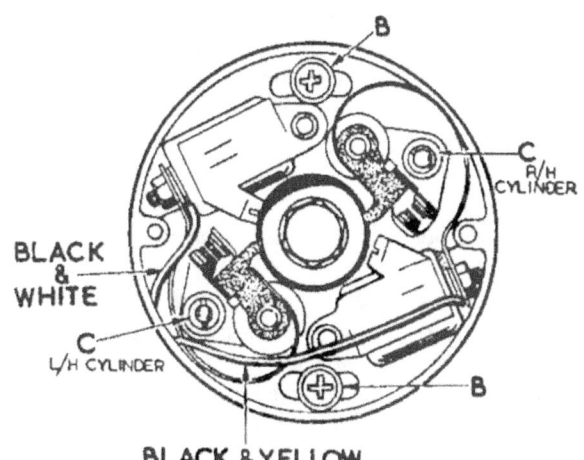

FIG. G.4. *Contact breaker and condenser assembly.*

Particular attention is called to the periodic lubrication procedure for the contact breaker which is given on pages A.11–12. When lubricating the parts ensure that no oil or grease gets on to the contacts.

If it is felt that the contacts require surface grinding then the complete contact breaker unit should be removed as described on page B.29 and the moving contacts disconnected by unscrewing the securing nuts from the condenser terminals. Grinding is best achieved by using a fine carborundum stone or very fine emery cloth, afterwards wiping away any trace of dirt or metal dust with a clean petrol (gasoline) moistened cloth. The contact faces should be slightly domed to ensure point contact. There is no need to remove the pitting from the fixed contact. When refitting the moving contacts do not forget to refit the insulating shields to the condenser terminals and apply a smear of grease to the contact breaker cam and moving contact pivot post. Lubricate the one felt pad.

ELECTRICAL SYSTEM

G2. Part E. Checking the High-Tension Circuit.

If ignition failure or misfiring occurs, and the fault is not in the low-tension circuit, then check the ignition coils as described in Part C. If the coils prove satisfactory, ensure that the high-tension cables are not the cause of the fault.

If a good spark is available at the high-tension cable, then the sparking plug suppressor cap or the sparking plug itself may be the cause of the fault. Clean the sparking plug and adjust the electrodes to the required setting as described on pages G.8–9 below and then retest the engine for running performance. If the fault recurrs then it is likely the suppressor caps are faulty and these should be renewed.

G2. Part F. Checking the Emergency Starting Circuit.

First, ensure that the contact breaker and sparking plug gap settings are satisfactory and then remove the contact breaker cover and place a small piece of insulating card between each set of contacts. Connect a D.C. voltmeter (0—15 volts) with the positive lead to earth and negative lead to the moving contact spring of the front set of contacts. A resistor is not required for this test.

Turn the ignition switch to IGN position. The voltmeter should indicate battery voltage. Repeat the test with the voltmeter negative lead connected to the rear moving contact spring.

Disconnect the green/yellow (green/black on 12-volt models) lead from the alternator (underneath the engine) and connect the voltmeter positive to green/yellow harness lead (green/black on 12-volt) and negative lead to frame. Turn the ignition switch to EMG position. The voltmeter should indicate battery voltage. If it does not the green/yellow lead (green/black on 12-volt) to number 17 ignition switch terminal, and black/white lead connecting ignition coil (+) terminal to ignition switch terminal number 15 should be checked. Reconnect alternator lead.

Finally, disconnect the battery, and then connect an A.C. voltmeter (0—15 volts) between the front moving contact spring and frame. With ignition switch in EMG position (both contacts still insulated with card) attempt to kickstart the engine. The A.C. voltmeter should deflect to about 7 to 10 volts. If it does not, the alternator should be checked as shown in Section G4, Part B, page G.12.

SPARKING PLUGS

It is recommended that the sparking plugs be inspected, cleaned and tested every 5,000 miles (4,800 km.) and new ones fitted every 10,000 miles (9,600 km.).

To remove the sparking plugs a box spanner (13/16 in. — 19.5 mm. — across flats) should be used and if any difficulty is encountered a small amount of penetrating oil should be placed at the base of the sparking plug and time allowed for penetration. When removing the sparking plugs identify each plug with the cylinder from which it was removed so that any faults on examination can be traced back to the cylinder concerned.

Due to certain features of engine design the sparking plugs will probably show slightly differing deposits and colouring characteristics.

Next examine the plugs for signs of petrol (gasoline) fouling. This is indicated by a dry, sooty, black deposit which is usually caused by over-rich carburation, although ignition system defects such as a discharged battery, faulty contact breaker, coil or condenser defects, or a broken or worn out cable may be additional causes. For this purpose it is recommended that any adjustments to carburation etc., which may be carried out to gain the required colour characteristics should always be referred to the left cylinder.

Examine both plugs for signs of oil fouling. This will be indicated by a wet, shiny, black deposit on the central insulator. This is caused by excessive oil in the combustion chamber during combustion and indicates that the piston rings or cylinder bores are worn.

ELECTRICAL SYSTEM

To rectify this type of fault the above mentioned items should be checked with special attention given to carburation system. Again, the left plug should be used as the indicator. The right plug will almost always have a darker characteristic.

Over-heating of the sparking plug electrodes is indicated by severely eroded electrodes and a white, burned or blistered insulator. This type of fault can be caused by weak carburation or over advanced ignition timing, although plugs which have been operating whilst not being screwed down sufficiently can easily become over-heated due to heat that is normally dissipated through to the cylinder head not having an adequate conducting path. Over-heating is normally symptomised by pre-ignition, short plug life, and "pinking" which can ultimately result in piston crown failure. Unnecessary damage can result from over-tightening the plugs. To achieve a good seal between the plug and cylinder head, screw the plug in by hand on to its gasket, then lightly tighten with a box spanner.

FIG. G.5. *Sparking plug diagnosis*.

A plug of the correct grade will bear a light flaky deposit on the outer rim and earth electrode, and these and the base of the insulator will be light chocolate brown in colour. A correct choice of plug is marked (A). (B) shows a plug which appears bleached, with a deposit like cigarette ash; this is too "hot-running" for the performance of the engine and a cooler-running type should be substituted.

A plug which has been running too "cold" and has not reached the self-cleaning temperature is shown at (C). This has oil on the base of the insulator and electrodes, and should be replaced by a plug that will burn off deposits and remove the possibility of a short-circuit. The plug marked (D) is heavily sooted, indicating that the mixture has been too rich, and a further carburation check should be made. At illustration (E) is seen a plug which is completely worn out and in need of replacement.

To clean the plugs it is preferable to make use of a properly designed proprietary plug cleaner. The makers instructions for using the cleaner should be followed carefully.

When the plugs have been carefully cleaned, examine the central insulators for cracking and the centre electrode for excessive wear. In such cases the plugs have completed their useful life and new ones should be fitted.

Finally, before refitting the sparking plugs the electrodes should be adjusted to the correct gap setting of .025 in. (.635 mm.). Before refitting sparking plugs the threads should be cleaned by means of a wire brush and a minute amount of graphite grease smeared on to the threads. This will prevent any possibility of thread seizure occurring.

If the ignition timing and carburation settings are correct and the plugs have been correctly fitted, but over-heating still occurs then it is possible that carburation is being adversely affected by an air leak between the carburettor, manifold and the cylinder head. This possibility must be checked thoroughly before taking any further action. When it is certain that none of the above mentioned faults are the cause of over-heating then the plug type and grade should be considered.

Normally the type of plugs quoted in GENERAL DATA are satisfactory for general use of the machine, but in special isolated cases, conditions may demand a plug of a different heat range. Advice is readily available to solve these problems from the plug manufacturer who should be consulted.

NOTE:—If the machine is of the type fitted with an air filter or cleaner and this has been removed it will affect the carburation of the machine.

CHARGING SYSTEM

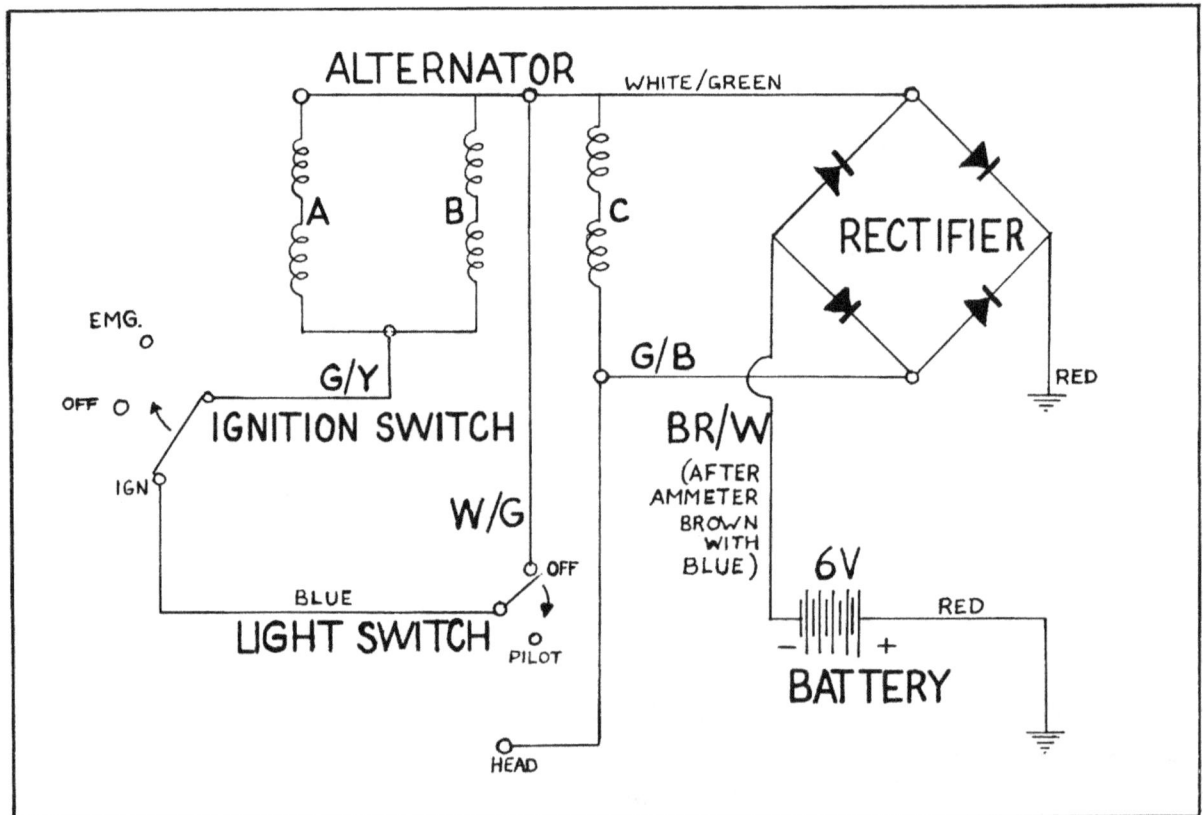

Fig. G.6. *Schematic illustration of 6-volt charging circuit.*

Description.

The charging current is supplied by the alternator, but due to the characteristics of alternating current the battery cannot be charged direct from the alternator. To convert the alternating current to direct current a full wave bridge rectifier is connected into the circuit. However, it is not satisfactory to have just this arrangement for battery charging, due to the varying applied load on the alternator, i.e. lights, state-of-charge of battery, etc. Hence to overcome the problem of variations in load, the output from the alternator has to be governed to meet requirements. This is achieved by interconnecting the generating coils and switch terminals as shown in the diagram above in Fig. G.6. With the lighting switch in OFF position the coils (A) and (B) are short-circuited and flux induced interacts with the rotor flux maintaining minimum output. With the switch in PILOT position the coils (A) and (B) are open-circuited and the flux interaction is thereby reduced causing coil (C) to give increased "medium" output. With the switch in HEAD position the coils (A), (B) and (C) are connected in parallel, giving maximum output.

On models with a 12-volt electrical system and Zener Diode charge control, the alternator leads are connected differently in the low output connection (i.e. lighting switch in OFF position). The alternator gives "medium" output for the lighting switch in both the OFF and PILOT positions, the four coils (B) and (C) being permanently connected across the rectifier. Switching to HEAD position connects the two remaining coils (A). (See Fig. G.7.) Excessive charge is absorbed by the Zener Diode which is connected across the battery. To ensure that back-leakage does not occur, the Zener Diode is connected to the battery, through the ignition switch so that there is no possibility of the battery discharging through the Diode. Always ensure that the ignition switch is in the OFF position whilst the machine is not in use.

To locate a fault in the charging circuit, first check the charging rate in the three switch position as shown in Part A. Proceed then to test the alternator as described in Part B. If the alternator is satisfactory, the fault must lie in the charging circuit, hence the rectifier must be checked as given in Part C, and then the wiring and connections as shown in Part D.

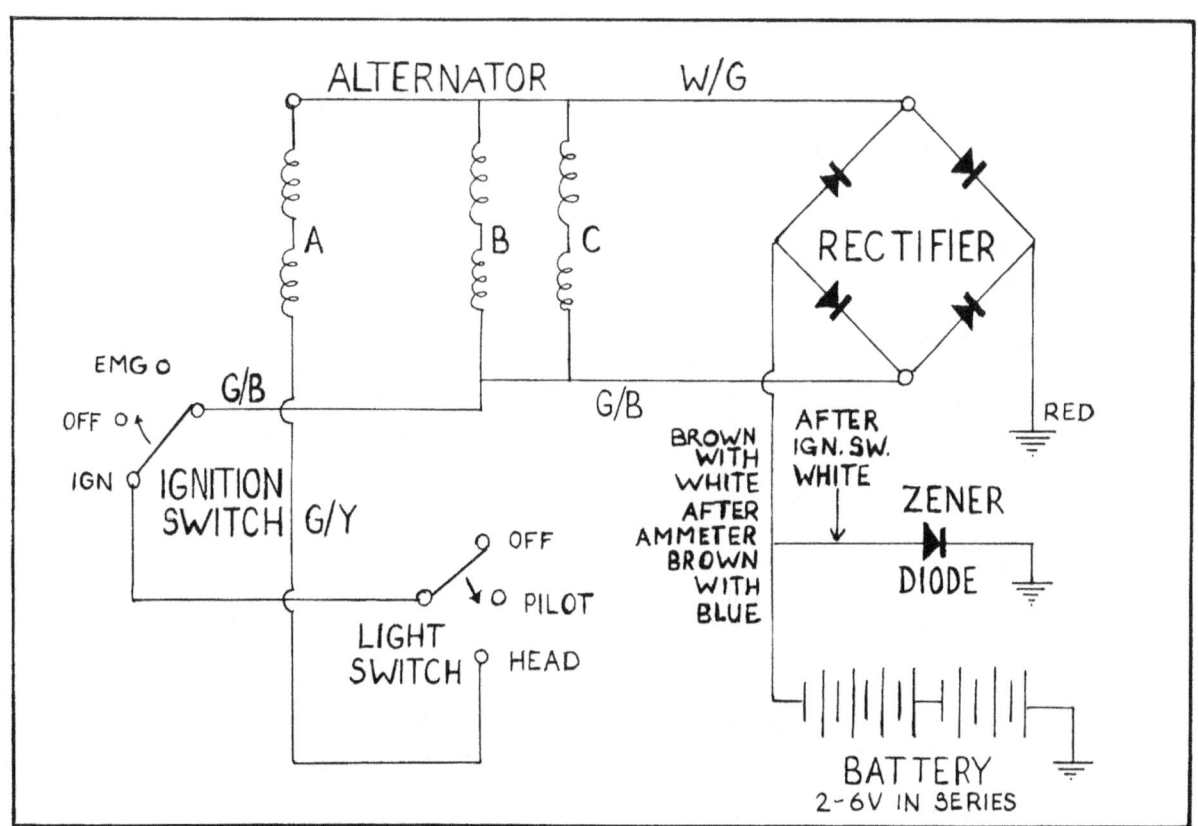

FIG. G.7. *Schematic illustration of 12-volt charging circuit.*

G4. Part A. Checking the D.C. Input to Battery.

For this test the battery must be in good condition and a good state of charge, therefore before conducting the test ensure that the battery is up to the required standard, or alternatively fit a good replacement battery.

Connect D.C. ammeter (0—15 amp.) in series between the battery main lead (brown/blue) and battery negative terminal and then start the engine and run it at approximately 3,000 r.p.m. (equivalent to 45 m.p.h. in top gear).

NOTE:—Ensure that the ammeter is well insulated from the surrounding earth points otherwise a short-circuit may occur.

Operate the lighting switch and observe the ammeter readings, for each position of the switch. The observed figures should not be less than those tabulated in Fig. G.18 for the particular model. If the readings are equal to or higher than those given, then the alternator and charging circuit are satisfactory. If the readings are lower than those quoted, then the alternator must be tested as described in Part B below.

G4. Part B. Checking the Alternator Output.

Disconnect the three alternator output cables underneath the engine and run the engine at 3,000 r.p.m. (equivalent to 45 m.p.h. in top gear).

Connect an A.C. voltmeter (0—15 volts) with 1-ohm load resistor in parallel with each of the alternator leads in turn as shown in the Table, Fig. G.18, and observe the voltmeter readings. A suitable 1-ohm load resistor can be made from a piece of nichrome wire as shown in Section G4, Part E, page G.15.

From the results obtained, the following deductions can be made:—

(1) If the readings are all equal to or higher than those quoted for the particular model then the alternator is satisfactory.

(2) A low reading on any group of coils indicates either that the leads concerned are chafed or damaged due to rubbing on the chains or that some turns of the coils are short-circuited.

(3) Low readings for all parts of the test indicates either that the green/white lead has become chafed or damaged due to rubbing on the chain(s) or that the rotor has become partially demagnetized. If the latter case applies, check that this has not been caused by a faulty rectifier or that the battery is of correct polarity, and only then fit a new rotor.

(4) A zero reading for any group of coils indicates that a coil has become disconnected, is open-circuit, or is earthed.

(5) A reading obtained between any one lead and earth indicates that coil windings or connections have become earthed.

If any of the above mentioned faults occur, always check the stator leads for possible chain damage before attempting repairs or renewing the stator.

It is beyond the scope of this manual to give instruction for the repair of faulty stator windings. However, the winding specification is given in the Table, Fig. G.18 for those obliged to attempt repair work.

G4. Part C. Rectifier Maintenance and Testing.

The silicon bridge rectifier requires no maintenance beyond checking that the connections are clean and tight, and that the nut securing the rectifier to the frame is tight. It should always be kept clean and dry to ensure good cooling, and spilt oil washed off immediately with hot water.

NOTE:—The nuts clamping the rectifier plates together must not be disturbed or slackened in any way.

ELECTRICAL SYSTEM

When tightening the rectifier securing nut, hold the spanners as shown in Fig. G.8, for if the plates are twisted, the internal connections will be broken. Note that the circles marked on the fixing bolt and nut indicate that the thread form is ¼ in. U.N.F.

FIG. G.8. *Refitting the rectifier.*

Testing the Rectifier.
To test the rectifier, first disconnect the brown/white lead from the rectifier centre terminal and insulate the end of the lead to prevent any possibility of a short-circuit occurring, and then connect a D.C. voltmeter (with 1-ohm load resistor in parallel) between the rectifier centre terminal and earth.

Disconnect the alternator green/yellow lead (green/black on 12-volt) and reconnect to rectifier green/black terminal (green/yellow on 12 volt) by means of a jumper lead.

NOTE:—Voltmeter positive terminal to frame earth (ground) and negative terminal to centre terminal on rectifier.

Ensure that all the temporary connections are well insulated to prevent a short-circuit occurring then turn the ignition switch to IGN position and start the engine.

With the engine running at approximately 3,000 r.p.m. (approximately 45 m.p.h. in top gear) observe the voltmeter readings. The reading obtained should be at least 7.5-volt minimum on 12-volt and 6-volt machines.

(1) If the reading is equal to or slightly greater than that quoted, then the rectifier elements in the forward direction are satisfactory.
(2) If the reading is excessively higher than the figures given, then check the rectifier earthing bolt connection. If the connection is good then a replacement rectifier should be fitted.
(3) If the reading is lower than the figures quoted or zero readings are obtained, then the rectifier or the charging circuit wiring is faulty and the rectifier should be disconnected and bench tested so that the fault can be located.

Note that all of the above conclusions assume that alternator A.C. output figures were satisfactory. Any fault at the alternator will, of course, reflect on the rectifier test results. Similarly any fault in the charging circuit wiring may indicate that the rectifier is faulty. The best method of locating a fault is to disconnect the rectifier and bench test it as shown below.

Bench Testing the Rectifier.
For this test the rectifier should be disconnected and removed. Before removing the rectifier, disconnect the leads from the battery terminals to avoid the possibility of a short-circuit occurring.

Connect the rectifier to a fully charged 12-volt battery of approximately 50 ampere/hours capacity at the 10 hour rate, and 1-ohm load resistor, and then connect the D.C. voltmeter in the V2 position, as shown in Fig. G.9.

Note the battery voltage (should be 12-volt) and then connect the voltmeter in V1 position whilst the following tests are conducted.

ELECTRICAL SYSTEM

FIG. G.9. *Rectifier (showing terminal connections for bench tests 1 and 2).*

A voltmeter in position V1 will measure the volt drop across the rectifier plate. In position V2 it will measure the supply voltage to check that it is the recommended 12-volts on load.

In Fig. G.11, the rectifier terminal markings (1), (2) and (3) are as shown physically in Figs. G.9 and G.10, while terminal (4) represents the rectifier centre bolt. (1) and (3) are the A.C. input terminals while (2) and (4) are the D.C. output terminals (—ve and +ve respectively).

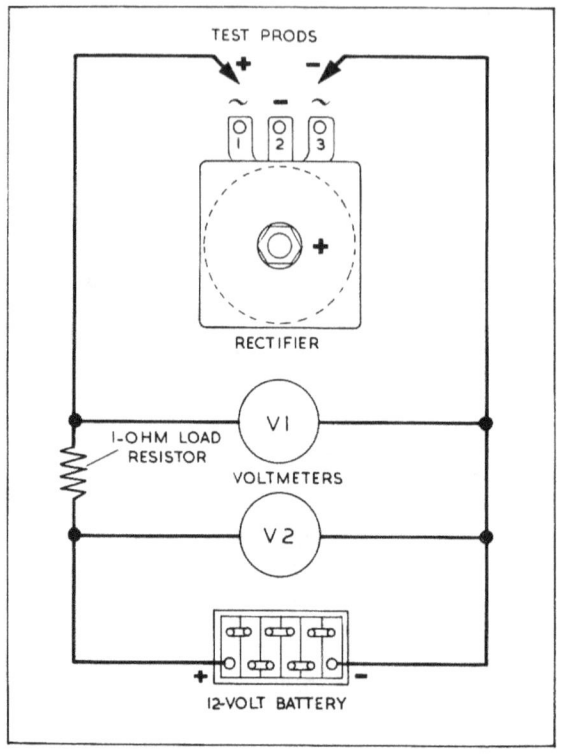

FIG. G.10. *Bench testing the rectifier.*

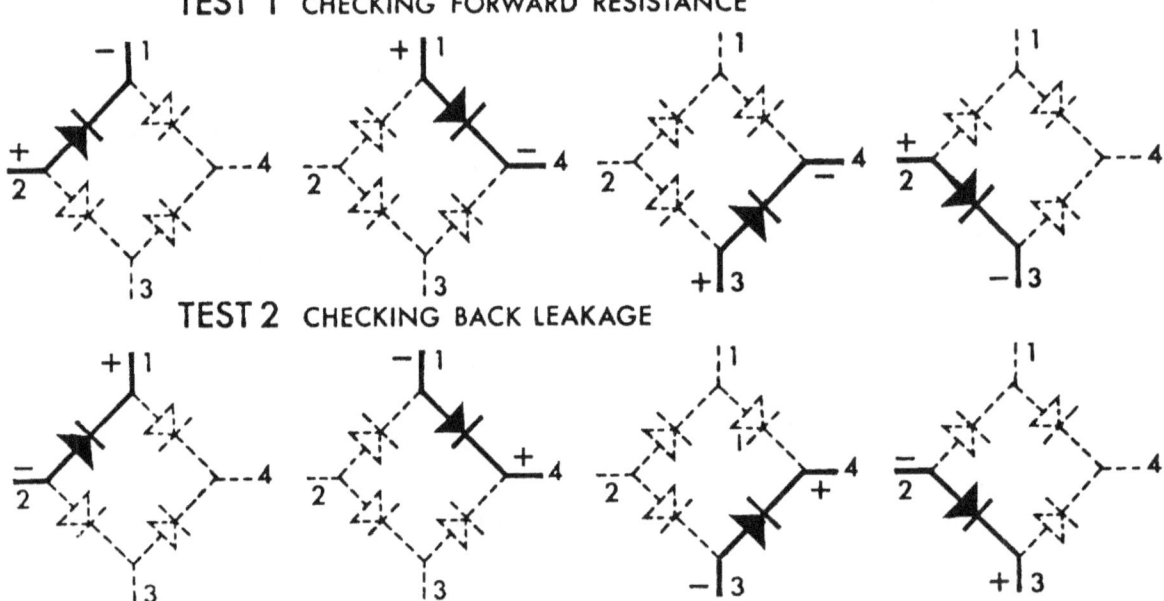

FIG. G.11. *Rectifier test sequence for checking forward resistance and back leakage.*

A5065 ELECTRICAL SYSTEM G15

Test 1. With the test leads, make the following connectings but keep the testing time as short as possible to avoid overheating the rectifier cell: (*a*) 1 and 2, (*b*) 1 and 4, (*c*) 3 and 4, (*d*) 3 and 2. Each reading should not be greater then 2.5-volts with the battery polarity as shown.

Test 2. Reverse the leads or battery polarity and repeat Test 1. The reading obtained should not be more than 1.5-volts below battery voltage (V_2), i.e. 10.5-volts minimum.

If the readings obtained are not within the figures given, then the rectifier internal connections are shorting or aged and the rectifier should be renewed.

G4. Part D. Checking the Charging Circuit for Continuity.

These three tests utilise the machines own battery to test for continuity or breakdown in the A.C. section of the charging system.

For this series of tests, the battery must be in a good state of charge and the **alternator leads must be disconnected** at the snap-connectors underneath the engine, so that there is no possibility of demagnetizing the rotor.

(1) First, check that there is voltage at the rectifier centre terminal by connecting a D.C. voltmeter, with 1-ohm load resistor in parallel, between the rectifier centre terminal and earth, remember (+ve) positive earth (ground). The voltmeter should read battery volts. If it does not, there is a faulty connection in the wiring and test (1), (3) and (4) in G2, Part B should be carried out to locate the fault.

(2) *This test does not apply to machines with 12-volt systems.*
Connect the green/yellow lead from the wiring harness (underneath the engine) to the rectifier centre terminal lead (brown/white), by means of a jumper lead, and turn the ignition switch to IGN position. Connect a D.C. voltmeter with load resistor in parallel between the white/green lead at the rectifier and earth (frame). With the lighting switch at OFF position, the voltmeter should read battery volts. If it does not the leads to ignition switch terminals 17 and 18 should be checked and also the leads to lighting switch terminals 4 and 5 must be checked.

(3) Connect the green/yellow lead (green/black lead for 12-volt system) from the wiring harness (underneath the engine) to the rectifier centre terminal, by means of a jumper lead, as in Test (2). Turn the ignition switch to IGN position and the lighting switch to HEAD position, and connect a D.C. voltmeter (with 1-ohm resistor in parallel) between green/black lead (green/yellow lead on 12-volt models) at rectifier (from harness on 12-volt models) and earth. The voltmeter should read battery voltage. If it does not, the leads to ignition switch terminals 17 and 18 should be checked and the leads to the lighting switch terminals 5 and 7 should also be checked. With the lighting switch in PILOT position no reading should be obtained between green/black (green/yellow on 12-volt models) and earth or green/white and earth at the rectifier.

G4. Part E. Constructing a 1-ohm Load Resistor.

The resistor used in the following tests must be accurate and constructed so that it will not overheat otherwise the correct values of current or voltage will not be obtained.

A suitable resistor can be made from 4 yards (3¾ metres) of 18 s.w.g. (.048 in., i.e. 1.2 mm., diameter) Nichrome wire by bending it into two equal parts and calibrating it as follows:—

(1) Fix a heavy gauge flexible lead to the folded end of the wire and connect this lead to the positive terminal of a 6-volt battery.

(2) Connect a D.C. voltmeter (0—10 volts) across the battery terminals and an ammeter (0—10 amp.) between the battery negative terminal and the free ends of the wire resistance, using a crocodile clip to make the connection.

(3) Move the clip along the wires, making contact with both wires until the ammeter reading is numerically equal to the number of volts shown in the voltmeter. The resistance is then 1-ohm. Cut the wire at this point, twist the the two ends together and wind the wire on an asbestos former approximately 2 in. (5 cm.) diameter so that each turn does not contact the one next to it.

ZENER DIODE CHARGE CONTROL

(12 volt machines only)

Description.

The Zener Diode output regulating system which uses four coils of the six-coil alternator connected permanently across the rectifier, provides automatic control of the charging current. It will only operate successfully on a 12-volt system where it is connected in parallel with the battery as shown in the wiring diagram, page G.26. The Diode is connected through the ignition switch to prevent any leakage when the motorcycle is not in use.

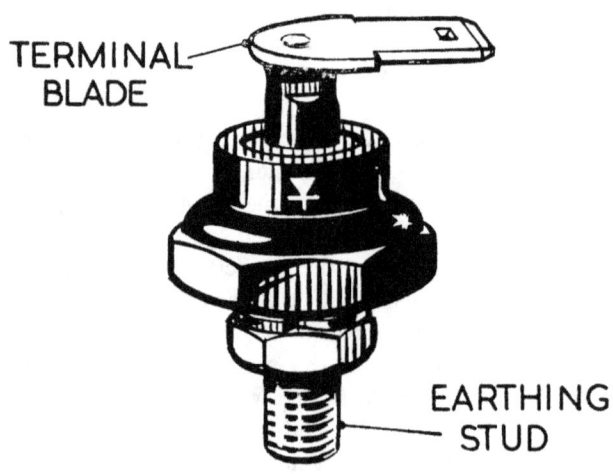

Fig. G.12. *Zener Diode.*

Assuming the battery is in a low state of charge its terminal voltage (the same voltage is across the Diode) will also be low, therefore the maximum charging current will flow into the battery from the alternator. At first none of the current is by-passed by the Diode because of it being non-conducting due to the low battery terminal volts. However, as the battery is quickly restored to a full state of charge, the system voltage rises until at 14 volts the Zener Diode becomes partially conducting, thereby providing an alternative path for a small part of the charging current. Small increases in battery voltage result in large increases in Zener conductivity until, at approximately 15 volts about 5 amperes of the alternator output is by-passing the battery. The battery will continue to receive only a portion of the alternator output as long as the system voltage is relatively high.

Depression of the system voltage, due to the use of headlamp or other lighting equipment, causes the Zener Diode current to decrease and the balance to be diverted and consumed by the component in use.

If the electrical loading is sufficient to cause the system voltage to fall to 14 volts, the Zener Diode will revert to a high resistance state of non-conductivity and the full generated output will go to meet the demands of the battery.

The Zener Diode is however unable to absorb the full output of the alternator. It is therefore necessary to retain some form of charge control through the lighting switch. This is achieved by permanently connecting four charging coils across the rectifier (white/green — green/yellow) and bringing in the other two coils (green/black) in the lighting switch headlamp position (Fig. G.7).

Maintenance.

The Zener Diode is mounted on an aluminium heat sink with an area of approximately 25 sq. in. Providing the Diode and the heat sink are kept clean, and provided with an adequate airflow, to ensure maximum efficiency, no maintenance will be necessary.

Checking Performance of Zener Diode.

The following procedure enables the Zener Diode to be tested on the machine. Only suitably calibrated first-grade moving coil instruments should be used.

(1) Withdraw the white cable from the Zener Diode terminal blade.

(2) Connect a suitable ammeter between the end of the cable removed and the Zener Diode terminal blade, using a suitable jumper lead.
N.B.—The ammeter positive terminal must be connected to the Zener Diode.

(3) Connect a suitable voltmeter between the Zener Diode terminal blade and the heat sink.
N.B.—The voltmeter positive terminal must be connected to the heat sink.

(4) Check that all lights are switched off.

(5) Start the engine and gradually increase the speed while observing both meters:
   (a) Up to 13.0 volts, the ammeter must indicate zero current. If any current is indicated below 13.0 volts, a replacement Zener Diode must be fitted.

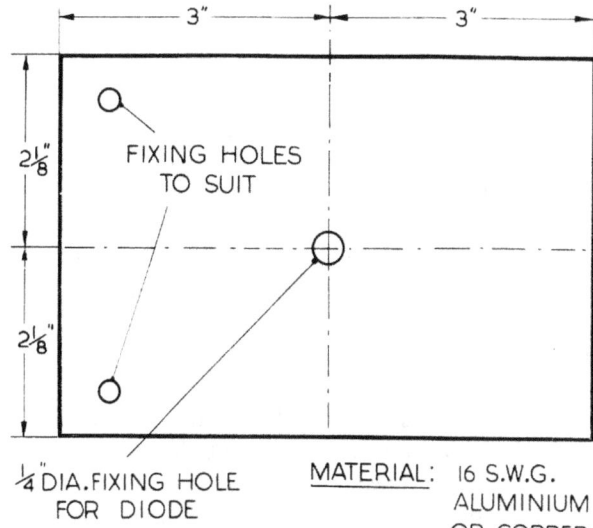

Fig. G.13. *Zener Diode heat sink.*

   (b) At a voltage between 13.5 and 15.3, the ammeter must indicate a current of 1.0 amperes. If a voltage higher than 15.3 is required before the ammeter will indicate 1.0 amperes, a replacement Zener Diode must be fitted.

(6) Disconnect the battery while the engine is still running and carry out the remaining check as quickly as possible to avoid overheating of the Zener Diode.
   (a) Slowly increase the engine speed.
   (b) At a voltage between 12.0 and 15.0, the ammeter must indicate a current of 5.0 amperes. If this current is not indicated between the voltage limits specified, a replacement Zener Diode must be fitted.

G18 ELECTRICAL SYSTEM A5065

A.C. IGNITION (E.T.) AND LIGHTING SYSTEMS

Description.

The A.C. magneto (energy transfer) system consists of two 3E.T. ignition coils, a contact breaker and an alternator specially wound for A.C. ignition and lighting. There are five leads from the alternator, two for ignition purposes and three for direct lighting purposes. The circuit diagram, on page G.27 illustrates the stator coil connections.

The main features of the A.C. ignition system for twin cylinder machines is that the ignition coil and contact breaker points are connected in parallel. In practice this means that when the contacts are closed the generated current flows from the alternator through the first set of contacts and then via earth through the second set, and so back to the alternator. When one set of contacts opens the current has to pass through an ignition coil primary winding and via earth through the second set of contacts which are arranged to be closed at the same instant. From this is can be seen that the availablity of a spark at either cylinder is dependent upon both contacts being clean and adjusted correctly (see Fig. G.14).

Another feature is that the energy transfer system operates on a rising current in the ignition coil primary winding and not falling primary current as in the conventional coil ignition system.

G6. Part A. A.C. Ignition.

The accurate and efficient working of the A.C. ignition system is dependent not only upon the piston/spark relationship that is involved but also the rotor/stator relationship at the instant of ignition. The stator is fixed to the left crankcase and requires no maintenance other than to check that the leads are not rubbing on either of the chains.

The rotor is located on the crankshaft by means of a dowel fitted to the timing disc. When the rotor is removed care should be taken to refit it in the appropriate position with the rotor hole located as shown in the Table below, in accordance with ignition timing requirements.

Dowel Location	Ignition Timing Full Advanced	Dowel Remarks
S	34° B.T.C.	500 c.c.
R	37° B.T.C.	650 c.c.

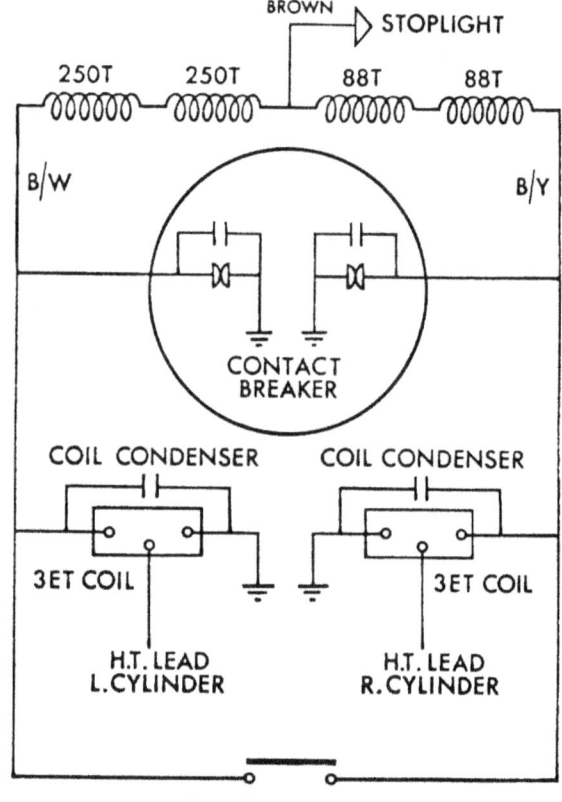

FIG. G.14.

The 3E.T. coil, condensers (capacitors), and high-tension leads must be kept clean and free from dirt or water. Also it is important that the sparking plug is maintained at the correct gap setting and that the centre electrode is kept clean.

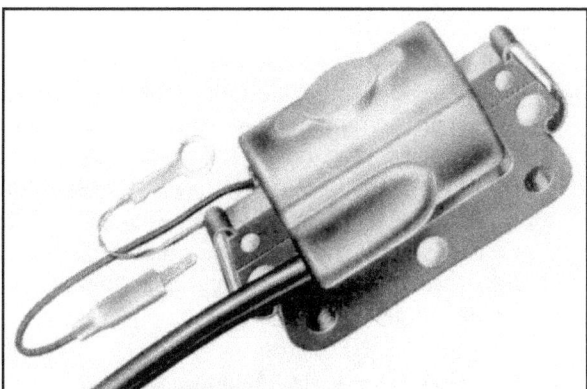

Fig. G.15.

Both sets of contact breaker contacts must be kept clean and adjusted correctly to the gap setting given in GENERAL DATA. A fault at either set of contacts will adversely affect the ignition spark at **both** cyclinders.

G6. Part B. Testing the A.C. Ignition System.

First, ensure that the timing, contact breaker and plug gaps are satisfactory, and then disconnect both high-tension leads and check that a spark is available by holding each of the cables about $\frac{3}{16}$ in. (4 mm.) from the cylinder head in turn and operate the kickstarter. A good spark should be produced. If it is not, then the 3ET coil and alternator ignition supply are suspect.

As it is not possible to test the 3ET coils accurately on the machine, the following test procedure should be adopted.

Two 6-volt external batteries are used for the next two tests, in conjunction with the A.C. ignition coils on the machine.

A.C. ignition coils are not designed to run under such conditions.

So, to prevent overheating occurring in the primary windings, **each test should be undertaken in as short a time as possible, and the batteries connected in circuit only when actually necessary to run the test.**

(1) Disconnect the five alternator leads under the engine.
(2) Unplug the black/yellow lead from the condenser at the right-hand side coil (under the petrol/gasolene tank).
(3) Connect the black/yellow lead to the positive (+ve) terminal of a 6-volt test battery.
(4) Connect the negative (—ve) battery lead to the condenser terminal.
(5) Unplug the black/white lead from the condenser at the left-hand side coil (under the petrol/gasolene tank).
(6) Connect the black/white lead to the positive (+ve) terminal of a second 6-volt test battery.
(7) Connect the negative (—ve) terminal of the second test battery to the left-hand condenser terminal.
(8) Remove the sparking plug wire from each plug in turn and with battery wires connected, open and close the contact breaker points. If the coils and condensers are satisfactory, a good spark will jump from the plug lead to earth (ground).
(9) If a poor spark (or no spark) is noted, check all wiring connections, and repeat (8) above. If the system still does not spark, instal new condensers and repeat (8). If still there is no spark, check the ignition coils by substitution.

G6. Part C. Checking the Alternator Output (A.C. Ignition Models).

To facilitate a check to be made on the alternator output, a separate ignition circuit must be used as given in Section G6, Part B above, so that the engine can be run at 3,000 r.p.m. (approximately 45 m.p.h. in top gear).

Pay careful regard to the warning given in the previous Section G6, Part B, concerning the possible overheating of the A.C. ignition coil primary windings.

The preferred alternative method is to use two MA6 ignition coils, bolted together, with the machines contact breaker leads, black/white, black/yellow connected to the (+ve) terminals on the test ignition coils. The test coil (—ve) terminals are linked together and fed to a test battery (—ve) negative terminal and the battery (+ve) positive connected to the ignition coils cases. A jumper lead is also required between battery (+ve) positive, and motorcycle frame earth (ground). The high-tension leads are connected to the appropriate sparking plugs.

With all five alternator leads disconnected under the engine start up the engine and run at 3,000 r.p.m. (equivalent to approximately 45 m.p.h. in top gear). Connect an A.C. voltmeter (0—10 volts) with a 1-ohm resistor in parallel between the pairs of alternator leads given in Table, Fig. G.18, page G.24.

(1) If the readings are equal to or higher than the figures quoted for the particular model, then the alternator is satisfactory.

(2) A low reading on any group of coils indicates either that the leads concerned are chafed through or damaged due to rubbing on the chains or that some of the coil turns are short-circuited.

(3) Low readings from all parts of the test indicates a partially demagnetized rotor. In this case the rotor must be renewed.

(4) A zero reading for any group of coils indicates that a coil has become disconnected and is open-circuit, in which case the stator should be replaced.

(5) A reading obtained between any one stator lead and earth (ground) indicates that some coil turns have become earthed (grounded) to the engine.

In this case, brush the stator with paraffin (kerosene) or petrol (gasoline). **Do not leave to soak.** Re-test on the machine. If still faulty, replace the stator.

If any fault does occur always check the stator leads for possible chain damage before attempting repair or renewing the stator. It is beyond the scope of this manual to give instruction for repair of faulty stator windings. However the winding specification is given in Table, Fig. G.18 to provide the required information for local repair work, should a correct replacement stator not be immediately available.

G6. Part D. Direct Lighting System.
The electrical power for the direct lighting system is supplied by three of the five alternator leads, namely the red, brown and brown/blue.

The leads are connected as shown in the wiring diagram (page G.27). In order that no one pair of coils is overloaded, the electrical loads are connected as shown and no deviation from the standard arrangement shown should be made.

An apparent loss or reduction of power at any of the lights may well be due to a high resistance caused by a loose or faulty connection. In the event of a fault occurring, always check the wiring connections, giving particular attention to the red earth (ground) lead from the alternator and headlamp. Note that a short-circuit in the brown stop lamp lead will result in the ignition system failing, hence the stop lamp switch connections should be always kept clean and dry.

In the event of a fault occurring which cannot be traced to the circuit connections the alternator should be checked as described in Section G6, Part C, page G.19.

ELECTRIC HORN

(Models 6H and 8H)

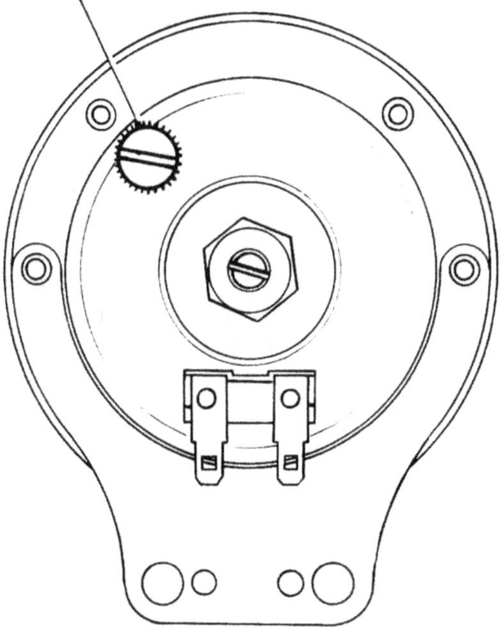

Description.
The horn is of a high frequency single-note type and is operated by direct current from the battery. (On A.C. models a similar horn specifically designed for A.C. current is fitted.) The method of operation is that of a magnetically operated armature, which impacts on the cone face, and causes the tone disc of the horn to vibrate. The magnetic circuit is made self-interrupting by contacts which can be adjusted externally.

If the horn fails to work, check the mounting bolts etc., and horn connection wiring. Check the battery for state of charge. A low supply voltage at the horn will adversely effect horn performance. If the above checks are made and the fault is not remedied, then adjust the horn as follows.

Horn Adjustment.
When adjusting and testing the horn do not depress the horn push for more than a fraction of a second or the circuit wiring may be overloaded.

A small serrated adjustment screw situated near the terminals (see Fig. G.16) is provided to take up wear in the internal moving parts of the horn. To adjust, turn this screw anti-clockwise until the horn just fails to sound, and then turn it back (clockwise) about one-quarter to half a turn.

FIG. G.16. *Horn adjustment screw.*

ELECTRICAL SYSTEM

HEADLAMP

Description.

The headlamp is of the pre-focus bulb light unit type and access is gained to the bulb and bulb holder by withdrawing the rim and light unit assembly. To do this slacken the screw at the top of the headlamp shell just behind and adjacent to the rim and prise off the rim and light unit assembly.

The bulb can be removed by first pressing the cylindrical cap inwards and turning it anti-clockwise. The cap can then be withdrawn and the bulb is free to be removed.

When fitting a new bulb, note that it locates by means of a cut-away and projection arrangement. Also note that the cap can only be replaced one way, the tabs being staggered to prevent incorrect reassembly. Check the replacement bulb voltage and wattage specification and type before fitting.

Focussing with this type of unit is unnecessary and there is no provision for such.

Beam Adjustments.

The beam must in all cases be adjusted as specified by local lighting regulations. In the United Kingdom the Transport Lighting Regulations reads as follows:—

> A lighting system must be arranged so that it can give a light which is incapable of dazzling any person standing on the same horizontal plane as the vehicle at a greater distance than twenty-five feet from the lamp, whose eye level is not less than three feet—six inches above that plane.

The headlamp must therefore be set so that the main beam is directed straight ahead and parallel with the road when the motorcycle is fully loaded. To achieve this, place the machine on a level road pointing towards a wall at a distance of 25 feet away, with a rider and passenger, on the machine, slacken the two small screws on the adaptor rim at either side and tilt the beam unit until the beam is focused at approximately two feet six inches from the base of the wall. Do not forget that the headlamp should be on "full beam" lighting during this operation.

TAIL AND STOP LAMP UNIT

Access to the bulbs in the tail and stop lamp unit is achieved by unscrewing the two slotted screws which secure the lens. The bulb is of the double filament offset pin type and when a replacement is carried out, ensure that the bulb is fitted correctly. Check that the two supply leads are connected correctly and check the earth (ground) lead to the bulb holder is in satisfactory condition.

When refitting the lens, do not overtighten the fixing screws or the lens may fracture as a result.

A5065 ELECTRICAL SYSTEM G23

ADDITIONAL INFORMATION

Alternator Model RM19 Having Stator Part No. 47162 (B.S.A. Nos. 19-8018 & 19-8019).

Fitted to A50 and A65 Star; Cyclone; Cyclone Clubman; Rocket; Lightning; Lightning Rocket and Clubman; Thunderbolt Rocket models.

Number of coils ... 6
Winding per coil ... 140 turns of 22 S.W.G.

D.C. output into lead-acid battery whose terminal voltage is maintained at 6.0—6.5 volts with alternator rotor driven at:—

2,000 rev./min. ... 7.5 amp. (min.)

5,000 rev./min. ... 10.0 amp. (max.)

N.B.—Above test requires green/yellow and green/black cables to be connected to one rectifier A.C. input terminal, and white/green cable to the other.

Energy Transfer Ignition Coil Model 3E.T. Part Nos. 45149 & 45150 (B.S.A. Nos. 19-1711 & 19-1746).

Number of turns on primary winding   160—165

Number of turns on secondary winding   12,000—12,500

Resistance of primary winding ...   0.45—0.55 ohm.

Contact Breaker Unit Model 4CA Part Nos. 47583 & 47612.

Part number 47583 is fitted to coil ignition machines and 47612 to energy transfer ignition machines. Both carry centrifugally operated timing advance mechanisms, the tests for which are as follows:—

47583 (B.S.A. Nos. 19-8113 & 19-8112).

(1) Set rotary spark gap to spark at zero degrees at less than 100 rev./min.
(2) Run contact breaker unit at 18,00 rev./min. Advance to be between $10\frac{1}{2}°$—$12\frac{1}{2}°$.
(3) Decelerate and check at the following speeds.

REV/MIN.	DEGREES
1,700	10—$12\frac{1}{2}$
1,300	8—$10\frac{1}{2}$
800	$1\frac{1}{2}$—$4\frac{1}{2}$

No advance to occur below 450 rev./min.

Lucas part number of control springs—54413020.

47612 (B.S.A. Nos. 19-8113 & 19-8111).

(1) Set rotary spark gap to spark at zero degrees at less than 100 rev./min.
(2) Run contact breaker unit at 1,750 rev./min. Advance to between 4°—6°.
(3) Decelerate and check at the following speeds.

REV/MIN.	DEGREES
1,200	6 (max.)
850	4—6
600	0—3
500	0—$1\frac{1}{2}$

No advance to occur below 375 rev./min.

Lucas part number of control springs—54415641.

ELECTRICAL SYSTEM

ALTERNATOR AND STATOR DETAILS—SPECIFICATIONS AND OUTPUT FIGURES

MODELS	SYSTEM VOLTAGE	IGNITION TYPE	ALTERNATOR MODEL	STATOR NUMBER
A50 and A65 (various)	12-volt	Coil	RM.19	47162
	6-volt			
A50 Cyclone Competition, A65 Spitfire Hornet	6-volt	A.C. IGN	RM.19	47197

FIG. G.17. *Electrical system details.*

STATOR NO.	SYSTEM VOLTAGE	D.C. INPUT TO BATTERY AMP. AT 3,000 R.P.M.			ALTERNATOR OUTPUT MINIMUM A.C. VOLTS AT 3,000 R.P.M.			STATOR COIL DETAILS		
		OFF	PILOT	HEAD Mainbeam	A	B	C	NO. OF COILS	TURNS PER COIL	S.W.G.
47162	6-volt	2.75	2.0	2.0	4.0	6.5	8.5	6	140	22
	12-volt	2.0*	2.1*	1.5*						
		4.8†	3.8†	1.8†						
47188	6-volt	Not applicable			5.0	2.0	5.0	*1	215	25—Ign.
								2	122	21—Lights
								3	88	20—lights
								4	98	21—Lights

Coil Ignition Machines.
A—White/green and green/black
B—White/green green/yellow
C—White/green and green/black—green/yellow connected.

A.C. Ignition Machines
A—Red and brown/blue
B—Black/yellow and black/white
C—Black/yellow and brown

*Zener in circuit
†Zener disconnected
‡With boost switch in circuit

*
1 Ignition
2 Stop lamp
3⎫
4⎭ Connected in series for other lighting
See also page G.23.

FIG. G.18. *Alternator—minimum output and stator details.*

ELECTRICAL SYSTEM

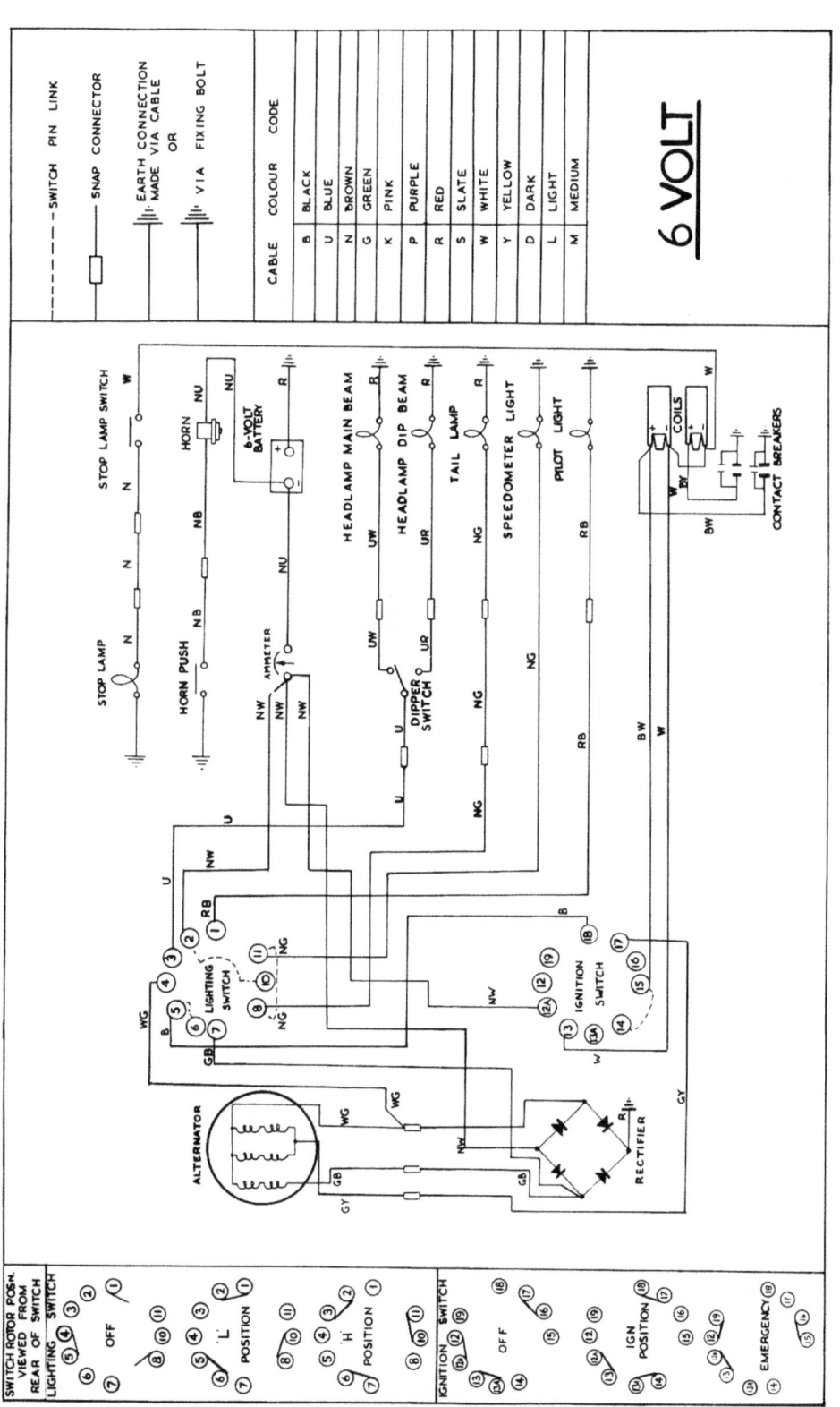

Fig. G.19. *Wiring diagram models A50 and A65.*

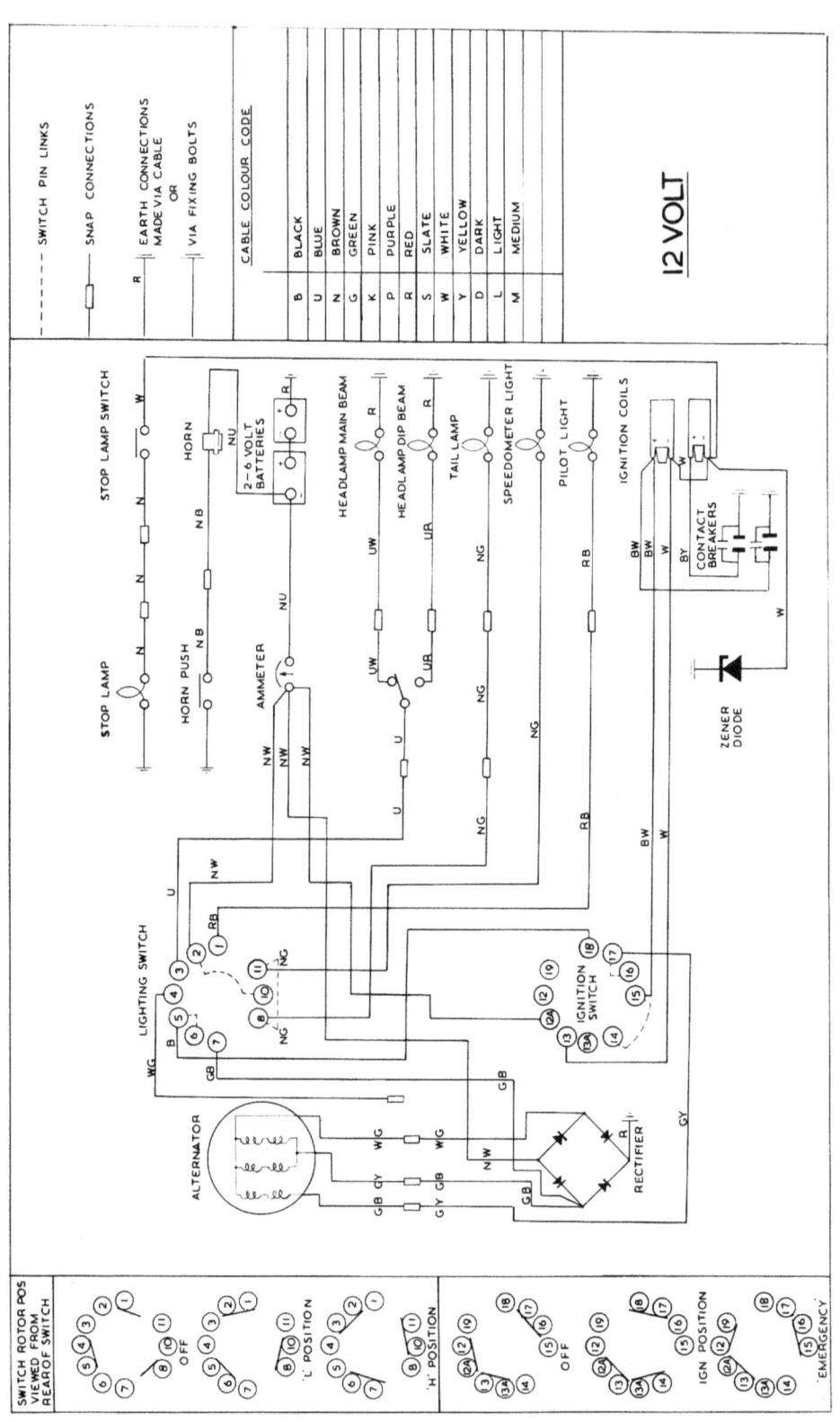

Fig. G.20. *Wiring diagram model A65 only.*

ELECTRICAL SYSTEM

MODELS A50 CYCLONE COMPETITION AND A65 SPITFIRE HORNET

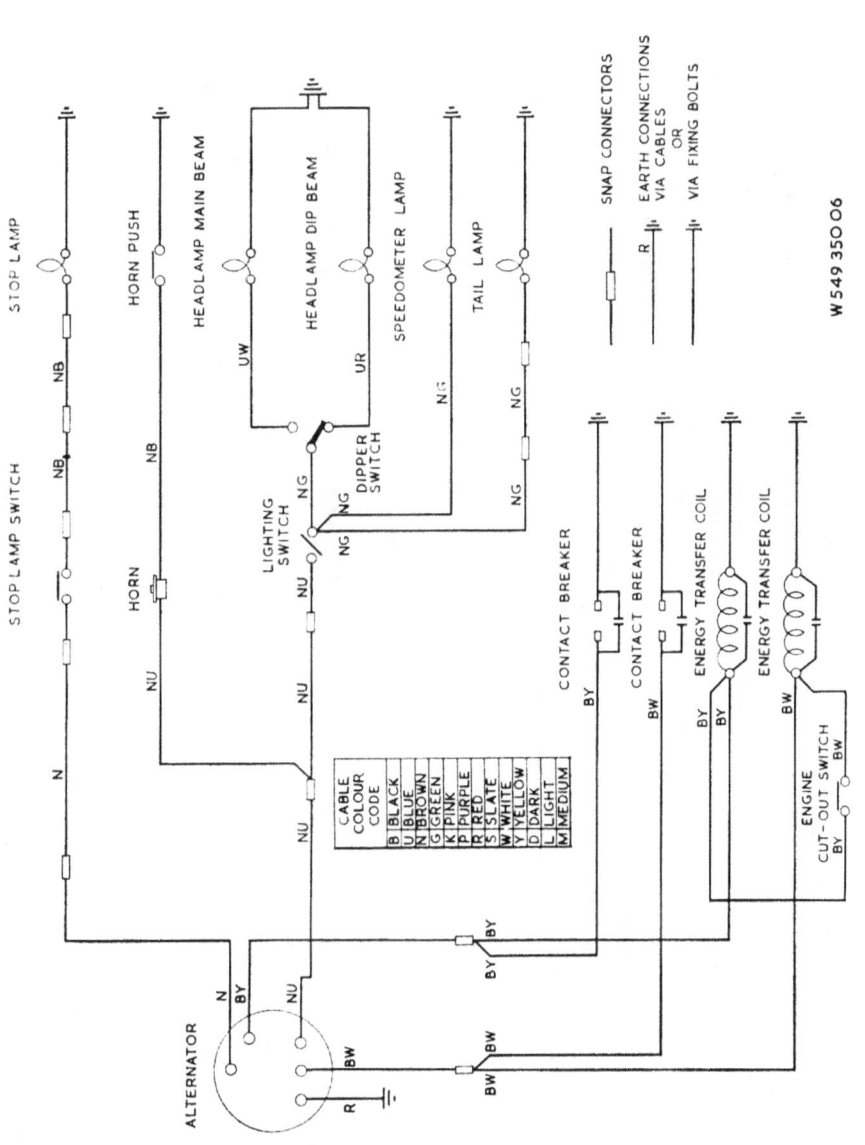

Fig. G.21. *Wiring diagram for "energy transfer" ignition system, with lighting circuit shown for use when required.*

G28 ELECTRICAL SYSTEM A5065

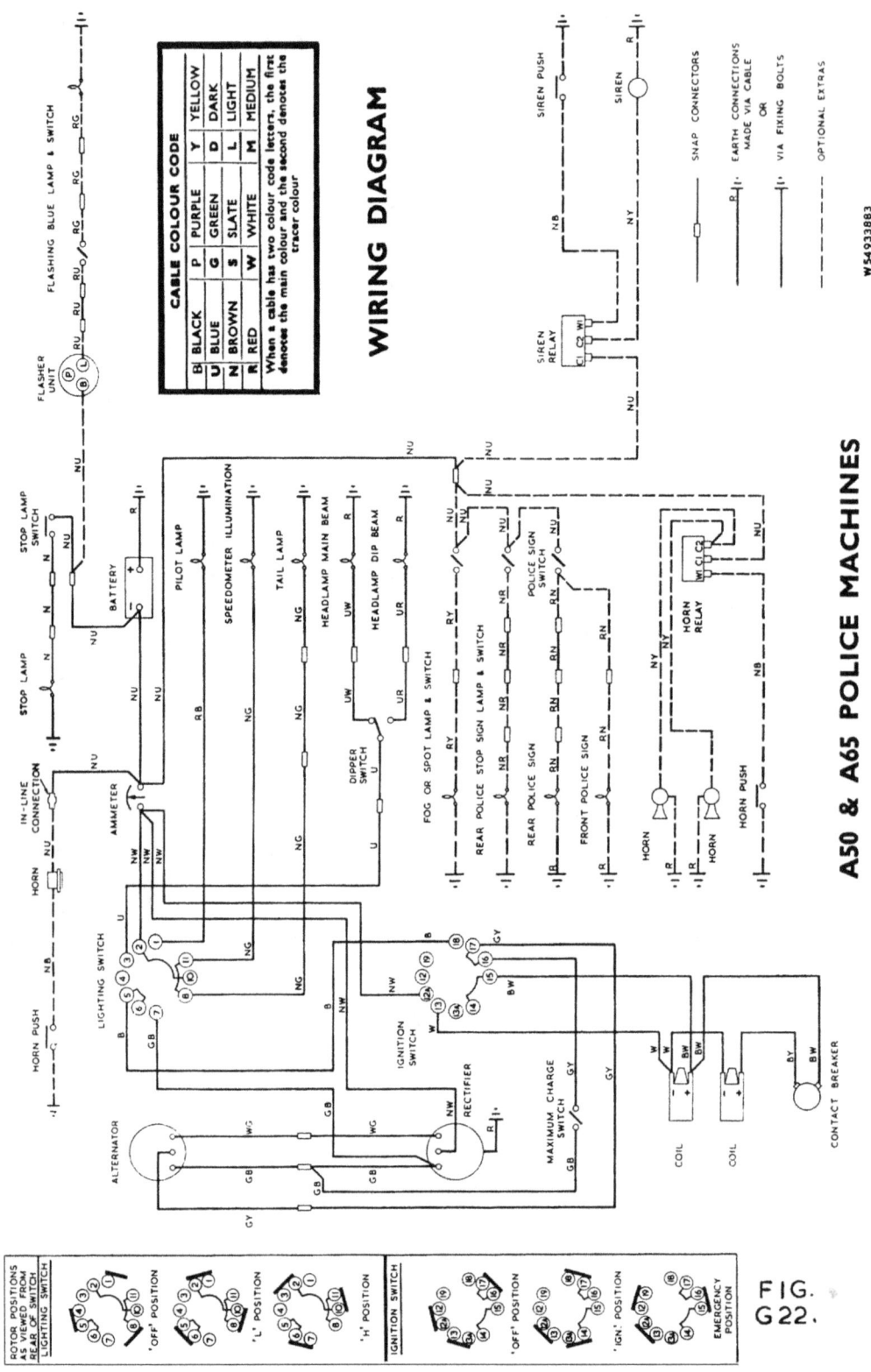

FIG. G22.

SERVICE TOOLS

INDEX

	Page
ENGINE	H.2–5
TRANSMISSION	H.6
FRONT FORKS	H.7–8

SERVICE TOOLS

ENGINE

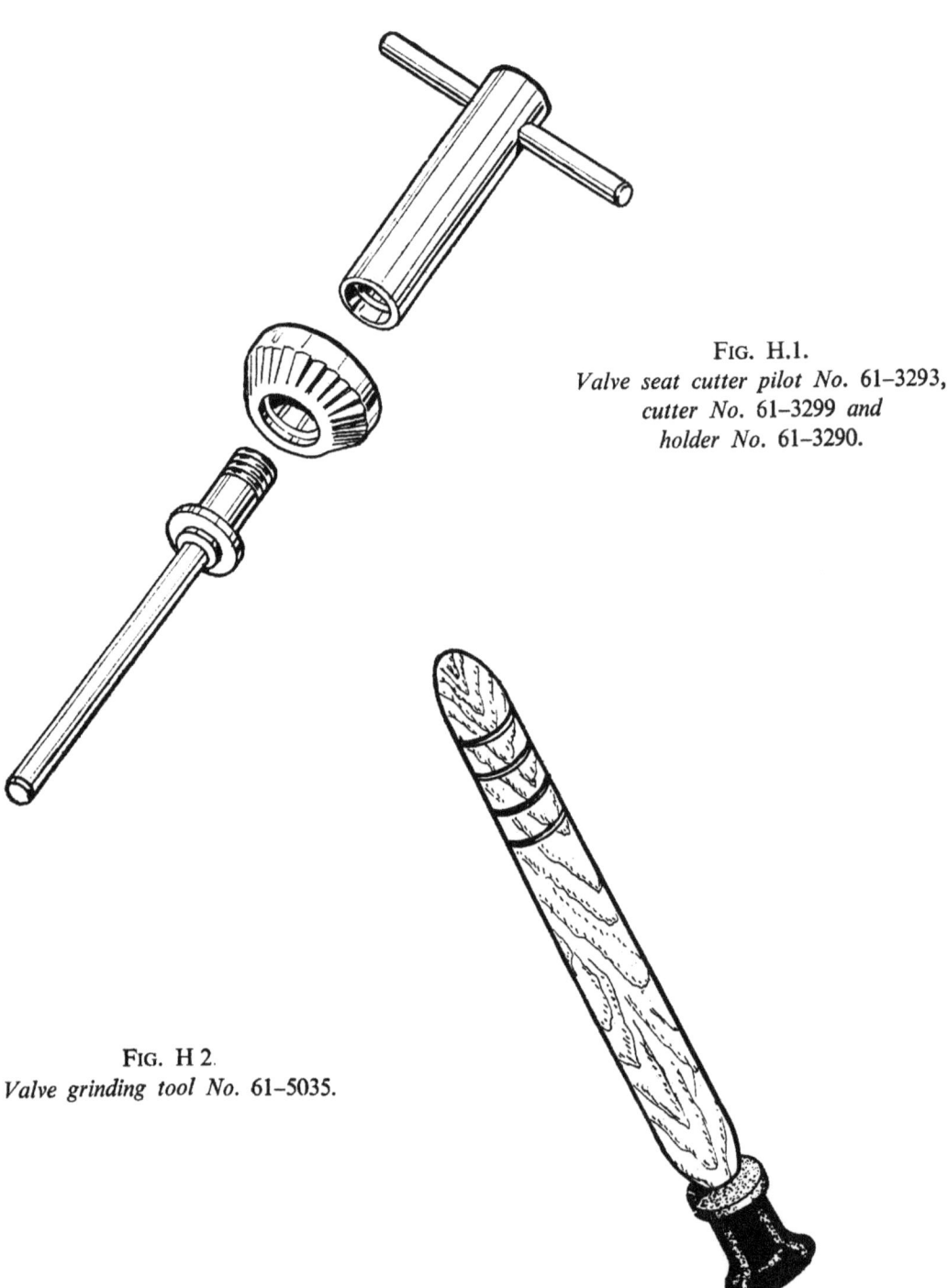

Fig. H.1.
Valve seat cutter pilot No. 61-3293, cutter No. 61-3299 and holder No. 61-3290.

Fig. H.2.
Valve grinding tool No. 61-5035.

SERVICE TOOLS

ENGINE

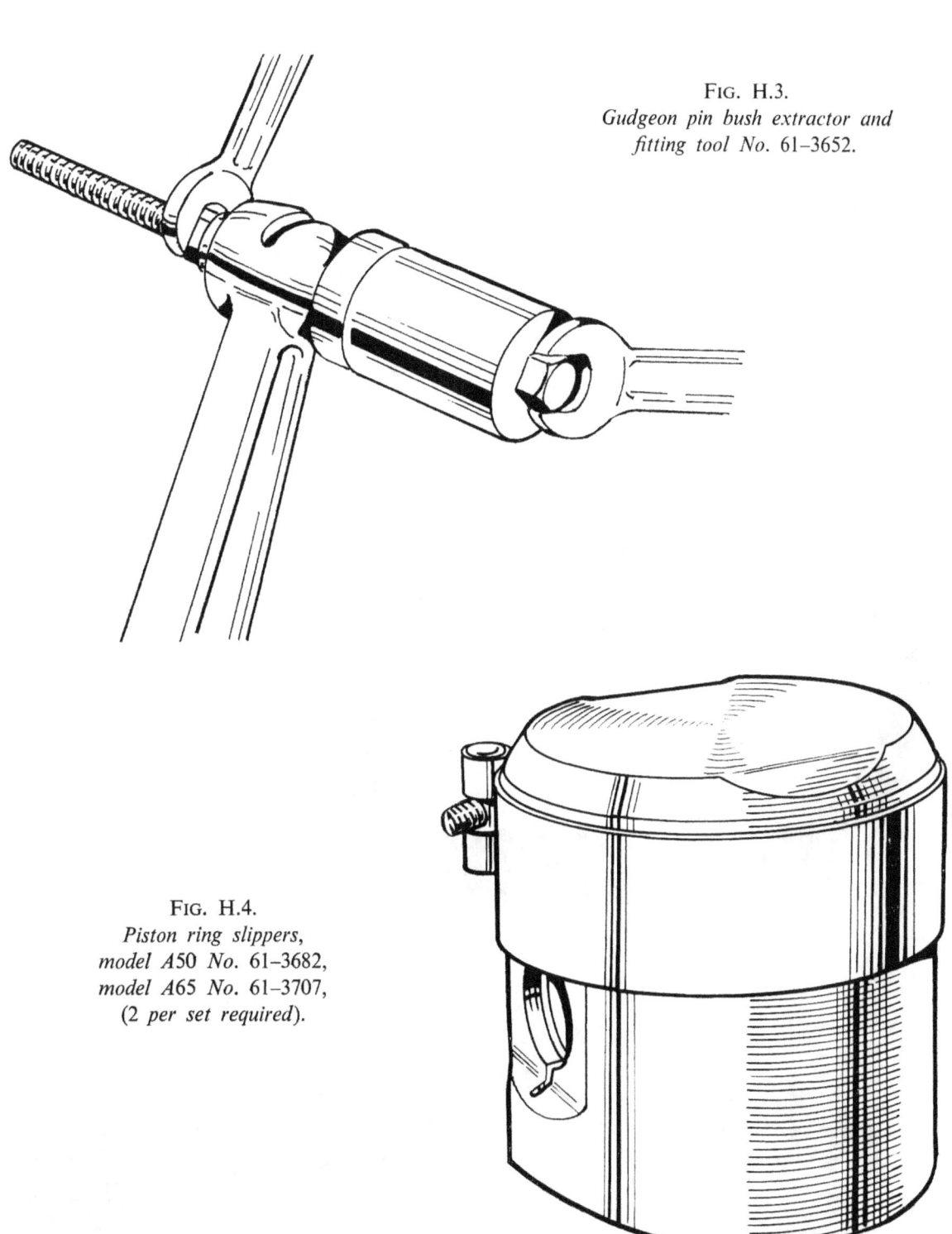

Fig. H.3.
Gudgeon pin bush extractor and fitting tool No. 61–3652.

Fig. H.4.
*Piston ring slippers,
model A50 No. 61–3682,
model A65 No. 61–3707,
(2 per set required).*

H4   SERVICE TOOLS   A5065

ENGINE

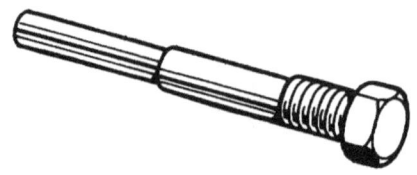

Fig. H.5.
*Contact breaker cam extractor
No. 61-5005.*

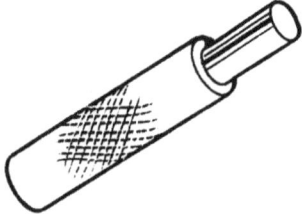

Fig. H.6.
*Valve guide fitting and extracting
punch No. 61-3382.*

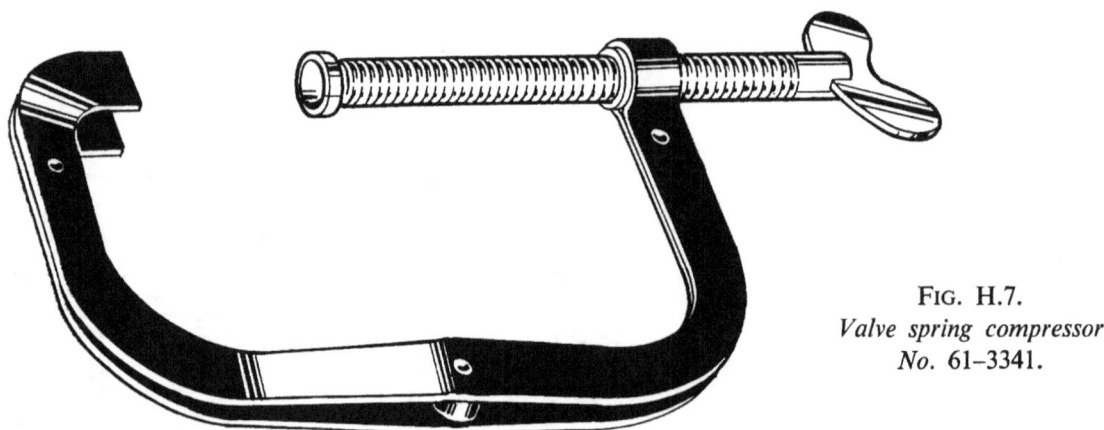

Fig. H.7.
*Valve spring compressor
No. 61-3341.*

Fig. H.8.
*Tappet circlip fitting tool
No. 61-3702.*

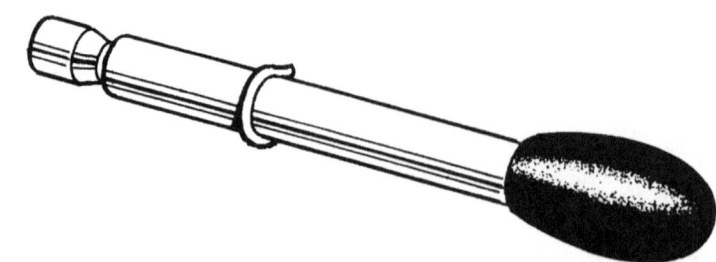

ENGINE

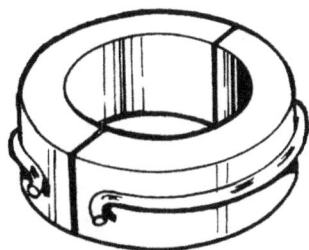

Fig. H.9.
*Crankshaft balance weights
(2 per set),*
No. 61–3710 (650 c.c. models),
No. 61–3711 (500 c.c. models).

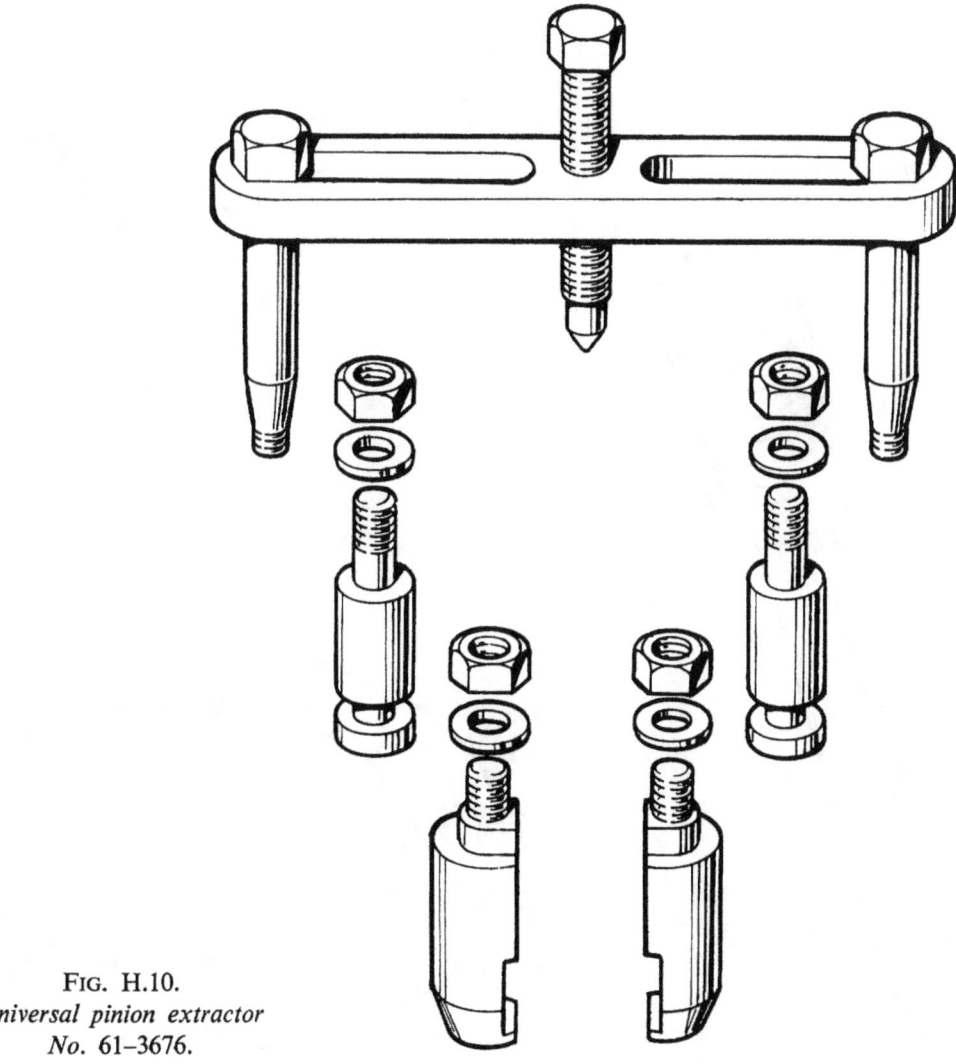

Fig. H.10.
Universal pinion extractor
No. 61–3676.

SERVICE TOOLS

TRANSMISSION

FIG. H.11.
*Clutch sleeve extractor
No. 61–1912.*

FIG. H.12.
*Camshaft bush extractor
No. 61–3159.*

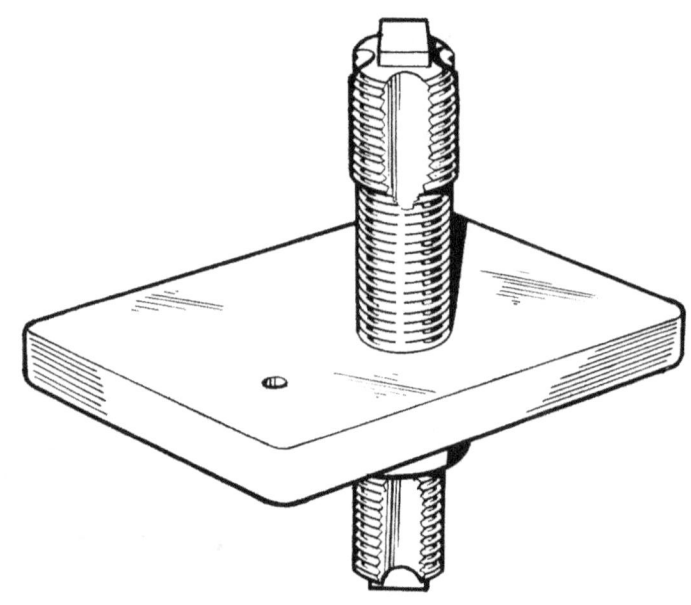

FIG. H.13.
*Clutch nut screwdriver
No. 61–3700.*

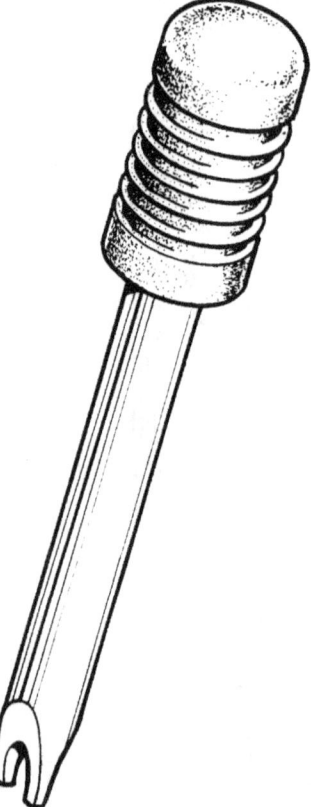

FIG. H.14.
*Clutch locking tool
No. 61–3760.*

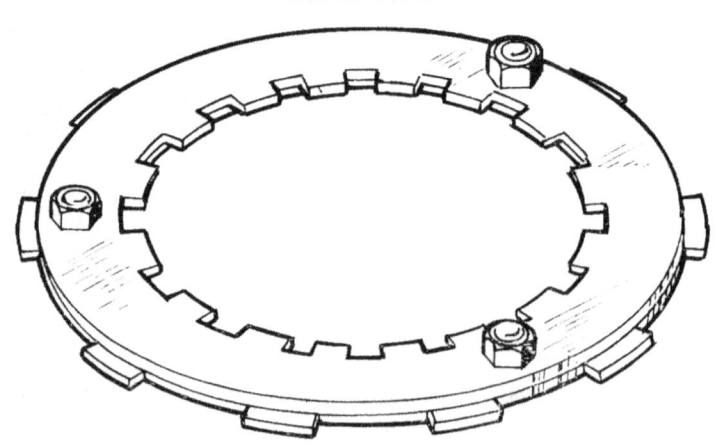

SERVICE TOOLS

FRONT FORKS

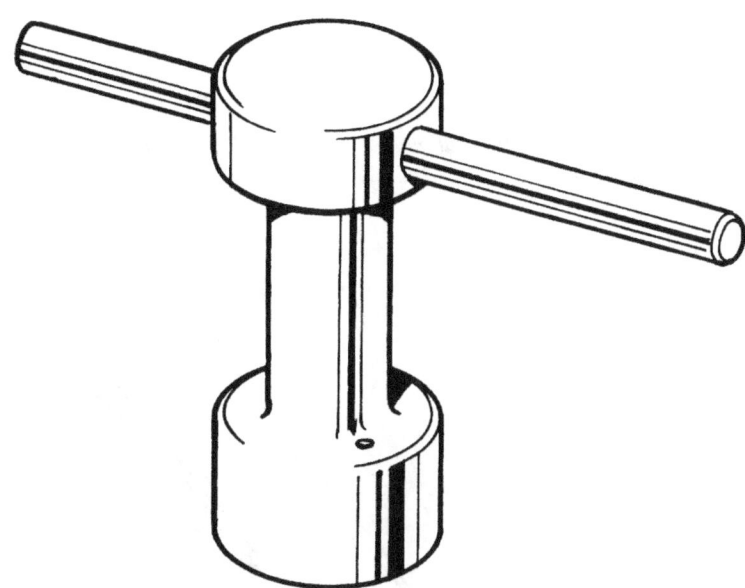

FIG. H.15.
*Steering head adjuster tool
No. 61-3008.*

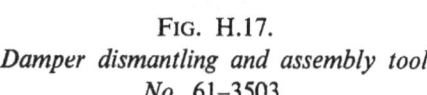

FIG. H.17.
*Damper dismantling and assembly tool
No. 61-3503.*

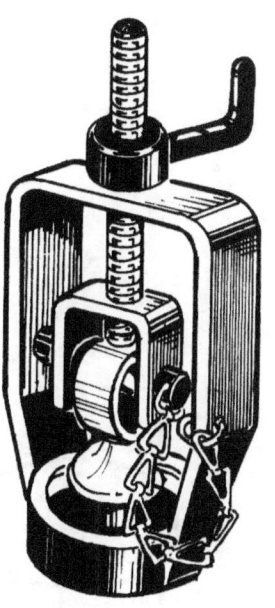

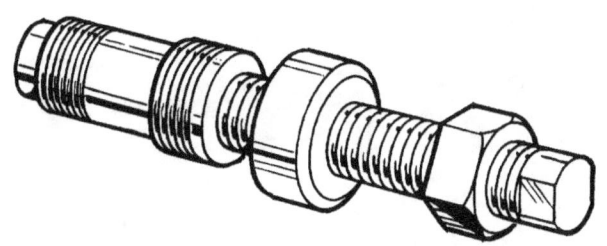

FIG. H.16.
*Fork leg fitting and removal tool
No. 61-3350.*

FRONT FORKS

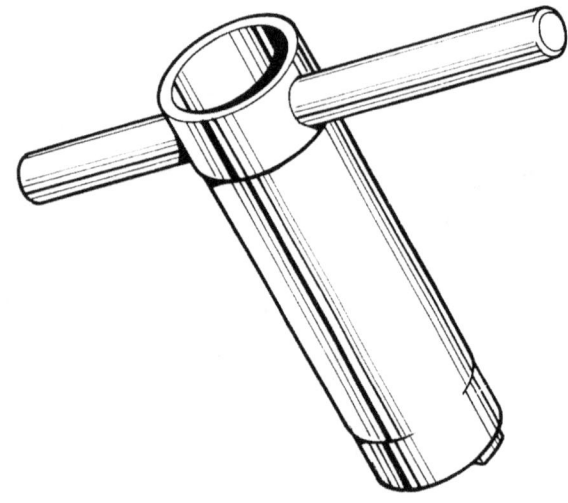

FIG. H.18.
Oil seal holder fitting and removal tool No. 61-3005.

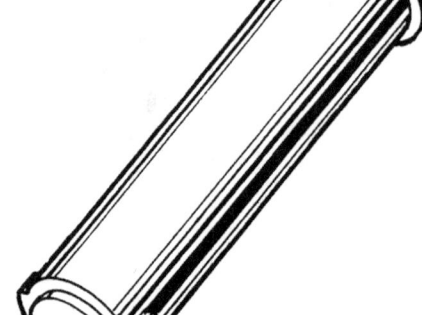

FIG. H.19.
Oil seal extractor punch No. 61-3006.

FIG. H.20.
Oil seal assembly tool No. 61-3007.

A5065   CONVERSION TABLES   J1

INDEX

	Page
Inches/Decimals to Millimetres	J.2
Fractions to Decimals and Millimetres	J.3
Millimetres to Inches	J.4
Drill Sizes and Wire Gauges	J.5
B.S.F. and B.S.W. Screw Threads	J.6
B.A. Screw Threads	J.7
Miles Per Gallon to Litres Per Killometre	J.7
Gallons to Litres	J.7
Pints to Litres	J.8
Pounds Per Square Inch to Kilograms Per Square Centimetre	J.8
Foot Pounds to Kilogrametres	J.8
Miles to Killometres	J.8
Pounds to Kilograms	J.8

CONVERSION TABLES

INCHES TO MILLIMETRES — UNITS

Inches	0	10	20	30	40
0		254.0	508.0	762.0	1016.0
1	25.4	279.4	533.4	787.4	1041.4
2	50.8	304.8	558.8	812.8	1066.8
3	76.2	330.2	584.2	838.2	1092.2
4	101.6	355.6	609.6	863.6	1117.6
5	127.0	381.0	635.0	889.0	1143.0
6	152.4	406.4	660.4	914.4	1168.4
7	177.8	431.8	685.8	939.8	1193.8
8	203.2	457.2	711.2	965.2	1219.2
9	228.6	482.6	736.6	990.6	1244.6

ONE INCH — 25.399978 millimetres.

ONE METRE — 39.370113 inches.

ONE MILE — 1.6093 kilometres.

ONE KILOmeter — .62138 miles.

DECIMALS TO MILLIMETRES — FRACTIONS

1/1000	
Inches	Mm.
.001	.0254
.002	.0508
.003	.0762
.004	.1016
.005	.1270
.006	.1524
.007	.1778
.008	.2032
.009	.2286

1/100	
Inches	Mm.
.01	.254
.02	.508
.03	.762
.04	1.016
.05	1.270
.06	1.524
.07	1.778
.08	2.032
.09	2.286

1/10	
Inches	Mm.
.1	2.54
.2	5.08
.3	7.62
.4	10.16
.5	12.70
.6	15.24
.7	17.78
.8	20.32
.9	22.86

CONVERSION TABLES

FRACTIONS TO DECIMALS AND MILLIMETRES

FRACTIONS			DECIMALS	MM.
		1/64	.015625	.3969
	1/32		.03125	.7937
		3/64	.046875	1.1906
1/16			.0625	1.5875
		5/64	.078125	1.9844
	3/32		.09375	2.3812
		7/64	.109375	2.7781
1/8			.125	3.1750
		9/64	.140625	3.5719
	5/32		.15625	3.9687
		11/64	.171875	4.3656
3/16			.1875	4.7025
		13/64	.203125	5.1594
	7/32		.21875	5.5562
		15/64	.234375	5.9531
1/4			.25	6.3500
		17/64	.265625	6.7469
	9/32		.28125	7.1437
		19/64	.296875	7.5406
5/16			.3125	7.9375
		21/64	.328125	8.3344
	11/32		.34375	8.7312
		23/64	.359375	9.1281
3/8			.375	9.5250
		25/64	.390625	9.9219
	13/32		.40625	10.3187
		27/64	.421875	10.7156
7/16			.4375	11.1125
		29/64	.453125	11.5094
	15/32		.46875	11.9062
		31/64	.484375	12.3031
1/2			.5	12.7000

FRACTIONS			DECIMALS	MM.
		33/64	.515625	13.0969
	17/32		.53125	13.4937
		35/64	.546675	13.8906
9/16			.5625	14.2875
		37/64	.578125	14.6844
	19/32		.59375	15.0812
		39/64	.609375	15.4781
5/8			.625	15.8750
		41/64	.640625	16.2719
	21/32		.65685	16.6687
		43/64	.671875	17.0656
11/16			.6875	17.4625
		45/64	.708125	17.8594
	23/32		.71875	18.2562
		47/64	.734375	18.6531
3/4			.75	19.0500
		49/64	.765625	19.4469
	25/32		.78125	19.8437
		51/64	.796875	20.2406
13/16			.8125	20.6375
		53/64	.828125	21.0344
	27/32		.84375	21.4312
		55/64	.859375	21.8281
7/8			.875	22.2250
		57/64	.890625	22.6219
	29/32		.90625	23.0187
		59/64	.921875	23.4156
15/16			.9375	23.8125
		61/64	.953125	24.2094
	31/32		.96875	24.6062
		63/64	.984375	25.0031
1				25.4000

CONVERSION TABLES

MILLIMETRES TO INCHES — UNITS

MM.	0	10	20	30	40
0		.39370	.78740	1.18110	1.57480
1	.03937	.43307	.82677	1.22047	1.61417
2	.07874	.47244	.86614	1.25984	1.65354
3	.11811	.51181	.90551	1.29921	1.69291
4	.15748	.55118	.94488	1.33858	1.73228
5	.19685	.59055	.98425	1.37795	1.77165
6	.23622	.62992	1.02362	1.41732	1.81103
7	.27559	.66929	1.06299	1.45669	1.85040
8	.31496	.70866	1.10236	1.49606	1.88977
9	.35433	.74803	1.14173	1.53543	1.92914

MM.	50	60	70	80	90
0	1.96851	2.36221	2.75591	3.14961	3.54331
1	2.00788	2.40158	2.79528	3.18891	3.58268
2	2.04725	2.44095	2.83465	3.22835	3.62205
3	2.08662	2.48032	2.87402	3.26772	3.66142
4	2.12599	2.51969	2.91339	3.30709	3.70079
5	2.16536	2.55906	2.95276	3.34646	3.74016
6	2.20473	2.59843	2.99213	3.38583	3.77953
7	2.24410	2.63780	3.03150	3.42520	3.81890
8	2.28347	2.67717	3.07087	3.46457	3.85827
9	2.32284	2.71654	3.11024	3.50394	3.89764

MILLIMETRES TO INCHES — FRACTIONS

1/1000	
MM.	INCHES
0.001	.000039
0.002	.000079
0.003	.000118
0.004	.000157
0.005	.000197
0.006	.000236
0.007	.000276
0.008	.000315
0.009	.000354

1/100	
MM.	INCHES
0.01	.00039
0.02	.00079
0.03	.00118
0.04	.00157
0.05	.00197
0.06	.00236
0.07	.00276
0.08	.00315
0.09	.00354

1/10	
MM.	INCHES
0.1	.00394
0.2	.00787
0.3	.01181
0.4	.01575
0.5	.01969
0.6	.02362
0.7	.02756
0.8	.03150
0.9	.03543

CONVERSION TABLES

DRILL SIZES

LETTER	SIZE	LETTER	SIZE
A	.234	N	.302
B	.238	O	.316
C	.242	P	.323
D	.246	Q	.332
E	.250	R	.339
F	.257	S	.348
G	.261	T	.358
H	.266	U	.368
I	.272	V	.377
J	.277	W	.386
K	.281	X	.397
L	.290	Y	.404
M	.295	Z	.413

NUMBER	SIZE	NUMBER	SIZE	NUMBER	SIZE	NUMBER	SIZE
1	.2280	14	.1820	27	.1440	40	.0980
2	.2210	15	.1800	28	.1405	41	.0960
3	.2130	16	.1770	29	.1360	42	.0935
4	.2090	17	.1730	30	.1285	43	.0890
5	.2055	18	.1695	31	.1200	44	.0860
6	.2040	19	.1660	32	.1160	45	.0820
7	.2010	20	.1610	33	.1130	46	.0810
8	.1990	21	.1590	34	.1110	47	.0785
9	.1960	22	.1570	35	.1100	48	.0760
10	.1935	23	.1540	36	.1065	49	.0730
11	.1910	24	.1520	37	.1040	50	.0700
12	.1890	25	.1495	38	.1015	51	.0670
13	.1850	26	.1470	39	.0995	52	.0635

WIRE GAUGES

NO. OF GAUGE	IMPERIAL STANDARD WIRE GAUGE		BROWN & SHARPE'S AMERICAN WIRE GAUGE	
	INCHES	MILLIMETRES	INCHES	MILLIMETRES
0000	.400	10.160	.460	11.684
000	.372	9.448	.410	10.404
00	.348	8.839	.365	9.265
0	.324	8.299	.325	8.251
1	.300	7.620	.289	7.348
2	.276	7.010	.258	6.543
3	.252	6.400	.229	5.827
4	.232	5.892	.204	5.189
5	.212	5.384	.182	4.621
6	.192	4.676	.162	4.115
7	.176	4.470	.144	3.664
8	.160	4.064	.128	3.263
9	.144	3.657	.114	2.906
10	.128	3.251	.102	2.588
11	.116	2.946	.091	2.304
12	.104	2.641	.081	2.052
13	.092	2.336	.072	1.827
14	.080	2.032	.064	1.627
15	.072	1.828	.057	1.449
16	.064	1.625	.051	1.290
17	.056	1.422	.045	1.149
18	.048	1.219	.040	1.009
19	.040	1.016	.035	.911
20	.036	.914	.032	.811
21	.032	.812	.028	.722
22	.028	.711	.025	.643
23	.024	.609	.023	.573
24	.022	.558	.020	.511
25	.020	.508	.018	.454
26	.018	.457	.016	.404
27	.0164	.416	.014	.360
28	.0148	.375	.012	.321
29	.0136	.345	.011	.285
30	.0124	.314	.010	.254

CONVERSION TABLES

B.S.F. SCREW THREADS

DIA. OF BOLT (INCH)	THREADS PER INCH	DIA. TAP DRILL (INCH)	CORE DIA.	AREA AT THD. ROOT SQ. IN.	PITCH DIAMETER NUT MAX.	PITCH DIAMETER NUT MIN.	PITCH DIAMETER BOLT MAX.	PITCH DIAMETER BOLT MIN.	HEX. FLATS (MEAN)	HEX. CORNERS	NUT THICKNESS (MEAN)
7/32	28	.1770	.1731	.0235	.2018	.1980	.1960	.1922	.412	.48	.166
1/4	26	.2055	.2007	.0316	.2313	.2274	.2254	.2215	.442	.51	.195
9/32	26	.238	.2320	.0423	.2625	.0586	.2565	.2527			
5/16	22	.261	.2543	.0508	.2897	.2854	.2834	.2791	.522	.61	.245
3/8	20	.316	.3110	.0760	.3495	.3450	.3430	.3385	.597	.69	.307
7/16	18	3/8	.3664	.1054	.4086	.4039	.4019	.3372	.707	.82	.370
1/2	16	27/64	.4200	.1385	.4670	.4620	.4600	.4550	.817	.95	.432
9/16	16	.492	.4825	.1828	.5295	.5245	.5225	.5175	.917	1.06	.495
5/8	14	35/64	.5335	.2235	.5866	.5813	.5793	.5740	1.006	1.17	.557
11/16	14	39/64	.5960	.2790	.6491	.6438	.6418	.6365	1.096	1.27	.620
3/4	12	21/32	.6433	.3250	.7044	.6986	.6966	.6908	1.196	1.39	.682
13/16	12	23/32	.7058	.3913	.7669	.7611	.7591	.7533			
7/8	11	25/32	.7586	.4520	.8248	.8188	.8168	.8108	1.296	1.50	.745
1	10	57/64	.8719	.5971	.9443	.9380	.9360	.9297	1.474	1.71	.870
1-1/8	9	1	.9827	.7585	1.0626	1.0559	1.0539	1.0472	1.664	1.98	.995
1-1/4	9	1-1/8	1.1077	.9637	1.1876	1.1809	1.1789	1.1722	1.852	2.15	1.115
1-3/8	8	1-15/64	1.2149	.1593	1.3041	1.2970	1.2950	1.2879	2.042	2.37	1.240
1-1/2	8	1.358	1.3399	.4100	1.4291	1.4220	1.4200	1.4129	2.210	2.56	1.365
1-5/8	8	1-31/64	1.4649	1.6854	1.5541	1.5470	1.5450	1.5379	2.400	2.78	1.400

B.S.W. SCREW THREADS

DIA. OF BOLT (INCH)	THREADS PER INCH	DIA. TAP DRILL (INCH)	CORE DIA.	AREA AT THD. ROOT SQ. IN.	PITCH DIAMETER NUT MAX.	PITCH DIAMETER NUT MIN.	PITCH DIAMETER BOLT MAX.	PITCH DIAMETER BOLT MIN.	HEX. FLATS (MEAN)	HEX. CORNERS	NUT THICKNESS (.005)
1/4	20	.1968	.1860	.0272	.2245	.2200	.2180	.2135	.522	.61	.245
5/16	18	1/4	.2412	.0458	.2836	.2789	.2769	.2722	.597	.69	.307
3/8	16	5/16	.2950	.0683	.3420	.3370	.3350	.3300	.707	.82	.370
7/16	14	23/64	.3460	.0940	.3991	.3938	.3918	.3865	.817	.95	.432
1/2	12	13/32	.3933	.1215	.4544	.4486	.4466	.4408	.917	1.06	.495
9/16	12	15/32	.4558	.1632	.5169	.5111	.5091	.5033	1.006	1.17	.557
5/8	11	17/32	.5086	.2032	.5748	.5688	.5668	.5608	1.096	1.27	.620
11/16	11	37/64	.5711	.2562		.6313	.6293		1.196	1.39	.682
3/4	10	41/64	.6219	.3038	.6943	.6880	.6860	.6797	1.296	1.50	.745
13/16	10	45/64	.6844	.3679		.7506	.7485				
7/8	9	3/4	.7327	.4216	.8126	.8059	.8039	.7972	1.474	1.71	.870
15/16	9	13/16	.7952	.4966		.8684	.8664				
1	8	55/64	.8399	.5540	.9291	.9220	.9200	.9129	1.664	1.93	.995

CONVERSION TABLES

B.A. SCREW THREADS

NO.	DIA. OF BOLT	THDS. PER INCH	DIA. TAP DRILL	CORE DIA.	AREA AT THD. ROOT SQ. IN.	PITCH DIAMETER NUT MAX.	PITCH DIAMETER NUT MIN.	PITCH DIAMETER BOLT MAX.	PITCH DIAMETER BOLT MIN.	HEX. FLATS	HEX. CORNERS	NUT THICKNESS
0	.2362	25.4	.1960	.1890	.0281	.2165	.2126	.2126	.2087	.413	.47	.236
1	.2087	28.2	.1770	.1661	.0217	.1908	.1875	.1873	.1838	.365	.43	.209
2	.1850	31.4	.1520	.1468	.0169	.1693	.1659	.1659	.1626	.324	.37	.185
3	.1614	34.8	.1360	.1269	.0126	.1472	.1441	.1441	.1409	.282	.33	.161
4	.1417	38.5	.1160	.1106	.0096	.1290	.1261	.1261	.1231	.248	.29	.142
5	.1260	43.0	.1040	.0981	.0075	.1147	.1119	.1119	.1091	.220	.25	.126
6	.1102	47.9	.0935	.0852	.0057	.1000	.0976	.0976	.0953	.193	.22	.110
7	.0984	52.9	.0810	.0738	.0045	.0893	.0869	.0869	.0845	.172	.20	.098
8	.0866	59.1	.0730	.0663	.0034	.0785	.0764	.0764	.0742	.152	.18	.087
9	.0748	65.1	.0635	.0564	.0025	.0675	.0656	.0656	.0636	.131	.15	.075
10	.0669	72.6	.0550	.0504	.0021		.0587	.0587		.117	.14	.067
11	.0591	81.9	.0465	.0445	.0016					.103	.12	.059
12	.0511	90.9	.0400	.0378	.0011					.090	.10	.051
13	.0472	102.0	.0360	.0352	.0010					.083	.09	.047
14	.0394	109.9	.0292	.0280	.0006					.069	.08	.039
15	.0354	120.5	.0260	.0250	.0005					.061	.07	.035
16	.0311	133.3	.0225	.0220	.0004							

MILES PER GALLON (IMPERIAL) TO LITRES PER 100 KILOMETRES

10	28.25	15	18.83	20	14.12	25	11.30	30	9.42	35	8.07	40	7.06	50	5.65
10½	26.90	15½	18.22	20½	13.78	25½	11.08	30½	9.26	35½	7.96	41	6.89	51	5.54
11	25.68	16	17.66	21	13.45	26	10.87	31	9.11	36	7.85	42	6.73	52	5.43
11½	24.56	16½	17.12	21½	13.14	26½	10.66	31½	8.97	36½	7.74	43	6.57	53	5.33
12	23.54	17	16.61	22	12.84	27	10.46	32	8.83	37	7.63	44	6.42	54	5.23
12½	22.60	17½	16.14	22½	12.55	27½	10.27	32½	8.69	37½	7.53	45	6.28	55	5.13
13	21.73	18	15.69	23	12.28	28	10.09	33	8.56	38	7.43	46	6.14	56	5.04
13½	20.92	18½	15.27	23½	12.02	28½	9.91	33½	8.43	38½	7.34	47	6.01	57	4.96
14	20.18	19	14.87	24	11.77	29	9.74	34	8.31	39	7.24	48	5.89	58	4.87
14½	19.48	19½	14.49	24½	11.53	29½	9.58	34½	8.19	39½	7.15	49	5.77	59	4.79

60	4.71	70	4.04			
61	4.63	71	3.98			
62	4.55	72	3.92			
63	4.48	73	3.87			
64	4.41	74	3.82			
65	4.35	75	3.77			
66	4.28	76	3.72			
67	4.22	77	3.67			
68	4.16	78	3.62			
69	4.10	79	3.57			

GALLONS (IMPERIAL) TO LITRES

	0	1	2	3	4	5	6	7	8	9	
—		4.546	9.092	13.638	18.184	22.730	27.276	31.822	36.368	40.914	—
10	45.460	50.005	54.551	59.097	63.643	68.189	72.735	77.281	81.827	86.373	10
20	90.919	95.465	100.011	104.557	000.000	113.649	118.195	122.741	127.287	131.833	20
30	136.379	140.924	145.470	150.016	000.000	159.108	163.645	168.200	172.746	177.292	30
40	181.838	186.384	190.930	195.476	200.022	204.568	209.114	213.660	218.206	222.752	40
50	227.298	231.843	236.389	240.935	245.481	250.027	254.573	259.119	263.605	268.211	50
60	272.757	277.303	281.849	286.395	290.941	295.487	300.033	304.579	309.125	313.671	60
70	318.217	322.762	327.308	331.854	336.400	340.946	345.492	350.038	354.584	359.130	70
80	363.676	368.222	372.768	377.314	381.860	386.406	390.952	395.498	400.044	404.590	80
90	409.136	413.681	418.227	422.773	427.319	431.865	436.411	440.957	445.503	450.049	90

CONVERSION TABLES

PINTS TO LITRES

	0	1	2	3	4	5	6	7	8
—	—	.568	1.136	1.705	2.273	2.841	3.410	3.978	4.546
¼	.142	.710	1.279	1.846	2.415	2.983	3.552	4.120	4.688
½	.284	.852	1.420	1.989	2.557	3.125	3.694	4.262	4.830
¾	.426	.994	1.563	2.131	2.699	3.267	3.836	4.404	4.972

POUNDS PER SQUARE INCHES TO KILOGRAMS PER SQUARE CENTIMETRE

	0	1	2	3	4	5	6	7	8	9	
—		0.070	0.141	0.211	0.281	0.352	0.422	0.492	0.562	0.633	—
10	0.703	0.773	0.844	0.914	0.984	1.055	1.125	1.195	1.266	1.336	10
20	1.406	1.476	1.547	1.617	1.687	1.758	1.828	1.898	1.969	2.039	20
30	2.109	2.179	2.250	2.320	2.390	2.461	2.531	2.601	2.672	2.742	30
40	2.812	2.883	2.953	3.023	3.093	3.164	3.234	3.304	3.375	3.445	40
50	3.515	3.586	3.656	3.726	3.797	3.867	3.937	4.007	4.078	4.148	50
60	4.218	4.289	4.359	4.429	4.500	4.570	4.640	4.711	4.781	4.851	60
70	4.921	4.992	5.062	5.132	5.203	5.273	5.343	5.414	5.484	5.554	70
80	5.624	5.695	5.765	5.835	5.906	5.976	6.046	6.117	6.187	6.257	80
90	6.328	6.398	6.468	6.538	6.609	6.679	6.749	6.820	6.890	6.960	90

FOOT POUNDS TO KILOGRAMETRES

	0	1	2	3	4	5	6	7	8	9	
—		0.138	0.277	0.415	0.553	0.691	0.830	0.968	1.106	1.244	—
10	1.383	1.521	1.659	1.797	1.936	2.074	2.212	2.350	2.489	2.627	10
20	2.765	2.903	3.042	3.180	3.318	3.456	3.595	3.733	3.871	4.009	20
30	4.148	4.286	4.424	4.562	4.701	4.839	4.977	5.116	5.254	5.392	30
40	5.530	5.668	5.807	5.945	6.083	6.221	6.360	6.498	6.636	6.774	40
50	6.913	7.051	7.189	7.328	7.466	7.604	7.742	7.881	8.019	8.157	50
60	8.295	8.434	8.572	8.710	8.848	8.987	9.125	9.263	9.401	9.540	60
70	9.678	9.816	9.954	10.093	10.231	10.369	10.507	10.646	10.784	10.922	70
80	11.060	11.199	11.337	11.475	11.613	11.752	11.890	12.028	12.166	12.305	80
90	12.443	12.581	12.719	12.858	12.996	13.134	13.272	13.411	13.549	13.687	90

MILES TO KILOMETRES

	0	1	2	3	4	5	6	7	8	9	
—		1.609	3.219	4.828	6.437	8.047	9.656	11.265	12.875	14.484	—
10	16.093	17.703	19.312	20.922	22.531	24.140	25.750	27.359	28.968	30.578	10
20	32.187	33.796	35.406	37.015	38.624	40.234	41.843	43.452	45.062	46.671	20
30	48.280	49.890	51.499	53.108	54.718	56.327	57.936	59.546	61.155	62.765	30
40	64.374	65.983	67.593	69.202	70.811	72.421	74.030	75.639	77.249	78.858	40
50	80.467	82.077	83.686	85.295	86.905	88.514	90.123	91.733	93.342	94.951	50
60	96.561	98.170	99.780	101.389	102.998	104.608	106.217	107.826	109.436	111.045	60
70	112.654	114.264	115.873	117.482	119.092	120.701	122.310	123.920	125.529	127.138	70
80	128.748	130.357	131.967	133.576	135.185	136.795	138.404	140.013	141.623	143.232	80
90	144.841	146.451	148.060	149.669	151.279	152.888	154.497	156.107	157.716	159.325	90

POUNDS TO KILOGRAMS

	0	1	2	3	4	5	6	7	8	9	
—		0.454	0.907	1.361	1.814	2.268	2.722	3.175	3.629	4.082	—
10	4.536	4.990	5.443	5.897	6.350	6.804	7.257	7.711	8.165	8.618	10
20	9.072	9.525	9.079	10.433	10.886	11.340	11.793	12.247	12.701	13.154	20
30	13.608	14.061	14.515	14.968	15.422	15.876	16.329	16.783	17.237	17.690	30
40	18.144	18.597	19.051	19.504	19.958	20.412	20.865	21.319	21.772	22.226	40
50	22.680	23.133	23.587	24.040	24.494	24.948	25.401	25.855	26.308	26.762	50
60	27.216	27.669	28.123	28.576	29.030	29.484	29.937	30.391	30.844	31.298	60
70	31.751	32.205	32.659	33.112	33.566	34.019	34.473	34.927	35.380	35.834	70
80	36.287	36.741	37.195	37.648	38.102	38.855	39.009	39.463	39.916	40.370	80
90	40.823	41.277	41.731	42.184	42.638	43.091	43.545	43.998	44.452	44.906	90

OVERSEAS DISTRIBUTORS

ADEN	Arabian Trading Co. Ltd., P.O. Box No. 426, Crater, Aden.
AFGHANISTAN	Indamar Afghan Ind. Inc., P.O. Box 37, Kabul.
ALASKA	B.S.A. Motor Cycles, Western, 3074 Broadway, Oakland 11, California.
ALGERIA	Movea, 96 Boulevarde du General Leclerc, Nanterre (Seine), France.
	Societe Algerienne de Distribution, 1 Rue d'Assus Alger, Algiers.
ARGENTINA	Ditlevsen & Cia. Ltda., Av. Ingeniero Huergo 1335, Buenos Aires.
AUSTRALIA:	
South Australia	J. N. Taylor & Co., 27 Gilbert Street, Box 579E G.P.O., Adelaide.
Victoria	L. F. Pratt Motor Cycles (Pty) Ltd., 291–293 Elizabeth Street, Melbourne.
N.S.W. and Queensland	Bennett & Wood Ltd., 288 Adelaide Street, Brisbane.
Tasmania	Sim King (Pty) Ltd., Box A.240G G.P.O., 95 George Street, Launceston.
West Australia	Mortlock Bros., 914 Hay Street, Perth.
AUSTRIA	Ferdinand Eichler, Hegelgasse 5, Vienna 1/1.
AZORES	Hayes & Travell Ltd., P.O. Box 56, Ponta Delgada, St. Michael's.
BAHAMAS	Nassau Bicycle Co., P.O. Box 191, Bay and Market Street, Nassau.
BAHREIN	United Commercial Agencies, P.O. Box 166, Bahrein Islands, Persian Gulf.
BELGIAN CONGO:	
Albertville	La Sima S.C.R.L., P.O. Box 671, Elizabethville.
Bukavu	Touriel Motors, P.O. Box 796, Bukavu.
Coquilhatville	Ets. Fr. Mechant et Fils, P.O. Box 786, Leopoldville.
Elizabethville	La Sima, Boite Postale 671, Elizabethville.
Leopoldville	Ets. Fr. Mechant et Fils, P.O. Box 786, Leopoldville.
Usumbura	Capelluto Touriel & Co., P.O. Box 501, Usumbura, Ruanda Urandi.
Stanleyville	Nassers Trading Co. Ltd., P.O. Box 71, Stanleyville.
BELGIUM	Ets. Moorkens S.A., 571 Grande Chaussee, Berchem, Antwerp.
BERMUDA	Holmes, Williams & Purvey Ltd., P.O. Box 444, Pembroke.
BORNEO:	
British North Borneo	Harrisons & Crosneld (Borneo) Ltd., Import Department, Jesselton.
Sarawak	The Borneo Co. Ltd., P.O. Box 141, Thomson Road, Kuching.
BOUGAINVILLE	Bennett & Wood Ltd., 114–120 Joynton Ave., Zeeland, Sydney, Australia.
BRAZIL	Mesbla S.A., Rua de Passeio 42/56, Rio de Janeiro.
(and branches at)	Sao Paulo (Est de Sao Paulo), Rua 24 de Maio 141.
	Porto Alegre (R. G. do Sul), Rua Voluntarios de Patria 524.
	Belo Horizonte (Minas Gerais), Rua Curitiba 444-464.
	Recife (Pernambuco), Rua de Palma 251.
	Pelotas (R. G. do Sul), Praca Cel. P. Osorio 152-154.
	Niteroi (Est do Rio), Rua Visconde Rio Branco 521-523.
	Marillia (Sao Paulo), Rua 9 de Julho 1001.
	Victoria (Espirato Santo), Av. Victoria 719-727.
	Salvador (Bahia), Av. Frederico Pontes 102-104.
BRITISH EAST AFRICA:	
Kenya	Hughes Ltd., P.O. Box 30060, Nairobi.
Tanganyika	International Motor Mart Ltd., P.O. Box 9060, Dar-es-Salaam.
Uganda	The Uganda Co. (Africa) Ltd., P.O. Box 1, Kampala.
Zanzibar	Musa Jusabani, P.O. Box 366, Zanzibar.
BRITISH GUIANA	Bookers Stores Ltd., Bookers Garage, 13–15 Water Street, Georgetown.
BRITISH HONDURAS	Santiago Castillo, P.O. Box 69, Belize.
BRITISH SOMALILAND	Arabian Trading Co., Berbera.
BRITISH WEST AFRICA:	
Gambia	Cie. F.A.O., P.O. Box 297, Bathurst.
Ghana	Cie. F.A.O., P.O. Box 70, Accra.
Nigeria	Cie. F.A.O., P.M.B. 2344, Lagos.
Sierra Leone	Cie. F.A.O., P.O. Box 70, Freetown.
(and other branches throughout territory)	
BRITISH WEST INDIES:	
Antigua (Leeward Is.)	The Carmart Ltd., P.O. Box 249, St. John's.
Barbados	Redman & Taylors Garage Ltd., P.O. Box 269, Church Street, Bridgetown.
Dominica (Leeward Is.)	A. C. Shillingford & Co., P.O. Box 123, The Garage, Roseau.
Grenada (Windward Is.)	Glean's Garage, St. Patricks.
Jamaica	B.S.A. Agency Ltd., P.O. Box 3, Denham Town, Kingston 14.
St. Kitts (Leeward Is.)	J. W. Thurston & Co. Ltd., Fort Street, Basselterre.
St. Lucia (Windward Is.)	Peter & Co., Castries.

OVERSEAS DISTRIBUTORS

BRITISH WEST INDIES (continued)
- Montserrat (Leeward Is.) — M. S. Osborne, Trescellian House.
- Nevis (Leeward Is.) — J. W. Thurston & Co. Ltd., Fort Street, Basselterre, St. Kitts.
- St. Vincent (Windward Is.) — Corea & Co. Ltd., P.O. Box 122, Bay Street, Kingston.
- Trinidad — J. K. Bayne Ltd., 19 Richmond Street, Port of Spain.

BURMA — Levetus Ltd., Ceylon House, 15–16 America Square, London E.C.3.
operating through:
Deacon Clarke & Co. Ltd., P.O. Box 1489, 67–69 Seikantha St., Rangoon.

CANADA:
- British Columbia and Alberta — Fred Deeley Ltd., 606E Broadway Avenue, Vancouver.
- Newfoundland — Edwin Murray Ltd., P.O. Box 1375, St. John's.
- Nova Scotia — L. C. Comeau, Comeauville, Nova Scotia.
- Ontario — Percy A. McBride Ltd., 69–71 Queen Street East, Toronto.
- Quebec — Bentleys Cycle & Sports Ltd., 2081 Bleury Street, Montreal 2.
- Saskatchewan and Manitoba — Nicholson Bros., 225 Third Avenue North, Saskatoon.

CANARY ISLANDS — J. Gonzales Suarez, Nicolas Estevanez 4, P.O. Box 9, Puerto de la Luz, Las Palmas.

CEYLON — Cargills (Ceylon) Ltd., P.O. Box 23, Fort, Colombo.

CHINA — M. D. Ewart & Co. Ltd., Finwell House, 26 Finsbury Sq., London E.C.2.

COLOMBIA — Balfour Williamson (Export Services) Ltd., Roman House, Wood Street, London E.C.2.

COOK ISLANDS — United Island Traders Ltd., P.O. Box 1500, Leopoldville.

COSTA RICA — Almacen la Granja S.A., Apartado Postal R, San Jose.

CUBA — Distribudora de Motocicletas Britanicas S.A., Padre Varela, P.O. Box 962, Havana.

CYPRUS — S. & G. Collocassides Ltd., 1–3 Heraclius Ave., P.O. Box 91, Nicosia.

CYRENAICA — Metcalfe Eng. Co. Ltd., P.O. Box 216, Benghazi.

DENMARK — H. V. Hansen Motors & Cycles A/S, Gl, Kongevej 127–131, Copenhagen.

DOMINICAN REPUBLIC — General Sales Co., Apartado 746, Santo Domingo R.D.

DUTCH GUIANA — The New Motor Supply & Importing Co., P.O. Box 422, Watermolen Street, Paramaribo.

ECUADOR — S.A. Comercial Anglo-Ecuatoriana, Casilla 410, Guayaquil.

EGYPT — T. W. M. Forsyth, 7 Sharira Maspero, Cairo.

ERITREA — Arabian Trading Co. Ltd., Viale Blatten, Chieta Lorenzo Tazaz 29–33, Asmara.

ETHIOPIA — Arabian Trading Co. Ltd., P.O. Box 23, 155 Cunningham St., Addis Ababa.

FALKLAND ISLANDS — The Falkland Island Co. Ltd., Port Stanley.
McAtasney & Sedgwick, Falkland Store, Stanley.

FAROE ISLANDS — Frits Jensen's Autowaerksted, Torshavn.

FIJI — Morris Hedstom Ltd., Suva.

FINLAND — S. & N. Osakeyhtio, N. Bulevar, Helsingfors.

FORMOSA (Taiwan) — Yah Sheng Chong Yung Kee Co. Ltd., 198 Nan King East Road, Section 2, Taipei, Taiwan, China.

FRANCE — Movea S.A., 96 Boulevarde de General Leclerc, Nanterre (Seine), France.

FRENCH ANTILLES:
- Guadeloupe — Maison F. d'Alexis, 44 Rue Frebault, Pointe-a-Pitre.

FRENCH INDIA — Levetus Ltd., Ceylon House, 15–16 America Square, London E.C.3.

FRENCH SOMALILAND — Arabian Trading Co., Djibouti.

FRENCH WEST AFRICA:
- Dahomey — Cie. F.A.O., Service Autos, Contonou.
- French Cameroons — Cie. F.A.O., Duala.
- Ivory Coast — Cie. F.A.O., Abidjan.
- Mauritania — The United Africa Co., P.O. Box 1, United Africa House, Blackfriars Road, London S.E.1.
operating through:
Cie. du Niger Francais, Boite Postale No. 230, Saint-Louis, Senegal.
- French Guinea — The United Africa Co.
operating through:
Cie. du Niger Francais, Conakry.
- French Sudan — The United Africa Co.
operating through:
Cie. du Niger Francais, Bamako.

OVERSEAS DISTRIBUTORS

FRENCH WEST AFRICA (continued)
    Senegal ... The United Africa Co.
operating through:
Nouvelle Societe Commerciale Africaine, 31 Boulevarde Pinet-Paprada, Dakar.

GERMANY (West) ... Detlevlouis, Renzelstrasse 7, Hamburg 13.
GIBRALTER ... English Garage Ltd., Queensway, Gibralter.
GILBERT AND ELLICE ISLANDS ... Morris Hedstrom Ltd., Apia, Samoa.
GOA ... M.S.B. Caculo, P.O. Box 68, Panjim, Goa.
GREECE ... D. F. Papoutsas, 56 Halcocondyli Street, Athens.
GUADELOUPE ... Maison F. d'Alexis, 44 Rue Frebault, Pointe-a-Pitre.
GUINEA (Republic) ... The United Africa Motors Ltd., P.O. Box 1, United Africa House, Blackfriars Road, London S.E.1.
operating through:
Cie. du Niger Francais, P.O. Box 619, Conakry.
HADRAMUT ... Arabian Trading Co., Esplanade, Aden.
HAITI ... J. Traverne, c/o Motor Services, Rue Dantes Destouches No. 22, P.O. Box 1225, Port-au-Prince.
HAWAII ISLANDS ... B.S.A. Motor Cycles Western, 3074 Broadway, Oakland 11, California.
HONDURAS ... M. Liebers, Apartado 51, Tegucigalpa, D.C.
HONG KONG ... Levetus Ltd., Ceylon House, 15–16 America Square, London E.C.3.,
operating through:
British Bicycle Co., P.O. Box 15694, 8 Hennessy Road.
ICELAND ... Falkinn Ltd., P.O. Box 997, Reikjavik.
INDIA ... Levetus Ltd., Ceylon House, 15–16 America Square, London E.C.3.,
  (*represented by*)
    Bombay ... M. N. Kamat, 166E Vincent Road, Sunder Bhuvan, Dadar, Bombay 14.
    Calcutta ... S. P. Bose, 56/1 Canning Street, Calcutta 1.
    Madras ... Wilson & Co. (Private) Ltd., North Railway Terminus Road, Royapuram, Madras.
INDONESIA ... P. T. Platow, P.O. Box DAK 1266, Djakarta.
IRAN ... H. Mohammed Tavakolipoor Trading Firm, Ave. Boozariomehri, Teheran.
IRISH REPUBLIC ... Huet Bros. Ltd., 7–8 Bachelor's Walk, Dublin 1.
ISRAEL ... S. Gousman & Son Ltd., P.O. Box 1730, Hakishon Street, Tel-Aviv.
ITALIAN SOMALILAND ... Arabian Trading Co., Esplanade, Aden.
IRAQ ... Emanuel Lirato, Tamimi Building, 23/196 Wathba Street, Baghdad.
ITALY (North) ... S.R.L. Ghe-Ba, Viale Gian Galeazzo 29, Milan.
JAPAN ... Balcom Trading Co. Inc., Fukoku Building No. 2, 2-Chome Uchisaiwai-Cho, Chiyoda-Ku, Tokyo.
KOREA ... Balcom Trading Co. Inc., Fukoku Building No. 2, 2-Chome Uchisaiwai-Cho, Chiyoda-Ku, Tokyo.
KUWAIT ... Abdul Rahman Albisher & Zaid Alkezemi, P.O. Box 47, Kuwait, Persian Gulf.
LAOS ... Garage et Atelier Mecanique Lao, 387 Avenue Foch That Khad, Vientianne.
LEBANON ... The Commercial & Contracting Co., P.O. Box 3120, Beirut.
LIBERIA ... Cie. F.A.O., Monravia.
LIBYA:
    Tripolitania ... Euafrica, Sciara Damasco 3, Tripoli.
    Cyrenaica ... Metcalfe Eng. Co. Ltd., P.O. Box 216, Benghazi.
LIECHENSTEIN ... Fibag, Postfach Zurich 4/39, Zurich, Switzerland.
LUXEMBOURG ... Ets. Moorkens S.A., 571 Grande Chaussee, Berchem, Antwerp, Belgium.
MADAGASCAR ... Movea S.A., 96 Boulevarde du General Leclerc, Nanterre (Seine), France.
MADEIRA ... Moto Strand, Avenida de Zarco 18, Funchal.
MALAYA ... Cycle & Carriage Co. (1926) Ltd., P.O. Box 142, Orchard Rd., Singapore.
MALI (Republic) ... United Africa Motors Ltd., P.O. Box 1, United Africa House, Blackfriars Road, London S.E.1.
operating through:
Compagnie du Niger Francais, P.O. Box 546, Bamako.
MALTA ... The John Bull Ironmongery Stores, St. John's Square, Valetta.
MAURITANIA (Republic) ... United Africa Motors Ltd., P.O. Box 1, United Africa House, Blackfriars Road, London S.E.1.,
operating through:
Cie. du Niger Francais, Boite Postale No. 230, Saint Louis, Senegal.

OVERSEAS DISTRIBUTORS

MAURITIUS	Lising & Co., P.O. Box 25, 32 Royal Street, Port Louis.
MEXICO	Watson Phillips & Cia., Apartado Postal No. 67, Mexico 6D.F.
	Alejandro Dominguez, Font Valle 60, Num. 536, Marida, Yucatan.
NETHERLANDS	Hart Nibbrig & Greeve N.V., Warmonder Damseweg 12, Sassenheim.
NETHERLAND ANTILLES	Caribbean Sales, P.O. Box 43, Noorstraat No. 543, Orangestrad, Aruba.
Dutch West Indies	Caribbean Sales, Joh. van Walbeek, Plein N.4.A., Curacao.
NEW BRITAIN	Bennett & Wood (Pty) Ltd., 114–120 Joynton Avenue, Zeeland, Sydney, N.S.W., Australia.
NEW CALEDONIA	Agence Automobile, Boite Postale 1, Noumea, Nouvelle Caledonia.
NEW GUINEA	Bennett & Wood Ltd., 114–120 Joynton Avenue, Zeeland, Sydney, N.S.W., Australia.
NEW HEBRIDES	Bennett & Wood Ltd., 114–120 Joynton Avenue, Zeeland, Sydney, N.S.W., Australia.
NEW IRELAND	Bennett & Wood Ltd., 114–120 Joynton Avenue, Zeeland, Sydney, N.S.W., Australia.
NEW ZEALAND	Skeates & White Ltd., P.O. Box 59, Auckland.
NICARAGUA	J. A. Estrada & Cia. Ltd., Apartado No. 11, Avenida Roosevelt, Managua.
NORTHERN MOROCCO	Abraham S. Levy, P.O. Box 132, Casa Riera 26–28, Tangier.
NORWAY	Erling Sande, Hausmannagt 27, Oslo.
NYASALAND	Mandala Motors, P.O. Box 467, Blantyre.
OKINAWA	Balcom Trading Co. Ltd., Fukoku Building No. 2, 2–Chome Uchisaiwai-Cho, Chiyoda-Ku, Tokyo.
PAKISTAN	Levetus Ltd., Ceylon House, 15–16 America Square, London E.C.3., operating through:
(West)	Shahnawaz Ltd., P.O. Box 4766, West Wharf Road, Karachi.
(East)	M. O. Rizvi, 78 Nawab Salin Ullan Road, Dacca.
(East)	Chowdbury & Co., 379 Sarrajuddoula Road, Chittagong.
PANAMA	Servicio de Autos Omphroy S.A., Apartado 3386, Estafeta No. 1, Panama.
PAPUA	Bennett & Wood Ltd., 114–120 Joynton Avenue, Zeeland, Sydney, N.S.W., Australia.
PARAGUAY	Fidencio Perez Cie. S.A., 14 De Mayo Pte Franco, Asuncion.
PERSIA (Iran)	H. Mohammed Travakolipoor, Ave. Boozarjomehri, Tehran.
PHILIPPINES	Campos Rueda & Sons Inc., P.O. Box 31, Manila.
PORTUGAL:	
(North)	Silva Neto & Cia. Lda., Anadia.
(South)	Stand Vidal, Rua Joaquim Bonifacio No. 13C, Lisbon.
PORTUGUESE EAST AFRICA	F. L. Simoes & Co., P.O. Box 13, Beira.
	A. A. Azevedo & Filhos, P.O. Box 482, Lourenco, Marques.
	Gordhandas Valabhdas & Filhos, P.O. Box 45, Mozambique.
	Auto Sobressalentes Ltd., P.O. Box 206, Quelimane.
PORTUGUESE WEST AFRICA	Casa Americaine Comercial S.A.R.L., Caixa Postal 1208, Luanda.
PORTUGUESE GUINEA	Nunes & Irmao, C.P. 83, Bissau.
PORTUGUESE INDIA	M.S.B. Caculo, Nova Goa.
PUERTO RICO	M. Castro Fernandez & Co. Ltd., P.O. Box 1579, San Juan 7, Puerto Rico.
QATAR	Kasem & Abdulla Sons of Darwish Fakhroo, P.O. Box 92, Doha-Qater, Arabian Gulf.
REUNION ISLES	Movea S.A., 96 Boulevarde du General Leclerc, Nanterre (Seine), France.
RHODESIA:	
(Northern)	Lusaka Auto Electrical Services, P.O. Box 628, Lusaka.
	British Cycle & Sports Co., P.O. Box 274, Livingstone.
	Jim Carter, P.O. Box 100, Ndola.
(Southern)	Van Rooyen Motor Cycle Works Ltd., 124 Gray Street, Bulawayo.
	Alick Stuart Ltd., P.O. Box 306, Bulawayo.
	Ray's Engineering Co., 69 5th-Street, P.O. Box 91, Gwelo.
	Gammon Bros., P.O. Box 151, Umtali.
	Johnstons Motor Cycle Supplies (Pty.) Ltd., 28 Pioneer Street, Salisbury.
Formashonaland	Sheps Motor Cycle Spares (Pvt) Ltd., P.O. Box 1126, Sachbury.
SALVADOR	La Agencia Nacional Ltda., Ave. Independencia, San Salvador.
SAMOA	Morris Hedstrom Ltd., Apia.
SARAWAK	Bormeo Co. Ltd., Thomson Road, Kuching.
SAUDI ARABIA	Ebrahim Abdullah Juffali & Bros., P.O. Box 297, Jeddah.

OVERSEAS DISTRIBUTORS

SENEGAL (Republic)	United Africa Motors Ltd., P.O. Box 1, United Africa House, Blackfriars Road, London S.E.1., operating through: Nouvelle Societe Commerciale Africaine, P.O. Box 397, Dakar.
SEYCHELLES	Mahe Trading Ltd., Victoria, Mahe.
SOLOMON ISLANDS	Bennett & Wood Ltd., 114–120 Joynton Avenue, Zeeland, Sydney, N.S.W., Australia.
SOMALIA	Arabian Trading Co., Aden.
SOUTHERN MOROCCO	Africa & Eastern (Near East) Ltd., P.O. Box 519, Casablanca. C. Dempers & Co. Ltd., P.O. Box 538, Windhoek.
SOUTH WEST AFRICA	C. Dempers & Co. Ltd., P.O. Box 538, Windhoek.
SPAIN	Talleres Sanglas S.A. Rbla, Justo Oliveras S/N Hospitalet, Barcelona.
SPANISH GUINEA	J. Gonzalez Suarez, Nicolas Estavez 4, P.O. Box 9, Puerto de la Luz, Las Palmas, Canary Islands.
SUDAN	Geo. Djerejian & Sons, P.O. Box 269, Khartoum.
SWEDEN	A–B E. Fleron, P.O. Box 155, Malmo.
SWITZERLAND	Fibag, Postfach Zurich 4/20, Zurich. Van Leisen S.A., 34 Rue de la Synagogue, Geneva.
SYRIA	M. Chafik el Khiami & Co., Rue el Nasr 169, Damascus, Syria.
TAHITI	H. Jean Hamon, Papeete.
TANGIER	Abraham J. Levy, P.O. Box 132, Casa Riera 26/28, Tangier.
THAILAND	Loxley (Bangkok) Ltd., P.O. Box 214, Loxley Building, 304 Suapan Road, Bangkok.
TONGA	E. M. Jones, P.O. Box 34, Nukualofa, Tonga Islands.
TRIPOLITANIA	Eurafrica, Sciara Damasco 3, Tripoli, Libya.
TUNISIA	Etabs. Jean Borg, 35 Rue de Marseille, Tunis.
TURKEY	Turkish Automobile Trade Co., Beyoglu Istikal Caddesi 239, P.O. Box 32, Beyoglu, Istanbul.
UGANDA	The Uganda Co. (Africa) Ltd., P.O. Box 1, Kampala.
UNION OF SOUTH AFRICA:	
Cape Province	Robb Motors Ltd., 102 Strand Street, Cape Town, P.O. Box 1100. Barnes Garage Ltd., P.O. Box 438, East London. The Union Cycle Works, P.O. Box 442, Kimberley. Sahds, P.O. Box 149, Queenstown. Scotts Garage, 4 Rhodes Street, Port Elizabeth. Du Plessis Cycle Store (Pty.), Lutz Street, Upington, District Gordonia.
Natal	W. Killerby (Natal) Ltd., 281 Umbilo Road, Durban, Natal. Jowett Bros., P.O. Box 201, Pietermaritzburg.
Orange Free State	E. Hoehne & Co., P.O. Box 619, Bloemfontein.
Transvaal	Jacks Motors (Pty.) Ltd., P.O. Box 8479, Johannesburg. Shimwell Bros. (Pty.) Ltd., P.O. Box 2035, Johannesburg, also at: P.O. Box 95, Pretoria.
UNITED STATES OF AMERICA:	
(East Coast)	B.S.A. Incorporated, 639 Passaic Avenue, Nutley 10, New Jersey.
(West Coast)	B.S.A. Motor Cycles Western, 3074 Broadway, Oakland 11, California.
URUGUAY	Linn & Cia. S.A., Casilla Correo 1027, Montevideo.
VENEZUELA	Moto Palace C.A., Grupo Oriol, Calle el Progreso, Urg las Acacias, Caracas. Casa del Motociclista (Rafael E. Montero), Calle 89-E, No. 3-A-52, Maracaibo (Zulia and Falcon).
VIRGIN ISLANDS	B.S.A. Incorporated, 637 Passaic Avenue, Nutley 10, New Jersey.
YEMEN	Arabian Trading Co., Esplanade, Aden.
ZANZIBAR	Musa Jusabani, P.O. Box 366.

VELOCEPRESS MANUALS - MOTORCYCLE

1930'S BRITISH MOTORCYCLE CARBS & ELEC COMPONENTS (BOOK OF)
1930'S BRITISH MOTORCYCLE ENGINES (OVERHAUL & MAINTENANCE)
1930'S BRITISH MOTORCYCLE GEARBOXES & CLUTCHES (BOOK OF)
AJS 1932-1948 SINGLES & TWINS 250cc THRU 1000cc (BOOK OF)
AJS 1945-1960 SINGLES 350cc & 500cc MODELS 16 & 18 (BOOK OF)
AJS 1955-1965 SINGLES 350cc & 500cc (BOOK OF)
ARIEL UP TO 1932 (BOOK OF)
ARIEL 1932-1939 PREWAR MODELS (BOOK OF)
ARIEL 1933-1951 (WORKSHOP MANUAL)
ARIEL 1939-1960 4 STROKE SINGLES (BOOK OF)
ARIEL 1958-1964 LEADER & ARROW (BOOK OF)
BMW R26 R27 (1956-1967) FACTORY WORKSHOP MANUAL
BMW R50 R50S R60 R69S (1955-1969) FACTORY WORKSHOP MANUAL
BRIDGESTONE 90 SERIES FACTORY WSM & PARTS CATALOGUE
BRIDGESTONE 175 SERIES FACTORY WSM & PARTS CATALOGUE
BRIDGESTONE 350 SERIES FACTORY WSM & PARTS CATALOGUES
BSA SERVICE SHEETS MASTER CATALOGUE ALL MODELS 1945-1967
BSA BANTAM D1 TO D7 1948-1966 FACTORY SERVICE SHEETS MANUAL
BSA BANTAM ALL MODELS FROM 1948 ONWARDS (BOOK OF)
BSA SINGLES & V-TWINS UP TO 1927 (BOOK OF)
BSA SINGLES & V-TWINS UP TO 1930 (BOOK OF)
BSA SINGLES & V-TWINS UP TO 1935 (BOOK OF)
BSA SINGLES & V-TWINS 1936-1939 (BOOK OF)
BSA C10, C11 & C12 1945-1958 FACTORY SERVICE SHEETS MANUAL
BSA OHV & SV SINGLES 250-600cc 1945-1959 (BOOK OF)
BSA C15 & B40 1958-1967 FACTORY SERVICE SHEETS MANUAL
BSA OHV & SV SINGLES 250cc (ONLY) 1954-1970 (BOOK OF)
BSA B31, B32, B33 & B34 1945-60 FACTORY SERVICE SHEETS MANUAL
BSA OHV SINGLES 350 & 500cc 1955-1967 (BOOK OF)
BSA M20, M21 & M33 1945-1963 FACTORY SERVICE SHEETS MANUAL
BSA TWINS A7 & A10 1948-1962 FACTORY SERVICE SHEETS MANUAL
BSA TWINS A7 & A10 1948-1962 (BOOK OF)
BSA TWINS A50 & A65 1962-1965 FACTORY WORKSHOP MANUAL
BSA TWINS A50 & A65 1962-1969 (SECOND BOOK OF)
CYCLEMOTOR (BOOK OF)
DOUGLAS 1929-1939 PREWAR ALL MODELS (BOOK OF)
DOUGLAS 1948-1957 POSTWAR ALL MODELS FACTORY SHOP MANUAL
DUCATI 160cc, 250cc & 350cc OHC MODELS FACTORY SHOP MANUAL
HONDA 50 ALL MODELS UP TO 1970 INC MONKEY & TRAIL (BOOK OF)
HONDA 90 ALL MODELS UP TO 1966 (BOOK OF)
HONDA 125-150cc TWINS C/CS/CB/CA FACTORY WORKSHOP MANUAL
HONDA 250-305 TWINS C/CS/CB FACTORY WORKSHOP MANUAL
HONDA 450 CB/CL 1965-1974 K0 TO K7 WORKSHOP MANUAL
HONDA C100 SUPER CUB FACTORY WORKSHOP MANUAL
HONDA C110 SPORT CUB 1962-1969 FACTORY WORKSHOP MANUAL
HONDA TWINS & SINGLES 50cc THRU 305cc 1960-1966 (BOOK OF)
HONDA TWINS ALL MODELS 125cc THRU 450cc UP TO 1968 (BOOK OF)
INDIAN PONYBIKE, BOY RACER & PAPOOSE ILL PARTS LIST & SALES LIT
J.A.P. ENGINES 1927-1952 & MOTORCYCLES 1934-1952 (BOOK OF)
LAMBRETTA 1947-1957 ALL 125 & 150cc MODELS (BOOK OF)
LAMBRETTA 1957-1970 LI & TV MODELS (SECOND BOOK OF)
MATCHLESS 1931-1939 ALL MODELS 250cc THRU 990cc (BOOK OF)
MATCHLESS 1945-1956 350 & 500cc SINGLES (BOOK OF)
MATCHLESS 1955-1966 350 & 500cc SINGLES (BOOK OF)
NEW IMPERIAL ALL SV & OHV FROM 1935 ONWARDS (BOOK OF)
NORTON 1932-1939 PREWAR MODELS (BOOK OF)
NORTON 1932-1947 (BOOK OF)
NORTON 1938-1956 (BOOK OF)
NORTON 1955-1963 MODELS 19, 50 & ES2 (BOOK OF)
NORTON 1955-1965 DOMINATOR TWINS (BOOK OF)
NORTON 1960-1970 TWIN CYLINDER FACTORY WORKSHOP MANUAL
NORTON 1970-1975 COMMANDO FACTORY WORKSHOP MANUAL
NORTON 1975-1978 MK 3 COMMANDO FACTORY WORKSHOP MANUAL
NSU PRIMA 1956-1964 ALL MODELS (BOOK OF)
NSU QUICKLY 1953-1963 ALL MODELS (BOOK OF)
PANTHER 1932-1958 LIGHTWEIGHT MODELS 250 & 350cc (BOOK OF)
PANTHER 1938-1966 HEAVYWEIGHT MODELS 600 & 650cc (BOOK OF)
RALEIGH MOPEDS 1960-1969 (BOOK OF)
RALEIGH MOTORCYCLES 1919-1933 (BOOK OF)
ROYAL ENFIELD 1934-1946 SINGLES & V TWINS (BOOK OF)
ROYAL ENFIELD 1937-1953 SINGLES & V TWINS (BOOK OF)
ROYAL ENFIELD 1946-1962 SINGLES (BOOK OF)
ROYAL ENFIELD 1958-1966 250cc & 350cc SINGLES (SECOND BOOK OF)
ROYAL ENFIELD 736cc INTERCEPTOR FACTORY WORKSHOP MANUAL
RUDGE 1933-1939 (BOOK OF)
SUNBEAM 1928-1939 (BOOK OF)
SUNBEAM 1946-1957 S7 & S8 (BOOK OF)
SUZUKI 50cc & 80cc UP TO 1966 (BOOK OF)
SUZUKI T10 1963-1967 FACTORY WORKSHOP MANUAL
SUZUKI T20 & T200 1965-1969 FACTORY WORKSHOP MANUAL
SUZUKI TWINS 1962 ONWARDS 125-500cc WORKSHOP MANUAL
TRIUMPH 1935-1939 PREWAR MODELS (BOOK OF)
TRIUMPH 1935-1949 (BOOK OF)
TRIUMPH 1937-1951 (WORKSHOP MANUAL)
TRIUMPH 1945-1955 FACTORY WORKSHOP MANUAL
TRIUMPH 1945-1958 TWINS (BOOK OF)
TRIUMPH 1956-1969 TWINS (BOOK OF)
VELOCETTE 1925-1970 ALL SINGLES & TWINS (BOOK OF)
VESPA 1951-1961 (BOOK OF)
VESPA 1955-1963 125 & 150cc & GS MODELS (SECOND BOOK OF)
VESPA 1955-1968 GS & SS (BOOK OF)
VESPA 1963-1972 90, 125 & 150cc (THIRD BOOK OF)
VILLIERS ENGINE UP TO 1959 INC. 3 WHEELERS (BOOK OF)
VILLIERS ENGINE UP TO 1969 (BOOK OF)
VINCENT 1935-1955 (WORKSHOP MANUAL)
YAMAHA 1961-1967 YA5 & YA6 (WORKSHOP MANUAL & ILL PARTS LIST)
YAMAHA 1971-1972 JT1& JT2 (WORKSHOP MANUAL & ILL PARTS LIST)

VELOCEPRESS TECHNICAL BOOKS – MOTORCYCLE

CATALOG OF BRITISH MOTORCYCLES (1951 MODELS)
LUCAS ELECTRONICS BRITISH M/CYCLES REPAIR & PARTS (1950-1977)
MOTORCYCLE ENGINEERING (P.E. Irving)
MOTORCYCLE ROAD TESTS 1949-1953 (Motor Cycle Magazine UK)
SPEED AND HOW TO OBTAIN IT (Motor Cycle Magazine UK)
TUNING FOR SPEED (P.E. Irving)

VELOCEPRESS MANUALS - THREE WHEELER'S

BSA THREE WHEELER (BOOK OF)
VINTAGE MORGAN THREE WHEELER (BOOK OF)

VELOCEPRESS MANUALS - AUTOMOBILE

ALFA ROMEO GIULIA WORKSHOP MANUAL 1300 TO 2000cc 1962-1975
ALFA ROMEO GIULIA TECH MANUAL CARBURETED CARS FROM 1962
ALFA ROMEO GIULIA TECH MANUAL FUEL INJECTED CARS FROM 1969
ALFA ROMEO GIULIETTA & GIULIA 750 & 101 SERIES 1955-1965 WSM
AUSTIN-HEALEY SPRITE & MG MIDGET WORKSHOP MANUAL 1958-1971
BMW 600 LIMOUSINE FACTORY WORKSHOP MANUAL
BMW 600 LIMOUSINE OWNERS HAND BOOK & SERVICE MANUAL
BMW 2000 & 2002 1966-1976 WORKSHOP MANUAL
BMW ISETTA FACTORY WORKSHOP MANUAL
CORVAIR 1960-1969 WORKSHOP MANUAL
CORVETTE V8 1955-1962 WORKSHOP MANUAL
FIAT 500 FACTORY WORKSHOP MANUAL 1957-1973
FIAT 600, 600D & MULTIPLA FACTORY WORKSHOP MANUAL 1955-1969
JAGUAR E-TYPE 3.8 & 4.2 SERIES 1 & 2 WORKSHOP MANUAL
JAGUAR MK 7, 8, 9 & XK120, 140, 150 WORKSHOP MANUAL 1948-1961
METROPOLITAN FACTORY WORKSHOP MANUAL
MGA & MGB OWNERS HANDBOOK & WORKSHOP MANUAL
MG MIDGET TC, TD, TF & TF1500 WORKSHOP MANUAL
PORSCHE 356 1948-1965 WORKSHOP MANUAL
PORSCHE 911 2.0, 2.2, 2.4 LITRE 1964-1973 WORKSHOP MANUAL
PORSCHE 911 2.7, 3.0, 3.2 LITRE 1973-1989 WORKSHOP MANUAL
PORSCHE 912 WORKSHOP MANUAL
TRIUMPH TR2, TR3, TR4 1953-1965 WORKSHOP MANUAL
VOLKSWAGEN TRANSPORTER, TRUCKS & WAGONS 1950-1979 WSM
VOLVO 1944-1968 ALL MODELS WORKSHOP MANUAL

VELOCEPRESS TECHNICAL BOOKS - AUTOMOBILE

FERRARI 250/GT SERVICE AND MAINTENANCE
FERRARI GUIDE TO PERFORMANCE
FERRARI OWNER'S HANDBOOK
FERRARI TUNING TIPS & MAINTENANCE TECHNIQUES
HOW TO BUILD A FIBERGLASS CAR
HOW TO BUILD A RACING CAR
HOW TO RESTORE THE MODEL 'A' FORD
MASERATI OWNER'S HANDBOOK
OBERT'S FIAT GUIDE
PERFORMANCE TUNING THE SUNBEAM TIGER
SOUPING THE VOLKSWAGEN
SOLEX CARBURETORS (EMPHASIS ON UK & EU AUTOMOBILES)
SU CARBURETORS (EMPHASIS ON UK AUTOMOBILES)
WEBER CARBURETORS (EMPHASIS ON ALFA & FIAT)

VELOCEPRESS BOOKS & GUIDES - AUTOMOBILE

ABARTH BUYERS GUIDE
COMPLETE CATALOG OF JAPANESE MOTOR VEHICLES
FERRARI 308 SERIES BUYER'S AND OWNER'S GUIDE
FERRARI BERLINETTA LUSSO
FERRARI BROCHURES AND SALES LITERATURE 1946-1967
FERRARI BROCHURES AND SALES LITERATURE 1968-1989
FERRARI OPP, MAINTENANCE & SERVICE H/BOOKS 1948-1963
FERRARI SERIAL NUMBERS PART I - ODD NUMBERS TO 21399
FERRARI SERIAL NUMBERS PART II - EVEN NUMBERS TO 1050
FERRARI SPYDER CALIFORNIA
HENRY'S FABULOUS MODEL "A" FORD
MASERATI BROCHURES AND SALES LITERATURE

VELOCEPRESS BOOKS – RACING

CARRERA PANAMERICANA - MEXICAN ROAD RACE (BOOK OF)
DIALED IN - THE JAN OPPERMAN STORY
IF HEMINGWAY HAD WRITTEN A RACING NOVEL
VEDA ORR'S NEW REVISED HOT ROD PICTORIAL

AUTOBOOKS WORKSHOP MANUALS & BROOKLANDS ROAD TEST PORTFOLIOS

FOR A COMPLETE LISTING OF THE AUTOBOOKS & BROOKLANDS TITLES THAT WE CURRENTLY HAVE AVAILABLE, PLEASE VISIT OUR WEBSITE.
www.VelocePress.com

www.ingramcontent.com/pod-product-compliance
Lightning Source LLC
Chambersburg PA
CBHW080429230426
43662CB00015B/2228